CHEESE:
CHEMISTRY, PHYSICS AND MICROBIOLOGY

Volume 2

Major Cheese Groups

CHEESE: CHEMISTRY, PHYSICS AND MICROBIOLOGY

Volume 2
Major Cheese Groups

Edited by

P. F. FOX

Department of Dairy and Food Chemistry, University College, Cork, Ireland

ELSEVIER APPLIED SCIENCE
LONDON and NEW YORK

ELSEVIER APPLIED SCIENCE PUBLISHERS LTD
Crown House, Linton Road, Barking, Essex IG11 8JU, England

Sole Distributor in the USA and Canada
ELSEVIER SCIENCE PUBLISHING CO., INC.
52 Vanderbilt Avenue, New York, NY 10017, USA

WITH 94 ILLUSTRATIONS AND 93 TABLES

© ELSEVIER APPLIED SCIENCE PUBLISHERS LTD 1987

British Library Cataloguing in Publication Data

Cheese: chemistry, physics and microbiology.
1. Cheese
I. Fox, P. F.
637′.3   SF271

Library of Congress Cataloging-in-Publication Data

Cheese: chemistry, physics, and microbiology.

Bibliography: p.
Includes index.
Contents: v. 1. General aspects—v. 2. Major cheese
groups.
1. Cheese. 2. Cheese–Varieties. I. Fox, P. F.
SF271.C43 1987   637′.3   86-24288

ISBN 1-85166-052-6 (v. 1)
ISBN 1-85166-053-4 (v. 2)
ISBN 1-85166-054-2 (set)

Printed in Great Britain by Galliard (Printers) Ltd, Great Yarmouth

Preface

Cheese manufacture is one of the classical examples of food preservation, dating from 6000–7000 BC. Preservation of the most important constituents of milk (i.e. fat and protein) as cheese exploits two of the classical principles of food preservation, i.e.: lactic acid fermentation, and reduction of water activity through removal of water and addition of NaCl. Establishment of a low redox potential and secretion of antibiotics by starter micro-organisms contribute to the storage stability of cheese.

About 500 varieties of cheese are now produced throughout the world; present production is $\sim 10^7$ tonnes per annum and is increasing at a rate of $\sim 4\%$ per annum. Cheese manufacture essentially involves gelation of the casein via isoelectric (acid) or enzymatic (rennet) coagulation; a few cheeses are produced by a combination of heat and acid and still fewer by thermal evaporation. Developments in ultrafiltration facilitate the production of a new family of cheeses. Cheeses produced by acid or heat/acid coagulation are usually consumed fresh, and hence their production is relatively simple and they are not particularly interesting from the biochemical viewpoint although they may have interesting physico-chemical features. Rennet cheeses are almost always ripened (matured) before consumption through the action of a complex battery of enzymes. Consequently they are in a dynamic state and provide fascinating subjects for enzymologists and microbiologists, as well as physical chemists.

Researchers on cheese have created a very substantial literature, including several texts dealing mainly with the technological aspects of cheese production. Although certain chemical, physical and microbiological aspects of cheese have been reviewed extensively, this is probably the first attempt to review comprehensively the scientific aspects of cheese manufacture and ripening. The topics applicable to most cheese varieties, i.e. rennets, starters, primary and secondary phases of rennet coagulation, gel formation, gel syneresis, salting, proteolysis, rheology and nutrition, are reviewed in Volume 1. Volume 2 is devoted to the more specific aspects of the nine major cheese families: Cheddar, Dutch, Swiss, Iberian, Italian, Balkan, Middle Eastern, Mould-ripened and Smear-ripened. A chapter is devoted to non-European cheeses, many of which are ill-defined; it is hoped that the review will stimulate scientific interest in these minor, but locally important, varieties. The final chapter is devoted to processed cheeses.

It is hoped that the book will provide an up-to-date reference on the scientific aspects of this fascinating group of ancient, yet ultramodern, foods; each chapter is extensively referenced. It will be clear that a considerable body of scientific knowledge on the manufacture and ripening of cheese is currently available but it will be apparent also that many major gaps exist in our knowledge; it is hoped that this book will serve to stimulate scientists to fill these gaps.

I wish to thank sincerely the other 26 authors who contributed to the text and whose co-operation made my task as editor a pleasure.

P. F. Fox

Contents

Preface v

List of Contributors ix

1. Cheddar Cheese and Related Dry-salted Cheese Varieties . 1
   R. C. LAWRENCE and J. GILLES

2. Dutch-type Varieties 45
   P. WALSTRA, A. NOOMEN and T. J. GEURTS

3. Swiss-type Varieties 93
   C. STEFFEN, E. FLUECKIGER, J. O. BOSSET and M. RUEGG

4. Mould-ripened Cheeses 121
   J. C. GRIPON

5. Bacterial Surface-ripened Cheeses 151
   A. REPS

6. Spanish and Portuguese Cheese Varieties 185
   A. MARCOS

7. Italian Cheeses 221
   P. F. FOX and T. P. GUINEE

Contents

8. Mediterranean Cheese Varieties: Ripened Cheese Varieties
   Native to the Balkan Countries 257
   MARIJANA CARIĆ

9. Domiati and Feta Type Cheeses 277
   M. H. ABD EL-SALAM

10. Some Non-European Cheese Varieties 311
    P. F. FOX

11. Processed Cheese Products 339
    MARIJANA CARIĆ and MILOSLAV KALÁB

Index 385

List of Contributors

M. H. ABD EL-SALAM
Laboratory of Food Technology and Dairying, National Research Centre, Tahrir Street, Dokki, Cairo, Egypt.

J. O. BOSSET
Federal Dairy Research Institute, CH-3097 Liebefeld-Bern, Switzerland.

MARIJANA CARIĆ
Faculty of Technology, Institute of Meat, Milk, Fat and Oil, Fruit and Vegetable Technology, University of Novi Sad, 2100 Novi Sad, V. Vlahovića 2, Yugoslavia.

E. FLUECKIGER
Federal Dairy Research Institute, CH-3097 Liebefeld-Bern, Switzerland.

P. F. FOX
Department of Dairy and Food Chemistry, University College, Cork, Ireland.

T. J. GEURTS
Department of Food Science, Agricultural University, De Dreijen 12, 6703 BC Wageningen, The Netherlands.

J. GILLES
New Zealand Dairy Research Institute, Private Bag, Palmerston North, New Zealand.

ix

J. C. Gripon
Laboratoire de Biochimie et Technologie Laitières, Institut National de la Recherche Agronomique, 78350 Jouy-en-Josas, France.

T. P. Guinee
Department of Dairy and Food Chemistry, University College, Cork, Ireland.

Miloslav Kaláb
Food Research Centre, Agriculture Canada, Ottawa, Ontario, Canada K1A OC6.

R. C. Lawrence
New Zealand Dairy Research Institute, Private Bag, Palmerston North, New Zealand.

A. Marcos
Departamento de Tecnología y Bioquímica de los Alimentos, Facultad de Veterinaria, Universidad de Córdoba, 44005 Córdoba, Spain.

A. Noomen
Department of Food Science, Agricultural University, De Dreijen 12, 6703 BC Wageningen, The Netherlands.

A. Reps
Institute of Food Engineering and Biotechnology, University of Agriculture and Technology, 10-957 Olsztyn-Kortowo, BL. 43, Poland.

M. Ruegg
Federal Dairy Research Institute, CH-3097 Liebefeld-Bern, Switzerland.

C. Steffen
Federal Dairy Research Institute, CH-3097 Liebefeld-Bern, Switzerland.

P. Walstra
Department of Food Science, Agricultural University, De Dreijen 12, 6703 BC Wageningen, The Netherlands.

Chapter 1

Cheddar Cheese and Related Dry-salted Cheese Varieties

R. C. Lawrence and J. Gilles

New Zealand Dairy Research Institute,
Palmerston North, New Zealand

1. INTRODUCTION

In the warm climates in which cheesemaking was first practised, cheeses would have tended to be of low pH as a result of the acid-producing activity of the lactic acid bacteria and coliforms in the raw milk. In colder climates, it would have been logical either to add warm water to the curds and whey to encourage acid production (the prototype of Gouda-type cheeses) or to drain off the whey and pile the curd into heaps to prevent the temperature falling. In the latter case, the piles became known as 'Cheddars', after the village in Somerset, England, where the technique is said to have been first used about the middle of the 19th century. The concept of cheddaring was quickly adopted also outside Britain. The first Cheddar cheese factory, as opposed to farmhouse cheesemaking, was in operation in the United States (NY State) in 1861, followed by Canada (Ontario) in 1864 and by New Zealand and England in 1871.

1.1 The Role of Cheddaring

Originally, Cheddar cheese was apparently made by a stirred curd process without matting, but poor sanitary conditions led to many gassy cheeses with unclean flavours.[1] Cheddaring was found to improve the quality of the cheese, presumably as a result of the greater extent of acid production. As the pH fell below about 5·4, the growth of undesirable, gas-forming organisms such as coliforms would have been increasingly inhibited. The piling and repiling of blocks of warm curd in the cheese vat for about 2 h

1

also squeezed out of the cheese any pockets of gas that formed during manufacture. Cheesemakers came to believe that the characteristic texture of Cheddar cheese was a direct result of the cheddaring process. It is now clear, however, that cheddaring and the development of the Cheddar texture are concurrent rather than interdependent processes. As will be described later, recently developed methods of manufacturing Cheddar cheese do not involve a cheddaring step but the cheese obtained is identical to traditionally-made Cheddar.

The development of the fibrous structure in the curd of traditionally-made Cheddar does not commence until the curd has reached a pH of 5·8 or less.[2] The changes that occur are a consequence of the development of acid in the curd and the loss of calcium and phosphate from the protein matrix. It is important, therefore, to recognize that 'cheddaring' is not confined only to Cheddar cheese. All cheeses are 'cheddared' in the sense that they all go through this same process of chemical change. The only difference is one of degree, i.e., the extent of flow varies due to differences in calcium level, pH and moisture.[3,4] In addition, the flow is normally restricted at an early stage in the manufacture of brine-salted cheeses by placing the curd in a hoop. If, however, Gouda curd is removed from a hoop, it flows in the same way as Cheddar curd. Similarly, the stretching that is induced in Mozzarella by kneading in hot water is best viewed as a very exaggerated form of 'cheddaring'. All young cheese, regardless of the presence of salt, can be stretched in the same way as Mozzarella provided that the calcium content and pH are within the required range.[5]

1.2 Development of Dry-salting

In the early days of cheesemaking, the surface of the curd mass was presumably covered with dry salt in an attempt to preserve the cheese curd for longer periods. In localities where the salt was obtained by the evaporation of sea-water, it would have been a rational step to consider using a concentrated brine rather than wait for all the liquid to evaporate. The technique of dry-salting, i.e. salting relatively small particles of curd before pressing, appears to have evolved in England. In addition to Cheddar and Cheshire, many other dry-salted cheeses were developed in Britain, the best known being Lancashire, Leicester, Derbyshire, Gloucester, Wensleydale, Dunlop, Caerphilly and Stilton.

Dry-salting overcomes the major disadvantage of brine-salting, i.e. the 'blowing' of the cheese due to the growth of such bacteria as coliforms and clostridia, but introduces new difficulties since the starter organisms are also inhibited by the salt. This inhibition is not a problem when the pH of the curd granules is allowed to reach a relatively low value prior to the application of salt, as in Cheshire and Stilton manufacture. The manufacture of a dry-salted cheese in the medium pH range (5·0–5·4), such as Cheddar, is however more difficult than that of the Gouda-type cheeses in which the pH is controlled mainly by the addition of water. At the time when the salt is added, a relatively large amount of lactose is still present in the Cheddar curd.[6] This is not, however, detrimental to the quality of the cheese provided that the salt-in-moisture (S/M) level is greater than 4·5% and the cheese is allowed to cool after pressing.[7]

Differences obviously exist in the procedures used for the manufacture of dry- and brine-salted cheeses but these have relatively little effect on the characteristics of the finished cheeses; the production of dry-salted cheeses is in principle similar to that of brine-salted cheeses. Clearly the rate of solubilization of the casein micelles and the activity of the residual rennet and plasmin in the curd will be affected more rapidly by dry-salting than by brining but only in the first few weeks of ripening. There is no evidence to suggest that the mechanisms by which the protein is degraded are affected by the changes in salt concentration as the salt diffuses into the curd. Any differences between dry- and brine-salted cheeses of the same chemical composition will therefore decrease as the cheeses age.

Traditional Cheddar cheese is visually different from the common brine-salted cheeses such as the Gouda- and Swiss-type cheeses, which are more plastic in texture and possess 'eyes'. Both these characteristics, however, are a result of the relatively high pH and moisture of these cheeses and not of brine-salting *per se*. The texture of a brine-salted cheese is closer than that of traditionally made Cheddar cheese since the curd is pressed under the whey to remove pockets of air before brining. As a close texture is a prerequisite for the formation of 'eyes', it has come to be generally believed that 'eyes' can only be obtained in brine-salted cheese. The recently developed technique of vacuum pressing, however, also allows the removal of air from between the particles of dry-salted curd. This can result in a closeness of texture similar to that of Gouda-type cheeses. It is now therefore possible to manufacture dry-salted cheese with 'eyes' provided that the chemical composition is similar to that of traditional brine-salted cheeses and if the starter contains gas-producing strains.[5]

2. MANUFACTURE OF CHEDDAR CHEESE

Dramatic changes in the manufacture of Cheddar cheese have occurred during the past 20 years. The single most important factor has been the availability of reliable starter cultures because the successful development of continuous mechanized systems for Cheddar manufacture has depended upon the ability of the cheesemaker to control precisely both the expulsion of moisture and the increase in acidity required in a given time. This in turn has led to the recognition that the quality of cheese, now being made on such a large scale in modern cheese plants, can only be guaranteed if its chemical composition falls within pre-determined ranges. Nevertheless, Cheddar cheese is still a relatively difficult variety to manufacture since the long ripening period necessary for the development of the required mature flavour can also be conducive to the formation of off-flavours. In addition, its texture, which is almost as important to consumers as its flavour, can vary considerably. The intermediate position of Cheddar cheese in the total cheese spectrum[3] (Fig. 1) is particularly exemplified by its textural properties which lie between the crumbly nature of Cheshire and the plastic texture of Gouda.

The traditional manufacture of Cheddar cheese consists of: (a) coagulating milk, containing a starter culture, with rennet; (b) cutting the resulting rennet coagulum into small cubes; (c) heating and stirring the cubes with the concomitant production of a required amount of acid; (d) whey removal; (e) fusing the cubes of curd into slabs by cheddaring; (f) cutting (milling) the cheddared curd; (g) salting; (h) pressing; (i) packaging and ripening. Although it is impossible to completely separate the

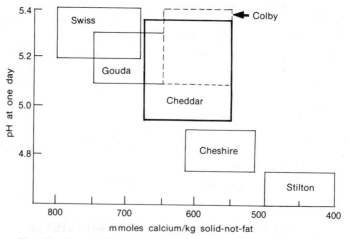

Fig. 1.   Classification of traditionally manufactured cheese varieties by their characteristic ranges of ratio of calcium/solids-not-fat and pH.

combined effects of some of these operations on the final quality of the cheese, they will as far as possible be considered individually.

2.1 Effect of Milk Composition and Starter Culture

Cheesemaking basically consists of the removal of moisture from a rennet coagulum (Fig. 2). The three major factors involved are the proportion of fat in the curd, the cooking (scalding) temperature and the rate and extent of acid production.[4] In order to achieve uniform cheese quality in large

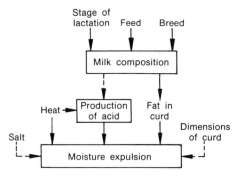

Fig. 2. Main factors in the expulsion of moisture from a rennet coagulum.

commercial plants, the manufacturing procedures must be as consistent as possible. The first requirement is uniformity of the raw milk. This is achieved by bulking the milk in a silo to even out differences in milk composition from the various districts supplying milk to the cheese plant. Preferably, the milk should be bulked before use so that its fat content can be accurately standardized. For Cheddar cheese varieties, the milk is normally standardized to a casein/fat ratio between 0·67 and 0·72. The more fat present in the cheese milk, and therefore in the rennet coagulum, the more difficult it is to remove moisture under the same manufacturing conditions since the presence of fat interferes mechanically with the syneresis process.[8]

The manufacture of Cheddar cheese is more dependent upon uniform starter activity than are washed curd cheeses such as Gouda. In this respect, at least, the manufacture of Cheddar-type cheese must be considered to be technically more sophisticated than that of other cheeses. The proper rate of acid development, particularly before the whey is drained from the curd, is essential if the required chemical composition of the cheese is to be obtained.[3,9] However, the curd is 'cooked', to expel moisture, at a temperature which normally adversely affects the starter bacteria. The cheesemaker must therefore exert judgement to ensure that the desired acid development in the curd is reached at about the same time as the required moisture content. It is not surprising that the defined single strain starter systems developed in New Zealand[3,10-12] have been based upon the temperature sensitivity of the selected strains as well as on their phage resistance and acid-producing ability. These defined starter systems have now also been widely adopted in the United States[13] and Ireland[14] and are replacing the undefined commercial mixed-strain cultures, of the type still almost universally used for the manufacture of Dutch-type cheeses.[15] If the cooking temperature is kept constant (for instance at 38°C) throughout the cheesemaking year and standardized milk is used, the most important factor by far in producing Cheddar cheese of uniform quality is the extent of acid production in the vats. To compensate for seasonal changes in milk composition it is normally only necessary to vary the percentage inoculum of starter to achieve the required acidity at draining.

2.2 Effect of Coagulant

The proportion of rennet added should be the minimum necessary to give a firm coagulum in 30 to 40 min. To achieve a similar firmness of coagulum throughout the season may involve the addition of calcium chloride and/or an increase in the temperature of the milk at which the rennet is added. The early stages of Cheddar cheese manufacture, specifically gel assembly and curd syneresis, have recently been reviewed in detail[16,17] (see Volume 1, Chapter 5). Electron microscopy studies[18-20] have shown that the casein micelles, which are separate initially, aggregate into a network, coalesce and finally form a granular mass. The fat globules, also separate at first, are gradually forced together as a result of shrinkage of the casein network. After the rennet coagulum is cut, the surface fat globules are exposed and washed away as the curd is stirred. This leaves a thin layer depleted of fat at the curd granule surface. During matting, the layers of adjacent curd granules fuse, leading to the formation of fat-depleted junctions.[21] Starter bacteria are trapped in the casein network near the fat–casein interface, which has been shown to be the region of highest water content in the mature cheese.[18] In all cheese varieties, the outline of the original particles of curd formed when the rennet coagulum is cut can be readily distinguished by scanning electron microscopy.[22] In addition, in traditionally made Cheddar cheese, the boundaries of the milled curd pieces can also be seen.[21] These curd granule and milled curd junctions in Cheddar cheese are permanent features which can still be distinguished in aged cheese.

The rennet coagulum consists of a continuous matrix of an aqueous protein mass interspersed with fat globules. The protein matrix, in turn, consists of small protein particles held together as a network by various binding forces. Several reports[23–25] conclude that the microstructure of the coagulum produced by the different types of milk coagulant is a major factor determining the structure and texture of Cheddar cheese. It has been suggested[24] that the 'structure of the protein network is laid down during the initial curd-forming process and is not fundamentally altered during the later stages of cheesemaking' and that the fibrous and more open framework of curd formed by bovine and porcine pepsins might be the reason for the softer curd associated with their use.[23] This implies that different milk coagulants significantly affect the initial arrangement of the network of protein structural units. It is more likely,[4] however, that the proportion of minerals lost from the rennet coagulum, as a result of the change in pH, largely determines the texture of a cheese. As one would expect, the type of rennet used greatly affects the degree of proteolysis as the cheese ripens[20,26] (cf. Volume 1, Chapters 3 and 10).

2.3 The Effect of Heating (Cooking) the Curd

During cooking, the curd is heated to facilitate syneresis and aid in the control of acid development. The moisture content of the curd is normally reduced from approximately 87% in the initial gel to below 39% in the finished Cheddar cheese. The expulsion of whey is aided by the continued action of rennet as well as the combined influence of heat and acid. The rate at which heat is applied was once considered to be important[27] but this is less relevant now that more reliable starter cultures are available. The temperature should be raised to 38–39°C over a period of about 35 min. The curd shrinks in size and becomes firmer during cooking.

2.4 Acid Production at the Vat Stage

The single most important factor in the control of Cheddar cheese quality is the extent of acid production in the vat (Fig. 3) since this largely determines the characteristic basic structure of the cheese[6] and its final pH.[28] Since the amount of rennet added and the cooking temperature profile are normally

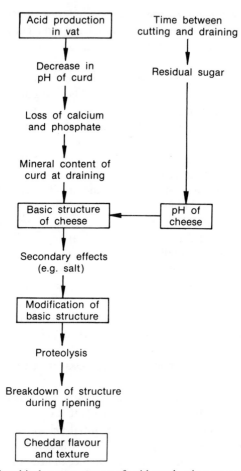

Fig. 3. Relationship between extent of acid production up to the draining stage and production of Cheddar cheese flavour.

constant in the manufacture of Cheddar cheese, the pH change in the curd becomes the important factor in regulating the rate of whey expulsion.[3,27] In mechanized cheesemaking systems, the cheese is usually made to a fixed time schedule. In New Zealand, the time between 'setting' (addition of milk coagulant) and 'running' (draining of whey from curd; also called 'pump out') is normally 2 h 30 min ± 10 min (Fig. 4). The percentage of starter added determines the increase in titratable acidity between 'cutting' and 'running'. The extent of acidity increase at this stage is particularly important since it also controls the increase in titratable acidity from 'drying' (when most of the whey has been removed) onwards.[29] The actual increase in titratable acidity may need to be adjusted at intervals throughout the year to achieve the required pH in the cheese at one day.

The basic factors which make such changes necessary appear to be connected with changes in the chemical composition of the milk and depend upon both the feed of the cow and the lactational cycle. The pH at draining also determines the proportions of residual chymosin (calf rennet) and plasmin in the cheeese.[3,30] The activities of these two enzymes play a major part in the degradation of the caseins during ripening and in the consequent development of characteristic cheese flavour and texture.

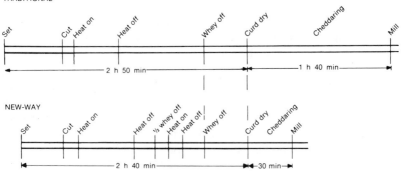

Fig. 4. Schedules for the manufacture of Cheddar cheese by the traditional and 'New-Way' processes.

While curd remains in the whey there is an equilibrium between the lactose in the curd and that in the whey. The whey thus provides a reservoir of lactose which prevents any great decrease in lactose concentration in the curd. After the whey has been removed, this reserve is no longer available and the lactose content of the curd falls rapidly as the fermentation proceeds. Curd which has been left in contact with the whey for a longer period has a higher lactose content than curd of the same pH value from which the whey has been removed earlier.[29,31] When high acidity is reached quickly in the vat, sufficient calcium is removed to alter the physical properties of the curd but insufficient phosphate is lost to seriously affect the buffering capacity of the cheese.[31] When high acidity is a consequence of an increase in the time between 'cutting' and 'running', a high loss of both calcium and phosphate occurs. The loss of phosphate is now sufficient to reduce the buffering capacity of the cheese significantly and the pH of the cheese is consequently lowered. Such cheese develops an acid flavour and a weak, pasty texture.

Acid production can only be under complete control if defined starter systems, such as the 'multiple strain' and 'single pair' systems recently developed in New Zealand,[3] are used. Use of these cultures has allowed New Zealand cheesemakers to reduce the time from 'set' to 'salt' to about 4 h 30 min (Fig. 4). Even shorter times are potentially possible but these are limited by the rate at which moisture can be expelled from the curd in the traditional Cheddar process. Experience has shown that it is preferable to produce lactic acid relatively slowly during the early stages of curd formation and cooking, followed by a steady and increasing rate after draining the curd from the whey, since this retains more of the calcium phosphate in the curd. Whitehead and Harkness[32] pointed out that a major acceleration of the process makes considerable demands on the skill of the cheesemaker. They doubted whether a manufacturing time of less than 3 h 30 min would be practical for traditional Cheddar cheesemaking since the rate of moisture expulsion must be kept in balance with acid development.

A 'New-Way' method has, nevertheless, been developed[33,34] in Australia in which the time from 'set' to 'salt' has been reduced to about 3 h 10 min. This method differs from traditional manufacture in four main respects (Fig. 4): (1) a thermophilic starter is used in addition to the normal mesophilic strains; (2) half the whey is run off about 25 min after the first 'cook' (38°C) has been completed; (3) a second 'cook' stage, 10 min later, further raises the temperature of the curd to 43–46°C; (4) the remaining whey is then run off and the curd cheddared for 30 min only. This method has been modified[35] with the maximum cooking temperature now used being 43°C. The main disadvantage of the New-Way method is the large amount of starter required (normally about 2% *Str. thermophilus* plus 2% mesophilic starter). While this short-time method has not been generally adopted, even in Australia, the technique of draining off part of the whey at some stage after the completion of 'cooking' is relatively common commercially.[36] The advantage of this practice is an increased rate of syneresis, probably due to a greater rate of impact of the curd particles during stirring.

Two other modifications of the Cheddar process, the Dariworld[37] and the USDA[38] methods, are unusual in that the curd is heated under brine to temperatures between 43° and 49°C. Neither has been adopted commercially.

2.5 The Effect of Cheddaring

The series of operations consisting of packing, turning, piling and repiling the slabs of matted curd is known as cheddaring. The curd granules fuse under gravity into solid blocks. Under the combined effect of heat and acid, matting of the curd particles proceeds rapidly. The original rubber-like texture gradually changes into a close-knit texture with the matted curd particles becoming fibrous. The importance attached to flow in the past varied markedly from country to country. In Britain, it was common for each Cheddar block to be made to spread into a thin, hide-like sheet covering an area of several square feet, whereas in New Zealand only moderate flow was induced, the final Cheddar block being little different in dimensions from when first cut. Investigations by Czulak and his colleagues initially led them to conclude[2,39–41] that extensive deformation and flow were essential in Cheddar cheesemaking. Further research in Australia,[42] New Zealand[43] and Canada,[21] however, has slowly led to the view that 'cheddaring' is not an essential step and serves no purpose other than to provide a holding period during which the necessary degree of acidity is developed and further whey can be released from the curd. This loss of whey is controlled by the acidity and temperature of the curd. The temperature is important both directly and indirectly since the rate of acid development is also influenced by temperature. In general, higher temperatures during cheddaring increase the expulsion of whey from the curd. In the traditional process manual manipulations of the curd, i.e. the cutting of the matted curd into different size blocks, the height of piling and the frequency of turning the curd blocks also aid in moisture control.

Mechanical forces—pressure and flow—were shown,[2,39] to be an important factor in the development of fibrous structure in the curd. This is clearly seen in the arrangement of the fibres, which follow the direction of the flow. Fibrous structure cannot be brought about by pressure and deformation, however, unless the curd has reached a pH of 5·8 or less.[2] This suggested that pressure and flow serve to knit, join, stretch and orientate the network of casein fibres already partly formed in response to rising acidity. The readiness to flow, the type of fibres and the density of their network are also influenced by temperature and moisture. The warmer the curd and the higher its moisture content, the more readily it flows and the finer, longer and denser are the fibres. These investigators[2] also concluded that it is possible to influence curd structure by manipulating pH, pressure and temperature and that a direct relationship exists between the structure and the water-holding capacity of the curd. This was confirmed by Olson and Price[44] who showed that extension and rapid flow of curd during cheddaring produced a higher moisture content in the resulting cheese.

Fluorescence microscope studies have demonstrated the change of the casein from spherical granular particles to a fibrous network.[41] While some granular structure was evident in curd grains, the conversion to the fibrous form was complete in cheddared curd. The fibrous shreds of cheddared curd consist of flattened, elongated curd particles which overlap each other, forming a network-type structure with the protein as a continuous phase. The exact mechanism responsible for these observed changes in cheddared curd is not known with certainty but the loss of minerals from the casein micelles in the curd is likely to be the major factor. The loss of calcium phosphate will destabilize the casein micelles resulting in a change in the conformation of the caseins. The concomitant loss of moisture from the casein micelles may also possibly contribute to the conformational change. It has been suggested[43] that if movement can occur within the curd the changes in protein structure allow the groupings of casein micelles to elongate and to establish a typical fibrous structure. If curd movement is prevented or restricted (no flow), the same changes occur at a molecular level. No elongation can, however, take place and no fibrous structure develops; the cohesive forces are, however, modified in the normal way, and when the restraint to movement is removed the mass quickly 'slumps' with the development of a fibrous texture.

Czulak[42] concluded that the characteristic close texture of Cheddar cheese could be obtained without cheddaring. He suggested, however, that in mechanizing the cheesemaking process it was probably most convenient, while holding the curd for acidity to develop, to allow the particles to mat together 'but to apply no labour or equipment for its fusing beyond that necessary for ready handling'. Almost all modern mechanized Cheddar cheesemaking systems are based upon these conclusions and involve little or no flow of the curd. This development was supported by the success achieved in the manufacture of cheese of normal Cheddar characteristics, particularly in the United States, by 'the stirred curd' process. This strongly indicated that flow and the cheddaring process itself are of little or no significance in the Cheddar cheesemaking process. Similar conclusions were also reached by research workers[43] in New Zealand. They considered that physical changes which may, under certain circumstances, become apparent in the macroscopic structure of the curd before pressing are of significance in relation to the texture of the final cheese only insofar as they may affect composition, particularly the moisture content of the curd.

2.6 The Effect of Milling

The milling operation consists of mechanically cutting the cheddared curd in small pieces in order to: (a) reduce the curd block and so enable more uniform salt distribution into the curd; (b) encourage whey drainage from the curd; (c) assemble the curd in a convenient form for hooping.

There is a practical upper limit to the cross-section of milled curd before salting for two reasons: (a) there is inadequate whey drainage after salting with large particles, (b) the larger the curd particles, the higher the salting rate required to achieve a given final level of salt-in-moisture (S/M) in the cheese. This increases the chance of seaminess[45] and gives higher salt losses in the whey.[46] The longer time required for salt penetration allows a greater development of acid in the centre of large curd particles than in smaller particles and this may result in a 'mottled' colour in the final cheese.

Gilbert[47] has pointed out that ideally the curd should be cut into spheres to obtain a uniform mass/surface area profile. The best that can be achieved,[47,48] however, is to use a curd mill that produces either a shredded curd, flakes of curd or pieces of curd resembling a finger. The more uniform the ratio of surface area to curd mass after milling, the more uniform will be the rate of salt diffusion into the milled curd particle and the proportion of salt retained. It is worth noting that these conditions are more closely satisfied if the curd is not cheddared but is kept in the granular state prior to salting.

2.6.1 Mellowing prior to salting

In the traditional procedure for Cheddar cheese manufacture, the milled 'chips' were left until the newly cut surfaces glistened as a mixture of whey and fat exuded from them. The mellowing period provided time to produce sufficient surface moisture to dissolve the salt crystals when they were applied and gave rise to higher salt retention. In a sense, therefore, the milled curd was being brine-salted.[47] The real purpose of the traditional mellowing period ('dwell time'), however, was to allow for further moisture release and acidity increase. In most modern mechanized Cheddar cheese manufacture a mellowing period of only 5–10 min has proved to be sufficient since the use of the improved culture systems now available has greatly simplified the control of moisture expulsion from the curd. In addition, the acidity at which curd is commonly salted these days has been considerably reduced. In some mechanized cheesemaking systems, salt is added to the curd immediately after milling and continuous agitation of the milled particles is used to encourage whey flow and brine development.

2.7 The Effect of Salting

The major difficulty in achieving cheese of uniform quality in modern Cheddar cheese plants results from the relatively wide variation in salt-in-moisture (S/M) levels that occurs in the cheese.[5] Salt (and more specifically S/M) plays a number of roles in the quality of Cheddar cheese by controlling: (a) the final pH of the cheese,[28,49] (b) the growth of micro-organisms, specifically starter bacteria and undesirable species such as coliforms, staphylococci and clostridia and (c) the overall flavour and texture of the cheese. The S/M level controls the rate of proteolysis of the caseins by the rennet, plasmin and bacterial proteases. Proteolysis, and thus the incidence of bitterness and other off-flavours, decreases with an increase in salt concentration.[49,50] At salt-in-moisture levels > 5·0, bitter flavours are rarely encountered;[51] below this level there is more or less a linear relationship between S/M and the incidence of bitterness. General aspects of salt in cheese were considered in Volume 1, Chapter 7; some specific aspects in relation to Cheddar are considered below.

2.7.1 Salting of milled curd

The salt crystals dissolve on the moist surfaces of the milled curd particles and form a brine. This diffuses into the curd matrix through the aqueous phase causing the curd to shrink in volume, and more whey is thereby released to dissolve more salt. The proportion of moisture in the curd and the amount of salt added both affect the rate of solution of the salt. The high salt content of the surfaces of the milled curd particles reduces the tendency of the particles to fuse together. The difference between dry-salting and brine-salting is, in effect, the availability of water at the surface of the curd. With brine-salting, salt absorption begins immediately. Release of whey occurs, as in dry-salting, but is not a prerequisite for salt absorption. The faster rate of salt absorption from brine has prompted the use of brine or salted whey in mechanized salting procedures[52] but none has yet met with commercial success.

While salt does promote syneresis, it should not be used in mechanized Cheddar cheesemaking as a means of making a significant adjustment to the moisture content of the curd. In modern cheese plants it is essential that the curd particles prior to salting are consistent from day to day with respect to moisture content, acidity levels, temperature, cross-sectional size and structure (degree of cheddaring), and that the application of salt is uniform. This gives the cheesemaker control over both the mean salt content and, equally important, the variation (standard deviation) within a day's manufacture. Cheese specifications normally require both moisture and S/M to be within specified ranges. This means in practice that variations in the moisture content of the curd prior to salting must not be greater than $\pm 1\%$.

It has been suggested[47,53] that the size of the salt crystals used is important for both salt uptake and moisture control. In practice, however, the major requirement in mechanized cheese plants is that the size range of the salt crystals should be narrow. If the range is variable, the delivery of salt from the equipment is erratic. The presence of high amounts of very fine crystals also results in excessive salt dust within the plant environment.

2.7.2 Mellowing after salting

Sufficient time must be allowed after salting (the mellowing period) to ensure the required absorption of salt on the curd surfaces and continued free drainage of whey. With the better starter systems now available there is no longer any necessity for cheesemakers to attempt to control the moisture content of the cheese by varying the amount of salt added. As a consequence, some mechanized Cheddar cheesemaking operations hoop the curd as soon as it has been salted. This has led to problems in cheese made by these shorter processes,[54] specifically to the entrapment of whey and consequently to excessive moisture and uneven colour in the cheese. As a result, a number of investigations have been carried out recently to determine the factors that influence the amount of salt absorbed and the speed of its absorption.[46-48,53]

The amount of salt absorbed by the curd and the rate of subsequent whey drainage is significantly influenced by those factors which influence diffusion rates in simple diffusion systems.[55] It is related to the availability of dissolved salt on the curd particle surfaces, and to the physical characteristics of the curd, e.g. fat-free curd allows faster diffusion. Even when a holding time of more than 30 min is maintained and the rate of salt addition is uniform, large variations may still occur in the salt content of cheeses because other conditions affecting salt absorption are not controlled. For instance, the curd temperature, the depth of curd, the extent of stirring after salt addition, and the degree of structure development in the curd were also found to be significant factors in the control of salt absorption and subsequent whey drainage.[46,53] It is not surprising therefore that there have been conflicting reports as to how long the mellowing period after salting should be. It is clear that at least 15 min holding is necessary to minimize loss of salt during pressing.[48] Other reports suggest that the pressing of the salted curd should be delayed for at least 30 min[46] and preferably for 45–60 min.[48] Some loss of salt occurs even when the holding period is extended to 60 min. An increase in the time of holding, however, substantially reduced the proportion of whey expelled during pressing and greatly improved the degree of salt absorption.[53] Nevertheless, in mechanized cheese plants, experience has shown that a mellowing period of only 15–20 min is usually adequate for satisfactory salt uptake and whey removal.[5]

The irregular effect of curd temperature on the extent of salt absorption was thought[48] to be caused by a protective layer of fat exuding from the surfaces of curd particles. Less fat was present on curd surfaces at 26°C than at 32°C. Above 38°C such fat was melted and dispersed in the brine solution that was present on the surface. In general, however, a decrease in temperature of the curd at salting increases the S/M of the final cheese.[53] Curd salted at a high pH retains more salt[29] and is more plastic than curd salted at a low pH. Similarly for a given salting rate, the S/M is high when the titratable acidity is low.[46] There is little doubt that salting the curd under the most favourable conditions for salt absorption reduces the proportion of salt required, and thereby reduces salt losses,[46] and also helps to overcome the defect of seaminess.[54,56]

2.7.3 Equilibration of salt within a cheese

The rate of penetration of salt into cheese curd is known to be very slow.[57] A mean diffusion rate of 0·126 cm²/day for salt in the water of Cheddar cheese has been reported.[55] This corresponds well with salt migration values for Gouda cheese of the same moisture content,[58] suggesting that the matrix structures of the two cheese types are similar. Despite the low salt diffusion rate it was nevertheless generally believed that the S/M component in Cheddar cheese was essentially uniform within a few days.[57,59] Reports[49,55,60–62] that wide variations in salt content occur between blocks from the same vat and even within a block, now suggest that, if salt distribution is not uniform initially, equilibrium will not be attained during the normal period of ripening of that cheese. The appreciable variation in the salt and moisture contents of small plug samples taken from different cheeses from the same vat[49,55,60] demonstrates how difficult it is to manufacture cheese to a uniform S/M level. As the consistency of cheese flavour is directly related to the extent of variability in S/M, the need to produce a curd mass consisting of particles of uniform cross-section at the time of salting cannot be over-emphasized (Fig. 5).

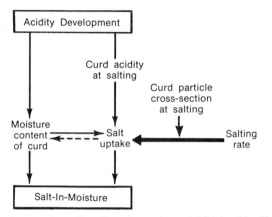

Fig. 5. Main factors that affect the salt uptake and S/M level in Cheddar cheese.

2.7.4 Seaminess and fusion

When curd particles are dry-salted, discrete boundaries are set up between the individual particles, in contrast to brine-salted cheeses where there is only one boundary, i.e. the cheese rind or exterior. The addition of dry salt results in shrinking of the curd and a rapid rate of release of whey containing calcium and phosphate, particularly in the first few hours of pressing. It has been suggested that the salted surface of the curd particle acts as a selective permeable membrane, thereby concentrating calcium and phosphate at the surface of the curd particle.[57] It is possible that this calcium gradient is also accentuated, under some circumstances, by the variations in pH between the surface and interior of the salted curd particle. These result from inhibition of starter activity by the high salt concentration at each curd boundary. The pH gradient set up leads, in turn, to a shallow calcium gradient,[63] the magnitude of which will depend upon the size of the curd particle and the proportion of salt added. In its most extreme form, the deposition of calcium phosphate crystals results in the phenomenon of seaminess in Cheddar cheese,[45,54,64] a condition in which the junctions of the milled curd particles are visible after pressing. Seaminess is more frequent and more marked with cheese of low moisture and high salt content and in some cases persists after the cheese has matured.[56] The binding between curd particles is usually weak, due to incomplete fusion. This often leads to crumbling when the cheese is sliced or cut into small blocks for packing.

Photomicrographs show that in both seamy and non-seamy Cheddar cheese, crystals of calcium orthophosphate dihydrate are dispersed throughout the cheese mass,[45] but in seamy cheese they are concentrated in the vicinity of the surfaces of the milled curd particles to which salt was applied. To a depth of about $20 \mu m$ below these surfaces, the protein appears to be denser than elsewhere, suggesting that severe dehydration of the surface has occurred on contact with dry salt. The observation[27,54] that seaminess is reduced by washing the curd after milling and before salting can be explained by the removal of calcium phosphate from the surface layer. In addition, the provision of more water, by reducing the concentration of salt on the surface of the curd particle, will lessen the dehydrating and contracting effect of salt on the surface layer.

Seaminess and poor bonding between the curd particles occur together and treatment with warm water corrects both defects. Poor fusion of the curd as a consequence of heavy salting results from irreversible changes in the protein at the surface, from poor contact between the hardened surfaces, from the physical separation brought about by the presence of salt crystals and, when these have disappeared, from the growth of the calcium orthophosphate crystals.[45] Fusion of the particles is improved by an increase in the pH, temperature or moisture of the curd.

2.8 The Effect of Pressing

Traditionally, Cheddar cheese was pressed overnight using a batch method. The recently developed 'block-former' system[65,66] has two major advantages for modern cheesemaking plants: firstly it is a continuous process and secondly the residence time is reduced to about 30 min. The curd is fed continuously into an extended hoop (tower) under a partial vacuum and a very short period of mechanical pressure is applied at the base of the tower, usually for about 1 min.

In traditionally-made Cheddar, the two common types of textural defect are mechanical- and slit-openness. Mechanical-openness (occurrence of irregularly shaped holes) is evident in very young cheese but decreases markedly during the first week or two after manufacture and thereafter changes little.[67-69] On the other hand, slit-openness is usually absent in freshly made cheese[70] but develops during maturation of the cheese.[71] The extreme expression of this defect, known as fractured texture, is found only in mature cheese. A comprehensive survey of commercial Cheddar cheese on the UK market carried out during 1958–61 found that mechanically open cheese was usually almost free of fractures and conversely that badly-fractured cheese usually had few mechanical openings.[72] The term 'fracture' is normally used to describe long slits, i.e. slits more than about 3·5 cm. As a result of the growth of the cheese pre-packaging trade in recent years, the importance attached to fractures in cheese has greatly increased since fractures can result in the breaking up of cheese during pre-packaging.

From the observation[73] that cheese hooped under whey had a completely close texture, and from their own studies of curd behaviour, Czulak and Hammond[39] concluded that air entrapped during compression of curd was responsible for mechanically open texture. They considered that during compression of the salted, granular curd, the spaces between the granules diminish until they form a complex of narrow channels filled with air. Under further pressure some of the air is forced out, the escape of the remainder being blocked by closure of the channels at various points and the high surface tension developed by traces of whey in the remaining narrowed outlets. The isolated pockets of entrapped air form numerous small irregular holes in the cheese. Conventionally made Cheddar cheese has a significantly closer texture than Granular cheese. The effect of cheddaring on texture appears to be due to the presence of milled strips of curd (fingers) compared to the relatively small granules of uncheddared curd present in Granular cheese. The larger the fingers of curd, the fewer the pockets of entrapped air and the closer the texture of the cheese. As mentioned previously, however, there is a practical limit to the size of milled curd since large curd fingers may result in inadequate whey drainage after salting.

During the last 30 years there has been a marked reduction in the incidence of both texture defects by: (a) the use of higher pressures during curd fusion;[74] (b) the change from the manufacture of rinded 80 lb (36 kg) cheese to smaller (20 kg), rindless cheese; (c) the introduction of vacuum pressing; (d) the use of defined single-strain cultures from which gas-producing strains have been omitted. The beneficial effects of these modifications are undoubtedly associated with a reduction in the gas content of the cheese. The production of carbon dioxide during ripening by non-starter bacteria has been associated with the development of slit-openness[71] but gas production is considered to be of secondary importance when compared to manufacturing conditions.[75] It is the relatively insoluble and biologically inactive nitrogen in the entrapped air which contributes to the ultimate openness of the cheese since the oxygen is rapidly metabolized during ripening.

2.8.1 Vacuum pressing
It was a logical step to prevent the entrapment of air between the curd particles by pressing the curd under vacuum, a procedure first[76] patented in

Canada in 1959. A moderately high vacuum is required, approximately 33 kPa pressure. Vacuum-treated cheese is free, or almost so, of mechanical openness when two weeks old and remains free throughout maturation.[70] There was some disagreement among the various groups of research workers as to the optimum conditions for vacuum pressing.[72] Initially, the cheddared and salted curd was pre-pressed under vacuum for 30 min before dressing, followed by normal pressing.[67] Later work suggested that pressures greater than 180 kPa appeared to be required during and after vacuum pressing to achieve close texture.[72]

An important development in Australia was the hooping of un-cheddared, granular, salted curd and pressing under vacuum.[42] It was found that the use of vacuum pressing ensured the characteristic close texture of Cheddar cheese, and thus eliminated the need for cheddaring. This observation was particularly significant for the complete mechaniz-ation of Cheddar cheese manufacture. Trials in New Zealand[70] quickly confirmed the Australian conclusions. Maximum reduction in openness was achieved with the combined use of vacuum pressing, a homofermenta-tive starter and a non-flow method of cheddaring.[71] Presumably, air can be removed more readily by vacuum from the relatively loose, granular, non-flow cheddared curd than from the closer textured cheddared curd. The recently developed technique used in the 'block-former' system of filling hoops under a partial vacuum is particularly effective in achieving a close texture. Mechanical-openness is never found in cheese made by the 'block-former' system but slit-openness does develop if gas-producing organisms are present.

A factor which formerly restricted the size of Cheddar cheese blocks was the tendency for large cheeses to show severe mechanical openness. With the aid of vacuum pressing it has been found quite practicable to form curd into very large blocks[77] which by extrusion into cutting equipment can be sub-divided into 20-kg blocks.

3. CHEMICAL COMPOSITION AND CHEDDAR CHEESE QUALITY

Recent developments in cheese marketing have resulted in a demand for cheese of greater uniformity of composition than in the past. Such uniformity is best achieved by a grading system based on compositional analysis, since a relationship between the composition and quality of Cheddar cheese is now well established.[52,78–82] Lyall[81] briefly reported on a procedure for evaluating chemical analyses of cheese, points being assigned on the basis of composition. However, the only scheme in commercial use for assessing Cheddar cheese quality by compositional analysis appears to be that proposed by Gilles and Lawrence.[80] Suggested ranges of moisture in the non-fat substance (MNFS), salt-in-moisture (S/M), fat-in-the-dry matter (FDM) and pH for both first and second grade cheeses are given in Fig. 6. All New Zealand export Cheddar cheese is now subject to compositional grading to ensure that atypical cheese is segregated. The principles and operation of this scheme have been

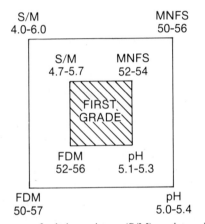

Fig. 6. Suggested ranges of salt-in-moisture (S/M), moisture in non-fat substance (MNFS), fat-in-the-dry matter (FDM) and pH for First grade (shaded) and Second grade Cheddar cheese. Analyses 14 days after manufacture.

reviewed[83] and it has been emphasized that, in addition to the compositional profile, a sensory flavour assessment should be carried out to ensure that the cheese is free from flavour defects. Cheese quality is determined, of course, ultimately by the texture and flavour of the cheese when eaten. These two properties are considered in greater detail in later sections.

Any grading system based on compositional analysis will be relatively complex since a further factor, the rate and extent of acid production at the vat stage, must also be considered.[3,80] Acid production in the vat not only determines, indirectly, the composition of the cheese but also governs the degree of acceptability of the cheese to the consumer. Grading cheese by composition and pH gives an indication as to whether or not acid production was normal. It is important to recognize that MNFS, S/M and pH are interrelated and that these three parameters must be controlled as a group to ensure first grade cheese. Nevertheless, the effect of each of these factors will, as far as possible, be examined separately.

3.1 Effect of MNFS

There is considerable circumstantial evidence that the main factor in the production of the characteristic flavour for the hard and semi-hard cheese varieties is the breakdown of casein.[84] This is supported by the finding that the ratios of moisture to casein and of salt to moisture are critical factors in cheese quality[80,83] since both parameters affect the rate of proteolysis in a cheese.[49] Traditionally, cheesemakers describe cheese in terms of its absolute moisture content, but the ratio of moisture to casein is much more important since it is the relative hydration of the casein in the cheese that influences the course of the ripening process.[83]

Since most commercial plants do not measure casein but only the fat and moisture in cheese, it is more practical to use the term MNFS, i.e. the ratio of moisture to non-fat substance. The non-fat substance is not the same as the casein in the cheese but is equal to the moisture plus the solids-not-fat. Approximately 85% of the solids-not-fat consists of casein. There is not, therefore, a strong relationship between the moisture to casein ratio and the MNFS. It is important to note however that *changes* in MNFS for any particular cheese variety correlate well with *changes* in the ratio of moisture to casein.

The MNFS value for cheese gives a much better indication of potential cheese quality than the moisture content of the cheese in the same way that the S/M ratio is a more reliable guide to potential cheese quality than is the salt content of the cheese *per se*.[83] In mechanized cheese plants, a significant relationship has been found to exist between the FDM and MNFS values in a cheese,[85] probably as a result of the relative inflexibility of the procedures available for the control of moisture. This is of commercial interest since changing the FDM is an effective way of controlling the MNFS in the cheese as the composition of the milk changes throughout the season.

The actual MNFS percentage for which a cheesemaker should aim depends upon the storage temperatures used and when the cheese is required to reach optimum quality. Experience has shown that if Cheddar cheese is to be stored at 10°C, and the cheese is to be consumed after 6–7 months, then the MNFS of the cheese should be about 53%. The higher the

MNFS percentage, the faster the rate of breakdown. Thus, if one anticipates that the cheese will be consumed after 3–4 months, the MNFS percentage can be increased to about 56%. However, the higher the MNFS the more rapidly Cheddar cheese will deteriorate in quality after reaching its optimum. The same is true for a Cheddar cheese with relatively low S/M, i.e. less than 4%, or with a high acid content (i.e. a low pH, < 4·95). Such cheeses tend to develop gas and sulphide-type off-flavours after they have reached maturity.

3.2 Effect of pH

Every cheese variety has a characteristic pH range.[3] Within this range the quality of the cheese is dependent upon both its composition and the way in which it is manufactured.[4] The pH value is important in that it provides an indication of the extent of acid production throughout the cheesemaking process. In normal manufacture, the curd acidity at salting is by far the most important factor in determining the pH of dry-salted cheese (Fig. 7). The salting acidity is, however, to a large extent controlled in turn by the acidity developed at draining.[28] The potential for a further decrease in pH after salting depends upon the residual lactose in the curd and its buffering capacity. The residual lactose will be determined by the rate at which an inhibitory level of NaCl is absorbed by the cheese curd and the salt tolerance of the starter strains used. The buffering capacity is largely determined by the concentrations of protein and phosphate present, and to

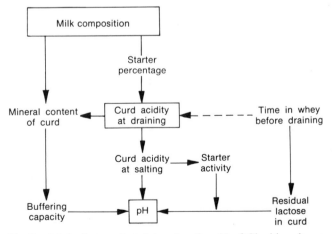

Fig. 7. Main factors that determine the pH of Cheddar cheese.

a much lesser extent by ions such as calcium. The percentages of phosphate and calcium retained in the cheese are influenced mainly by the rate of acidification prior to the separation of the whey from the curd. The buffering capacity is also influenced by seasonal, regional and lactational factors but little is known about these relationships at present.

Given reliable starter activity at the vat stage, the actual pH reached in dry-salted cheeses is determined by the S/M value since this controls the extent of starter activity after salting, the rate of lactose utilization in the salted curd and thus the pH reached. A S/M concentration of 6% will inhibit the activity of all *Streptococcus cremoris* strains, the starter organisms of choice for Cheddar manufacture.[12] The proportion of residual lactose that remains unmetabolized in such cheese will be high even after 2 months. In a cheese with a S/M of 4·5%, however, the starter will not be completely inhibited and the lactose will be rapidly metabolized. This explains why the pH values of one-day Cheddar cheese may range from 5·3 (which is about the pH of the curd at salting) down to pH 4·9. In general, the higher the pH the greater the amount of lactose left unmetabolized. Under normal circumstances this residual lactose does not affect the quality of Cheddar cheese at maturity.[5]

The importance of measuring the pH at one day has been generally overlooked in the past, probably because it is relatively difficult to measure the pH of cheese accurately. This has led to a lack of appreciation of the significance of relatively small changes in pH. In addition, a pH value *per se* is sometimes difficult to interpret unless considered in conjunction with the calcium level in the cheeses.[83]

3.3 The Effect of S/M

The main factors that determine the S/M percentage of Cheddar cheese are summarized in Fig. 5. In young Cheddar cheese the S/M ratio is the major influence controlling water activity. This in turn determines the rate of bacterial growth and enzyme activity in the cheese, specifically the proteolytic activity of chymosin,[50,86] plasmin[87] and starter proteinases.[88] If the S/M value is low (<4·5%), the starter numbers will reach a high level in the cheese and the chance of off-flavours due to starter is greatly increased.[89,90] For this reason, cheesemakers normally aim for a S/M value in Cheddar cheese between 4·5% and 5·5%.[28,83] Within this S/M range the rate of metabolism of the lactose is controlled by a second factor, the temperature of the cheese during the first few days of ripening, since this controls the rate of growth of non-starter bacteria such as lactobacilli and pediococci.[7] While non-starter bacteria grow on constituents other than lactose in cheese, undoubtedly the presence of lactose encourages their rapid growth. This tends to result in a more heterolactic metabolism of lactose, usually with the production of acetate, ethanol and carbon dioxide and may lead to flavour and textural defects. Clearly, the initial numbers of non-starter bacteria in the salted curd should be controlled by attention to hygiene during manufacture. Thereafter, their rate of growth, particularly during the first few days of ripening, should be kept to a minimum and this is largely controlled by the temperature of the cheese.[7]

The necessity to introduce compositional ranges into the grading system is well illustrated by the fact that it is not yet possible to produce a uniform line of cheese within a day's manufacture, particularly with respect to S/M values. This does not necessarily mean, however, that some of the cheese produced is of poorer quality than the rest. The rate of ripening will differ, but all of the cheese is likely to be acceptable as long as its composition is within the required compositional range. For instance, variations in the moisture content and acidity of the curd before salting, in the accuracy of salt delivery by salting equipment and in the dimensions and structure of the milled curd will all result in considerable variation in salt uptake.[28] Even within a single 20-kg block of cheese, S/M values vary by as much as 1%. Nevertheless as long as the titratable acidity at salting is normal, S/M values between 4·5 and 6·0% will tend to result in acceptable cheese.[83]

3.4 Effect of FDM

The FDM percentage in Cheddar cheese is of less importance than MNFS, S/M or pH, in that it normally only influences cheese quality indirectly through its effect on MNFS.[91] Nevertheless, the FDM percentage has more relevance to the cheesemaker than the fat content *per se* because moisture is volatile and legal limits for fat are usually specified in terms of FDM. Use of FDM has the further advantage that it can be controlled directly by milk standardization whereas the fat content of cheese cannot.

A prerequisite for the manufacture of cheese of a desired composition is the use of milk with a standardized casein/fat ratio. The actual ratio required to obtain a specified FDM must be found from experience for each cheese plant since the composition of the milk will vary significantly between different milk supply areas. Milk composition fluctuates as a result of many factors, some of which, such as seasonal changes, the stage of lactation and the health of the cows' udders, are not under the cheesemaker's control. An increase of about 0·02–0·04 in the casein/fat ratio will generally cause a decrease of 1% in the FDM.[92]

4. TEXTURE OF CHEDDAR CHEESE

The texture of Cheddar cheese is recognized as being important to the consumer, yet it has not been studied extensively. This is partly due to the complexity of the situation since several variables affect the texture[91,93] and the effect of any one variable depends on the magnitude of the others. It is difficult, if not impossible, to make cheeses that differ with respect to one variable only, leaving the other variables unaltered. Our knowledge of cheese texture is therefore still mostly of a qualitative nature. A further problem is that individual teams of workers use different nomenclature for defining textural properties. For example, the properties which they claim to be measuring are variously described as body, structure, firmness, hardness, consistency, cohesiveness, crumbliness, toughness or shortness, yet the methods used may be almost identical. On the other hand, a single property, the 'firmness' of cheese, has been measured by various research groups in several different ways, i.e. using compression, penetration, tensile and breaking methods (see Volume 1, Chapter 8).

Cheddar cheese is unusual in that its texture is intermediate (Fig. 1) between those of the relatively high pH cheeses, which flow readily when a force is applied, and the low pH cheeses which tend to deform, by shattering, only at their yield point. Scanning electron microscopy has established that cheese consists of a continuous protein matrix but that this matrix is clearly different in the various cheese types.[94] The structural units in the protein matrix of Gouda are essentially in the same globular form (10–15 nm in diameter) as in the original milk. In contrast the protein aggregates in Cheshire are much smaller (3–4 nm) and are apparently in the form of strands or chains, i.e. the original sub-micellar protein aggregates appear to have lost almost all their identity. Cheddar is intermediate between Gouda and Cheshire, i.e. much of the protein in Cheddar is in the form of smaller particles than in Gouda. As the pH decreases towards that of the isoelectric point of paracasein, the protein assumes an increasingly more compact conformation and the cheese becomes shorter in texture and fractures at a smaller deformation.[95,96] Cheddar is a popular cheese to manufacture since the texture can vary from curdy to mealy but still be within a range that the consumer is willing to accept as characteristic of Cheddar.

The high moisture and relatively high pH (5·2) of American Cheddar resulted traditionally in a more cohesive and waxy texture[1] than English and New Zealand Cheddar. In North America, relatively low levels of acid are developed in the curd up to the salting stage (less than 0·65% titratable acidity). In contrast, English cheesemakers strove for a high salting acidity (about 0·85%) with a consequently low final pH (about 4·9). New Zealand cheesemakers aimed for a final pH of 5·0 and a moisture content of about 35% in contrast to the 38–39% moisture level found in both American and English Cheddar. In recent times, however, most Cheddar-producing countries have tended towards the American style of 'sweet' Cheddar cheese with a final pH between 5·1 and 5·3 now being common. Care must be taken, however, not to exceed a pH of 5·3 since the cheese will then be curdy in texture and will take longer to reach the smoothness of texture normally associated with mature Cheddar.

4.1 Effect of pH, Calcium and Salt

While the calcium content, and probably phosphate, plays an important part in establishing the characteristic structure,[3,4] the texture of Cheddar cheese appears to be more dependent upon pH than on any other factor. For the same calcium content, the texture at 35 days can vary from curdy (pH > 5·3) to waxy (pH 5·3–5·1) to mealy (pH < 5·1). Recent trials in New Zealand have shown that for any given pH value, the calcium level of Cheddar can vary over a range of ± 15 mmoles/kg with only a slight effect on the texture[5] although there is a general tendency for the cheese to become less firm as the calcium content decreases.

An explanation for the marked changes in the texture of Cheddar curd as the pH decreases from pH 5·4 to 5·0 now appears possible following the recent observation[97,98] that the hydration of casein micelles in milk reaches a maximum at about pH 5·45. More importantly, Creamer[99] found that casein hydration in renneted milk greatly increased in the presence of NaCl between about pH 5·1 and 5·5. Furthermore at any given pH the extent of solubilization of the micelles by the NaCl decreased as the calcium concentration in the solution increased. This finding is in agreement with the effects of calcium in brine on the solubilization of the rind of Gouda-type cheese[100] and on the quantity of brine-soluble protein (BSP) fractions that can be extracted from Cheddar curd,[101] and the observation that in general a higher Ca^{2+}/Na^+ ratio results in a firmer cheese.[95] The marked changes in the texture of Cheddar cheese that occur as the pH varies between pH 5·5 and 4·9 appear to result from the combined effects of pH, NaCl and the calcium concentration on the extent of the interaction between casein and water. It may also be significant that renneted case in 5% NaCl binds very little calcium below pH values of about 5·1.[99]

It has long been known[102] that fresh Cheddar curd is insoluble in warm (50°C) sodium chloride solution (5%, w/v) but that as lactic acid develops in the curd during manufacture its solubility increases. This increase in the fraction that is soluble in brine has been attributed to the loss of calcium salts in the whey. The development of a fibrous texture and the formation of strings on a hot iron were related to the increase in quantity of the BSP fractions.[102] The enrichment of milk with calcium reduced the proportion of casein extracted from Cheddar curd in the BSP.[101] Furthermore, the Cheddar cheese ripened more slowly and did not become salts in the whey. The development of a fibrous texture and the formation of strings on a hot iron were related to the increase in quantity of the BSP fractions.[102] The enrichment of milk with calcium reduced the calcium present in buffalo milk[105] may also account for the difficulty in manufacturing Cheddar cheese from buffalo milk. The extent of proteolysis is low,[106] presumably because the degree of solubilization of the casein micelles by the NaCl is reduced. As a result the cheese needs to be stored for long periods before the characteristic Cheddar texture and flavour develop.

Salt also has a more direct effect on the texture of Cheddar cheese: excessive salting (i.e. a S/M > ~6%) produces a firm-textured cheese which is drier and ripens at a slow rate,[27] while under-salting (i.e. a S/M < ~4%) results in pasty cheese with abnormal ripening and flavour characteristics. Such factors as enzyme activity and the conformation of α_{s1}- and β-caseins in salt solutions,[86] solubility of protein breakdown products, hydration of the protein network,[58] and interactions of calcium with the paracaseinate complex in cheese[100] are all influenced by salt concentration.

4.2 Effect of Protein, Fat and Moisture

Basically, cheeses consist of an aggregation of water, fat and protein (mainly casein) in roughly equal proportions by weight, plus small amounts of NaCl and lactic acid. Since protein is considerably denser than either water or fat, it occupies only about one-sixth of the total volume. Nevertheless, it is largely the protein matrix which gives rise to the rigid form of the cheese. Any modification of the nature or the amount of the protein present in the cheese will modify its texture. Thus, reduced-fat Cheddar cheese (17% fat) is considerably firmer and more elastic than full-fat Cheddar cheese (35% fat) even though the MNFS levels of the cheese are the same.[107] This difference was explained by the presence in the reduced-fat cheese of about 30% more protein matrix, which must be cut or deformed in texture assessments, but such a large reduction in fat must also affect the texture of the cheese.

Fat in cheese exists as physically distinct globules, dispersed in the aqueous protein matrix.[18] In general, increasing the fat content results in a slightly softer cheese, as does an increase in moisture content, since the protein framework is weakened as the volume fraction of protein molecules decreases. Relatively large variations in the fat content are, however, necessary before the texture of the cheese is significantly affected.[83] Commercial cheese with a high FDM usually has a high MNFS[85] and this causes a decrease in firmness. An inverse relationship between the fat content and cheese hardness has been reported,[91,108] but so, strangely, has a direct relationship.[109] This apparent anomaly is due to the use of the term 'hardness' to describe different textural characteristics and also to the different temperatures at which the hardness test was carried out.

4.3 Effect of Ripening

Considerable changes in texture occur during ripening as a consequence of proteolysis. The rubbery texture of 'green' cheese changes relatively rapidly as the framework of α_{s1}-casein molecules is cleaved by the residual coagulant.[96] A group of Cheddar cheeses examined over a period of nearly a year increased in hardness and decreased in elasticity with the age of the cheese, the greatest changes occurring during the first 30 days.[108] In part, this is caused by the loss of structural elements but another feature of proteolysis is probably important:[96] as each peptide bond is cleaved two new ionic groups are generated and each of these will compete for the available water in the system. Thus, the water previously available for solvation of the protein chains becomes tied up by the new ionic groups making the cheese firmer and less easily deformed. This change, in combination with loss of an extensive protein network, gives the observed effect.

Clearly, the change in texture during ripening depends upon the extent of proteolysis which, for any individual cheese, is determined by the duration and temperature of maturation. The main factor that influences the rate of proteolysis appears to be S/M.[50,86] A direct relationship between S/M and residual protein was established whereas the correlation between moisture and residual protein was relatively weak. A cheese with a low S/M value has a higher rate of proteolysis and is correspondingly softer in texture than a cheese with a high S/M. The concentrations of residual rennet and plasmin in the cheese, together with the starter and non-starter proteinases present, must, however, also be important factors that determine the rate of proteolysis.[4] An increase in the heat treatment of the milk before manufacture reduces the rate of formation of water-soluble nitrogenous products[110] but this effect would be minor relative to the other factors cited.

5. FLAVOUR OF CHEDDAR CHEESE

Cheese ripening is essentially the controlled slow decomposition of a rennet coagulum of the constituents of milk. Hydrolysis of the casein network, specifically α_{s1}-casein, by the coagulant appears to be responsible for the initial changes in the coagulum matrix.[96] The levels of both chymosin and plasmin retained in the curd are pH-dependent.[4,30] In fresh milk, plasmin, the native milk proteinase, is associated with the casein micelles but it dissociates as the pH is decreased.[87] Both the proportion of plasmin and its activity will therefore decrease as the pH of the cheese decreases. The role of plasmin in Cheddar cheese flavour has yet to be elucidated but it has been reported that the rate and extent of characteristic flavour development in Cheddar cheese slurries appeared to be related directly only to the degradation of β-casein.[111] Plasmin may well, therefore, prove to be an enzyme of considerable importance in the development of cheese flavour.

As the original casein network is broken down the desired balance of flavour and aroma compounds is formed. However, the precise nature of the reactions which produce flavour compounds and the way in which their relative rates are controlled is poorly understood. This has been due firstly to the lack of knowledge of the compounds which impart typical flavour to Cheddar cheese, and secondly to the complexity of the cheese microflora as the potential producers of flavour compounds. Any organism that grows in the cheese, whether starter or non-starter, and any active enzyme that may be present such as chymosin or plasmin, must have an influence on subsequent cheese flavour (Fig. 8). Research in New Zealand has clearly established, however, that if starter and non-starter growth is controlled so as not to reach levels that give discernible off-flavours[4,7] and if as little chymosin as possible is used,[112,113] the flavour which develops in Cheddar cheese is likely to be acceptable to most consumers.

There appear to be only two 'facts' on which all research workers on Cheddar cheese flavour seem to agree. Firstly, that milk fat has to be present for the perception of flavour[114] and secondly that lactic starters

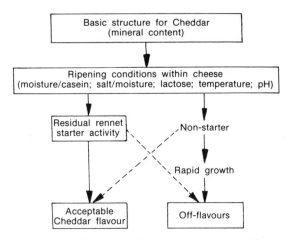

Fig. 8.   The main factors that determine the development of flavour in Cheddar cheese.

must be used for the development of a typical balanced Cheddar flavour. However, the mechanisms by which fat and starter carry out their functions is not at all well understood. Virtually every finding and conclusion reached by any research group have become subsequently a matter of controversy. Totally contradictory conclusions have appeared, sometimes from the same group, on, for example, the role of starter and non-starter organisms in Cheddar cheese. Not surprisingly, therefore, many reviews have been written recently on Cheddar flavour.[84,115–118] This section is an attempt by the present authors to summarize what they consider to be relevant.

5.1 Effect of Milkfat

It is well accepted that Cheddar cheese made from skim-milk does not develop a characteristic flavour. Cheese with a FDM greater than 50% developed a typical flavour whereas cheese with a FDM less than 50% did not.[114] When, in this study, a series of batches of cheese were made from milk of increasing fat content (from 0 to 4·5%), the quality of the flavour improved as the fat content increased. If, however, the fat content was increased above a certain limit the flavour was not further improved. Substituting vegetable or mineral oil for milkfat still resulted in a degree of Cheddar flavour.[119] This suggests that the water–fat interface in cheese is important and that the flavour components are dissolved and retained in the fat. Clearly, although milk proteins and lactose are the most likely sources of the flavour precursors in Cheddar cheese, the milkfat plays an important but not yet completely defined role.

5.2 Effect of Protein

As described earlier, it is likely that the breakdown of casein is involved in the production of Cheddar cheese flavour. A further consequence of proteolysis could also be the release of flavour components which were previously bound to the protein.[120] Most research has concentrated on the aroma aspect of Cheddar flavour but it now appears to have been established that the non-volatile, water-soluble fraction makes the greater contribution to flavour intensity. It has been suggested[84,120] that the importance of low levels of such non-volatile compounds as peptides, amino acids and salts has been under-rated in the past. This view is supported by the highly significant correlations found between the levels of proteolysis products and the extent of flavour development.[121] The level of phosphotungstic acid-soluble amino nitrogen was found to be a reliable indicator of flavour development. Above certain limits, however, the level of specific low molecular weight peptides results in bitterness. Cheddar cheeses made with temperature-insensitive starter strains were found to become bitter because large numbers of starter cells contributed excessive levels of proteinases. These released bitter-tasting peptides from high molecular weight peptides which had been produced mainly as a result of chymosin action.[89] The subject of bitterness, the single most common defect in Cheddar cheese, has been extensively reviewed (for instance Ref. 122).

Manning and his colleagues have published several reports (see Ref. 123 for review) that strongly implicate the volatile sulphur compounds, specifically methanethiol, in Cheddar cheese flavour, but an Australian report[124] concludes that none of these sulphur compounds is a reliable indicator of flavour development. It is conceivable, however, that although the volatiles do not make a measurable contribution to the intensity of Cheddar flavour, they may still be an essential factor in the quality of the flavour.[120] This is supported by the finding[125,126] that the quality of blocks of Cheddar cheese decreased, and off-flavours increased, with decrease in block size. Headspace analysis showed that the concentrations of H_2S and CH_3SH, compounds that are extremely susceptible to oxidation, decreased as the quality of the cheese decreased.

5.2.1 Effect of redox potential

Since the redox potential determines the status of disulphide/sulphydryls in both the casein and the enzymes in cheese, the redox potential would be expected to affect the rate of proteolysis during cheese ripening. The data supporting the view that the development of characteristic cheese flavour is determined by the ability of protein-based sulphur groups to accept hydrogen resulting from oxidative ripening processes have been extensively reviewed.[115,126] Whenever active —SH groups failed to appear early in ripening, as a consequence of atypical manufacturing conditions, the resulting cheese was found to lack flavour.[115]

In all cases, the formation of —SH groups has been related to the development of desirable cheese flavour. For example, the unsuccessful attempts to duplicate the flavour of cheese made from unheated milk by the addition of 'flavour-producing' bacteria to heated milk is considered to be the result of the heat-induced interaction of sulphur-containing groups of milk proteins, which reduces the ability of the groups to accept hydrogen during fermentation.[115] A more recent finding,[127] however, suggests that non-starter bacteria vary in their ability to maintain the required low redox potential in cheese. This might account for the many conflicting reports concerning the effect of non-starter bacteria on cheese flavour.

5.3 Role of Starter

The absence of any Cheddar flavour in gluconolactone-acidified cheese and the development of typical, balanced Cheddar flavour in starter-only cheese[128] established that starter has a role in the development of cheese flavour. What exactly that role is has been much more difficult to determine. The concept of an indirect contribution of starters to the production of flavour compounds was first suggested by New Zealand research workers.[129] They considered that the main role of the starter might be limited merely to providing a suitable environment which allows the elaboration of characteristic cheese flavour. They were careful, however, to leave open the question of whether the starter also produced chemical compounds that contribute to this desirable flavour. Other research workers have surprisingly concluded that some of the key flavour compounds are produced non-enzymically and that starter enzymes are not directly responsible for Cheddar flavour,[116,130–132] a view that has recently had to be modified.[133] It seems more reasonable at this stage to assume that the enzymes of both viable and dead starter cells are involved in flavour development.

It is clear that one role of the starter streptococci is to provide the required redox potential, pH and moisture content in the cheese that allows enzyme activity to proceed favourably. In addition, the temperature during manufacture and the S/M must be so controlled as to ensure that the net metabolic activity of the starter organisms is low[113,129] but nevertheless adequate to allow the required pH at one day to be reached. Should the starter reach too high a population or survive too long, flavour defects such as bitterness, which mask or detract from cheese flavour, are produced. Accumulated circumstantial evidence suggests strongly that the reduction or removal of unpleasant flavours is associated with improved perception of the Cheddar flavour.[89,129]

A second role for starter in flavour development may be more direct in that lactic streptococci can metabolize lactose and citrate to diacetyl.[134] It has been suggested[135] that cheese flavour may in part be the consequence of the formation of addition compounds between diacetyl and —SH groups. These, together with low levels of free amino acids and specific peptides,[120] acetic acid,[136,137] carbon dioxide,[137] lactic acid,[137] and NaCl, may well form the basis of Cheddar cheese flavour.

5.4 Role of Non-starter

Cheddar cheese made under controlled bacteriological conditions and containing only starter streptococci develops balanced, typical flavour[128] but it is intriguing that cheeses made in open vats develop such flavour more rapidly.[138–140] This would suggest that a non-starter flora, present as a result of post-pasteurization contamination, is beneficial. There have, nevertheless, been reports that conclude that non-starter bacteria have little effect on normal Cheddar cheese flavour development.[131,141]

The role of non-starter bacteria in Cheddar cheese flavour has clearly yet to be elucidated. However, as has been amply shown for starter organisms, it is probable that relatively low densities of non-starter bacteria are beneficial but high densities are not.[4] It appears that the rate of growth of the non-starter bacteria during the early days of ripening is important. The rate of cooling of the cheese, after pressing the curd, appears to be the single most significant factor in controlling the cheese flora[7] and appears to offer the easiest method of controlling cheese flavour.[142]

An alternative to actually determining the numbers of non-starter bacteria in cheese is to measure a compound such as acetate, since this provides an index of the degree of hetero-fermentative metabolism that may have taken place (T. F. Fryer, personal communication). When such growth is extensive, cheese quality is often less than satisfactory because of fermented and sour off-flavours and one of the compounds responsible is undoubtedly acetic acid. More recently, it has been shown that the L-lactate originally present in the cheese is slowly converted to D-lactate.[143] Racemization, which normally takes about 90 days, represents a significant change during Cheddar cheese ripening since about half of the lactate (0·7% of the cheese mass) is transformed. All pediococci that have been isolated from Cheddar cheese have had racemizing activity, and the level of this activity was up to seven times greater than in the small proportion of lactobacillus isolates which could convert L-lactate to D-lactate.[143] An interesting point is that the calcium salt of D,L-lactic acid is less soluble than that of L-lactic acid. Racemization will therefore encourage the formation of undesirable white deposits in cheese.

6. GRADING OF CHEDDAR CHEESE

There is no absolute standard for measuring cheese quality. Young Cheddar cheese is judged on the basis of whether it has properties characteristic of its variety. Compositional analysis provides an objective method of detecting atypical cheese and is to be preferred to subjective grading methods. In the case of mature cheese, quality assessment is largely a matter of personal preference, with consumers differing considerably in their requirements with respect to cheese flavour.

The assignment of a grade to a consignment of cheese may be improperly influenced by the sample since differences may exist between blocks of cheese made from the same vat of milk and even within the same block of cheese. Flavour defects, such as fruitiness and sulphide off-flavours, have sometimes been located in particular areas within a cheese.[5] Such lack of uniform flavour usually results from variations in S/M.[28] Differences between cheeses has also been attributed to an uneven cooling of cheese blocks stacked closely on pallets while the cheese is still warm.[144] It is clear that a grade score is likely to be highly biased if the assessment of a whole vat depends on a single, randomly-drawn sample.[55]

It has long been recognized that the texture of Cheddar cheese changes dramatically during the first few days of ripening. The simplest explanation for this observation is that the cheese microstructure consists of an extensive network of α_{s1}-casein and that cleavage by chymosin (or rennet substitute) of just a few peptide bonds of α_{s1}-casein greatly weakens this network.[96] This results in a relatively large change in the force necessary for deformation. It is differences in this force that a grader attempts to assess when he rubs down a plug of cheese between his thumb and fore-finger. From this assessment of the texture, after the cheese has been allowed to ripen for at least seven days, the grader proceeds to predict what the quality of the cheese will be after it has matured.[4]

The sensory method of prediction traditionally used by graders has therefore some validity since the rate of change in the cheese texture during the first few days of ripening is determined by the same factors, i.e. the pH at one day, the salt to moisture ratio and the moisture to casein ratio, which also influence the quality of the cheese at maturity (Fig. 9). In addition,

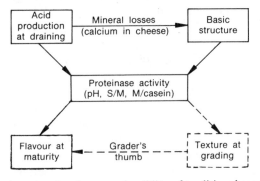

Fig. 9.   An explanation for the general validity of traditional sensory testing of Cheddar cheese.

experience has long shown that a Cheddar cheese with an atypical texture seldom, if ever, develops a characteristic flavour. Unfortunately, however, the reverse is not true. A good-textured cheese does not always result in an acceptable flavour, since off-flavours can still be produced if unsuitable manufacturing and ripening procedures are used.[4] Essentially, the grader, using his thumb, is attempting to assess that acid production at draining was normal for the particular variety of cheese. However, this can be achieved more directly and objectively by measurement of the cheese composition, which would also partly overcome the confusion in nomenclature used in grading circles. 'Body', 'texture', 'firmness' and 'hardness' may all be synonymous if different experts are judging the same batch of cheese and there is a need to define and standardize the various terms.

6.1 The Role of Calcium

The calcium content of Cheddar cheese has an important effect upon both texture and long-term keeping quality.[5] Variations in the calcium content occur as a result of differences in the starter percentage used, the time allowed from 'set' to 'run' during manufacture and because of both seasonal and lactational changes. The point in the process at which the curd is drained from the whey is the key stage in the manufacture of Cheddar cheese since it controls to a large extent its mineral content, the proportions of residual chymosin and plasmin in the cheese, the final pH and the moisture to casein ratio.[3] All of these influence the rate of proteolysis in the cheese. Furthermore, a relationship has been found between the calcium content of the cheese, the concentration of residual chymosin and the protein breakdown during ripening[4] and also between the rate of acid development in the early stages of manufacture and the proteolysis in the cheese.[145] It follows then that the calcium level is an index of both the extent of acid production up to the draining stage and also an indication of the rate of proteolysis that is likely to occur during ripening. Significant differences in the calcium content of Cheddar cheese manufactured on the same day would suggest differences in the proportions of residual chymosin and plasmin in the cheeses. Consequently, one would expect differences in the rate of proteolysis and thus in the development of flavour.

The introduction of minimum calcium levels into the cheese specifications would further improve the prediction rate when grading a young cheese, since a calcium content above a predetermined level would indicate that acid production up to the draining stage had been normal. It must be stressed, however, that the variations in the calcium content of Cheddar cheese have a much smaller effect than S/M or MNFS on cheese quality[5] and calcium data should only be used to complement these more important quality parameters. It should also be noted that the routine determination of calcium in cheese presents some problems,[146] with a precision of only $\pm 5\%$.

7.   VARIANTS OF CHEDDAR CHEESE

7.1 Low Fat Cheddar Cheese

Much interest has been shown in the potential market for a reduced-fat Cheddar cheese in today's calorie-conscious society. It is proving difficult, however, to produce a low fat cheese with the same flavour and texture characteristics as a full-fat cheese.[147,148] Cheddar cheeses containing only 15–30% fat are noticeably more firm and less smooth when young than full-fat cheese. The differences in texture, although marked in the early stages of ripening, apparently narrow after the cheese has matured for one or two months.[148]

7.2 Stirred Curd or Granular Cheese

As discussed earlier, granular cheese preceded, historically, the manufacture of traditional Cheddar cheese. It is made as for normal Cheddar cheese except that the cheddaring step is omitted. More acid, therefore, has to be developed at the vat stage to compensate for the shorter total manufacturing time but starter systems are now available which allow very acceptable granular cheese to be produced. Maintaining curd in the granular form, without the need for milling prior to salting, has obvious attractions. There is, however, a tendency for the curd to mat after drying unless it is agitated and continued stirring may lead to high fat losses. Moisture expulsion is also faster than during cheddaring.

The salted curd particles take some time to fuse together, the rate of bonding depending largely upon the pH of the curd at salting. There are, however, advantages in mechanized cheesemaking systems in having the curd in a granular form at the hooping stage. The salt readily mixes with the curd, the salted granules flow readily and can be easily hooped. Stirred curd cheesemaking is now widely used in the manufacture of 'barrel' (bulk pressed) cheese, although there is still, apparently, a problem with variations in moisture levels.[149]

Granular, stirred curd gives rise to open-textured cheese as a result of air being entrapped within the cheese.[39] Following the development of methods of pressing cheese under vacuum[76] the problem of open texture has been eliminated and good quality Cheddar cheese can be produced without cheddaring by vacuum pressing the dry-stirred curd. It thus appears that the main purpose of cheddaring is to achieve a reduction in entrapped air. Granular cheese resembles Cheddar cheese in composition but it does mature somewhat differently because of the relatively low acidity at which the curd is salted. Curd hooped in the granular form gives a texture at 14 days which, although completely close, is just perceptibly different from normal Cheddar cheese.[42] This difference in texture, however, becomes increasingly less obvious as the cheese matures.

7.3 Washed Curd Varieties

There has been a substantial increase in recent years in the consumption of dry-salted washed-curd varieties of cheese.[150] Varieties such as Colby and Monterey, which are milder in flavour and have a more plastic texture than Cheddar, apparently have filled a need for consumers. They are high-moisture cheeses (39–40%) and ripen rapidly.

7.3.1 Colby and Monterey

The recent improvements in the production of granular Cheddar for processing are also indirectly responsible for the increase in production of Colby and Monterey since these varieties are in fact washed-curd, granular cheeses. Traditionally, whey is drained off until the curd on the bottom of the vat is just breaking the surface and cold water is added to reduce the temperature of the curds/whey to about 27°C (Fig. 10). The moisture content of the cheese can be controlled by the temperature of the curd/whey/water mix. The moisture content decreases as the temperature is increased

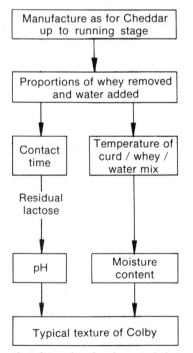

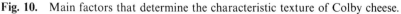

Fig. 10. Main factors that determine the characteristic texture of Colby cheese.

between 26°C and 34°C. The pH of the cheese is determined both by the proportions of whey removed and water added. The length of time the water is in contact with the curd is also important since this determines the level of residual lactose. Since salt penetration into the interior of the granular curd particles is rapid, no pH gradient occurs and seaminess is not a problem.

The calcium content of Colby (Fig. 1) tends to be lower than that of Cheddar because of the slightly higher starter percentage used and a further loss of calcium at the washing stage. As discussed previously, however, it is the pH that determines to a large extent the texture of a cheese. The addition of water results in a small increase (about 0·1–0·2 units) in pH of the finished cheese but this is sufficient to give the cheese a more plastic texture than Cheddar. Recent trials[5] have shown that the calcium level of Colby cheese can vary between 120 and 180 mmoles/kg cheese without influencing significantly the texture of the cheese as long as the pH is greater than about 5·2. The characteristic texture of Colby cheese is thus influenced almost entirely by its pH and moisture level (Fig. 10). Traditionally, Colby had a mechanically open texture but the use of short-time pressing systems,[65,66] in which the curd is transported to the press under a partial vacuum, results in a texture that is as close as that of Gouda-type cheese varieties. Monterey cheese has many similarities to Colby but is usually softer.[1]

REFERENCES

1. Kosikowski, F. V., *Cheese and Fermented Milk Foods*, 2nd edn, Edwards Brothers Inc., Ann Arbor, Michigan, 1977.
2. Czulak, J., *Proc. 15th Int. Dairy Congress, London*, 1959, Vol. 2, p. 829.
3. Lawrence, R. C., Heap, H. A. and Gilles, J., *J. Dairy Sci.*, 1984, **67**, 1632.
4. Lawrence, R. C., Gilles, J. and Creamer, L. K., *N.Z. J. Dairy Sci. Technol.*, 1983, **18**, 175.
5. Gilles, J. and Lawrence, R. C., Unpublished results.
6. Turner, K. W. and Thomas, T. D., *N.Z. J. Dairy Sci. Technol.*, 1980, **15**, 265.
7. Fryer, T. F., *Proc. 21st Int. Dairy Congress, Moscow*, 1982, Vol. 1, Book 1, p. 485.
8. Sammis, J. L., *Res. Bull. Univ. Wis. Agric. Exp. Stn*, No. 7, 1910.
9. Whitehead, H. R. and Harkness, W. L., *Aust. J. Dairy Technol.*, 1954, **9**, 103.
10. Lawrence, R. C. and Pearce, L. E., *Dairy Ind.*, 1972, **37**, 73.
11. Lawrence, R. C., Heap, H. A., Limsowtin, G. K. Y. and Jarvis, A. W., *J. Dairy Sci.*, 1978, **61**, 1181.
12. Lawrence, R. C., Thomas, T. D. and Terzaghi, B. E., *J. Dairy Res.*, 1976, **43**, 141.

13. Richardson, G. H., Ernstrom, C. A. and Hong, G. L., *Cult. Dairy Prod. J.*, 1981, **16**, 11.
14. Daly, C., *Irish J. Food Sci. Technol.*, 1983, **7**, 39.
15. Stadhouders, J. and Leenders, G. J. M., *Neth. Milk Dairy J.*, 1984, **38**, 157.
16. Fox, P. F. In: *Developments in Food Proteins*, Vol. 3 (Ed. B. J. F. Hudson), Elsevier Applied Science, London, p. 69, 1984.
17. Green, M. L. In: *Advances in the Microbiology and Biochemistry of Cheese and Fermented Milk* (Eds F. L. Davies and B. A. Law), Elsevier Applied Science, London, p. 1, 1984.
18. Kimber, A. M., Brooker, B. E., Hobbs, D. G. and Prentice, J. H., *J. Dairy Res.*, 1974, **41**, 389.
19. Kalab, M., *Milchwissenschaft*, 1977, **32**, 49.
20. Stanley, D. W. and Emmons, D. B., *J. Inst. Can. Sci. Tech. Aliment.*, 1978, **10**, 78.
21. Lowrie, R. J., Kalab, M. and Nichols, D., *J. Dairy Sci.*, 1982, **65**, 1122.
22. Kalab, M., Lowrie, R. J. and Nichols, D., *J. Dairy Sci.*, 1982, **65**, 1117.
23. Eino, M. F., Biggs, D. A., Irvine, D. M. and Stanley, D. W., *J. Dairy Res.*, 1976, **43**, 113.
24. Green, M. L., Turvey, A. and Hobbs, D. G., *J. Dairy Res.*, 1981, **48**, 343.
25. Green, M. L., Marshall, R. J. and Glover, F. A., *J. Dairy Res.*, 1983, **50**, 341.
26. Creamer, L. K., Gilles, J. and Lawrence, R. C., *N.Z. J. Dairy Sci. Technol.*, 1985, **20**, 185.
27. Van Slyke, L. L. and Price, W. V., *Cheese*, 4th edn, Orange Judd Publishing Co., New York, 1952.
28. Lawrence, R. C. and Gilles, J., *N.Z. J. Dairy Sci. Technol.*, 1982, **17**, 1.
29. Dolby, R. M., *N.Z. J. Sci. Technol.*, 1941, **22**, 289A.
30. Holmes, D. G., Duersch, J. W. and Ernstrom, C. A., *J. Dairy Sci.*, 1977, **60**, 862.
31. Czulak, J., Conochie, J., Sutherland, B. J. and Van Leeuwen, H. J. M., *J. Dairy Res.*, 1969, **36**, 93.
32. Whitehead, H. R. and Harkness, W. L., *Proc. 15th Int. Dairy Congress, London*, 1959, Vol. 2, p. 832.
33. Czulak, J., Hammond, L. A. and Meharry, J., *Aust. Dairy Rev.*, 1954, **22**(6), 18.
34. Czulak, J. and Hammond, L. A., *Aust. Dairy Rev.*, 1956, **24**, 13.
35. Hammond, L. A., *Proc. 1st Biennial Marschall Int. Cheese Conf.*, 1979, p. 495.
36. Patel, M. C., Lund, D. B. and Olson, N. F., *J. Dairy Sci.*, 1972, **55**, 913.
37. Irvine, D. M. and Price, W. V., 1958, *U.S. Patent* 2 850 390.
38. Walter, H. E., Sadler, A. M., Malkames, J. P. and Mitchell, C. D., *J. Dairy Sci.*, 1956, **39**, 917.
39. Czulak, J. and Hammond, L. A., *Aust. J. Dairy Technol.*, 1956, **11**, 58.
40. Czulak, J., *Dairy Eng.*, 1958, **75**, 67.
41. King, N. and Czulak, J., *Nature, Lond.*, 1958, **181**, 113.
42. Czulak, J., *Dairy Eng.*, 1962, **79**, 183.
43. Harkness, W. L., King, D. W. and McGillivray, W. A., *N.Z. J. Dairy Sci. Technol.*, 1968. **3**, 124.
44. Olson, N. J. and Price, W. V., *J. Dairy Sci.*, 1970, **53**, 1676.
45. Conochie, J. and Sutherland, B. J., *J. Dairy Res.*, 1965, **32**, 35.
46. Gilles, J., *N.Z. J. Dairy Sci. Technol.*, 1976, **11**, 219.
47. Gilbert, R. W., *Proc. 1st Biennial Marschall Int. Cheese Conf.*, 1979, p. 503.

48. Breene, W. M., Olson, N. F. and Price, W. V., *J. Dairy Sci.*, 1965, **48**, 621.
49. Thomas, T. D. and Pearce, K. N., *N.Z. J. Dairy Sci. Technol.*, 1981, **16**, 253.
50. Pearce, K. N., *Proc. 21st Int. Dairy Congress, Moscow*, 1982, Vol. 1, Book 1, p. 519.
51. Lawrence, R. C. and Gilles, J., *N.Z. J. Dairy Sci. Technol.*, 1969, **4**, 189.
52. Robertson, P. S., *J. Dairy Res.*, 1966, **33**, 343.
53. Sutherland, B. J., *Aust. J. Dairy Tech.*, 1974, **29**, 86.
54. Czulak, J., *Aust. J. Dairy Technol.*, 1963, **18**, 192.
55. Sutherland, B. J., *Aust. J. Dairy Technol.*, 1977, **32**, 17.
56. Czulak, J., Conochie, J. and Hammond, L. A., *Aust. J. Dairy Technol.*, 1964, **19**, 157.
57. McDowall, F. H. and Dolby, R. M., *J. Dairy Res.*, 1936, **7**, 156.
58. Guerts, T. J., Walstra, P. and Mulder, H., *Neth. Milk Dairy J.*, 1974, **28**, 102.
59. Hoeker, W. H. and Hammer, B. W., *Food Res.*, 1944, **9**, 278.
60. McDowall, F. H. and Whelan, L. A., *J. Dairy Res.*, 1933, **4**, 147.
61. Fox, P. F., *Irish J. Agric. Res.*, 1974, **13**, 129.
62. Morris, T. A., *Aust. J. Dairy Technol.*, 1961, **16**, 31.
63. Le Graet, Y., Lepienne, A., Brule, G. and Ducruet, P., *Le Lait*, 1983, **63**, 317.
64. Al-Dahhan, A. H. and Crawford, R. J. M., *Proc. 21st Int. Dairy Congress, Moscow*, 1982, Vol. 1, Book 1, p. 389.
65. Wegner, F., *Proc. 1st Biennial Marschall Int. Cheese Conf.*, 1979, p. 213.
66. Brockwell, I. P., *Proc. 2nd Biennial Marschall Int. Cheese Conf.*, 1981, p. 208.
67. Czulak, J., Freeman, N. H. and Hammond, L. A., *Aust. J. Dairy Technol.*, 1962, **17**, 22.
68. Irvine, O. R. and Burnett, K. A., *Can. Dairy Ice Cream J.*, 1962, **41**, 24.
69. Price, W. V., Olson, N. F. and Grimstad, A., *J. Dairy Sci.*, 1963, **46**, 604.
70. Robertson, P. S., *Aust. J. Dairy Technol.*, 1965, **20**, 155.
71. Hoglund, G. F., Fryer, T. F. and Gilles, J., *N.Z. J. Dairy Sci. Technol.*, 1972, **7**, 150.
72. Robertson, P. S., *Dairy Ind.*, 1965, **30**, 779.
73. Walter, H. E., Sadler, A. M., Malkames, J. P. and Mitchell, C. D., *U.S. Dept. Agric. Bur. Dairy Ind.*, 1953, BDI-Inf-158.
74. Whitehead, H. R. and Jones, L. J., *N.Z. J. Sci. Technol.*, 1946, **27**, A 406.
75. Hoglund, G. F., Fryer, T. F. and Gilles, J., *N.Z. J. Dairy Sci. Technol.*, 1972, **7**, 159.
76. Smith, A. B., Roberts, M. J. and Wagner, D. W., 1959, *Canadian Patent* No. 578 251.
77. Robertson, P. S., *Dairy Ind.*, 1967, **32**, 32.
78. O'Connor, C. B., *Irish Agric. Creamery Rev.*, 1971, **24**(6), 5.
79. Fox, P. F., *Irish J. Agric. Res.*, 1975, **14**, 33.
80. Gilles, J. and Lawrence, R. C., *N.Z. J. Dairy Sci. Technol.*, 1973, **8**, 141.
81. Lyall, A., *Aust. J. Dairy Technol.*, 1968, **23**, 30.
82. Pearce, K. N. and Gilles, J., *N.Z. J. Dairy Sci. Technol.*, 1979, **14**, 63.
83. Lawrence, R. C. and Gilles, J., *N.Z. J. Dairy Sci. Technol.*, 1980, **15**, 1.
84. Adda, J., Gripon, J. C. and Vassal, L., *Food Chem.*, 1982, **9**, 115.
85. Lelievre, J., *J. Soc. Dairy Technol.*, 1983, **36**, 119.
86. Fox, P. F. and Walley, B. F., *J. Dairy Res.*, 1971, **38**, 165.
87. Richardson, B. C. and Pearce, K. N., *N.Z. J. Dairy Sci. Technol.*, 1981, **16**, 209.

88. Martley, F. G. and Lawrence, R. C., *N.Z. J. Dairy Sci. Technol.*, 1972, **7**, 38.
89. Lowrie, R. S. and Lawrence, R. C., *N.Z. J. Dairy Sci. Technol.*, 1972, **7**, 51.
90. Breheny, S., Kanasaki, M., Hillier, A. J. and Jago, G. R., *Aust. J. Dairy Technol.*, 1975, **30**, 145.
91. Whitehead, H. R., *J. Dairy Res.*, 1948, **15**, 387.
92. Dolby, R. M. and Harkness, W. L., *N.Z. J. Sci. Technol.*, 1955, **37A**, 68.
93. Weik, R. W., Ph.D. thesis, University of Michigan, Ann Arbor, Michigan, 1964.
94. Hall, D. M. and Creamer, L. K., *N.Z. J. Dairy Sci. Technol.*, 1972, **7**, 95.
95. Walstra, P. and Van Vliet, T., *Int. Dairy Fed.*, Doc-153, 1982, p. 22.
96. Creamer, L. K. and Olson, N. F., *J. Food Sci.*, 1982, **47**, 631.
97. Snoeren, T. H. M., Klok, H. J., Van Hooydonk, A. C. M. and Damman, A. J., *Milchwissenschaft*, 1984, **39**, 461.
98. Tarodo de la Fuente, B. and Alais, C., *J. Dairy Sci.*, 1975, **58**, 293.
99. Creamer, L. K., *Milchwissenschaft*, 1985, **40**, 589.
100. Guerts, T. J., Walstra, P. and Mulder, H., *Neth. Milk Dairy J.*, 1972, **26**, 168.
101. Gupta, S. K., Whitney, R. M. and Tuckey, S. L., *J. Dairy Sci.*, 1974, **57**, 540.
102. Van Slyke, L. L. and Bosworth, A. W., *N.Y. Agric. Exp. Stn Tech. Bull.*, 1907, No. 4.
103. Ernstrom, C. A., Price, W. V. and Swanson, A. M., *J. Dairy Sci.*, 1958, **41**, 61.
104. Babel, F. J., *Nat. Butter Cheese J.*, 1948, **39**, 42.
105. Rajput, Y. S., Bhavadasan, M. K. and Ganguli, N. C., *Milchwissenschaft*, 1983, **38**, 211.
106. Neogi, S. B. and Jude, T. V. R. *Proc. 20th Int. Dairy Congress, Paris*, 1978, Vol. E, p. 810.
107. Emmons, D. B., Kalab, M. and Larmond, E., *J. Texture Studies*, 1980, **11**, 15.
108. Baron, M., *Dairy Ind.*, 1949, **14**, 146.
109. Weik, R. W., Combs, W. R. and Morris, H. A., *J. Dairy Sci.*, 1958, **41**, 375.
110. Call, A. O. and Price, W. V., *J. Dairy Sci.*, 1944, **27**, 681.
111. Harper, W. J., Carmona, A. and Kristoffersen, T., *J. Food Sci.*, 1971, **36**, 503.
112. Lawrence, R. C. and Gilles, J., *N.Z. J. Dairy Sci. Technol.*, 1971, **6**, 30.
113. Lawrence, R. C., Creamer, L. K., Gilles, J. and Martley, F. G., *N.Z. J. Dairy Sci. Technol.*, 1972, **7**, 32.
114. Ohren, J. P. and Tuckey, S. L., *J. Dairy Sci.*, 1969, **52**, 598.
115. Kristoffersen, T., *J. Agric. Food Chem.*, 1973, **21**, 573.
116. Law, B. A., *Dairy Sci. Abstr.*, 1981, **43**, 143.
117. Law, B. A. In: *Advances in the Microbiology and Biochemistry of Cheese and Fermented Milk* (Ed. F. L. Davies and B. A. Law) Elsevier Applied Science, London, p. 187, 1984.
118. Aston, J. W. and Dulley, J. R., *Aust. J. Dairy Technol.*, 1982, **37**, 59.
119. Foda, E. A., Hammond, E. G., Reinbold, G. W. and Hotchkiss, D. K., *J. Dairy Sci.*, 1974, **57**, 1137.
120. McGugan, W. A., Emmons, D. B. and Larmond, E., *J. Dairy Sci.*, 1979, **62**, 398.
121. Aston, J. W., Durward, I. G. and Dulley, J. R., *Aust. J. Dairy Technol.*, 1983, **38**, 55.
122. Crawford, R. J. M., *Ann. Bull. Int. Dairy Fed.*, 1977, No. 97.
123. Green, M. L. and Manning, D. J., *J. Dairy Res.*, 1982, **49**, 737.
124. Aston, J. W. and Douglas, K., *Aust. J. Dairy Technol.*, 1983, **38**, 66.

125. Manning, D. J., Ridout, E. A., Price, J. C. and Gregory, R. J., *J. Dairy Res.*, 1983, **50**, 527.
126. Kristoffersen, T., *J. Dairy Sci.*, 1967, **50**, 279.
127. Thomas, T. D., McKay, L. L. and Morris, H. A., *Appl. Environ. Microbiol.*, 1985, **49**, 908.
128. Reiter, B., Fryer, T. F., Sharpe, M. E. and Lawrence, R. C., *J. appl. Bact.*, 1966, **29**, 231.
129. Lowrie, R. J., Lawrence, R. C. and Peberdy, M. F., *N.Z. J. Dairy Sci. Technol.*, 1974, **9**, 116.
130. Law, B. A., Castanon, M. J. and Sharpe, M. E., *J. Dairy Res.*, 1976, **43**, 301.
131. Law, B. A. and Sharpe, M. E., *Dairy Ind. Int.*, 1977, **42**(12), 10.
132. Law, B. A. and Sharpe, M. E., *J. Dairy Res.*, 1978, **45**, 267.
133. Law, B. A. and Wigmore, A. S., *J. Dairy Res.*, 1983, **50**, 519.
134. Lawrence, R. C. and Thomas, T. D. In: *Microbial Technology: Current State, Future Prospects* (Ed. A. T. Bull, D. C. Ellwood and C. Ratledge), Cambridge University Press, Cambridge, p. 187, 1979.
135. Lawrence, R. C., *J. Dairy Res.*, 1963, **30**, 235.
136. Forss, D. A. and Patton, S., *J. Dairy Sci.*, 1966, **49**, 89.
137. Morris, H. A., *J. Dairy Sci.*, 1978, **61**, 1198.
138. Law, B. A., Castanon, M. and Sharpe, M. E., *J. Dairy Res.*, 1976, **43**, 117.
139. Law, B. A., Hosking, Z. D. and Chapman, H. R., *J. Soc. Dairy Technol.*, 1979, **32**, 87.
140. Reiter, B., Fryer, T. F., Pickering, A., Chapman, H. R., Lawrence, R. C. and Sharpe, M. E., *J. Dairy Res.*, 1967, **34**, 257.
141. Law, B. A. and Sharpe, M. E., *Proc. 20th Int. Dairy Congress, Paris*, 1978, Vol. E, p. 769.
142. Miah, A. H., Reinbold, G. W., Hartley, J. D., Vedamuthu, E. R. and Hammond, E. G., *J. Milk Food Technol.*, 1974, **37**, 47.
143. Thomas, T. D. and Crow, V. L., *N.Z. J. Dairy Sci. Technol.*, 1983, **18**, 131.
144. Conochie, J. and Sutherland, B. J., *Aust. J. Dairy Technol.*, 1965, **20**, 36.
145. O'Keeffe, R. B., Fox, P. F. and Daly, C., *J. Dairy Res.*, 1975, **42**, 111.
146. Pearce, K. N., *N.Z. J. Dairy Sci. Technol.*, 1977, **12**, 113.
147. Olson, N. F., *Dairy Field*, 1980, **163**(2), 64.
148. Olson, N. F., *Dairy Record*, 1984, **85**(10), 115.
149. Olson, N. F., *Dairy Record*, 1984, **85**(11), 102.
150. Olson, N. F., *J. Dairy Sci.*, 1981, **64**, 1063.

Chapter 2

Dutch-type Varieties

P. Walstra, A. Noomen and T. J. Geurts

Department of Food Science, Agricultural University,
Wageningen, The Netherlands

1. DESCRIPTION

We define Dutch-type varieties of cheese as those that:

—are made of fresh cows' milk;
—the milk being at most partly skimmed (generally leading to at least 40% fat in the dry matter of the cheese);
—are clotted by means of rennet (usually extracted from calves' stomachs);
—use starters consisting of mesophilic streptococci and usually leuconostocs, that generally produce CO_2;
—have a water content in the fat-free cheese below 63% (ratio of water to solids-not-fat < 1·70);
—are pressed to obtain a closed rind;
—are salted after pressing, usually in brine;
—have no essential surface flora;
—are at least somewhat matured (a few weeks) and thus have undergone significant proteolysis.

Consequently, the cheese usually has a semi-hard to hard consistency and a smooth texture, usually with small holes; the flavour intensity varies widely.

So defined, Dutch-type varieties constitute one of the most important (if not the most important) types of cheese produced in the world (in terms of tonnage), comparable in that respect to Cheddar and the group of white, fresh cheeses.

45

Variation within the type is considerable:

—loaf size may be between 0·2 and 20 kg;
—loaf shape may be a sphere (Edam), a flat cylinder with bulging sides
    (Gouda), a block, like a loaf of bread, etc.;
—fat content in the dry matter ranges from 40 to over 50%;
—water content in the fat-free cheese ranges from 53 to 63%;
—salt content in the cheese water ranges from 2 to 7%;
—pH may be anywhere from 5·0 to 5·6;
—maturation may take from 2 weeks to 2 years.

Generally, a larger loaf is likely to have a lower water content (initially) and is matured for a longer time. The character (taste, consistency) ranges almost from that of a typical St Paulin to Parmesan, even within a type of the same designation, e.g. Gouda. Further variation occurs because of the use of different starters, different degrees of acidification during curd making, whether the cheese milk is pasteurized or not, contamination with different micro-organisms (lactobacilli, in particular, can grow in the cheese) and different conditions during maturation. Finally, herbs or spices are sometimes added, particularly cumin (i.e. the seeds of *Cuminum cyminum*, not of *Carum carvi*—caraway or 'Kümmel'—as applied in other varieties).

Traditionally, two main types of cheese were made in the Netherlands: Gouda and Edam. Gouda cheese (Dutch: Goudse kaas) was made in fairly large loaves of flat cylindrical shape (mostly 4–12 kg) from fresh unskimmed milk, and was matured for variable periods (6–60 weeks); it is still made on some farms in much the same way ('Goudse boerenkaas'). Edam (Edammer kaas), a sphere of, for example, 2 kg, was made from a mixture of skimmed evening milk and fresh morning milk, leading to about 40% fat in the dry matter; the cheese had a somewhat shorter texture than Gouda, and was usually matured for 6 months or more. Later, a greater range of cheeses, differing in shape, body and taste, evolved from these types; one reason for change was to obtain better sliceability. The same or similar types are made in several countries, having either evolved in the country itself or as an imitation of cheese as made in the Netherlands; the phylogeny is not always clear. Table I lists several of these; the table is not complete and may even contain some inaccuracies as it is difficult to obtain reliable data from all over the world. Other derived types have, for example, a higher (Dutch: roomkaas) or a lower fat content. The method of making the cheese has altered greatly. Some Italian varieties are similar to Dutch-type varieties, although higher scalding temperatures are applied;

Dutch-type cheeses[a]

Country	Designation	Weight (kg)	Maturation (months)	Fat in DM[b] (%)	Wff[c] (%)	Remarks
The Netherlands	Amsterdammer kaas	2·5-5	0·7-1·5	49	62	Gouda shape
	Goudse kaas	2·5-30	1-20	49	59	
	Lunchkaas (baby Gouda)	0·2-1·1	0·7-2	49	62	Gouda shape
	Edammer kaas	1·7-2·5	1-15	41	59	
	Baby-Edammer	0·9-1·1	0·7-2	41	61	Sphere
	Commissie-kaas	3-4·5	4-12	41	59	Sphere
	Middelbare kaas	5-6·5	4-12	41	59	Sphere
Argentina	Pategrás Argentino	5		40	58	
Brazil	Bola (Prato Esférico)	2		45	56	
	Prato Estepe	4		46	60	
	Reino	1·5-1·8		45	53	
Czechoslovakia	Javor	12		50	57	
Denmark	Danbo	1-14	1·5	47	61	Loaf
	Elbo	5·5	1·5	47	61	Gouda shape
	Fynbo	7	≥1·5	47	61	Part of salt added to curd
	Maribo	14	2-3	47	59	
	Molbo	1·5-3	1·5	47	60	Sphere
	Samsø	14	1·5-3	47	59	
	Tybo	3	1·5	47	61	Loaf
Egypt	Memphis (Menfis)	4	2·5	48	52	
Finland	Kartano	4·5	1·5	42-47	59	
	Lappi (Pehtori, Vouti)	1·8-3	1-1·5	42-47	58	
	Turunmaa (Korsholm)	6	2	52	61	
France	Mimolette	2·5-4	>1·5	41	59	Sphere
Germany (F.R.)	Brotedamer	2·5-4·5	≥1	41	58	Loaf
	Geheimratskäse	0·5	1	45	61	

continued

TABLE I—contd.

Country	Designation	Weight (kg)	Maturation (months)	Fat in DM[b] (%)	Wff[c] (%)	Remarks
Hungary	Balaton sajt	9–12	1	46	55	
Ireland	Blarney			48	57	
Italy	Fontal	11–13	1·5	46	60	
Jugoslavia	Trapist sir	1·5–2	1–1·5	45	63	
Norway	Norvegia	4–12	3	46	58	
	Nøkkelost	4–15	4	46	56	Spiced
Poland	Mazurski	18		50	58	
	Salami	1·2		40–45	58	Sausage shape
	Warmiński	4·5		40–45	58	
Sweden	Drabantost	4–12	2–4	45–50	59	Block
	Herrgårdsost	12–15	3–4	43–46	55	
	Hushållsost	1–2	2	45–50	60	
	Prästost	12–14	4–5	52	58	
	Sveciaost	12–15	4	47	57	Part of salt added to curd
USSR	Västerbottensost	18	8	50	52	
	Jaroslavskij syr	3–10	2	45–50	59	
	Kostromskoj syr	5–12	2·5	45	55	
	Pošechonskij syr	5–6	1·5	45	59	
	Rossiskij syr	5–18	3·5	50	60	Part of salt added to curd
	Stepnoj syr	5–10	2·5	45	58	
	Uglišskij syr	3	2	45	59	

[a] Partly after Refs 1 and 2. The numerous varieties of which the designation includes words like Dutch, Gouda or Edam have been deleted, although the specifications for such cheeses often differ somewhat from those of the original types.

[b] Fat content in the dry matter

even varieties like Colby and Monterey are rather similar to Gouda, although they are made in a different way, e.g. with dry salting. After all, it is the composition of the cheese, more than the way in which it is made, that determines its properties, as was, for example, pointed out by Lawrence *et al.*[3]

Some cheese types, although clearly outside our definition of Dutch-type varieties, have, nevertheless, evolved from traditional Dutch cheeses. These include:

—'Meshanger', originally an Edam cheese that failed to develop sufficient acidity and so obtained a high water content, a soft body and a flat shape.[4]

—Tilsiter, originally derived from Gouda, from which it differs mainly in having a red slime on the surface.[2]

—'Maasdammer', a cheese very much like Jarlsberg, and thus containing propionic acid bacteria (considered to be a defect in true Gouda).

For the sake of completeness, we mention also some other varieties that were traditionally made in the area which now constitutes the Netherlands.

—Leyden cheese (Dutch: Leidse kaas), still made on a few farms from raw milk, skimmed a few times and thus pre-acidified. Shape: flat cylindrical; weights: 8–12 kg; fat content in the dry matter: about 30%; dry and hard and containing cumin seeds; matured for 6–12 months. A type with 40% fat-in-dry matter, but otherwise much the same as Gouda (the shape is slightly different), is now being produced industrially.

—Friesian cheese (Dutch: Friese kaas), made from raw milk, skimmed several times which was, therefore, rather acid at the time of renneting. A kind of 'cheddaring' was applied and it was salted at the curd stage. It contained about 20% fat-in-dry matter, was very hard and dry, and was matured for a long time. It was made in three varieties: without spices ('kanterkaas'), with cumin ('kruidkaas') and with cumin and cloves ('nagelkaas'). 'Friese nagelkaas' is still produced, but its texture and composition are more like Leyden cheese, and it is made from fresh, pasteurized, partly skimmed milk.

—Limburger (Dutch: Limburgse kaas) is the same as the 'Hervekaas' or 'Fromage d'Herve', made in the Belgian provinces Limburg and Liège.

—'Witte meikaas', a soft but pressed, white cheese consumed when a few days old.

—Ewes' milk cheese, e.g. from the Texel (made like a small Gouda) or from Friesland (somewhat like Brynzda).

At the present time, several other types of cheese are being produced in the Netherlands.

2. MANUFACTURE

The authors assume that the reader is familiar with the general principles of cheesemaking, e.g. as outlined in Volume 1 of this book.

2.1 Treatment of Milk

Treatment of milk aims at improving or maintaining the quality of the milk for cheesemaking, with respect to cheese quality and composition, yield and ease of manufacture.

Milk quality may be defined so as to include composition. The fat and casein content of the milk naturally affect cheese yield and fat content; lactose content affects cheese acidity (Section 3.2). Off-flavours, particularly if associated with the fat, may be carried over into the cheese. In a well-ripened cheese, such flavours may be masked and flavour due to lipolysis may even be desirable, but in the milder varieties this is not so. Physical dirt should be absent as it shows up in the cheese, but can be removed easily by filtering and/or centrifuging.

The bacteriological quality of cheese milk is of great importance. Pathogenic organisms may survive in cheese, which may be a problem in raw-milk cheese. Pathogenic enterobacteriaceae and staphylococci may even grow in cheese, although not if the cheese contains no sugar. Proper manufacturing procedures ensure that anywhere in the cheese, either the sugar is fully and rapidly converted into acid by the starter organisms[5], or the salt content is already high enough to prevent the growth of pathogens. *Staph. aureus* can grow somewhat if salt is present, but then normally does not produce toxin. Several bacteria present can cause defects in the cheese: coliforms, *Lactobacillus* spp., *Str. thermophilus*, faecal streptococci, propionic acid bacteria, *Clostridium tyrobutyricum* (see further Section 3·5). Growth of psychrotrophic bacteria in the raw milk may lead to the production of sufficient thermostable lipolytic enzymes to cause undesired lipolysis in the cheese;[6] bacterial proteinases do not seem to cause undesirable effects.[6,7] Milk to be stored for long periods before cheesemaking is usually given a mild heat-treatment ('thermization'), sufficient to kill several types of bacteria, including most psychrotrophs, but not to greatly alter the milk otherwise, e.g. 10 s at 65°C.

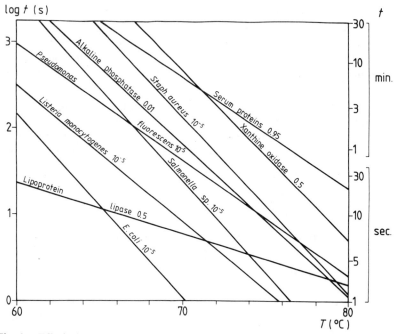

Fig. 1. Effect of heat treatments of various severity on the denaturation of serum proteins, the inactivation of some enzymes, and the killing of some micro-organisms, important for cheese quality or safety. The figures indicate the fraction left unchanged after the treatment. Approximate average results after various sources.

The milk is commonly pasteurized, usually HTST, e.g. 20 s at 72°C. Figure 1 gives time–temperature relations for effects that are important for cheesemaking; it should be realized that these are only examples since there is considerable variation in the thermolability of micro-organisms, etc. Pasteurization serves the following functions:

—Killing of pathogens; those that possibly occur are killed if heating is sufficient to inactivate alkaline phosphatase. Toxin produced by *Staphylococcus aureus* is not inactivated by such treatment.[8]

—Killing of spoilage organisms. Spores of *Clostridium tyrobutyricum* survive but enterobacteriaceae, propionic acid bacteria and most lactic acid bacteria are killed. Some species of *Lactobacillus* and *Streptococcus* are not fully killed, but they are seldom present in great numbers in the milk. However, *Str. thermophilus* may grow in the regenerating section of the heat exchanger[9,10] and thus attain high numbers if it is

continuously used for a long time (e.g. 10 h); this may lead to undesirable flavour and texture of the cheese.
—Inactivation of milk enzymes. Probably, this may be useful only with regard to lipoprotein lipase (EC 3.1.1.34), but even the usefulness of this is variable (see below). Several lipases and proteinases produced by psychrotrophic bacteria are not inactivated.[6]
—If the milk is pasteurized shortly before renneting it also serves to undo, more or less, the adverse effects of cold storage on the casein micelles and salt equilibrium (which in turn affects renneting properties, Volume 1, Chapter 3), to melt the fat in the globules and to bring the milk to renneting temperature.

Heat treatment can also have undesirable effects, particularly if its intensity is more than that needed to inactivate alkaline phosphatase:

—Denaturation of serum proteins leads to slow renneting, a weak curd and poor syneresis (Volume 1, Chapters 3–5). It may also easily cause a cheese of poorer quality, particularly the development of a bitter flavour; the explanation is not clear (more rennet may be retained in the curd, rapid proteolysis of denatured serum proteins?). Since heat denaturation also causes a profitable increase in cheese yield, fairly rigorous control is exerted in some countries, e.g. via the nitrogen content of the whey (which, for example, should be at least 95% of that of the whey made from raw milk).
—Useful milk enzymes may be inactivated, especially xanthine oxidase (EC 1.2.3.2). This enzyme is needed to slowly convert (added) NO_3^- into NO_2^-, which is essential for the desired action of nitrate against clostridia (Section 3.5).

Although pasteurization of cheese milk is widespread, and has certainly helped to considerably improve average cheese quality, it is often held to be responsible for a certain lack of flavour, especially in well-matured varieties. This may be due to inactivation of lipoprotein lipase or to killing of bacteria that may impart in a raw-milk cheese some flavour that is desirable to some people and that anyway may be more variable than the flavour of cheese made from pasteurized milk. A less severe pasteurization may improve flavour. If the bacterial quality of the milk is very good, cheese can be made from raw milk or from mixtures of raw and pasteurized milk. An old-fashioned way of improving milk quality is to let the fresh milk cream at low temperatures (5–10°C); in this way, most bacteria accompany the cream because of agglutination.[11] By pasteurizing the cream, and not the skim-milk, most bacteria are killed without greatly affecting milk enzymes.

Another way to enhance microbiological quality is by bactofugation. This may be applied when cheese is made from raw milk. Another purpose is the removal of spores of *Clostridium tyrobutyricum*. This treatment reduces the number of spores drastically, even to about 3%.[12,13] The sediment obtained contains the spores but also casein and its removal would cause a significant reduction in cheese yield (about 6%). Consequently, the sediment is commonly UHT-heated to kill the spores and added again to the milk; the concomitant denaturation of serum proteins involves a small enough quantity to be acceptable. Double bactofugation increases the efficacy of spore removal, but is, of course, costly.

Homogenization of cheese-milk is rarely practised. It may enhance lipolysis, depending on conditions, and this may be either desirable or not, but generally not. However, it causes the cheese to attain an undesirable, sticky texture. Damage to the fat globules, e.g. by foaming, may also enhance lipolysis. Splashing milk from a height into the cheese vat may even cause some 'churning', leading to significant creaming in the vat; this happens if cold milk is warmed to 30°C and then brought into the vat. The remedy is to warm the milk sufficiently to melt the fat and then cool it to 30°C.[14]

In most cases, the milk is standardized so as to yield the desired fat content in the dry matter of the cheese (Section 3.1). This generally implies some skimming of the milk. Usually, part of the milk is passed through a separator (which also removes dirt particles) and sufficient cream is removed.

Substances added to the milk may include:

— $CaCl_2$ to speed up and particularly to diminish variability in renneting and syneresis.
— Nitrate, to prevent early blowing by coliforms and growth of *C. tyrobutyricum*. Nowadays, nitrate is often added later, i.e. to the curd–whey mixture after about half of the whey has been removed. This is both to save on nitrate and to avoid producing large quantities of whey that contains nitrate.
— Colouring matter, either β-carotene or annatto (an extract of the fruits of *Bixa orellana*), for obvious reasons. Its use appears to be waning and it is often omitted. Some types are highly coloured, e.g. Mimolette.

Spices, if any, are commonly added to the curd.

2.2 Main Process Steps

Figures 2 and 3 are examples of flow-sheets for the production of Edam and Gouda cheese. Some essential process steps in the transformation of milk into fresh cheese are discussed below. Those steps largely determine cheese composition and the efficiency of production. Important aims are to obtain maximum yield, to control cheese composition (hence quality), and to keep the process as short as possible, while following a fixed time schedule. The main points to be considered in relation to cheese composition are: final water content, pH of the cheese, quantity of calcium phosphate remaining in the cheese, and the quantity of rennet retained in the curd. To regulate the process, syneresis rate is paramount. The effects of several process parameters on these variables are summarized in Fig. 4; the relationships are, of course, only very approximate and they often depend on the level of other parameters.

Another essential variable is the bacterial population in the fresh cheese, as it greatly affects ripening (Section 3.4) and the possible development of defects (Section 3·5). This concerns starter bacteria (Section 3.3) as well as contaminating organisms. Strictly enforced hygienic measures must be taken to prevent undesirable growth of lactobacilli[21] and the propagation of bacteriophages.[22]

Pre-acidification (which is rarely practised today), quantity of starter added, rate of growth of starter bacteria and the time needed until the curd is separated from the whey, all affect the pH of the curd at the latter moment and consequently, the concentrations of calcium and inorganic phosphate left in the cheese. Lower concentrations of these give a somewhat lower cheese yield, a lower buffering capacity and consequently a slightly lower pH, and may somewhat affect cheese texture, the consistency becoming slightly softer and shorter. The concentration of rennet retained in the cheese increases markedly with a lower pH and a lower temperature at the moment of whey separation.

Renneting is usually done at about 30°C and cutting starts 20–30 min afterwards. About 20 ml rennet with a specific activity of 10 800 Soxhlet units and about 7 g $CaCl_2$ are usually added to 100 litres of cheese milk. The aim is to produce a curd that can be cut easily and stirred without undue losses of 'fines' in the whey and that shows rapid syneresis. If the milk is drawn from a very large quantity and moreover if the calving pattern of the cows is fairly evenly spread throughout the year, milk composition is generally sufficiently constant to always give good results with fixed quantities of rennet and $CaCl_2$.

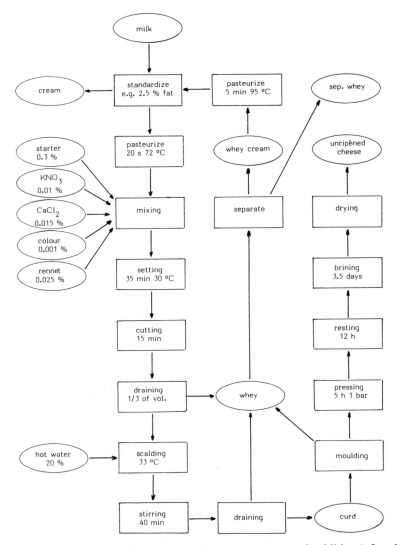

Fig. 2. Example of a flow sheet (main process steps and additions) for the manufacture of Edam cheese (until curing) in a fairly traditional way. Wooden moulds and cheese cloth were used during pressing.

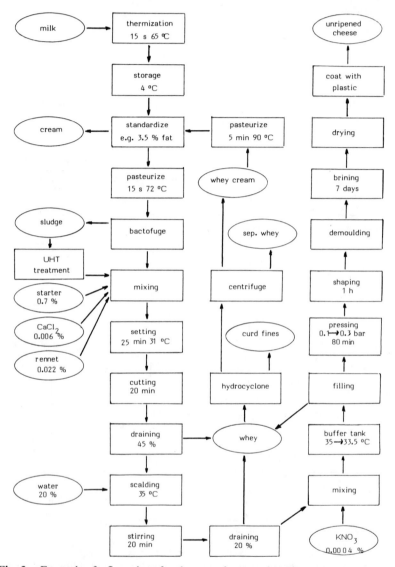

Fig. 3. Example of a flow-sheet for the manufacture of 12 kg Gouda cheese (until curing) by a modern method. Time from start of cutting to start of filling: 60 min. A curd filling machine with vertical columns and plastic moulds with a nylon gauze lining are used. NaCl content of brine: 14%, brine temperature: 14°C. If bactofugation is omitted, about 0·0016% KNO₃ is added.

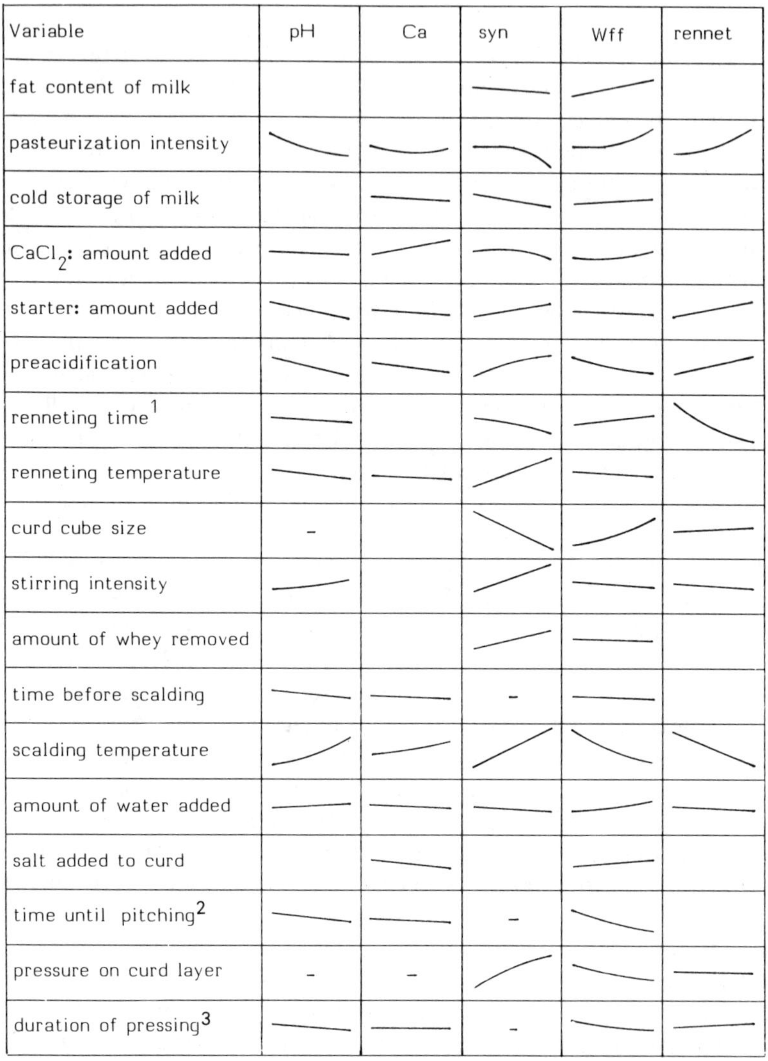

Variable	pH	Ca	syn	Wff	rennet
fat content of milk					
pasteurization intensity					
cold storage of milk					
CaCl$_2$: amount added					
starter: amount added					
preacidification					
renneting time[1]					
renneting temperature					
curd cube size					
stirring intensity					
amount of whey removed					
time before scalding					
scalding temperature					
amount of water added					
salt added to curd					
time until pitching[2]					
pressure on curd layer					
duration of pressing[3]					

Fig. 4. The effects of milk properties and conditions during curd making on the pH of the curd at the end of curd making (moment of separation of curd and whey), the amount of Ca retained in the curd, the rate of syneresis (syn), the water content of the fat-free (Wff) cheese (before brining) and the quantity of rennet retained in the curd. The figure is meant only to illustrate trends for cheese of average water content. If no curve is given, the relation is unknown but probably is weak; a dash implies no relation. Notes: (1). This generally implies reciprocal of rennet quantity. (2). Total time between cutting and pitching. (3). On the curd layer (not in the moulds). After various sources, e.g. Refs 15–20, and authors' observations.

The curd is cut, usually in cubes of some 8–15 mm size. Stirring, at first gently (to minimize loss of fines, etc.) and later more vigorously, is done either with the knives used for cutting or with special stirrers. After a while, part of the whey is removed so that stirring becomes more effective, i.e. the forces acting on the curd grains are higher and thus promote syneresis. The temperature is increased (scalding), also to speed up syneresis, but not to temperatures high enough to injure the starter organisms, which usually implies keeping below 38°C. Scalding can be done by indirect heating, by adding heated whey, or by adding hot water. The latter practice is the most common, since water usually has to be added anyway to regulate pH. The higher the moisture content of the cheese, the higher its ratio of lactose to buffering substances, and hence the lower its pH becomes, since, ideally, all lactose is converted into lactic acid. Independent control of the water content and the pH of cheese can thus be achieved by more or less diluting the cheese moisture with added water or 'washing' the curd. These aspects are further discussed in Section 3.2.

For some varieties, part of the salt is added to the curd–whey mixture at the end of curd making to inhibit growth of undesired micro-organisms.

After the curd has lost enough moisture (the water content being, for example, 65% in the case of Gouda cheese and the pH 6·5), stirring is stopped and the curd grains are allowed to sediment. Partial fusion of curd grains now occurs and a continuous mass of curd is formed that can be cut into blocks and taken out of the whey. Considerable loss of whey from the curd occurs during these stages[23] and this is promoted by applying some pressure (e.g. 400 Pa) by placing perforated metal plates on top of the curd or by the curd layer itself being deep enough; pressure also promotes curd fusion. If a very low water content is desired, the drained curd may be stirred or worked; this causes considerable additional syneresis, but also loss of fines and fat and a cheese with a rather open texture (many irregular, small holes).

The whey obtained at various stages may be collected separately, because it differs in pH, added water and added nitrate and, rarely, salt. The whey is usually separated and the cream obtained is pasteurized, e.g. 5 min at 90°C, to fully destroy any bacteriophages that may be present; it is used to adjust the fat content of the next lot of cheese milk. Curd fines are sometimes separated from the whey by means of hydrocyclones or filters, but are not recycled to the curd because of the danger of contamination (bacteria and phages).

The blocks of curd obtained are put into moulds and pressed. Originally, wooden moulds were used, and the curd was wrapped in cloth; a pressure of

50–100 kPa was applied for several hours and the cheese developed a very distinct, firm rind. Nowadays, cheese loaves are formed in perforated metal or plastic moulds, sometimes lined with a gauze or some kind of cloth to promote drainage and rind formation. The pressure is usually much lower and is applied for a shorter time. Consequently, only a weak rind is formed, although the rind should be fully 'closed' (i.e. free of visible openings). Closing of the rind is due to complete fusion of the outermost layer of curd grains. Pressing as it is applied nowadays is generally insufficient to cause complete fusion throughout the mass of the freshly pressed loaf. This implies that some moisture can still move fairly freely through the cheese mass, possibly leading to uneven moisture distribution. Within 24 h, however, curd fusion is generally complete.

The cheese loses considerable moisture during pressing, but moisture loss is slight once a closed rind has formed. This implies that starting the pressing earlier and applying a higher pressure lead to less moisture loss, and hence to a cheese with a higher water content. By varying the moment of applying pressure, water content can thus be regulated to some extent, especially to ensure the same water content in cheese loaves of the same batch. During stirring in the whey, syneresis proceeds faster than in a block of curd. Consequently, the blocks formed last have the lowest water content immediately after shaping and pressure should be applied to those loaves directly to 'keep in the moisture', while the blocks formed earlier should be left for a much longer time before pressing[24] (see also Section 3.2).

In traditional cheesemaking, the freshly pressed loaves were turned in the moulds and left there till the next day for 'shaping' (Dutch: omlopen), i.e. to attain a symmetrical shape. The main change occurring was, however, complete conversion of lactose into lactic acid. This is important because during brining the action of the starter bacteria is slowed down and even effectively stopped in the rind, owing to the combined effects of low temperature and high salt content. Nowadays, a greater quantity of a faster growing starter is usually added, which implies that much more lactic acid has already been produced a few hours after adding starter. Often, the cheese is put into brine within 1 h after pressing when some lactose is not yet converted into acid. (Incidentally, this means that even in a 3 week old cheese, the outermost layer may contain about 0·2% lactose in the cheese moisture and that the brine also contains lactose.) The use of pasteurized milk, strict hygiene and adequate rind treatment (Section 2.4) are needed to prevent undesirable growth of micro-organisms.

Brining is primarily done to provide the cheese with the necessary salt. Moreover, it serves to cool the loaves rapidly to below 15°C (to stop further

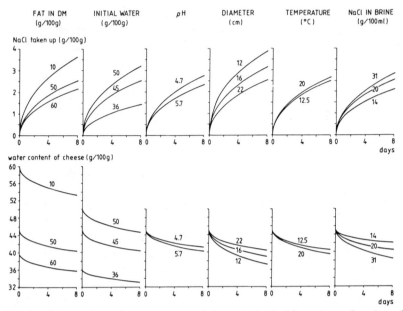

Fig. 5.   Salt uptake and water content of cheese (spherical loaves) as a function of the duration of brining. Unless mentioned otherwise, a cheese of 50% fat in dry matter and 45% water, diameter 22 cm, pH 5·0 and a brine of pH 5·0, containing 20 g NaCl/100 ml, temperature 12·5°C, were used (from Ref. 25).

syneresis, and prevent or slow down the growth of undesirable bacteria), and to give them a certain rigidity (due to the high salt content in the rind) during the necessary handling shortly after brining. Brining further causes a considerable loss of water (2–3 times the quantity of salt taken up) and loss of a little soluble matter (<0·2% of the cheese mass). Factors affecting these processes are discussed in Chapter 7, Volume 1. Figure 5 summarizes the effects of several variables on salt uptake and water loss. The average salt content is generally 3–5 g/100 g water in the cheese; of course, it takes considerable time (up to some weeks in a large loaf) for the salt to become more or less evenly distributed throughout the cheese.

The brine generally contains about 18% NaCl, but weaker brines are sometimes used to allow brining the loaves for exactly one week. This poses the problem of growth of salt-tolerant lactobacilli in the brine that may even to some extent penetrate the cheese and cause flavour defects.[26,27] Regular cleaning of the equipment is desirable. The brine should contain enough Ca (0·3%) and acid (pH 4·5) to prevent dissolution of cheese protein in the brine, which would cause a slimy rind.[28]

2.3 Mechanization

The past 30 years especially have witnessed drastic changes in the cheese industry. Refrigeration of milk at the farm ($\sim 4°C$) and every second or third day collection of this milk has become the accepted system in many countries. Rigorous control of the hygienic quality of the milk leads to far smaller variation in composition, thus facilitating the introduction of systems for process control. Thermization of raw milk (e.g. 10 s at 65°C), which prevents the growth of psychrotrophic spoilage organisms, enables further storage of milk at the factory for some days. Moreover, cheese factories have been modernized and merged into plants with high capacity. Plants with an annual production of 10 000 tonnes of cheese, manufactured in a 5 day working week, are not exceptional. These plants are highly mechanized, automated and computerized, producing cheese of the desired quality at relatively low labour costs but with very costly equipment. In the majority of cases, individual plants specialize in the manufacture of a single cheese variety.

The main developments in the mechanization and automation of cheese production can be described briefly as follows.

Curd making and moulding. The size of cheese vats has been increased very considerably. This initially became possible with the introduction of specific curd-sedimentation vats (strainers), with a moving, perforated belt. At one end of this vat, the sedimented and drained curd layer is mechanically cut into pieces of desired dimensions, which are put into moulds, pressed, etc. This method allows for the production of cheese with less variation in composition, moisture content in particular, and loaf weight. The capacity of cheese vats has been increased from 5000 to 12 000 litres. This system is still applied, but in many cases has been superseded by the following technique. Curd is made batch-wise in vats of up to 20 000 litres and the time schedule for successive batches (vats) is programmed in such a way that finished curd–whey mixtures can be pumped separately into a buffer tank, whence the mixture is fed into continuously working machines that separate the whey from the curd, shape the curd blocks and fill them into moulds. (Most machines operate with a downward curd stream, but machines with an upward stream are used also.) Technologically, these machines have the advantage that the weight of the loaves can be controlled accurately, the relative standard deviation being 0·5–1·5%; this is especially important for small loaves, e.g. Edam cheese. During the mould filling process, syneresis of the curd proceeds and would cause the water content of cheese to decrease if no precautions were taken. Therefore, syneresis during moulding is slowed down by stirring only gently and by gradually decreasing the temperature of the curd–whey mixture in the buffer tank by 0·5 to 2°C. In this way, the moisture content of the cheese can be controlled fairly accurately.

Pressing. Instead of pressing cheese loaves in stacks, it has become increasingly common to press them in a single layer. Presses are filled and emptied continuously. Continuous pressing, however, is not applied because differences still exist in water content between loaves of a batch at the beginning and the end of moulding, due to differences in the extent of syneresis of the curd. Consequently, to obtain a uniform water content in all loaves, special attention is given to the order in which loaves are set tight under the press. With respect to demoulding, systems have been designed which prevent damage to the relatively weak cheese rind.

Brining. Two brining systems are in use. One employs racks composed of several horizontal compartments; the racks can be moved up and down in a deep brine basin (2–3 m). Filling and, after brining, emptying of successive compartments is realized by circulation of the brine, which also enhances the rate of salt uptake by the cheese. In the other system, the loaves are salted while floating in a shallow layer of circulating brine (∼0·4 m); brine sprinkling machines or rollers that periodically immerse the loaves take care of salting of the top of the loaves.

Storage. Treatments in curing rooms also have been highly mechanized: transport, plastifying and turning of cheese, cleaning of shelves, etc. Much progress has been made to control the temperature, relative humidity and velocity of air, in order to approximate the ideal situation in which each loaf is stored under identical conditions.

2.4 Rind Treatment and Curing

For Dutch-type cheese varieties according to our definition (Section 1), development of micro-organisms on the cheese surface is undesirable, because they may negatively affect cheese quality. In particular, the growth of moulds must be prevented, since some species may produce mycotoxins, e.g. sterigmatocystine by *Aspergillus versicolor.* In former days, cheese was pressed in such a way as to obtain a thick and very tough rind; mould development was reduced by regular rubbing of the cheese rind with a dry cloth and unboiled linseed oil. After hardening, the coat formed also reduced water evaporation from the cheese rind, thus permitting it to remain supple and springy. Mineral oils, e.g. paraffin, were applied as well. This practice was abandoned after the introduction of plastic emulsions, which offer superior protection and permit production of cheese with a much weaker rind. Without this, mechanization and marked speeding up of cheesemaking would not have been possible. These polymer dispersions form, on drying, a coherent plastic film that offers protection against mechanical damage and slows down, but does not prevent, evaporation of water. The film mechanically hinders mould growth, but it may also contain fungicides, e.g. natamycin (pimaricin), an antibiotic produced by *Streptomyces natalensis*, or calcium and sodium sorbate. In the Netherlands, only natamycin is allowed while in some other countries only sorbates are permitted. When compared to sorbates, natamycin offers the advantages that its migration into the cheese is generally limited to the outer 1 mm of the rind and that it does not adversely affect the appearance, taste and flavour of the cheese.[29] Moreover, natamycin is much more effective than sorbates; for comparable protection from mould growth, the amount of sorbate needed is about 200 times that of natamycin. With respect to public health, an acceptable daily intake of 0·3 mg natamycin per kg body weight per day has been established;[30] Dutch cheese regulations limit the quantity to 2 mg/dm^2 of cheese surface when the cheese is sold.

In practice, successive treatments (2–3 times) with plastic emulsion are applied to all sides of the cheese shortly after manufacture. Care is taken that the cheese surface is sufficiently dry before each treatment. Treatment is repeated during long curing.

Generally, cheese is cured at 12–16°C and 85–90% RH. The conditions must allow the plastic emulsion to dry quickly, otherwise undesired organisms like coryneform bacteria and yeasts may develop and cause off-flavours. However, if the emulsion dries too quickly, cracks may form in the plastic layer, allowing microbial growth. Particularly at the beginning of ripening, the cheese inevitably expels a little moisture, causing a high humidity between the loaf and the shelf, which favours bacterial growth. To prevent this and to allow the cheese to retain a good shape, loaves are turned frequently during this period. Upon prolonged ripening, this frequency is reduced. Regular cleaning and drying of the shelves and control of the microbial condition of the air in curing rooms form part of a general programme on hygiene.

Just before they are put on the market, cheeses may be treated with paraffin, generally after they have been treated with a plastic emulsion; in the

Netherlands this especially concerns Edam-type cheese. Before waxing, the loaves must have a very clean and dry surface, since a high humidity between the cheese and the wax layer favours bacterial growth, causing off-flavours and gas formation. Consequently, wax is applied predominantly to mature cheese.

Some cheese is made in rectangular or square loaves for curing while wrapped in saran foil. This particularly suits the processed cheese industry and those customers who prefer this type of cheese when it is to be sold in prepacked portions or slices. Compared to normal cheese, important differences are the lack of a firm rind, the almost complete absence of moisture loss and the consequently more homogeneous composition. The cheese should have a lower (1–2%) water content immediately after manufacture, because this content must meet the standards for normal cheese after ripening. Prolonged curing, however, tends to produce cheese of poor flavour, unless the cheese is kept at low temperatures ($< 8°C$). A starter with low CO_2-producing capacity is used to prevent loosening of the wrapping. It is not necessary to turn the cheese which may be ripened at a lower relative humidity (e.g. 70%).

3.   IMPORTANT TOPICS

3.1 Standardization and Yield

Standardization of milk for cheesemaking means adjustment of its fat content to ensure that the cheese being made contains the legally required percentage of fat in the dry matter (FDM). The yield is the mass of cheese obtained from a certain quantity of this milk.

It is of importance to calculate precisely the desired fat content of the cheese milk. The yield of cheese should also be predictable. Comparison with the ultimate analytical results may enhance our understanding of the cheesemaking process.

Usually, all the cheese made from one vat of milk is weighed. If this is always performed in much the same way it may be a valuable help, since it gives a first indication of cheese composition.

3.1.1 Standardization
Under practical cheesemaking circumstances, establishing the correct fat content of the milk causes specific problems. Firstly, the cheese mass is always inhomogeneous, causing difficulties in establishing its real fat in dry

matter content. For this reason, borer samples may give considerable bias and the whole loaf, a sector from it, or a quarter from a square-shaped cheese, is ground. Secondly, one has to take into account that, generally, the fat content of different loaves from one batch is not identical, the standard deviation often amounting to about 0·5% FDM. Moreover, FDM decreases during ripening, since proteolysis involves 'conversion' of some water into dry matter.

For these reasons, a safety margin is taken into account, i.e. the fat content is adjusted to a somewhat higher level than is required. As a rule, a surplus value of ~ 1·5% FDM is taken. The plus sign in notations like 40 + or 60 + refers to this margin.

Difficulties in standardization are also caused by the multiplicity of variables affecting the ratio of fat to dry matter in the finished product:

1. The composition of the milk changes with season and shows short-term fluctuations. Moreover, changes may occur during prolonged cold storage. Until some 30 years ago the fat content of the whole milk was taken as the basis of standardization, based on an assumed constant fat/protein ratio. The higher the fat content of whole milk, the higher the fat content of the cheese milk has to be. The ratio between the fat and protein contents of the whole milk is, however, not constant. Hence, this method is not very precise. Much greater certainty is obtained if the protein content of the milk is estimated, or still better, its casein content. Almost fixed proportions of the fat and of the Ca-caseinate Ca-phosphate complex are carried over from the milk into the cheese.

2. The method of making the cheese. Important aspects are:

    —The cutting of the curd, which affects fat losses into the whey and the amount of curd fines. (The latter fraction has a lower fat content than the curd itself.)
    —The quantity of wash water, which affects the SnF content in the moisture of the cheese.
    —The amount of acid produced in the curd, and thereby the loss of calcium phosphate into the whey.
    —The quantity of salt absorbed by the cheese.
    —The pasteurization of the milk; denatured serum proteins are incorporated in the curd, increasing its SnF content.

3. The maturation of the cheese; the quantity of fat hardly changes but the SnF does, since water is converted in dry matter during the hydrolysis processes.

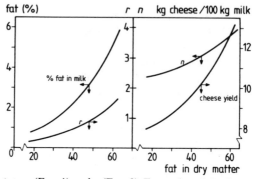

Fig. 6. The factors r (Eqn 1) and n (Eqn 3). Examples of the fat content (v) of the cheese milk (3·4% protein) and of the yield of cheese (12 days old, 58% Wff, 4% salt in dry matter).

To standardize the cheese milk, the ratio between its fat content (v) and its (crude) protein content (p) may, in fact, be used as a directive. Suppose that F is the fraction of the fat that is transferred from the milk to the cheese, and that K kg fat-free dry cheese, including added salt, originates from 1 kg of milk protein, then Fv/Kp represents the ratio between fat and SnF in the cheese. As far as the making of Dutch-type cheese is concerned, both F and K approximate 0·9.[18] Hence, the ratio of fat to protein in the milk may be adjusted to the ratio that is desired between fat and SnF in the cheese. Schulz and Kay[31] accordingly arranged their 'Käse-Tabellen'. If p is known, the appropriate value of v may be found in the table for any cheese being made.

In the Dutch cheesemaking industry, more detailed formulae are in use, e.g. (Ref. 32):

$$v = rp + q \qquad (1)$$

Under normal conditions of Gouda and Edam cheesemaking, r depends primarily on the desired fat in dry matter content of the cheese. For 40% FDM, $r \approx 0·67$, for 48% FDM, $r \approx 0·91$ (see also Fig. 6). The factor, q, refers to the fat lost in the first and second whey. The loss increases more than proportionally with v. For cheese with 20% FDM, $q \approx 0·05$, for 40% FDM, $q \approx 0·14$, for 48% FDM, $q \approx 0·20$, for 60% FDM, $q \approx 0·40$. In Fig. 6, v is shown as a function of FDM; note the strong increase of v with increasing FDM. Some cheesemakers use more elaborate calculations to arrive at v.

3.1.2 Yield
The yield of cheese can be defined as kg of product (y) obtained from 100 kg of cheese milk.

$$y = \text{kg (fat + protein + other solids + water)} \qquad (2)$$

Most factors affecting the ratio of fat to dry matter also influence cheese yield.

An important variable is undoubtedly the water content of the cheese and, hence, the loss of whey (syneresis) during curd making and pressing. Many factors affect the water content (Section 3.2). Its standard deviation between loaves of one batch often amounts to 0.5–1%.[24,33] It has been observed that y increases by ~ 0.2 kg if the water content increases with 1 percentage unit.[32]

If we consider the water content as given, additional factors affecting y are:

Season. Under Dutch conditions, y is relatively high in autumn and low in spring, the discrepancy amounting to over 10%.

Mastitis. Severe mastitis leads to the production of milk with a reduced casein content and a reduced casein/total N ratio.[34,35] Actually, since large quantities of bulk milk are used, real problems are never met.

Genetic variants of milk proteins. These may affect cheese yield,[36,37] but there is doubt about the correlations being causative.

Cold storage of the milk. Literature reports on this effect are confusing, presumably because no distinction has been made between purely physical and bacterial changes.

Pasteurization of the milk. A higher heating temperature will increase y (Section 2.1).

Rennet type. Differences in proteolysis, other than the splitting of κ-casein, would decrease y but they are usually negligible, unless some microbial rennets are used.[104]

Starter. A change in the amount added introduces several other changes. Firstly, the incorporation into the curd of denatured serum proteins may increase with the starter quantity. Banks *et al.*[38,39] reported such an effect with Cheddar cheese. The higher yield is caused by the increased retention of serum proteins from the starter, since it is prepared from severely heated milk. Secondly, in Dutch-type cheese manufacture the use of more starter inevitably requires more curd wash water (Section 3.2) which increasingly dilutes the whey and hence reduces the yield. The net result of both factors may be almost nil. Increasing the rate of acidification (more or more active

P. Walstra, A. Noomen and T. J. Geurts

starter) decreases the pH of milk and curd, inducing more dissolution of Ca and inorganic phosphate. Probably, the subsequent loss in y is small, say 30 g for 10 kg cheese produced if the pH at separation of curd from whey is as low as 6·25 instead of 6·5. Moreover, more proteose peptone will leave the micelles at a lower pH, and will be lost in the whey. A lower yield (a higher protein content of the whey) might be expected since O'Leary et al.[34] and Richardson[40] found more proteolysis when more starter was used. The findings of van den Berg and de Vries[16] do not, however, point to such an effect.

CaCl₂. Addition to the milk causes some accumulation of colloidal calcium phosphate in the micelles.[41] Usually, about 1 mmol/litre $CaCl_2$ is added to enhance the clotting, presumably yielding ~ 30 g 'cheese' from 100 kg milk.

Washing. The dilution of whey with water at scalding affects y. Increasing the quantity of added water, e.g. from 30 to 40% (expressed per mass of curd and whey after part of the whey has been removed) reduces y by 0·5 to 1%. The effect is illustrated in Fig. 7. In the calculation of y, the efficiency of decreasing the concentration in the curd particles by the washing was taken to be 90% for lactose and other low-molecular substances, and 50% for the serum proteins.

Ultrafiltration. An increase in cheese yield is obtained because of the accumulation of serum proteins in the curd.[43]

Salting. Absorption of NaCl obviously causes a gain in weight. Against this profit there is usually a greater loss of moisture,[25] hence a net loss of weight. The quantity of absorbed salt varies, e.g. from 1 to 3% and the net weight loss may vary from, say, 0·02 to 0·06 kg/kg cheese produced; the loss of solids-not-salt, including losses caused by mechanical damage during salting, ranges from 1 to 3 g/kg (see also Fig. 5).

Strictly speaking, y refers to the ultimate product, excluding curd remnants, fines, and any rind trimmings which have to be discarded; y includes the plastic coating. Clearly, y can in no way be predicted very precisely, the cheesemaking process being too complex. Even the random variation in water content (see above) makes exact prediction difficult. To predict the yield of cheese from a given vat of standardized milk one obviously will proceed on its protein content. In the tables of Schulz and Kay,[31] the y value can be looked up if cheese of certain fat and water

kg cheese / 100 kg milk

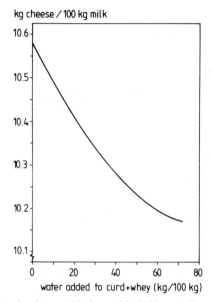

water added to curd+whey (kg/100 kg)

Fig. 7. Yield of Gouda cheese (12 days old, 41% water) as a function of the quantity of 'curd wash' water used. Water content and pH of the cheese are assumed to remain constant (recalculated from Ref. 42).

content and with 5% salt-in-moisture has to be made, starting with milk of known protein content. The yield of 12 day old cheese may be calculated[32] from:

$$y = np - 0.084 \qquad (3)$$

where n depends mainly on FDM. In the case of full-cream cheese, $n \approx 3.1$, and y amounts, for example, to 10.7 kg (see also Fig. 6).

An example of calculations with respect to the standardization of cheese milk and to cheese yield is given in Ref. 24, which also deals with applications under practical manufacturing conditions.

3.2 Control of pH and Water Content

Very few quantitative data have been published on this subject. Process control has made considerable progress during the last decades but some variations in the cheese composition cannot yet be explained satisfactorily. The degree of acidification in curd and freshly made cheese shows unexplained fluctuations.

It is not easy to adjust the water content and pH of cheese independent of each other. In Section 3.2.3, interrelationships under varying conditions are considered.

3.2.1 The control of the water content

The basic information with respect to this subject is outlined in Chapter 5, Volume 1. Moreover, the effects of several factors involved are illustrated in Fig. 4. In fact we have to deal here with the amount of water in the fat-free cheese (Wff), rather than with the absolute water content of the cheese which, within one cheese type, decreases fairly proportionally with increasing fat content.[44] Wff is characteristic for the type of cheese considered (see also Table I).

As a matter of fact, numerous factors affect the water content. Under normal manufacturing conditions, however, the number of process parameters available to really adjust Wff turns out to be restricted. Important are:

(a) The cutting of the curd. The smaller the grains, the higher the syneresis rate, causing a lower water content. Cutting the curd very finely, however, seems to increase Wff, and it causes a greater loss of fines and of fat into the whey. A very inhomogeneous cheese mass may result if the initial size of the grains differs widely.

(b) The stirring of the curd–whey mixture. This concerns the intensity of stirring, which increases with the stirring rate and on any removal of part of the whey; the duration of stirring; and (scalding) temperature. Figure 6 in Chapter 5, Volume 1 shows, among other things, that extended stirring causes a lower ultimate water content. If the temperature of the curd mass is kept constant after separation of the whey, then the time of separation should affect the final water content only slightly. This illustrates that in practical cheesemaking the lowering of the temperature after the whey drainage rapidly restrains syneresis.

(c) The above process steps also play a part in the acidification rate, since the temperature affects the virulence of the starter bacteria, and since stirring can be stopped earlier at a higher syneresis rate, hence at a higher pH. Figure 6 in Chapter 5, Volume 1 illustrates the great importance of acidification.

Other variables occurring at renneting, pressing, shaping and salting have effects also but they are not suitable process parameters to adjust the water content.

3.2.2 Control of the pH

Here, we deal with the pH at one or a few days after making the cheese; after this, the pH gradually but slowly increases as a result of maturation.

The pH of the cheese results mainly from the amount of lactic acid on the one hand, and that of the buffering compounds on the other. The acid is produced by the starter bacteria, metabolizing the available lactose. The main buffering substance in curd and cheese is the Ca-paracasein Ca-phosphate complex, of which colloidal calcium phosphate (CCP) contributes roughly one third of the buffering capacity. Some compounds in the curd moisture are also involved, e.g. phosphates, serum proteins, citrates.

It is worthwhile to distinguish between different situations with respect to pH control. Some lactose may remain in the finished cheese, because the acidification process is hindered or stopped. Adding salt at an early stage, as is done when making Meshanger cheese,[4] may bring this about. If Dutch-type cheese is brined shortly after pressing, some lactose is usually left in the outer rind portion (Section 2.2). The lactic acid fermentation may also be restrained by cooling, which is practised in the manufacture of Quarg, Cottage cheese and Bel Paese. Lactic acid produced by starter bacteria may be metabolized by organisms of the surface flora on soft cheese, thereby increasing the pH. In the majority of cheese types, including the Dutch, all lactose is converted, mainly into lactic acid. If we now presume that the water content of the fat-free cheese (Wff) is adjusted to its desired value, important compositional characteristics of the milk in relation to the final pH are:

(a) The lactose content of the milk serum (rather than the lactose to casein ratio in the milk).

(b) The quantity (and composition?) of CCP in the casein micelles; a changed buffering capacity of the curd is due predominantly to a different CCP concentration.

As soon as the cheese milk has been collected and bulked, these variables (a and b) are fixed. To make the desired type of cheese from this milk, important process parameters involved are:

(A) Factors affecting the water content of the cheese. The higher the water content, the more lactose, or its equivalent lactic acid, is present in the cheese, and the lower the pH will be. In other words, from the moment the cheese loaf is formed, the ratio between incorporated lactose and buffering substances controls the pH. It

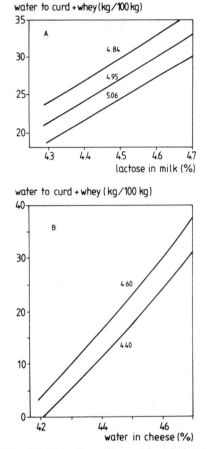

water to curd + whey (kg/100 kg)

Fig. 8. Amount of curd wash water to be used in relation to the lactose content of the milk (A), and the water content of the cheese before brining (B). Figures near the curves indicate lactose (%) in the fat-free dry cheese (A) and in the milk (B). In A, water content of the cheese is 46%; in B, lactose content in the fat-free dry cheese is 4·85% (from Ref. 15).

has been observed that, *ceteris paribus*, increasing the water content of Gouda cheese by one percentage unit, decreases the pH by 0·1 unit.

(B)   The decrease in pH during curd making, and the ensuing loss of Ca and phosphate into the whey, may play a part too. These phenomena depend on the buffering capacity of the curd, on the amount of added $CaCl_2$ (which decreases the pH slightly), and on the degree of acid production which is, in turn, affected by the amount and type of starter added, the temperature, any pre-acidification, infection with bacteriophage and the presence of inhibiting components (antibiotics and disinfectants, agglutinins (active in milk but not in curd and cheese), and the peroxidase–H_2O_2–thiocyanate system). In many cases, however, the pH will have changed by only ~0·2 units at moulding and this drop causes dissolution of very little CCP and hence it would have only a minor effect on the final pH. On the other hand, a decrease in pH increases the syneresis rate, which affects the water content and hence the pH (via point A above). If the water content is kept constant by other means, a small effect still remains since now a slightly smaller quantity of the buffering calcium phosphate is incorporated into the curd, causing a lower final pH and a lower cheese yield (Section 3.1).

(C) The best process parameter through which to adjust the pH, independently of the water content, is washing. After the addition of the water to the whey–curd mixture, lactose diffuses from the grains into the whey to equalize the lactose concentrations inside and outside the particles, although equilibrium is rarely reached. When the size distribution of the particles is normal and the contact time with the wash-water is 25 min, the efficiency of reducing the lactose concentration in the curd is ~90%.[45] More water causes a lower yield (Section 3.1) as well as a less valuable whey.

Figure 8 illustrates the quantities of water to be added under conditions related to normal Gouda cheese manufacture. The 'lactose in the fat-free dry matter' represents the ratio between lactose and buffering substances (see point A). Note that increasing the water content before salting from 44 to 46%, increases the amount of water to be added by 15 percentage units. A 0·2% higher lactose content of the milk necessitates 5 percentage units more added water.

3.2.3 Interrelations

Table II tentatively illustrates the feasibility of adjusting the pH and the water content at various levels. If a cheese with a high water content is desired, e.g. 47%, and a normal pH of 5·1, then in addition to gentle cutting and stirring, much water at a relatively low temperature must be added. To obtain a normal water content and a high pH, whey drainage and water addition may be repeated.

TABLE II
Feasibility of making Dutch-type cheese of desired pH and
water content; very qualitative

		Low	Normal	High
	High	+ +	+	?
pH ↑	Normal	+	+ +	+
	Low	?	+	+ +

Low   Normal   High
→ water content

+ + = easy
+ = possible
? = hardly feasible

If the water content is to be normal and the pH rather low ($\sim 5\cdot 0$), addition of water should be omitted. Scalding can preferably be achieved by means of hot water in the vat jacket, or by adding heated whey (which formerly was common practice in Edam cheese manufacture). If an extremely low pH is desired, giving a typical short consistency, the milk may be more or less pre-ripened and/or extra lactose supplied.

To obtain a low water content and a normal pH, the curd should be cut rather finely and, after removal of part of the whey, it should be stirred vigorously at a rather high scalding temperature. Heating should, again, be indirect and slow to prevent the formation of curd particles with a 'skin'. Moreover, a high amount of starter should be added, and possibly some pre-acidification applied. A further lowering of the water content can be obtained by 'working' the drained curd (Section 2.2).

3.3 Starters: Composition and Handling

Use is made of mesophilic starters, usually composed of strains of *Str. cremoris* and/or *Str. lactis* as acid-producing micro-organisms and citric-acid fermenting organisms, either *Leuconostoc lactis* and/or *Leuc. cremoris* (B-starters) or both the leuconostocs and *Str. lactis var. diacetylactis* (BD-starters). Whether B- or BD-starters are selected depends largely on the desired degree of eye formation in the cheese: BD-starters ferment citric acid more rapidly and produce more CO_2 than B-starters. Detailed information on these organisms, for example as to their taxonomy, physiology, biochemical characteristics, phages and phage resistance, and on the composition of starters and their propagation can be found in various publications (e.g. Refs 46–48; see also Chapter 6, Volume 1).

In many European countries spontaneously-developed mixed-strain starters have been used traditionally. These so called Practice(P)-starters[49] are phage-carrying and partially phage resistant, contrary to single-strain starters. Mechanisms involved in the protection of P-starters against phages have been described recently.[22] Daily propagation of these starters in cheese factories is possible without any controlled protection against air-borne bacteriophages. They do not show complete failure of acid production when they become contaminated with disturbing phages, but the strain composition of the starter is greatly affected and the rate of acidification may vary considerably.

Modern large-scale cheese factories require the use of starters with constant activity. Acid production in cheese must proceed fairly quickly and at a constant rate, the latter being essential for the control of syneresis and the water content of the cheese. Therefore traditional methods for starter production are increasingly being replaced by the use of starter concentrates, enabling more uniform bacterial composition of starters and their rate of acidification when they are propagated under complete protection from phage. In the Netherlands, P-starters in use at cheese factories have been selected according to their taste and flavour formation, rate of acidification, eye formation and phage-resistance. They are kept as inoculated milk in a frozen condition and are rarely transferred to preserve their P-properties, phage-resistance in particular. These starters serve for the production of concentrates for bulk starter preparation (thus eliminating the use of mother cultures at the factory), and the concentrates are distributed to the cheese factories in a frozen state.[22] The manufacture of bulk starter concentrates is under development.

The most common procedure now is as follows. Bulk starter milk is pasteurized, e.g. for 10 min at 90°C (batch-pasteurization) or 1 min at 95°C (HTST-pasteurization). The intensity of the heat treatment should be at least equal to that for 3 min at 90°C to destroy any phages present. Specially designed bulk starter equipment offers an effective barrier against air-borne contamination with phages: generally, tanks provided with HEPA (High Efficiency Particulate Air) filters and a special device enabling decontamination of the outer side of boxes of starter concentrate with hypochlorite solution before the starter is introduced into the tank, are used.[50,51] Additional precautions should be taken to avoid accumulation of disturbing phages in the factory, which especially could affect the rate of acidification of the curd in the vat. These measures include: the manufacture of bulk starters in separate rooms; use of closed equipment, cheese vats in particular; and frequent cleaning and disinfection of all installations. Cheese whey is a specially dangerous source of phage contamination. Starters are propagated for 18–24 h at $\sim 20°C$. In almost all modern factories, the starter is automatically metered and added to the cheese vat. Starters may be kept for a limited time (e.g. 24 h) below $5°C$ without loss of activity.

The activity of the bulk starter should be the same on successive days of manufacture. Activity is usually tested in a standardized activity test[52] performed with a standard, pasteurized, reconstituted, high-quality skim-milk powder, and also with the pasteurized cheese milk, which ought to be skimmed. The activity of the starter in either of these milks should be constant. Any change in activity may indicate either: contamination of the starter with disturbing bacteriophages, a decreased activity of the starter (e.g. if it had been kept too long at a low temperature), the presence of antibiotics and/or disinfecting agents in the cheese milk, or gross variations in the composition of the milk. To a certain extent, variation in activity may be corrected by adjusting the quantity of starter added to the cheese milk, or by adjusting other conditions during curd making, e.g. the scalding temperature. It must be remarked that results of the activity test and the acidification rate of cheese do not always agree because of different conditions in milk and fresh cheese, notably phage concentration. According to practical standards for the Dutch cheese industry, the pH of cheese should be 5·7–5·9 after 4 h from the start of manufacture, and 5·3–5·5 after 5·5 h.[53]

3.4 MATURATION

Maturation is the resultant of numerous changes occurring in the cheese. Some changes start during curd making, but most become manifest during storage. The structure and the composition of cheese alter greatly and so do organoleptic properties. Biochemical, microbiological, chemical and physical aspects are involved. Development of cheese properties is due particularly to the conversion of lactose, protein, fat and, in Dutch-type varieties, of citric acid.

3.4.1 Fermentation of lactose and citric acid
Formation of lactic acid by the starter bacteria is paramount for the preservation of cheese. By their action they:

—Ferment lactose quickly and almost completely; consequently, the cheese soon lacks available carbohydrate.

starter cfu/g cheese

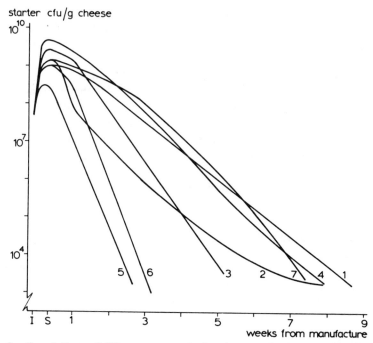

Fig. 9. Populations of different starters during the manufacture and ripening of aseptically made Gouda cheese. Plate counts of samples I (milk after inoculation with starter) and S (cheese immediately before brining) are expressed as per gram of finished cheese: cfu = colony forming units (from Ref. 55).

—Produce lactic (and a little acetic) acid and reduce the pH of the cheese to 5·1–5·2. At this pH, about half of the lactic acid is present in its undissociated (i.e. bacteriostatic) form.
—Reduce the redox potential of the cheese to about − 140 to − 150 mV at pH ≈ 5·2[53,54] as measured with a normal hydrogen electrode.

All these changes aid in inhibiting the growth of undesired micro-organisms; salt uptake by the cheese, the presence of a protective cheese rind and adequate treatment of this rind contribute also (Section 2.4). However, microbial defects cannot be always prevented (Section 3.5).

Starter bacteria may differ greatly as to growth rate, the maximum number to which they grow in cheese and the rate at which they lose viability during cheese ripening (Fig. 9). Cheese milk is commonly inoculated at a level of 10^7 starter bacteria/ml of milk. Mechanical inclusion in the curd leads already to $\sim 10^8$ cfu/g of curd, where they grow to, at most, $\sim 10^9$; this implies that starter bacteria generate (divide) only a few times in the fresh cheese. After growth, fermentation is far from complete (pH of cheese ~ 5.7), and during further conversion of lactose, growth and fermentation are uncoupled.

Fermentation of citric acid is of particular importance to eye formation in Dutch-type cheese. The BD- and B-starters used in the manufacture of Dutch-type varieties ferment citric acid, but BD-starters do so more rapidly and produce more CO_2; they are, therefore, selected if more extensive eye formation is desired. The rate of decrease of the citric acid content in the young cheese may be used as an index for the desired degree of eye formation;[53] the rate of citric acid fermentation is, however, not the only factor involved in eye formation (see Section 3.4.5).

3.4.2 Proteolysis

Protein breakdown in Dutch-type varieties is due mainly to the action of (calf) rennet enzymes, enzymes of the starter bacteria and, to a much lesser extent, milk proteinases. Basic information about these proteolytic systems is given in Chapter 10, Volume 1. The separate and combined actions of these systems in Gouda cheese have been studied intensively by Kleter[56–59] and Visser,[55,60–63] making use of aseptic milking and cheesemaking techniques.

Effectively, the action of calf rennet is determined predominantly by the amount remaining in the curd. This depends primarily on:[20]

—the quantity of rennet used in cheesemaking;
—the water content of the cheese;
—the pH during cheese manufacture; the lower the pH, the more calf rennet becomes associated with the paracasein. The amount of starter used, its rate of acidification and the initial pH of the cheese milk and its composition are, therefore, of importance;
—the scalding temperature of the curd; the higher this temperature, the less active rennet is included;
—the heat treatment of the milk; the more intensive, the more rennet the curd will contain (see also Fig. 4).

The action of rennet enzymes, predominantly chymosin, is characterized by the rapid degradation of α_{s1}-casein at the onset of maturation, about 80% being decomposed within one month. β-Casein is degraded far more slowly, about 50% remaining even after six months.[62] Rapid breakdown of α_{s1}-casein is particularly favoured by the pH of the cheese being near to the optimum (about 5) for rennet action, and a moderate NaCl content ($\sim 4\%$)

TABLE III

Quantity of soluble N compounds as produced in aseptically made Gouda cheese by the combined and separate actions of rennet, starter bacteria and milk proteinase (after Ref. 61). Data to illustrate trends; the blank values differed slightly

Ripening time (months)	Proteolytic system	Soluble nitrogen, as percentage of total nitrogen			
		Total	As peptides of MW		As amino acids
			>14 000	14 000–1 400	<1 400
1	Rennet	6·7	2·7	2·7	1·2	0·1
	Starter	2·5	0·2	0·6	0·4	1·3
	Milk proteinase	2·0	0·2	0·4	1·3	0·1
	All systems (cheese)	12·2	1·8	2·3	6·1	2·0
3	Rennet	12·7	3·6	5·2	3·7	0·2
	Starter	4·7	0·3	0·7	1·4	2·3
	Milk proteinase	3·3	0·4	0·7	1·9	0·3
	All systems (cheese)	19·5	2·3	3·3	9·1	4·8
6	Rennet	17·3	4·4	4·1	8·4	0·3
	Starter	7·6	0·9	0·3	2·4	4·0
	Milk proteinase	4·7	0·5	1·0	2·7	0·5
	All systems (cheese)	26·0	5·5	2·3	10·8	7·4

in the cheese moisture. β-Casein degradation is slowed down considerably, even at this low NaCl content.[64] The decomposition of α_{s1}-casein is an important factor in the development of cheese consistency (see Chapter 8, Volume 1). Calf rennet appears to be responsible for the formation of the greater part of soluble N and the liberation of high and low molecular weight (MW) peptides, but only very low amounts of amino acids (Table III).

When acting separately in cheese, starter bacteria are able to decompose paracasein gradually, proteolytic activity becoming manifest only after several weeks of ripening. Therefore, this capacity, in particular the ability to degrade α_{s1}-casein, seems of minor importance because in the meantime, the casein will have been largely degraded by rennet.[62] Contrary to rennet, starter bacteria predominantly produce low-MW peptides and amino acids (see Table III). Starters may vary greatly in this respect.[61] Rennet and/or starter bacteria may cause bitterness in cheese; for the underlying mechanisms, reference is made to Chapter 10, Volume 1.

When acting alone in cheese, milk proteinases may decompose α_{s1}- and

β-caseins to some extent during prolonged ripening. It can be seen from Table III that small amounts of low-MW peptides and amino acids are liberated.[61] The pH and NaCl Content of Dutch-type varieties are not very favourable for the activity of most enzymes; in particular, plasmin activity is reduced greatly.[65]

In normal cheeses, where all enzyme systems act together, no clear mutual stimulation or inhibition of the systems in the formation of soluble N components is observed. From Table III it can, however, be deduced that the action of rennet clearly stimulates the starter bacteria to accumulate amino acids and low-MW peptides, which is most likely due to the progressive degradation by starter peptidases of the higher MW products of rennet action.

Contents of soluble N compounds reflect the 'width' of ripening. The 'depth' of ripening is defined as the ratio between the amount of degradation products of low MW, e.g. amino acids or peptides with $MW < 1400$, and the total amount of soluble breakdown products. In that sense, the width of ripening of Dutch-type cheese varieties is predominantly determined by rennet action, and the depth by the action of starter bacteria.

Serum proteins (at least if undenatured) seem to be hardly degraded in cheese.[66]

3.4.3 Lipolysis

In Dutch-type varieties some lipolysis usually occurs and is even desired, but it should be limited. Factors affecting lipolysis have been intensively studied by Stadhouders and co-workers.[67-73] Cheese made from raw milk shows distinct action of milk lipase; if made from aseptically drawn milk containing a negligible number of lipolytic bacteria, fat acidity increases gradually.[67,68] HTST-treatment of milk, e.g. 15 s at 72°C, largely but not completely inactivates milk lipase[6] (see also Fig. 1). Cheese made from aseptically drawn, low-temperature pasteurized milk still shows an increase of fat acidity during maturation, although this increase is slight or even scarcely noticeable.[58,59] One may question as to what extent variations in results were caused by differences in susceptibility of the milk to lipolysis, e.g. due to mechanical damage of the fat globules.

Under well-controlled conditions during making and curing of cheese made from pasteurized milk, a good bacteriological quality of the milk prior to thermization of pasteurization and the absence of microbial growth on the cheese surface during maturation in particular, lipolysis in cheese will result predominantly from the action of starter bacteria, residual milk lipase and heat-stable lipases of psychrotrophic organisms which, however, should only be present in small numbers. Enzymes of the starter bacteria hardly decompose triglycerides, but are able to produce free fatty acids from mono- and diglycerides formed by milk lipase and/or microbial lipases.[73] The activity of milk lipase is reduced by the NaCl in the cheese.[67] Milk lipase action is also affected by the pH of the cheese. Although this action has been found to decrease markedly with decreasing pH when assayed on substrates greatly different from cheese (e.g. Ref. 67), the acidity of cheese fat has been reported to increase faster in cheese of low pH.[67,74] The explanation is unclear, though it should be noted that at a lower pH a higher proportion of any short-chain fatty acids present will be in the fat phase. Lipase activity in cheese increases markedly with temperature.[67,75] In cheese made from milk containing high numbers of psychrotrophic bacteria (or their heat-stable lipases), lipolysis may be increased to undesirable levels. Also, growth of organisms on the cheese surface, e.g. moulds, coryneform bacteria, yeasts,[67,70] may contribute to increased acidity of the fat. Growth of such organisms, however, is usually kept down, but cannot be fully prevented; consequently, the rind portion of the cheese generally acquires a somewhat higher fat acidity.

3.4.4 Flavour

Flavour is defined as the complex sensation comprising aroma, taste and texture (see Ref. 76). Little is known about the nature of the aroma compounds in Dutch-type cheese, but it is clear that the breakdown products of lactose and citric acid (lactic acid, diacetyl, CO_2, etc.), of paracasein (peptides and amino acids), and of lipids (free fatty acids) are essential for the flavour. A correct balance must exist between the various flavour substances.[77] Lactic acid causes the refreshing acid taste, which is particularly noticeable in young cheese; an excess of lactic acid renders the cheese sour, a shortage insipid. Indirectly, lactic acid exerts influence on the texture of cheese. Large changes in flavour develop during maturation. Numerous secondary products formed during the fermentation of lactose and the subsequent partial transformation of lactic acid affect aroma and taste (e.g. aldehydes, ketones, alcohols, esters, organic acids, CO_2). Proteolysis is also crucial in flavour formation. Paracasein is tasteless, but many degradation products are not; for example, peptides may be bitter and many amino acids have specific tastes, sweet, bitter or brothlike, in particular.[77] Short peptides and amino acids contribute at least to the basic flavour of cheese.[77,78] Higher temperatures, a higher pH, a higher water content and a lower NaCl content in cheese appear to favour proteolysis, in particular the formation of amino acids.[79] Mature cheese contains numerous volatile compounds, usually in small amounts. These are predominantly degradation products of amino acids, e.g. NH_3, various amines, H_2S, phenylacetic acid.

Protein degradation greatly affects cheese consistency and thereby probably flavour perception. Carbon dioxide, although tasteless, appears to influence the flavour; loss of CO_2 may contribute to the rapid loss of typical flavour from grated cheese. NaCl accentuates the flavour; saltiness of cheese is governed by the NaCl content of the cheese rather than that in the cheese moisture. In mature cheese, free fatty acids may render the cheese flavour very piquant. However, in cheese lacking sufficient basic flavour, free fatty acids soon produce a rancid flavour.

3.4.5 Texture

Cheese rheology is discussed in Chapter 8, Volume 1 of this book (see also Ref. 80). The main factors affecting consistency in Dutch-type varieties probably are moisture content, extent of proteolysis, pH, NaCl and fat contents, any inhomogeneity of these variables throughout the cheese mass and, of course, temperature.

During maturation, several changes occur that may be important to texture:

—Structure and composition become more uniform, particularly in the early stages due to further fusion of curd grains, and reduction of salt, moisture and pH gradients.
—The cheese loses water by evaporation and ongoing syneresis (especially near the rind) and due to proteolysis.
—Maturation primarily implies breakdown of the paracaseinate network; it also causes a slight increase in pH (formation of alkaline groups by proteolysis, degradation of lactic acid).
—Gas is formed.

The common result is that during maturation the apparent elastic modulus of the cheese increases, the deformation at which fracture occurs decreases and the fracture stress at first decreases and subsequently increases again.[81] The only rheological parameter that appears to correlate well with the degree of maturation of the cheese is the deformation at fracture, as was, for instance, found in a study of several, widely different cheeses ranging in age from 4 to 20 weeks.[82] The relative deformation at fracture is, say, 1·6 for unsyneresed curd, 0·7 directly after pressing and 0·3 after 3 months of maturation.

In several Dutch-type varieties, the number, size and shape of holes is considered an important texture characteristic. Holes are formed if gas pressure exceeds saturation and if sufficient nuclei are present. The gas is usually CO_2 produced by starter organisms or CO_2 and possibly H_2 produced by undesirable bacteria (Section 3.5). Gas pressure can be high enough if its rate of production is relatively fast (which depends on temperature, type and number of bacteria and possibly citrate content), if its rate of diffusion out of the cheese is slow (mainly depending on loaf size) and if the milk had been saturated with air (so that a certain CO_2 pressure corresponds with a higher overall gas pressure). Nuclei are usually small air bubbles, either incorporated as such in the curd when the curd mass is 'worked' after draining off all whey, or present in the milk. The latter presumably exist as tiny air bubbles adhering to dirt particles and very small granules of partially coalesced fat globules; they can remain only if the milk is (almost) saturated with air. Nucleation predominantly determines the number of holes and their shape depends on cheese consistency, while both characteristics also depend on rate of gas production. If the latter is not too fast and the cheese consistency allows for slow viscous flow of the cheese material, eyes (i.e. spherical holes) develop. If the consistency is short, or more precisely if the breaking stress of the material at slow deformation is low, slits may develop because the cheese mass fractures in the vicinity of the holes. Such may be the case for a cheese of low pH, low calcium phosphate content and considerable proteolysis at the time of gas production, but quantitative relations cannot be given yet.

3.5 Microbial Defects

Whether or not deteriorative micro-organisms will develop in cheese is determined by the microbial composition of the cheese milk, any contamination during cheesemaking, the composition of the cheese and curing conditions. Most undesirable organisms are killed by HTST-treatment of milk, e.g. 15 s at 72°C. Consequently, the nature and the degree of the defects may differ greatly between cheese made from raw milk and pasteurized milk. However, in spite of rigorous hygienic standards, contamination of milk or curd with undesired organisms cannot be fully prevented; moreover conditions of modern cheesemaking, e.g. the almost continuous use of moulding machines, may allow considerable growth. Some defects may even originate specifically from the introduction of modern technology. Nevertheless, to guarantee the microbial quality of cheese, practical GMP standards for the Dutch cheese industry have been drawn up.[53] It must be noted that any organisms in the milk are almost completely entrapped in the curd, thus raising their number per gram of fresh cheese by a factor of 10, as compared to their number per gram of curd (gel) at the end of renneting.

3.5.1 Coliform bacteria

These bacteria require lactose for growth in cheese. They grow only during the early stages of cheesemaking and can multiply very rapidly during the first few hours when other conditions, such as pH and temperature, are also favourable. According to the species or strains involved, varying amounts of metabolites are formed; most important are lactic acid, acetic acid, formic acid, succinic acid, ethanol, 2,3-butyleneglycol, hydrogen and carbon dioxide. In cases of excessive growth, cheeses develop off-flavours (yeasty, gassy, unclean) and show 'early blowing' due to the formation of CO_2 and, in particular, of H_2, which has very low solubility in cheese. Strains may differ in their potency to produce free H_2 in cheese; those that ferment citric acid readily show a reduced risk for early blowing, because hydrogenation of intermediate metabolites occurs.[83] HTST-treatment of milk, e.g. 15 s at 72°C, kills the coliform organisms and consequently, early blowing is unlikely to occur in cheese made from pasteurized milk, but in industrial practice a slight recontamination of this milk with coliform bacteria of non-faecal origin, e.g. *Enterobacter aerogenes*, is inevitable and growth during cheesemaking must be well controlled to limit their number in cheese. Apart from hygienic conditions, rapid acidification of the curd, thereby decreasing the pH and the amount of lactose, is of great importance.

Formation of H_2 by coliform bacteria is inhibited by nitrate which suppresses the formation of the hydrogen lyase system normally involved in the production of hydrogen from lactose via formate under sufficiently anaerobic conditions, and induces the formation of a formate dehydro-genase/nitrate reductase system.[84,85] The nitrite formed induces the production of a formate dehydrogenase/nitrite reductase system.[86] Nitrate and nitrite act as terminal hydrogen acceptors and their nitrogen is used for bacterial growth or for ammonia production.[83,87] Hence, no H_2 is produced from formate. Growth of coliform bacteria is not prevented (e.g. Ref. 88), CO_2 is normally produced and development of off-flavour is not inhibited.

Nitrate is, however, used primarily to prevent the 'late blowing' defect caused by butyric acid bacteria.

3.5.2 Butyric acid bacteria

Butyric acid fermentation is characterized by the breakdown of lactic acid principally to butyric acid, CO_2 and H_2:

$$2CH_3CHOHCOOH \rightarrow CH_3CH_2CH_2COOH + 2CO_2 + 2H_2$$

Consequently, growth of anaerobic, spore-forming, lactate-fermenting butyric acid bacteria, especially of *Clostridium tyrobutyricum*, may cause 'late blowing' of cheese due to excessive production of CO_2 and H_2, and a very bad off-flavour. Silage, used as a feed in winter, represents the main source of contamination of the milk, especially when it is insufficiently preserved. Such silage contains large numbers of *Cl. tyrobutyricum* spores, which survive passage through the digestive tract of the cow and concentrate in dung. The degree of contamination of the milk with spores therefore strongly depends on hygienic conditions during milking,[89,90] but even with modern methods of milking, a slight contamination with dung present on the udder cannot be prevented. This problem is the more serious since the spores fully survive the HTST-treatment normally applied to the cheese milk.

Dutch-type varieties are especially vulnerable to butyric acid fermentation, the more so for larger cheese loaves. Because of the serious nature of the defect, much research has been undertaken to find ways to reduce the number of spores in milk and to prevent their germination and growth in cheese. Factors studied include: bactofugation of the milk; addition to the milk of nitrate, hydrogen peroxide and other oxidizing substances, or lysozyme; the use of a nisin-producing starter; the salt content and pH of the cheese; cheese ripening temperature; amount of (undissociated) lactic acid (for relevant literature information, see Refs 12, 91, 105).

Nitrate may be used effectively to prevent butyric acid fermentation and has been used for such for about 150 years. The mechanism of inhibition requires the presence of xanthine oxidase (EC 1.2.3.2) which reduces nitrate to nitrite.[92] Nitrite is considered to delay the germination of spores for a certain period after brining (but the actual mechanism may well be more complicated[105]). Later on, the inhibitory action is taken over by NaCl when it has become evenly distributed throughout the cheese and if it is present at sufficient concentration.[93] If nitrite is the only factor involved in the initial inhibition, it must be very effective, since it is present at only very small concentrations (see also Fig. 10).

At a given curing temperature, usually about 14°C, the combined effect of several factors determines whether growth of *Cl. tyrobutyricum* is

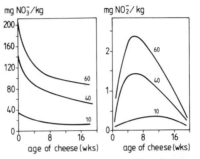

Fig. 10. Contents of nitrate and nitrite per kg of Gouda cheese, made from HTST-pasteurized milk (5 s at 76°C) during storage at 13°C. Parameter is the amount of NaNO$_3$ added to the cheese milk (g/100 litre) (after Ref. 94).

possible or not. Important factors promoting growth are a large number of spores in the cheese milk, a low content of undissociated lactic acid (hence usually a high pH), a low nitrate content in the cheese and a low level of NaCl in the cheese moisture. The rate at which salt becomes homogeneously distributed throughout the cheese mass, its final concentration and the initial nitrate content of the cheese are, therefore, crucial.[95] For example, a cheese with a high pH requires a higher than normal final salt concentration to inhibit growth. Any discrepancy in conditions may allow growth of *Cl. tyrobutyricum* to start. Since the pH of the cheese is increased by the butyric acid fermentation, growth conditions for the organism then become more and more favourable and consequently the rate of fermentation is accelerated.

Low numbers of spores in the cheese milk, which can also be achieved by bactofugation, permit the amount of nitrate to be reduced considerably. A certain amount remains necessary because without nitrate the critical concentration of spores in milk capable of causing the butyric acid fermentation is extremely low, 5–10 spores/litre, which generally cannot be achieved.[13]

Increased numbers of coliform bacteria, e.g. > 10^5/g in a one-day old cheese, may cause nitrate to disappear too quickly from the cheese, increasing the risk of butyric acid fermentation. Growth of some particular strains of mesophilic lactobacilli also may have this effect.[96]

Heat treatments of milk that inactivate xanthine oxidase render cheese made from such milk very vulnerable to late blowing.

3.5.3 Lactobacilli

Growth of mesophilic normal or salt-tolerant lactobacilli may introduce flavour and texture defects, especially in mature cheese. Even when initially present in small numbers, e.g. 10/ml of cheese milk, some strains of common lactobacilli (*L. plantarum*, *L. casei*, *L. brevis*) may grow slowly in cheese to more than $2 \times 10^7/g$ in 4–6 weeks,[21] causing gassy and putrid flavours and an excessively open texture. Probably, amino acids are used as a carbon source.[97] The organisms are killed by adequate pasteurization of milk, e.g. 15 s at 72°C. In industrial practice, continuously working curd-drainage machines are the main source of contamination.

In particular, if the salting of cheese is carried out in brine of reduced strength there is a risk of defects caused by salt-tolerant lactobacilli, some strains being able to survive even in the presence of >15% NaCl. Furthermore, they differ from normal lactobacilli by their continuing growth in cheese and their active amino acid metabolism, causing phenolic, putrid, mealy and H_2S-like flavours in 4–6 month-old cheese. Some strains also produce excessive quantities of CO_2, causing the formation of holes, either eyes or cracks according to the consistency of cheese.[98] More than 10^3 of these gas-forming lactobacilli per ml of brine is considered to be dangerous. The lactobacilli enter the cheese through penetration of the rind during brining, this being facilitated if the cheese is insufficiently pressed and the rind not well closed.[99] Of course, contamination of the cheese milk with these bacteria must be prevented. If a weak brine (e.g. 14% NaCl) is kept sufficiently acid (pH ≤ 4.6) and cold (~ 13°C), growth of the organisms usually does not occur, and they die gradually. Increased numbers in brine originate from their growth in deposits, which are often present on the walls of basins just above the brine level, on racks and other equipment, and so contaminate the brine. Growth conditions for the lactobacilli are more favourable in these deposits as a result of the action of salt-tolerant yeasts increasing pH, a lower NaCl concentration (due to absorption of water), and a somewhat higher temperature than that of the brine, which usually is ~ 13°C. Measures to keep the number of lactobacilli low in brine include good hygiene in the brining room with removal of deposits, adjustment of the NaCl content of the brine to at least 16% and of its pH to ≤ 4.5.[100]

3.5.4 Thermoresistant streptococci

These bacteria are normally present in raw milk. In particular, strains of *Str. thermophilus* may be responsible for cheese of inferior quality. Contrary to the mesophilic streptococci, they can grow at 45°C and survive thermization (e.g. 10 s at 65°C) and HTST-pasteurization (e.g. 15 s at 72°C) of milk. During such heat treatments the organisms may become attached to the walls of the cooling section of the heat exchanger and may start to multiply very rapidly (minimum generation time, ~ 15 min), this among other things depending on their initial number in the milk. Continuous use of heat exchangers for too long a period without cleaning may cause heavy contamination of the cheese milk (about 10^6 per ml). As a result of their concentration in curd and growth during the early stage of cheesemaking, their number may increase to more than 10^8/g of cheese. They render the flavour of cheese 'unclean' and 'yeasty'. Moreover, CO_2-production by these bacteria may yield cheese with an excessively open texture, especially when a starter with high CO_2-producing capacity is used for cheesemaking.[101,102]

3.5.5 Propionic acid bacteria

Very considerable growth of these organisms in cheese results in the development of a sweet taste and a very open texture, due to excessive gas formation. Propionic acid bacteria can convert lactates into propionic acid, acetic acid and CO_2, according to:

$$3CH_3CHOHCOOH \rightarrow 2CH_3CH_2COOH + CH_3COOH + CO_2 + H_2O$$

Consequently, the pH of the cheese does not change significantly. Because they develop very slowly in cheese, any serious defects occur only after prolonged ripening. Several conditions determine their growth in cheese. The pH is decisive, significant growth starting only from 5·1 and increasing at higher values. Increasing concentrations of NaCl retard their growth, but the effect of the variation in NaCl content in Dutch-type cheeses (4–5% NaCl in the water) is small. Higher salt concentrations, e.g. near the rind of the cheese, may be inhibitory. Higher storage temperatures favour the growth of propionic acid bacteria. Nitrate hinders their development. When conditions allow growth of these bacteria in cheese, the development of butyric acid bacteria (if present) may also be expected, provided that growth of the latter is not prevented otherwise. Propionic acid bacteria are killed by low-temperature treatment of milk, e.g. 15 s at 72°C. Therefore, they are predominantly of interest in the manufacture of cheese made from raw milk, farm-made cheese in particular.

3.5.6 Coryneform bacteria, yeasts and moulds

Abundant growth of yeasts and coryneform bacteria on the cheese surface may lead to a somewhat slimy rind and a part-coloured or pink appearance. Growth of these organisms is favoured by: insufficient acidification of the cheese leading to a significant lactose content in the rind; salting of cheese in brine with a low NaCl content and a high pH; inadequate drying of the cheese rind after brining (this is the main factor in practice); and the use of insufficiently cleaned shelves. Growth of moulds causes discoloration and may under extreme conditions produce a health hazard because of mycotoxin formation. To prevent their development, special attention must be paid to treatment of the cheese rind and the hygienic conditions in curing rooms (see Section 2.4).

3.5.7 Minor defects

Growth of *Lactobacillus bifermentans* may contribute to textural defects. This organism is characterized by its ability to ferment both sugars and lactic acid;[103] acetic acid, ethanol, CO_2 and H_2 are produced. Its growth in cheese proceeds slowly and defects due to its action are, therefore, only occasionally observed. Since the organism does not withstand low-temperature pasteurization of cheese milk, it very rarely causes problems in cheese made from pasteurized milk.

Growth of certain lactobacilli (e.g. *L. büchneri*) and/or faecal streptococci (e.g. *Str. durans*) occasionally cause undesired high levels of biogenic amines, histamine and tyramine in particular. This problem is most frequently encountered in cheese made from raw milk.

Various micro-organisms may sometimes cause flavour defects, predominantly in cheese made from raw milk. These include *Str. lactis var. maltigenes* (burned flavour), *Str. faecalis var. malodoratus* (H_2S flavour), and yeasts (yeasty, fruity flavour). Increased levels of psychrotrophic organisms or of their thermostable lipases in the cheese milk may cause the cheese to become rancid.

ACKNOWLEDGEMENT

We are indebted to Mr G. van den Berg, Netherlands Institute for Dairy Research, for scrutinizing the manuscript.

REFERENCES

1. Burkhalter, G. (Rapporteur), IDF-Catalogue of cheeses. *FIL-IDF Bulletin*, 1981, Doc. 141, p. 3.
2. Mair-Waldburg, H. (Ed.), *Handbuch der Käse*, Volkswirtschaftlicher Verlag, Kempten, 1974.
3. Lawrence, R. C., Gilles, J. and Creamer, L. K., *New Zealand J. Dairy Sci. Technol.*, 1983, **18**, 175.
4. Noomen, A. and Mulder, H., *Neth. Milk Dairy J.*, 1976, **30**, 230.

5. van Schouwenburg-van Foeken, A. W. J., Stadhouders, J. and Witsenburg, W. W., *Neth. Milk Dairy J.*, 1979, **33**, 49.
6. Driessen, F. M., Lipases and proteinases in milk. Occurrence, heat inactivation, and their importance for the keeping quality of milk products. Doctoral thesis, 1983, Agricultural University, Wageningen.
7. Law, B. A., Andrews, A. T., Cliffe, A. J., Sharpe, M. E. and Chapman, H. R., *J. Dairy Res.*, 1979, **46**, 497.
8. Bergdoll, M. S. In *Food Borne Infections and Intoxications*, 2nd Edn (Ed. H. Riemann and F. Bryan) Academic Press, 1979, New York, pp. 444–95.
9. Hup, G., Bangma, A., Stadhouders, J. and Bouman, S., *Zuivelzicht*, 1979, **71**, 1014.
10. Driessen, F. M. and Bouman, S., *Zuivelzicht*, 1979, **71**, 1062.
11. Stadhouders, J. and Hup, G., *Neth. Milk Dairy J.*, 1970, **24**, 79.
12. van den Berg, G., Hup, G., Stadhouders, J. and de Vries, E., *Rapport Nederlands Instituut voor Zuivelonderzoek*, 1980, **R112**.
13. Stadhouders, J., *Neth. Milk Dairy J.*, 1983, **37**, 233.
14. Mulder, H. and Walstra, P., *The Milk Fat Globule. Emulsion Science as Applied to Milk Products and Comparable Foods*, Pudoc, Wageningen, 1974.
15. van den Berg, G. and de Vries, E., *Zuivelzicht*, 1976, **68**, 878, 924 (NIZO-nieuws, 1976, No. 6, 7).
16. van den Berg, G. and de Vries, E., *Neth. Milk Dairy J.*, 1975, **29**, 181.
17. Birkkjaer, H. E., Sørensen, E. J., Jørgensen, J. and Sigersted, E., *Beretn. Statens Forsøgsmejeri*, 1961, No. 128.
18. Lolkema, H. and Blaauw, J., *Kaasbereiding*, Landelijke Stichting Beroepsopleiding Levensmiddelenindustrie, Apeldoorn, 1974.
19. Monib, A. M. M. F., *Meded. Landbouwhogeschool Wageningen*, 1962, **62**(10).
20. Stadhouders, J. and Hup, G., *Neth. Milk Dairy J.*, 1975, **29**, 335.
21. Stadhouders, J., Kleter, G., Lammers, W. L. and Tuinte, J. H. M., NIZO-nieuws M.9, 1983; *Voedingsmiddelentechnologie*, 1983, **26**, 20; *Zuivelzicht*, 1983, **75**, 1118.
22. Stadhouders, J. and Leenders, G. J. M., *Neth. Milk Dairy J.*, 1984, **38**, 157.
23. Walstra, P., van Dijk, H. J. M. and Geurts, T. J., *Neth. Milk Dairy J.*, 1985, **39**, 209.
24. Wilbrink, A., *Neth. Milk Dairy J.*, 1979, **33**, 202.
25. Geurts, T. J., Walstra, P. and Mulder, H., *Neth. Milk Dairy J.*, 1980, **34**, 229.
26. Wilbrink, A., Spoelstra, T. and Strampel, J., *Zuivelzicht*, 1981, **73**, 16.
27. Stadhouders, J., Hup, G. and Hassing, F., *Voedingsmiddelentechnologie*, 1974, **27**, 17.
28. Geurts, T. J., Walstra, P. and Mulder, H., *Neth. Milk Dairy J.*, 1972, **26**, 168.
29. de Ruig, W. G. and van den Berg, G., *Neth. Milk Dairy J.*, 1985, **39**, 165.
30. Het Additievenboekje. Een overzicht van toevoegingen aan drink- en eetwaren, Staatsuitgeverij, 's-Gravenhage, 1981.
31. Schulz, M. E. and Kay, H., *Käse-Tabellen*, Milchwirtschaftlicher Verlag Th. Mann KG, Hildesheim, 1957.
32. Posthumus, G., Klijn, C. J. and Booy, C. J., *Off. Orgaan Kon. Ned. Zuivelbond FNZ*, 1967, **59**, 712, 740, 749, 769.
33. Straatsma, J., de Vries, E., Heijnekamp, A. and Kloosterman, L., *Zuivelzicht*, 1984, **76**, 956 (NIZO-nieuws, 1984-8).

34. O'Leary, J., Hicks, C. L., Aylward, E. B. and Langlois, B. E., *Res. Food Sci. Nutr.*, 1983, **1**, 150.
35. Steffen, C. and Rentsch, F.,|*Schweiz. Milchztg*, 1981, **107**, 129, 137.
36. McLean, D. M., Graham, E. R. B., Ponzoni, R. W. and McKenzie, H. A., *J. Dairy Res.*, 1984, **51**, 531.
37. Schaar, J., *Scand. J. Dairy Technol. Know-How*, 1984, **8**, 43.
38. Banks, J. M. and Muir, D. D., *Milchwissenschaft*, 1985, **40**, 209.
39. Banks, J. M., Tamime, A. Y. and Muir, D. D., *Dairy Ind. Internat.*, 1985, **50**, 11.
40. Richardson, G. H., *Cultured Dairy Products J.*, 1984, **19**, 6.
41. Walstra, P. and Jenness, R., *Dairy Chemistry and Physics*, John Wiley, New York, 1984.
42. Posthumus, G., Booy, C. J. and Klijn, C. J., *Off. Orgaan Kon. Ned. Zuivelbond FNZ*, 1963, **55**, 986.
43. Maubois, J. L. In: *Le Fromage*, A. Eck (Ed.), Lavoisier, Paris, p. 157, 1984.
44. Pearce, K. N., *N.Z. J. Dairy Sci. Technol.*, 1978, **13**, 59.
45. van den Berg, G. and de Vries, E., *Milchwissenschaft*, 1974, **29**, 214.
46. Davies, F. L. and Law, B. A. (Eds). *Advances in the Microbiology and Biochemistry of Cheese and Fermented Milk*, Elsevier Applied Science Ltd, London, New York, 1984.
47. Daly, C., *Antonie van Leeuwenhoek*, 1983, **49**, 297.
48. Stadhouders, J., *Milchwissenschaft*, 1974, **29**, 329.
49. Galesloot, T. E., Hassing, F. and Stadhouders, J., *Proc. 17th Int. Dairy Congr.*, Munich, 1966, Vol. D, p. 491.
50. Lankveld, J. M. G., *Voedingsmiddelentechnologie*, 1984, **17**, 33.
51. Stadhouders, J., Bangma, A. and Driessen, F. M., *Zuivelzicht*, 1976, **68**, 180.
52. Starters in the manufacture of cheese. *FIL-IDF Bulletin*, 1980, Doc. 129.
53. Northolt, M. D. and Stadhouders, J., *Zuivelzicht*, 1985, **77**, 324, 488.
54. Langeveld, L. P. M. and Galesloot, T. E., *Neth. Milk Dairy J.*, 1971, **25**, 15.
55. Visser, F. M. W., *Neth. Milk Dairy J.*, 1977, **31**, 120.
56. Kleter, G. and de Vries, Tj., *Neth. Milk Dairy J.*, 1974, **28**, 212.
57. Kleter, G., *Neth. Milk Dairy J.*, 1975, **29**, 295.
58. Kleter, G., *Neth. Milk Dairy J.*, 1976, **30**, 254.
59. Kleter, G., *Neth. Milk Dairy J.*, 1977, **31**, 177.
60. Visser, F. M. W., *Neth. Milk Dairy J.*, 1977, **31**, 188.
61. Visser, F. M. W., *Neth. Milk Dairy J.*, 1977, **31**, 210.
62. Visser, F. M. W., *Neth Milk Dairy J.*, 1977, **31**, 247.
63. Visser, F. M. W., *Neth. Milk Dairy J.*, 1977, **31**, 265.
64. Noomen, A., *Neth. Milk Dairy J.*, 1978, **32**, 49.
65. Noomen, A., *Neth. Milk Dairy J.*, 1978, **32**, 26.
66. de Koning, P. J., de Boer, R., Both, P. and Nooij, P. F. C., *Neth. Milk Dairy J.*, 1981, **35**, 35.
67. Stadhouders, J., De hydrolyse van vet bij de kaasrijping in verband met de smaak van kaas, Doctoral thesis, 1956, Agricultural University, Wageningen.
68. Stadhouders, J. and Mulder, H., *Neth. Milk Dairy J.*, 1957, **11**, 164.
69. Stadhouders, J. and Mulder, H., *Neth. Milk Dairy J.*, 1958, **12**, 238.
70. Stadhouders, J. and Mulder, H., *Neth. Milk Dairy J.*, 1959, **13**, 291.
71. Stadhouders, J. and Mulder, H., *Neth. Milk Dairy J.*, 1960, **14**, 141.
72. Driessen, F. M. and Stadhouders, J., Lipolysis in hard cheese made from pasteurized milk, *FIL-IDF Bulletin*, Doc. **86**, p. 101.

73. Stadhouders, J. and Veringa, H. A., *Neth. Milk Dairy J.*, 1973, **27**, 77.
74. Raadsveld, C. W. and Mulder, H., *Neth. Milk Dairy J.*, 1949, **3**, 222.
75. Raadsveld, C. W. and Mulder, H., *Neth. Milk Dairy J.*, 1949, **3**, 117.
76. Badings, H. T., Flavors and Off-Flavors. in: *Dairy Chemistry and Physics*, (Ed. P. Walstra and R. Jenness), John Wiley, New York, p. 336, 1984.
77. Mulder, H., *Neth. Milk Dairy J.*, 1952, **6**, 157.
78. Ali, L. A. M., The amino acid content of Edam cheese and its relation to flavour, Doctoral thesis, Agricultural University, Wageningen, 1960.
79. Raadsveld, C. W., *Neth. Milk Dairy J.*, 1952, **6**, 342.
80. Walstra, P. and van Vliet, T., Rheology of cheese, *IDF-Bulletin*, 1982, Doc. **153**, p. 22.
81. Mulder, H., *Versl. Landbouwk. Onderz.*, 1945, **51C**, 467.
82. Oortwijn, H., Unpublished report 84.80 of the Rijkskwaliteitsinstituut voor Land- en tuinbouwprodukten (RIKILT), Wageningen, 1984.
83. Galesloot, T. E., Over de vroeg beginnende gasvorming in kaas. Doctoral thesis, Agricultural University, Wageningen; Publication L.E.B. Fonds, No. 29, Wageningen, 1946.
84. Ruiz Herrera, J. and De Moss, J. A., *J. Bact.*, 1969, **99**, 720.
85. Ruiz Herrera, J. and Alvarez, A., *Antonie van Leeuwenhoek*, 1972, **38**, 479.
86. Abou-Jaoudé, A., Chippaux, M., Pascal, M. C. and Casse, F., *Biochem. Biophys. Res. Comm.*, 1977, **78**, 579.
87. Cole, J. A. and Brown, C. M., *FEMS Microbiol. Lett.*, 1980, **7**, 65.
88. Galesloot, T. E. and Hassing, F., *Neth, Milk Dairy J.*, 1983, **37**, 1.
89. de Vries, Tj. and Stadhouders, J., *Zuivelzicht*, 1977, **69**, 196.
90. de Vries, Tj. and Brouwer, J., *Boerderij*, 1980, **64**, 50.
91. Kleter, G., Lammers, W. L. and Vos, E. A., *Neth. Milk Dairy J.*, 1984, **38**, 31.
92. Galesloot, T. E., *Neth. Milk Dairy J.*, 1961, **15**, 31.
93. Galesloot, T. E., *Neth. Milk Dairy J.*, 1961, **15**, 395.
94. Goodhead, K., Gough, T. A., Webb, K. S., Stadhouders, J. and Elgersma, R. H. C., *Neth. Milk Dairy J.*, 1976, **30**, 207.
95. Galesloot, T. E., *Neth. Milk Dairy J.*, 1964, **18**, 127.
96. Nieuwenhof, F. F. J., *Neth. Milk Dairy J.*, 1977, **31**, 153.
97. Kristoffersen, T. and Nelson, F. E., *Appl. Microbiol.*, 1955, **3**, 268.
98. Stadhouders, J., Hup, G. and Hassing, F., *Voedingsmiddelentechnologie*, 1974, **27**, 17.
99. Hup, G., Stadhouders, J., de Vries, E. and van den Berg, G. *Zuivelzicht*, 1982, **74**, 270.
100. Stadhouders, J., Leenders, G. J. M., Maessen-Damsma, G., de Vries, E. and Eilert, J. G., *Zuivelzicht*, 1985, **77**, 892.
101. Hup, G., Bangma, A., Stadhouders, J. and Bouman, S., *Zuivelzicht*, 1979, **71**, 1014.
102. Driessen, F. M. and Bouman, S., *Zuivelzicht*, 1979, **71**, 1062.
103. Pette, J. W. and van Beynum, J., *Versl. Landb. Onderz.*, Dep. Landb., 's-Gravenhage, 1943, **49**(9) C, 315 (see DSA 1946-47, **8**, 248).
104. Emmons, D. B., Beckett, D. C. and Binns, M., *Proc. 20th Intern. Diary Congr.*, Paris, 1978, Vol. *E*, p. 491.
105. Stadhouders, J., Hup, G. and Nieuwenhof, F. F. J., *Mededelingen Ned. Inst. voot Zuivelonderzoek*, 1983, **M19**.

Chapter 3

Swiss-type Varieties

C. Steffen, E. Flueckiger, J. O. Bosset and
M. Ruegg

Federal Dairy Research Institute,
Liebefeld-Bern, Switzerland

1. GENERAL

There is no internationally recognized definition of Swiss-type cheese that differentiates it from other varieties. Swiss-type cheeses have round regular eyes which vary in size from medium to large (Fig. 1). The body and texture correspond to those of hard or semi-hard cheeses. Swiss-type cheese was originally manufactured in the Emmen valley in Switzerland, its precursors were mountain cheeses.[1] Emmentaler is probably the best-known Swiss-type cheese and is frequently referred to simply as 'Swiss cheese'. Gruyère and Appenzeller are other Swiss cheeses belonging to the Swiss-type group.

The characteristics of Swiss manufactured Emmentaler are:

—cylindrical shape;
—firm dry rind;
—weight: 60–130 kg;
—1000–2000 round eyes, diameter 1–4 cm, caused by propionic acid fermentation;
—flavour: mild, slightly sweet, becoming more aromatic with increasing age;
—cheese body: ivory to light-yellow, slightly elastic.

Today, Swiss-type varieties are manufactured in many countries by methods differing from traditional Swiss procedures. Thus, the treatment of milk, the extent of mechanization, the weight, shape, ripening time and shelf life of foreign Swiss-type cheeses are often different from the original.

C. Steffen, E. Flueckiger, J. O. Bosset, M. Ruegg

TABLE I

Constituents of ripe Emmentaler, Gruyère and Appenzeller $(N = 60)$[5-8]

	Emmentaler		Gruyère		Appenzeller	
	$\bar{x}$	s	$\bar{x}$	s	$\bar{x}$	s
Protein g/kg	291	5·8	268	6·4	249	7·0
Fat g/kg	314	9·8	322	12·0	318	8·0
Water g/kg	351	7·9	358	8·6	392	11·0
NaCl g/kg	4·4	1·5	15·9	2·4	16·2	1·9
Calcium g/kg	10·1	0·5	8·9	0·3	7·4	0·4
Manganese mg/kg	0·3	0·01	0·3	0·08	0·3	0·06
Copper[a] mg/kg	14·5	3·6	13·1	3·8	14·0	3·7
Iron mg/kg	3·4	1·1	3·9	1·3	2·7	0·7
Volatile fatty acids mmol/kg	128	19·5	33·0	12·1	74·0	24·9
Acetic acid mmol/kg	44·0	9·3	18·0	8·3	42·0	11·0
Propionic acid mmol/kg	84·0	15·8	10·0	9·0	24·0	13·5
Lactic acid mmol/kg	34·0	22·0	106·0	14·0	45·0	16·7
Free amino acids g/kg	30·0	9·6	39·0	8·8	39·0	8·6
Age days	134	13	195	8	150	9

[a] Values for cheese manufactured in copper kettles.
For definition of $\bar{x}$ and s, see Table IV.

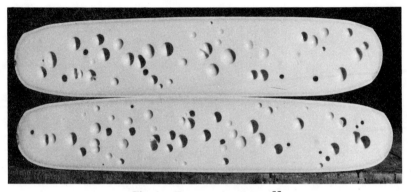

Fig. 1. Emmentaler cheese.[77]

Various authors[2-4] classify different cheeses as being Swiss type; these include the following: Samsoe, Jarlbergost, Herregardsost, Maasdamer, Comté, Iowa-style Swiss cheese.
Table I shows the main constituents of ripe Emmentaler, Gruyère and Appenzeller cheeses.

2. FERMENTATION

The quality of Swiss-type cheese depends principally on the course of lactic acid fermentation, propionic acid fermentation (essential for Emmentaler), proteolysis and smear ripening (valid for Gruyère and Appenzeller).

2.1 Lactic Acid Fermentation

Every cheese type firstly undergoes homofermentative lactic acid fermentation, with over 90% of the lactose being converted to lactic acid. Controlled lactic acid fermentation is obtained by adding thermophilic and sometimes mesophilic lactic acid bacterial cultures to the cheese milk. Lactic acid bacteria are morphologically dissimilar[9,10] and consist of long and short rods (lactobacilli) as well as cocci (streptococci). They are all Gram-positive. Lactic acid bacteria have complex nutritional requirements for growth and milk is an ideal medium. They tolerate a high degree of acidity. The starter cultures used in Swiss cheese manufacture contain both thermophilic species such as *Streptococcus thermophilus*, *Lactobacillus lactis*, *Lactobacillus helveticus*, *Lactobacillus bulgaricus* and mesophilic

TABLE II
Characteristics of lactic acid bacteria used for cheesemaking[10,76,77]

	S. lactis	S. thermophilus	L. helveticus	L. lactis
Generation time min (optimal conditions)	15–20	15–20	35–45	35–45
Lactic acid production in milk g/litre (total acid possible)	5–8	8–10	20–30	10–25
Optimal growth temperature °C	20–30	38–42	38–45	38–45
Optimal pH	6·0	6·0–6·5	5·0–5·5	5·0–5·5
Proteolysis	medium	weak	strong	strong
Lactic acid pattern	L(+)	L(+)	L(+)/D(−)	D(−)

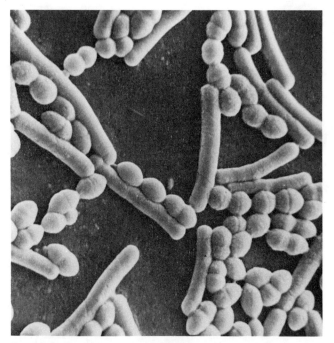

Fig. 2. Scanning electron micrograph of a culture of lactic acid bacteria (Streptococci and Lactobacilli).[77]

species, e.g. *Streptococcus cremoris, Streptococcus lactis* (Fig. 2). Table II shows the properties of lactic acid bacteria species frequently used in cheesemaking.

Lactose breakdown normally follows the fructose-1,6-diphosphate pathway described by Emden–Meyerhof–Parnas.[10] Its catabolism starts with processing in the vat, and 4–6 h after dip filling of the moulds, the sugar is entirely hydrolysed. Whereas free glucose is never detected at high concentrations in the cheese, free galactose is found during the early stages. The complete lactic acid fermentation lasts about 24 h (Fig. 3).

The lactic acid produced in the cheese loaf influences the quality of cheese in several ways. It acts as a preservative since the lower pH values (milk 6·6–6·8, 1-day old cheese: 5·1–5·3) inhibit the growth of strongly proteolytic and other bacteria. Moreover, it removes calcium from the paracasein–calcium phosphate complex; this influences syneresis, body characteristics and proteolysis. Finally, lactic acid is an appropriate

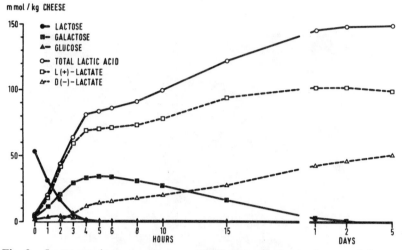

Fig. 3. Lactose, glucose, galactose and lactate concentrations and lactate configuration in Emmentaler cheese.[11]

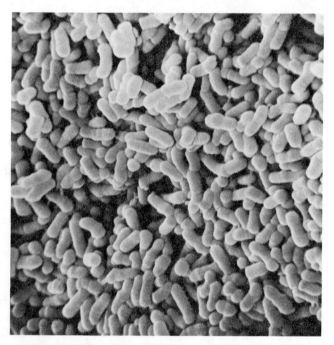

Fig. 4. Scanning electron micrograph of a *Propionibacterium freudenreichii* culture.[74]

substrate for the subsequent propionic acid fermentation or for the surface flora of smear-ripened cheese (Gruyère, Comté, Appenzeller).

2.2 Propionic Acid Fermentation

Most Swiss-type cheeses undergo a more or less pronounced propionic acid fermentation, which is brought about by Gram-positive, short-rod propionic acid bacteria. They grow under anaerobic conditions, at low oxygen concentrations only, and occur naturally in the rumen and intestine of ruminants.[9] Lactate is transformed into propionate, acetate and carbon dioxide in the following proportions:

$$3CH_3CHOHCOO^- \rightarrow 2CH_3CH_2COO^- + CH_3COO^- + CO_2 + H_2O$$

Hygienic milk production calls for the inoculation of cheese milk in the vats with a culture of propionic acid bacteria (mostly *Propionibacterium freudenreichii* subsp. *shermanii*) before processing (Fig. 4). To initiate propionic acid fermentation, the ripening temperature for the cheese must be raised to approximately 18–25°C for a certain period of time. As a result,

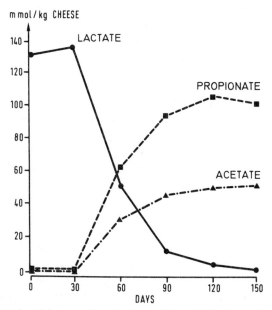

Fig. 5. Lactate breakdown and production of the volatile fatty acids, propionate and acetate, during ripening of Emmentaler cheese.[77]

these lactate fermenters, originally at low concentrations in cheese milk, develop to levels of 10^8–10^9 organisms/g cheese. Emmentaler cheese undergoes propionic acid fermentation 20–30 days after the start of manufacture. The resulting metabolites, propionic acid and acetic acid, essentially contribute to the development of the characteristic flavours of Swiss-type cheese, whereas the carbon dioxide produced is responsible for eye formation. As soon as the development of sufficient eyes is accomplished, the propionic acid fermentation is usually retarded by storing the cheese at a lower temperature (Fig. 5).

2.3 Proteolysis

In Swiss-type cheese with a dry rind, proteolysis is, apart from propionic acid fermentation, the most important factor for ripening and flavour development. In Cheddar and Gouda type cheeses, rennet plays an important role in proteolysis. However, this enzyme is absent from Swiss-type cheeses since it is denatured during cooking at the high temperatures used. In Swiss-type cheeses, milk proteinase and the proteolytic enzymes of lactic acid bacteria are principally responsible for protein breakdown.[62,63] Generally, thermophilic lactobacilli exert a stronger proteolytic effect than mesophilic streptococci, whereas thermophilic streptococci have very little influence on protein breakdown. The proteolytic activity of propionic bacteria is insignificant. When raw milk is processed, certain micro-organisms of the wild (indigenous) flora of milk (e.g. enterococci, micrococci) may possibly be involved in proteolysis. The proteolytic enzymes of psychrotrophs from milk after prolonged cold storage sometimes influence ripening and flavour development. Proper selection of strains of lactic acid bacteria for starter cultures and the application of appropriate measures during manufacture in order to obtain the desired number of lactobacilli in the young cheese are the best means of controlling proteolysis. The activities of proteolytic enzymes in cheese further depend on the water content, lactic acid concentration, pH, storage temperature, storage time, NaCl concentration, water activity (a_w) and copper content.

Casein in unripened cheese is odourless, tasteless and water-insoluble and has a tough and rubbery consistency. The proteolytic enzymes of micro-organisms in cheese split this casein network into short-chain water-soluble compounds, e.g. peptones, polypeptides, peptides and amino acids (Fig. 6). These metabolites also contribute to the development of the characteristic flavour, body and texture of Swiss-type cheese. Indices of proteolysis are the concentration of the water-soluble nitrogen (WSN),

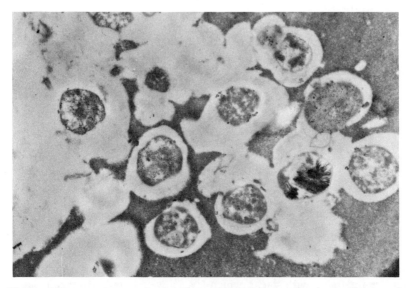

Fig. 6. Electron micrograph of a 12-month-old Emmentaler cheese. Note casein breakdown in the neighbourhood of micro-organisms: the white areas around the bacteria represent the casein matrix degraded by proteolytic enzymes.[75]

non-protein nitrogen (NPN), and different proteolytic enzymes (e.g. leucine-aminopeptidase). In recent years, the measurement of peptides, free amino acids and amines has also been used in order to better determine protein breakdown (Table III). The amino acids may be further decomposed enzymatically by decarboxylation, deamination and trans-amination, but non-enzymic reactions are also involved. The products arising from amino acid breakdown are: amines, ammonia, α-keto-acids, aldehydes, aromatic acids, mercaptans and fatty acids.

Some Swiss-type cheeses, such as Gruyère, undergo a smear ripening process. The surface of the cheese is first de-acidified by yeasts. Early in the ripening process various salt-tolerant micro-organisms develop (e.g. *Micrococcus, Enterococcus, Brevibacterium linens*). These micro-organisms degrade the lactic acid and influence the flora and the colour of the surface of the cheese.[64]

In cheese with surface ripening, proteolysis is further affected although the proteolytic enzymes of the surface flora, such as the leucine-aminopeptidase, arginine-iminopeptidase, phenylalanine-aminopeptidase and proline-aminopeptidase do not penetrate or penetrate only slightly into the cheese mass.[12] An indirect, but strong proteolytic effect arises from

TABLE III
Development of proteolysis in Emmentaler Cheese[6,42,77]

Age (days)	Total N (g/kg)	Water-soluble N (g/kg)	Non-protein N (g/kg)	Free amino acids	
				Total (g/kg)	Glutamic acid (mmol/kg)
1	69·0	3·7	1·3	1·61	1·8
30	68·2	8·8	3·1	4·91	4·2
60	68·9	14·9	6·0	11·40	11·1
90	69·2	15·5	7·7	17·70	17·5
120	68·9	16·2	8·5	22·80	21·8
150	68·5	17·0	9·6	27·50	25·2

the accelerated increase of the pH in the outer zones of the cheeses due to de-acidification of the surface by the smear flora as well as from regular surface treatment with smear, which gives a wetter rind. Moreover, sapid substances from the smear flora diffuse into the cheese mass.

Insufficient proteolysis may bring about different cheese defects. If the level of protein breakdown is too low, the taste is flat and the body consistency too 'long'. Sometimes, uneven openings also result. Excessive proteolysis gives an overripe and sharp taste and a shorter body consistency. This defect becomes particularly evident when a large amount of casein is decomposed into low-molecular compounds (high non-protein nitrogen level). Additional carbon dioxide production by decarboxylation

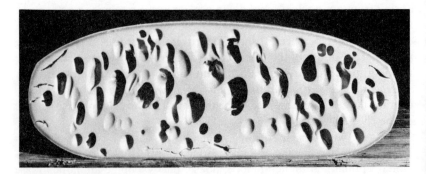

Fig. 7. Emmentaler cheese with secondary fermentation; note cracks due to excessive gas pressure from CO_2 produced by amino acid decarboxylases.[77]

clearly reduces the keeping quality of the cheese and leads to oversized eye formation. The cheese body often cannot withstand the pressure of the gas and cracks appear. This defect is called late or secondary fermentation.[13,36]

Frequently, the course of proteolysis in a cheese loaf varies from one zone to the other, a phenomenon that is due to temperature changes in the cheese loaf during lactic acid fermentation. Since the outer zone cools down fastest, it often develops a bacterial flora which is proteolytically more active than the micro-organisms in the centre of the loaf. This usually leads to cheese defects such as short and firm body, or sharp taste, or the development of white colour under the rind.

A particularly serious defect results from the eventual presence of *Clostridium sporogenes*. This sporeformer brings about non-specific proteolysis, which may be local and very intensive. The cheese mass then shows putrid spots and is inedible.

2.4 Other Fermentation Processes

Besides the desired fermentation process, there are other possible metabolic processes caused by microbial activities, which may even lead to cheese defects.

Lipolysis is unwanted because of the atypical rancid taste it produces. However, it is sometimes supposed that a slight amount of fat hydrolysis in milk contributes to the development of the characteristic aroma of raw milk Swiss-type cheese.

Butyric acid fermentation is totally undesirable, since lactate decomposition by *Clostridium butyricum* and *Cl. tyrobutyricum* into butyric acid, acetic acid, carbon dioxide and hydrogen causes the cheese loaf to blow. Even in small amounts, butyric acid is unfavourable to flavour development. Therefore, in Switzerland, silage feeding of cows is prohibited for cheese production. This prohibition, together with hygienic milk production, helps prevent contamination with these butyric acid bacteria. In other countries, spores are either eliminated by bactofugation of milk or germination is restricted by additives, e.g. nitrates.

Heterofermentative lactic acid fermentation is of minor importance. In Emmentaler cheese it provokes abundant eye formation and in other cheese varieties such as Gruyère and Appenzeller it may contribute to the development of the eyes.

Mixed acid fermentation may occur due to the growth of Enterobacteriaceae, leading to an excess of eye formation in Swiss-type cheese due to the low water solubility of hydrogen produced by these bacteria.

2.5 Eye Formation

The characteristic eye formation of Emmentaler cheese is due mainly to the presence of carbon dioxide produced by propionic acid bacteria during lactate breakdown.[14] We can follow carbon dioxide production by measuring continually the carbon dioxide diffusing out of the cheese loaf.[15,16]

As shown in Fig.8, carbon dioxide diffusion begins before propionic acid fermentation since small quantities of carbon dioxide are already produced during lactic acid fermentation. The steep rise in the production of carbon dioxide, however, coincides with the onset of the propionic acid fermentation. At the peak, carbon dioxide production and carbon dioxide diffusion rates are identical. The diffusion rate drops as soon as the cheese loaves are transferred from the ripening room (22°C) to the cold room (12°C). A new equilibrium then develops at a lower level between carbon dioxide production and carbon dioxide diffusion.

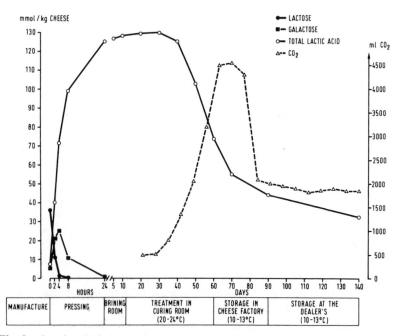

Fig. 8.   Lactic acid fermentation, lactate breakdown and CO_2 loss during ripening of Emmentaler cheese.[15,36,77]

The different stages of carbon dioxide production and eye formation may be schematized as follows:

CO$_2$ Production and Eye Formation

CO$_2$ production and CO$_2$ diffusion

(starts at the beginning of the lactic acid fermentation)

↓

Accumulation of CO$_2$ in the cheese body
(propionic acid fermentation)

↓

Oversaturation at the centres of future eye formation
(propionic acid fermentation)

↓

Onset of eye formation at these centres
(after approximately 20–30 days)

↓

Increase in the number of eyes and their enlargement
(propionic acid fermentation + decarboxylation of amino acids)

The development of eye formation depends mainly upon:

—time, quantity and intensity of CO$_2$ production;
—number and size of the areas of future eye formation;
—CO$_2$ pressure and diffusion rates;
—body texture and temperature.

Eye formation is a lengthy process. At the beginning, i.e. about 30 days after manufacture, only a few eyes appear; thereafter, the number of new holes increases progressively. The maximum rate is attained after about 50 days, which is also the time of rapid eye enlargement. The appearance of new eyes declines with decreasing carbon dioxide production and the simultaneous hardening of the cheese body. Nevertheless, eye formation sometimes continues in the cold room.

The quantity and distribution of the eyes also depend on other factors such as those mentioned above. The number of eyes is increased by the in-homogeneity of the curd, physical openness and hydrogen-forming micro-organisms. Centrifugation and thermization of the milk or application of vacuum after filling of the curd and during pressing of the cheese are performed in order to obtain a larger number of eyes (overset).[14,65] In a cheese loaf of approximately 80 kg, total carbon dioxide production is about 120 litres before the cheese is sufficiently aged for consumption. About 60 litres remain dissolved in the cheese body, approximately 20 litres are found in the eyes and approximately 40 litres diffuse out of the loaf.

The actual carbon dioxide production in Emmentaler cheese is higher than the amount calculated according to the equation of Fitz[17] on the basis of lactate breakdown and production of volatile fatty acid (acetate, propionate). Therefore, there must be further sources of carbon dioxide besides propionic acid fermentation. It has been demonstrated that lactic acid fermentation and protein breakdown are also sources of carbon dioxide.

In contrast to Emmentaler, Gruyère and Appenzeller cheeses do not strictly need propionic acid fermentation for eye formation, though it may be of some importance. In these cheese types, eye formation starts with lactic acid fermentation, probably because of the activity of heterofermentative lactic acid bacteria. Some carbon dioxide arises from oxidative decarboxylation of 6-phospho-gluconate during the formation of lactate and acetate or ethanol from glucose.[9] Enlargement of the eyes, which takes place at a later stage, is probably due to a slight propionic acid fermentation and particularly to the carbon dioxide liberated by decarboxylation of amino acids.

Carbon dioxide pressure passes through two major phases (Fig. 9). The

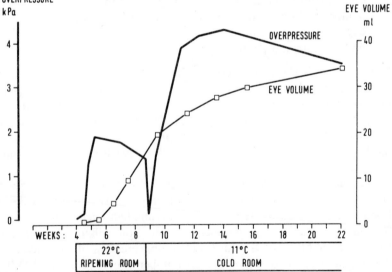

Fig. 9.   Eye formation, volume and CO_2 overpressure in Emmentaler cheese.[15,18]

first covers the period of proper eye formation in the ripening room. During this period, the carbon dioxide pressure remains relatively low, between 1500 and 2500 Pa, because of the low resistance of the soft cheese mass to gas compression at 22–24°C. During storage, i.e. the second stage, the carbon dioxide pressure increases to 4000–8000 Pa. The differences in pressure between the various loaves are higher in the second stage than in the first. The pressure increase in the second stage is explained by the higher resistance to gas compression of the cheese mass, which is due to a decrease in temperature from 22 to 12°C, and by continued gas production. During the first stage, carbon dioxide pressure mainly causes enlargement of the eyes, but in the second stage there is a marked pressure increase within the eyes.

3. FLAVOUR

Cheese flavour depends firstly on the properties of the cheese milk. Certain plants and feed-stuffs such as bulbous plants, leeks, vegetable wastes, herb mixtures and different mineral salt mixtures fed to dairy cows can influence the taste of milk and produce off-flavours. The chemical composition of milk also varies throughout lactation and is thus another factor of influence. Certain milk enzymes can induce flavours, e.g. lipase can cause rancidity. The microbial composition of milk plays an important role.[20,21] Whilst the wild flora of milk is generally composed of unwanted micro-organisms,[22–24] which can influence the flavour directly by their fermentative activities or indirectly by other enzymatic reactions, the desired lactic acid bacteria must be added to the cheese milk in the form of starter cultures. Rennet is also a flavour influencing factor.

Cheese flavour secondly depends on the different operations involved in cheesemaking and cheese ripening. In Switzerland, Swiss-type cheese is made from raw milk. Certain sapid compounds in milk are in fact lost and others are produced when it is subjected to thermization or pasteurization before processing. The high temperatures applied during the early stages of manufacture and pressing of Swiss cheeses are essential for flavour development. Other important factors are the fermentation and ripening processes (pH, water activity), the conditions prevailing at the surface of the loaves, and even their size and shape. As regards brining and smearing, the salt concentration in these solutions affects the water activity in cheese and hence bacterial growth, thus indirectly contributing to cheese taste. The principal pathways of biosynthesis of cheese flavours are dealt with in many publications.[25–35] For analytical reasons, the flavour components

TABLE IV
Mean volatile fatty acid and lactic acid contents (mmol/kg) of ripe Swiss-type cheeses [6-8.36]

Components	Emmentaler			Gruyère			Appenzeller		
	Age: approx. 5 months			Age: approx. 6·5 months			Age: approx. 4·5–5·5 months		
	$\bar{x}$	s	N	$\bar{x}$	s	N	$\bar{x}$	s	N
Total volume fatty acids	124·0	17	60	33·1	12·1	62	73·7	24·9	59
Acetic acid	41·9	8·8	60	18·3	8·3	62	41·8	11·0	59
Propionic acid	83·7	15·8	60	9·9	9·0	62	24·1	13·5	59
i-butyric acid	—	—	60	—	—	62	0·4	1·8	59
n-butyric acid	—	—	60	3·1	2·8	62	4·4	4·3	59
i-valeric acid	—	—	60	0·9	0·7	62	2·2	2·2	59
i-caproic acid	—	—	60	—	—	62	0·9	1·4	59
n-caproic acid	—	—	60	—	—	62	—	—	59
Lactic acid	29·0	15·1	25	106	14·0	62	44·9	16·7	59

$\bar{x}$ = arithmetic mean $\Big\}$ formally calculated although some distributions are asymmetric.
s = standard deviation
N = number of samples.
— = traces or data missing.

are generally divided into two major groups, the volatile and the non-volatile compounds.

The *volatile compounds* include volatile fatty acids, primary and secondary alcohols, methyl ketones, aldehydes, esters, lactones, alkanes, aromatic hydrocarbons and different sulphur and nitrogen containing compounds (Table IV).

The *non-volatile group* is composed of peptides, peptones, amino acids, amines, organic and inorganic salts and fat.[7] Some compounds have been determined quantitatively, others have been identified qualitatively only, but a comprehensive study of flavours in Swiss-type cheese is lacking (Tables V–VII). In a recent review, Ney[27] proposed a key which suggests the possible contribution of each of these components to cheese flavour. This key is used here to present the available data for Swiss-type cheese.

TABLE V
Mean free amino acid contents in ripe Swiss-type cheeses (mmol/kg)[7,37,42]

Free amino acids	Emmentaler	Gruyère	Appenzeller
Phosphoserine	4·23	5·85	5·00
Aspartic acid	1·07	6·32	5·82
Threonine	6·56	8·54	6·86
Serine	5·73	9·32	2·41
Asparagine	0	17·40	14·16
Glutamic acid	33·65	43·61	46·38
Glutamine	1·44	5·37	5·53
Proline	18·33	30·81	28·66
Glycine	6·14	9·54	9·98
Alanine	9·21	9·71	10·39
Citrulline	2·89	5·02	2·04
Aminobutyric acid	0	0	0·71
Valine	17·08	20·33	26·16
Methionine	4·68	5·82	6·18
Isoleucine	6·99	14·50	15·22
Leucine	24·24	28·71	31·84
Tyrosine	3·01	5·48	4·88
Phenylalanine	11·51	17·19	15·43
β-alanine	0	0·53	0
γ-aminobutyric acid	0·43	7·52	2·09
Ethanolamine	0·91	0·25	0
Ornithine	6·98	4·96	8·56
Lysine	20·38	27·63	31·29
Histidine	3·90	8·23	6·97
Arginine	0	0·91	0

TABLE VI

Mean amine contents in ripe Swiss-type cheeses (mmol/kg)[43]

Amines	Emmentaler	Gruyère	Appenzeller
Putrescine	0	0–0·25	0–0·4
Histamine	0	0	0·5–2·0
Cadaverine	0	0·4–1·00	0·5–2·0
Tyramine	0·4–2·5	0·1–1·00	1·0–2·5
Phenylethylamine	0	0–0·02	0–0·2

TABLE VII

Mean contents of water and major non-volatile components in ripe Swiss-type cheeses (% w/w)[6-8]

Component	Emmentaler	Gruyère	Appenzeller
Water	35·00	35·80	39·20
Fat	31·50	32·20	31·80
Total N	4·55	4·35	3·90
Water-soluble N	1·20	1·40	1·65
Non-protein N	0·70	0·85	0·90
NaCl	0·65	1·45	1·60

As regards other volatile flavour components not mentioned above, only Swiss Gruyère cheese has been studied thoroughly. Liardon et al.[38] and Bosset and Liardon[39] have identified 8 alkylpyrazines, indole and benzothiozole in the alkaline fraction,[39-41] 16 primary alcohols, 6 secondary alcohols, 5 ketoalcohols, 19 ketones (mainly methylketones with odd carbon number), 6 aldehydes, 7 esters, 1 lactone as well as 9 miscellaneous components, particularly aromatic hydrocarbons, sulphur and nitrogen containing compounds in the neutral fraction,[39] and 11 compounds, i.e. fatty acids and phenols, in the acid fraction.[41] For certain components, the changes in their concentrations were followed over 12 months of ripening.[40,41] Some of these volatile and non-volatile flavour components have also been found in Emmentaler and Gruyère-type cheese manufactured abroad.[44-53]

4. BODY CHARACTERISTICS

Cheese body and texture are very important qualities for both dealers and consumers. Variations from what is considered normal in body and texture within the same cheese variety is not tolerated since there is a close relationship between the body and texture and other qualities such as eye

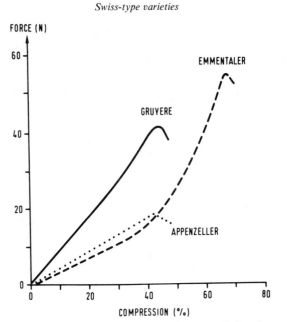

Fig. 10. Typical force–compression diagrams for some Swiss cheese varieties.[55]

formation, taste and shelf-life. By texture we understand the structure and the consistency of the cheese body. The structure depends to a great extent on the microstructure inside the curd particles, whereas the body consistency is characterized by the reaction of the cheese mass to compression. The structure of the cheese body can be firm or soft, the consistency short (coarse, brittle) or long (tough, elastic). The quality of the cheese body is evaluated in sensorial assessments by skilled panellists or scientifically analysed by objective determination of chemical and physical parameters. In Switzerland, the Instron universal testing machine, the most frequently used measuring instrument, is used to determine the body characteristics of Swiss hard and semi-hard cheese: cylindrical cheese samples are submitted to compression.[54] Figure 10 shows typical force–compression diagrams resulting from such measurements.[55] These graphs permit the determination of:

—the force at breaking point which causes the body to crack;
—the compression at breaking point, expressed as a percentage of the original height of the sample; this is a description of the length of the body;
—the force required to compress the sample by 33%; this is characteristic of the firmness of the body.

The force at the breaking point therefore depends on the length and firmness of the cheese body. The force required to cause cracking is higher for Emmentaler than for Gruyère (Fig. 10). The body of Emmentaler is soft and long, whereas a Gruyère has firmer and shorter body consistency. Differences in texture, within the same cheese variety, are partly due to differences in chemical composition. The correlations between body characteristics and chemical composition have been calculated for 195 5-month-old Emmentaler cheeses (Table VIII).

Firmness depends on the total nitrogen content, which is the main support of cheese body structure, as well as on the water content, which lends softness to the body. There is a negative correlation between the length (compression) of the cheese body and its lactate content. In hard and semi-hard cheese, the body characteristics change during ripening, mainly as a result of proteolysis (Fig. 11).

In Emmentaler, the body becomes longer during the first 30 days of ripening. Continued curd fusion changes the cheese body so that a higher

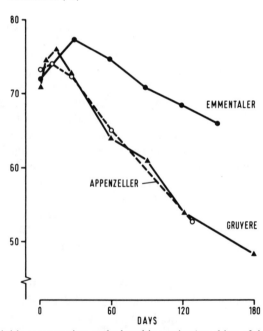

Fig. 11. Variable compression at the breaking point (cracking of the cheese body) throughout ripening.[57]

TABLE VIII
Correlations between analytical data for 195 150-day-old Emmentaler cheeses[57]

Parameter	1	2	3	4	5	6	7	8
1 Compression	1·00							
2 Force	0·63	1·00						
3 Firmness	−0·26	0·52	1·00					
4 Water	−0·11	−0·35	−0·35	1·00				
5 Fat	0·13	−0·04	−0·19	−0·69	1·00			
6 Total N	0·19	0·63	0·62	−0·30	−0·29	1·00		
7 Lactate	−0·36	−0·38	−0·07	0·36	−0·30	−0·19	1·00	
8 pH	0·19	0·33	0·14	−0·02	−0·06	0·14	−0·26	1·00

compression is required to crack the samples. Comparison with Gruyère and Appenzeller (Fig. 11) shows that this increase in compression is less pronounced in these varieties than in Emmentaler. After the beginning of eye formation, at the age of 35 days approximately, the cheese body again becomes shorter. In Gruyère and Appenzeller, the body becomes much shorter during the course of ripening.

These differences are due to divergent intensities of proteolysis. In smear-ripened cheeses, such as Gruyère and Appenzeller, the protein breakdown

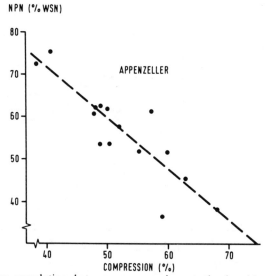

Fig. 12. Linear correlation between compression at the breaking point and protein breakdown (non-protein nitrogen as % of water-soluble nitrogen); 15 130-day-old Appenzeller cheese loaves were studied.[57]

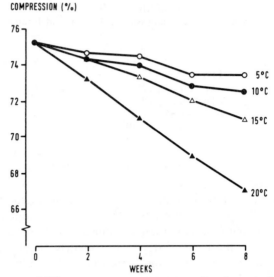

Fig. 13. Influence of different storage temperatures after the main fermentation on compression at the breaking point of Emmentaler.[57]

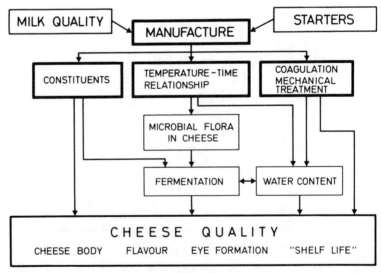

Fig. 14. Influences of factors throughout manufacture on the quality of Swiss-type cheese.[58]

'in depth', i.e. from peptones and polypeptides into smaller peptides and free amino acids, is greater than in dry-ripened Emmentaler.

The good correlation between protein breakdown 'in depth' and compression at the breaking point is evident from Fig. 12. The intensity of proteolysis is represented by the increasing quantity of water soluble NPN. In this example of an Appenzeller cheese, the slope value of linear regression was −0·87. Similar relationships have been found in other cheese varieties.

It is possible to accelerate proteolysis by increasing the storage temperature. Figure 13 shows the influence of temperature on the development of cheese body. Blocks of the same Emmentaler loaf were stored at 5, 10, 15 and 20°C after eye formation had terminated, i.e. after approximately 70 days of ripening. It is evident that the storage temperature clearly influences the compression at breaking point. The greatest difference was found between 15 and 20°C; the greatest difference in protein breakdown was also found at these temperatures. Thus it appears that the typical body and texture of a variety can be obtained more rapidly by increasing the storage temperature. This, however, generally gives rise to pronounced off-tastes.[56]

5. INFLUENCES OF CHEESEMAKING OPERATIONS

The characteristics of eyes, flavour, body and texture and shelf-life of Swiss-type cheese originate mainly from the starter cultures, the quality of the milk and the different cheesemaking operations. Figure 14 shows the relationship between the factors that determine cheese quality.

The milk used for cheese manufacture should contain as few bacteria as possible so that the added starter cultures have an optimum effect. If raw milk is processed, the bacteriological requirements are particularly stringent. The microbial and hygienic state of farm milk, of course, also depends on the duration and temperature of storage and secondary contamination before or after processing must be avoided.

The temperature–time relationship during manufacture, pressing and ripening determines the development of lactic acid bacteria of the starters added. Most Swiss-type cheese varieties need high cooking or scalding temperatures. Emmentaler is heated to 52–54°C after curd-making. During pressing, the temperature remains at around 50°C for many hours (Fig. 15). At this temperature, the curd dries and most of the undesirable micro-organisms are eliminated.

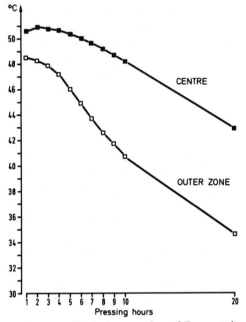

Fig. 15.   Temperature profile during pressing of Emmentaler cheese.[72]

The fat, protein, water and salt contents are essential for body texture and taste. All Swiss-type varieties are rennet cheeses. This means that the milk coagulation is induced by animal rennet or rennet substitutes. The water content of the curd can be adjusted by controlled coagulation and mechanical treatment of the whey–curd mixture.[59] As regards eye formation, proper dip filling of the moulds is imperative since air inclusions can lead to undesirable openness (Fig. 16).

Swiss-type cheeses are very often manufactured in copper vats. The copper content of the cheese inhibits the formation of lactic and propionic acids, and influences the ripening, formation of aroma as well as the distribution of the eyes.[66–70]

For many decades, Swiss-type cheeses were manufactured in vats (Kessi) with a capacity of 800–1400 litres. Many manufacturing processes had to be mechanized or rationalized when the volume of production increased. Today, up to 15000 litres of milk are transformed at one time in 'Käsefertiger'. Cheese loaves are then formed in automatic presses and ripened in mechanically equipped cellars. In various countries, Swiss-type cheeses are manufactured in the form of blocks and ripened in plastic

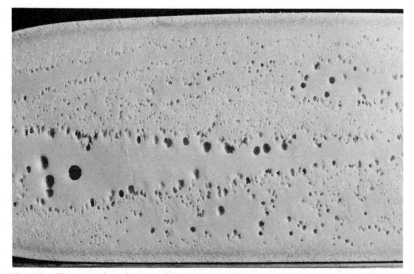

Fig. 16. Emmentaler cheese with air inclusion after dipping of the curd; note openness of texture.[77]

bags.[4,5,71] The development of the texture and flavour is further controlled by the storage conditions (temperature, storage time, relative air humidity, curing).

6. CONTROL OF RIPENING REACTIONS

As can be seen from preceding data, the ripening processes in Swiss-type cheese are influenced by different factors, among which the water activity (a_w) is important (Table IX). It directly influences the growth and metabolism of the micro-organisms as well as the enzymatic activities in cheese.[60,61] The rather low a_w in Swiss-type cheese is not only a

TABLE IX
Typical a_w values for Appenzeller, Emmentaler and Gruyère cheese[60,61,73]

Type	Age (months)	Average a_w	Standard deviation	a_w range in rind
Appenzeller	4–5	0·962	0·006	0·97–0·98
Emmentaler	4–5	0·972	0·007	0·90–0·95
Gruyère	6–7	0·948	0·012	0·92–0·98

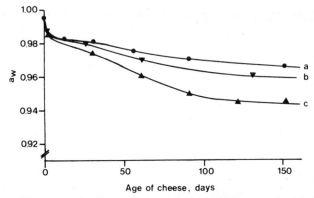

Fig. 17. Influence of the degree of ripening on a_w of Emmentaler (a), Gruyère (b) and Appenzeller (c) cheese (a_w at time 0, 0·995, corresponds to the value for milk estimated from its freezing point).[60]

characteristic of its ripening process, but is also responsible for its good keeping quality. The a_w value varies with the concentration of low-molecular water-soluble cheese components, i.e. the salt and soluble products of protein breakdown as well as with the pH. It decreases with the progress of proteolysis during ripening (Fig. 17). Most cheeses show zonal differences.

REFERENCES

1. Peter, A. and Zollikofer, E., *Lehrbuch der Emmentalerkäserei*, Verlag K. J. Wyss Erben AG, Bern, 1959.
2. Kosikowski, F. V., *Cheese and Fermented Milk Foods*, Edwards Brothers Inc., Michigan, 1977.
3. Reinbold, G. W., *Swiss Cheese Varieties*, Pfizer, New York, 1972.
4. Mair-Waldburg, H., *Handbuch der Käse*, Volkswirtschaftl. Verlag, Kempten, 1974.
5. Steffen, C., Glaettli, H. and Nick, B., *Schweiz. milchw. Forschung*, 1979, **8**(2), 19.
6. Steiger, G. and Flueckiger, E., *Schweiz. milchw. Forschung*, 1979, **8**(3), 39.
7. Steffen, C., Glaettli, H., Steiger, G., Flueckiger, E., Buehlmann, C., Lavanchy, P. and Nick, B., *Schweiz. milchw. Forschung*, 1980, **9**(2), 19.
8. Steffen, C., Glaettli, H., Steiger, G., Flueckiger, E., Buehlmann, C., Lavanchy, P., Nick, B., Schnider, J. and Rentsch, F., *Schweiz. milchw. Forschung*, 1981, **10**(3), 51.
9. Schoen, G., *Mikrobiologie*, Verlag Werder, Freiburg, 1978.
10. Carr, J. G., Cutting, C. V. and Whiting, G. C., *Lactic Acid Bacteria in Beverages and Food*, Academic Press, London, 1973.
11. Steffen, C., *Schweiz. milchw. Forschung*, 1975, **4**(3), 16.
12. Meyer, J., Casey, M. and Gruskovnjak, J., *Schweiz. milchw. Forschung*, 1985, **14**(2), 11.

13. Steffen, C., *Schweiz. milchw. Forschung*, 1979, **8**(3), 44.
14. Steffen, C., *Schweiz. Milchztg*, 1973, **99**(63), 478, 488.
15. Flueckiger, E., *Schweiz. Milchztg*, 1980, **106**(71), 473(72), 479.
16. Flueckiger, E., Montagne, D. H. and Steffen, C., *Schweiz. milchw. Forschung*, 1978, **7**(4), 73.
17. Clark, W. M., US Dept. of Agr. Bulletin, 1912, p. 151.
18. Kurmann, J. L. and Wuethrich, A., *Schweiz. Milchztg*, 1975, **101**(1), 1.
19. Van Straten, S. and Maarse, H. (Eds) In: *Volatile Compounds in Food*; *Qualitative Data*, Division for nutrition and food research tno, Institute CIVO-Analysis TNO, Zeist, p. 481, 1983.
20. Gallmann, P. and Puhan, Z., *Schweiz. milchw. Forschung*, 1982, **11**(1 and 2), 3.
21. Gallmann, P. and Puhan, Z., *Schweiz. milchw. Forschung*, 1982, **11**(4), 64.
22. Kielwein, G., *Dte Molk.-Ztg*, 1975, **96**, 1112.
23. Bolliger, O. and Zahnd, L., *Proc. XV Int. Milchwirtschaftskongress*, London, 1959, Vol. 2, Section 3, p. 751.
24. Dellaglio, F. and Bottazzi, V., *Dairy Sci. Abstr.*, 1972, **34**, 703.
25. Adda, J. In: *Le Fromage* (Ed. A. Eck), Diffusion Lavoisier, Paris, p. 330, 1984.
26. Adda, J., Gripon, J.-C. and Vassal, L., *Food Chemistry*, Vol. 9, Elsevier Applied Science, London, p. 115, 1982.
27. Ney, K. H. In: *The Quality of Foods and Beverages: Chemistry and Technology*, Vol. 1 (Ed. G. Charalambous and G. Inglett), Academic Press, New York, p. 389, 1981.
28. Law, B. A., *Dairy Sci. Abstr.*, 1981, **43**, 143.
29. Moskowitz, J. J. In: *The Analysis and Control of Less Desirable Flavors in Foods and Beverages* (Ed. G. Charalambous), Academic Press, New York, p. 53, 1980.
30. Behnke, U., *Die Nahrung*, 1980, **24**, 71.
31. Badings, H. T. and Neeter, R., *Neth. Milk Dairy J.*, 1980, **34**, 9.
32. Dumont, J. P. and Adda, J. In: *Progress in Flavour Research* (Ed. D. G. Land and H. E. Nursten), Elsevier Applied Science, London, p. 245, 1979.
33. Forss, D. A., *J. Dairy Sci.*, 1979, **46**, 691.
34. Adda, J., Roger, S. and Dumont, J. P. In: *Flavor of Foods and Beverages; Chemistry and Technology* (Ed. G. Charalambous and G. E. Inglett), Academic Press, New York, p. 65, 1978.
35. Panouse, J. J., Masson, J. D. and Truong Thanh Tong, *Industr. alim. agr.*, 1972, **83**, 133.
36. Steffen, C. and Nick, B., *Schweiz. milchw. Forschung*, 1981, **10**(2), 32.
37. Lavanchy, P. and Buehlmann, C., *Schweiz. milchw. Forschung*, 1983, **12**(1), 3.
38. Liardon, R., Bosset, J. O. and Blanc, B., *Lebensmittel Wissenschaft u.-Technol.*, 1982, **15**, 143.
39. Bosset, J. O. and Liardon, R., *Lebensmittel Wissenschaft u. -Technol.*, 1984, **17**, 359.
40. Bosset, J. O. and Liardon, R., *Lebensmittel Wissenschaft u. -Technol.*, 1985, **18**, 178.
41. Bosset, J. O., Liardon, R. and Collomb, M. in preparation.
42. Lavanchy, P., Buehlmann, C. and Blanc, B., *Schweiz. milchw. Forschung*, 1979, **8**(1), 9.
43. Lavanchy, P., Buehlmann, C. and Steiger, G., *Schweiz. milchw. Forschung*, 1985, **14**, in press.

44. Mocquot, G., *J. Dairy Res.*, 1979, **46**, 133.
45. Langsrud, T. and Reinbold, G. W., *J. Milk Food Technol.*, 1973, **36**, 593.
46. Langler, J. E. and Day, E. A., *J. Dairy Sci.*, 1966, **49**, 91.
47. Langler, J. E., Libbey, L. M. and Day, E. A., *J. Agr. Food Chem.*, 1967, **15**, 386.
48. Mitchell, G. E., *Aust. J. Dairy Technol.*, 1981, **36**, 21.
49. Biede, S. L., A study of the chemical and flavor profiles of Swiss cheese. PhD. Dissertation, Iowa State University, 1977.
50. Biede, S. L. and Hammond, E. G., *J. Dairy Sci.*, 1979, **62**, 227, 238.
51. Kiermeier, F., Mayr, A. and Hanusch, J., *Z. Lebensmittelunters. u. -Forsch.*, 1968, **136**, 193 and **137**, 273.
52. Vamos-Vigyazo, L. and Kiss-Kutz, N., *Acta Alimentaria*, 1974, **3**, 309.
53. Schormueller, J., *Adv. Food Res.*, 1968, **16**, 231.
54. Eberhard, P. and Flueckiger, E., *Schweiz. Milchztg*, 1978, **104**(4), 24.
55. Eberhard, P. and Flueckiger, E., *Schweiz. Milchztg*, 1981, **107**(5), 23.
56. Flueckiger, E. and Eberhard, P., *Proc. XXI Int. Milchwirtschaftskongress*, Moskau, 1982, Vol. I (1), p. 481.
57. Eberhard, P., Thesis, Eidg. Techn. Hochschule, Zürich, 1985.
58. Steffen, C. In: *Käsereitechnologischer Sonderlehrgang '85*, Landesverband Bayerischer Molkereifachleute und Milchwirtschaftler E.V., Füssen, Jahresbroschüre, p. 151, 1985.
59. Schwartz, M. E., *Cheese-making technology*, Noyes Data Corporation, London, 1973.
60. Ruegg, M. and Blanc, B. In: *Water Activity: Influences on Food Quality* (Ed. L. B. Rockland and G. F. Stewart), Academic Press, New York, p. 791, 1981.
61. Ruegg, M. In: *Properties of Water in Food* (Ed. D. Simatos and J. L. Multon), Martinus Nijhoff, Dordrecht, p. 603, 1985.
62. Richardson, B. C. and Pearce, K. N., *N.Z. J. Dairy Sci. Technol.*, 1982, **16**, 209.
63. Casey, M. *et al.*, in press.
64. Keller, S. and Puhan, Z., *Schweiz. Milchw. Forschung*, 1985, **14**(2), 3.
65. Gehriger, G., Kurmann, J. L. and Kaufmann, H., *Schweiz. Milchztg*, 1974, **100**(84), 573, (85) 581.
66. Burkhalter, G., *Schweiz. Milchztg*, 1956, **82**, 41.
67. Kiermeier, F. and Weiss, G., *Z. f. Lebensm.-Unters. u. Forschung*, 1970, **142**, 397.
68. Oehen, V., Haenni, H. and Bolliger, O., *Schwiez. Milchztg*, 1962, **88**, 423.
69. Ritter, W., *Schweiz. Milchztg*, 1967, **93**, 115.
70. Maurer, L., *Oesterr. Milchwirtsch.*, 1972, **27**(14), 249.
71. Scott, R., *Cheesemaking Practice*, Elsevier Applied Science, London, p. 274, 1981.
72. Steffen, C. and Schnider, J., *Schweiz. Milchztg*, 1978, **104**, 383.
73. Blanc, B., Ruegg, M., Baer, A., Cassey, M. and Lukes, A., *Schweiz. Milchw. Forschung*, 1982, **11**, 22.
74. Ruegg, M., Moor, U. and Blanc, B., *Milchwissenschaft*, 1980, **35**, 329.
75. Ruegg, M. and Blanc, B., *Schweiz. Milchw. Forschung*, 1972, **1**(1), 1.
76. Steffen, C., Nick, B. and Blanc, B., *Schweiz.. Milchw. Forschung*, 1973, **2**(4), 37.
77. Unpublished data from Federal Dairy Research Institute, 3097 Liebefeld-Bern.

Chapter 4

Mould-ripened Cheeses

J. C. Gripon

*Laboratoire de Biochimie et Technologie Laitières,
Institut National de la Recherche Agronomique,
Jouy-en-Josas, France*

1. INTRODUCTION

Mould-ripened cheeses represent a small proportion of world cheese production. However, these cheeses are becoming increasingly popular with consumers and there is an increasing demand for them. Blue-veined cheeses have long been produced in various countries; Roquefort, Gorgonzola, Stilton and Danish Blue are typical examples. The production of surface-mould ripened soft cheeses, such as Camembert, was limited to France for a long time, but in recent years many countries have tried to develop the production of such cheeses.

The presence of mould within the cheese (*Penicillium roqueforti*) or on the surface (*P. camemberti*) gives these cheeses a different appearance and the high biochemical activities of these moulds produce very typical aroma and taste. These moulds also lead to more complex ripening than in other varieties of cheese with simple flora.

The present paper, after reviewing briefly the composition of the flora of these cheeses, considers the various biochemical changes occurring during their ripening, their aroma and textural properties and, finally, the control of their ripening. The more technological aspects have been treated in other reviews[1-4] and so are not discussed here. Coghill[5] briefly reviewed the microbiology and biochemistry of the ripening of blue-veined cheeses.

2. THE FLORA OF MOULD-RIPENED CHEESES

The composition and evolution of the flora of mould-ripened cheeses are complex, particularly when raw milk is used. Traditional Camembert is a

121

good example: starters used are primarily mesophilic lactic streptococci (*Streptococcus lactis*, *S. cremoris*) and after 24 h, a firm, drained demineralized curd is obtained with a pH of 4·5–4·6. The flora is then essentially composed of mesophilic lactic streptococci.[6] After curd-making, yeasts grow on the surface,[6-8] forming a dense layer about 200 μm thick;[9] *Kluyveromyces lactis*, *Saccharomyces cerivisiae*, *Debaryomyces hansensi* are the most common yeast species.[7,8] The mould, *Geotrichum candidum*, appears at the same time as the yeasts but its growth is limited by salting. After 6 or 7 days of ripening, the growth of *Penicillium camemberti* is observed and a white felt covers the entire surface of the cheese. After 15–20 days, when the *Penicillium* has consumed the lactic acid and de-acidified the cheese, an aerophilic acid-sensitive bacterial flora becomes established on the surface. This flora is formed of micrococci and coryneform bacteria (a high percentage are *Brevibacterium linens*).[6,10,11] Coliform bacteria can also be observed,[6,10-13] *Hafnia alvei* being the dominant species.[11] Inside the cheese, lactic streptococci are clearly dominant, the yeast population remaining lower than on the surface (about 10^6 cells/g instead of 10^8 cells/g),[7] as well as the coliform population.[10] In the production of these cheeses from pasteurized milk (which is the case for the large majority of Camembert cheeses), the flora is less diverse, containing mostly organisms added as starters, i.e. mesophilic streptococci and *P. camemberti*. The populations of other micro-organisms are reduced and the cheese obtained is different from that made from raw milk: its taste and aroma are more neutral and less accentuated.

Blue-veined cheeses made from raw milk also have a complex flora. In 1966–1968, Devoyod[14-16] showed that besides having *P. roqueforti* and lactic bacteria, the flora of Roquefort cheese (which is made with raw ewe's milk) also contains yeasts, lactobacilli, micrococci, staphylococci and coliform bacteria (Fig. 1). Lactic streptococci are always clearly dominant inside the cheese but yeasts and leuconostocs are also present from the beginning of ripening.[17,18] Lactobacilli (mainly *Lactobacillus casei* and *L. plantarum*) reach a maximum just before salting.[15] The staphylococci decrease markedly during the first 48 h[19] and the coliform bacteria decrease regularly during the first month.[14] After salting, the surface flora primarily contains yeasts and micrococci.

Piercing the cheese admits enough air to allow the growth of *P. roqueforti* whose sporulation is visible inside the curd of 'bleu d'Auvergne' 2–3 weeks after manufacture.[20]

It is clear that in both surface-mould and blue-veined cheeses, *Penicillium* spp. are the major components of the flora and the cheeses are marked by

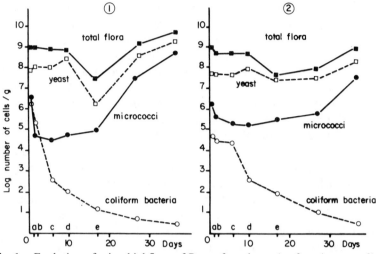

Fig. 1. Evolution of microbial flora of Roquefort cheese (surface:1; centre:2). a: 21 h after rennet; b: in warm room (18°C); c: in cold room (10°C); d: before salting; e: after salting (from Devoyod and Bret[16]).

their characteristics. However, in traditional cheese made from unheated milk, the secondary flora plays an essential complementary role in the development of its organoleptic properties.

The morphological and physiological properties of *P. roqueforti* and *P. camemberti* have been reviewed by Moreau[21,22] and Choisy *et al.*[23] Up to the last few years, two species of the latter were distinguished: *P. caseicolum* and *P. camemberti*. As *P. caseicolum* is considered as a white mutant of *P. camemberti*,[24] only the name *P. camemberti* is now used.[24,25] Moreau distinguished 4 different forms of *P. camemberti*:

—a form with fluffy mycelium, first white becoming grey-green (*P. camemberti sensus stricto*);
—a form with 'short hair', rapid growth; white, dense, close-napped mycelium;
—a form with 'long hair', slow growth; white, loose, tall mycelium;
—'neufchatel' form: vigorous, rapid growth giving a thick white-yellow mycelium.

The last three forms correspond to the old name of *P. caseicolum*. The 'neufchatel' form has slightly higher lipolytic and proteolytic activities than the others.[26-28] Only the white forms are actually used as starters in cheesemaking.

Mould-ripened cheeses are generally thought to be limited to surface-mould-ripened soft cheeses and blue-veined cheeses. In fact, there are a small number of other, less known, varieties of mould-ripened cheese that are produced in more limited quantities. In France, these are semi-hard cheeses called 'Saint-Nectaire' and 'Tome de Savoie'. The surface of these cheeses is covered by a complex fungal flora containing *Penicillium*, *Mucor*, *Cladosporium*, *Geotrichum*, *Epicoccum* and *Sporotrichum*.[29] Mould has also been reported on the surface of Italian cheeses such as Taleggio (*Penicillium*, *Mucor*) and Robiola (*Geotrichum*).[30,31]

Gammelost is a semi-hard cheese made in Norway from skimmed milk. After acidification, the milk is heated to 65°C and the casein precipitated and collected. After moulding, the curd is held for about 2 h in boiling whey, and the next day a suspension of *Mucor* is sprayed on the surface. The brown colour of the cheese is due to the development of this mould.[32] The inside of the cheese is brown-yellow and this colour intensifies as the cheese ripens. Gammelost has a piquant, aromatic taste. *P. roqueforti* has also been reported to develop inside Gammelost. In this case, the cheese is pierced with metal needles covered with *P. roqueforti* spores to permit the mould to develop.[33]

The physico-chemical data on these latter varieties of mould-ripened cheese are, unfortunately, very limited so we shall treat here only blue-veined cheeses and surface-mould-ripened soft cheeses.

3. PROTEOLYSIS AND AMINO ACID CATABOLISM

3.1 Intensity of Proteolysis

Proteolysis is very intense in blue-veined cheese. More than 50% of the total nitrogen (TN) is soluble at pH 4·6 in ripe Roquefort[14] and about 65% in Danish Blue.[34] This soluble fraction contains a large number of small peptides and the non-protein nitrogen (NPN: nitrogen soluble in 12% trichloracetic acid) is about 30% of TN.[35] Free amino acids are also abundant, representing 10% of the total nitrogen in Danish Blue.[36] Equivalent or higher amounts (280–500 mg/10 g of cheese) were reported by Kosikowski and Dahlberg.[37] Godinho and Fox[35] noted that proteolysis is more limited in the outer parts than in the centre of the cheese and suggested that NaCl limits *Penicillium* growth and its proteolytic action.

In the outer part of a ripe raw-milk Camembert, about 35% of the nitrogen is soluble;[38] within the cheese, there is less breakdown and only 25% of the nitrogen is soluble. These values are lower than for blue-veined cheese but nevertheless show extensive proteolysis. The soluble nitrogen fraction contains many small peptides (the NPN is about 20% of the total N).[38,39] In traditional Camembert cheeses, ammonia represents 7–9% of total N[39,40] and results from extensive deamination of amino acids. The profile of free amino acids obtained by Do Ngoc *et al.*[39] is different from that of whole casein hydrolysate: alanine, leucine and phenylalanine occur in higher proportions and aspartic acid, tyrosine and lysine in lower proportions; arginine and serine occur in particularly low amounts.[39] This shows preferential release during proteolysis and also the catabolism of free amino acids.

Electrophoretograms of blue-veined cheese show evident breakdown of α_{s1}- and β-caseins;[20,34,41] at the end of ripening, these caseins have almost disappeared and the major products on the electrophoretograms show low mobility.[20,41] Trieu-Cuot and Gripon[20,42] noted that the electrophoretic profiles of surface-mould-ripened cheese are very similar to those of blue-veined cheese but reveal less proteolysis.

Compared to proteolysis in other cheeses, that in mould-ripened cheeses is higher (particularly in blue-veined cheeses), and β-casein is degraded more extensively than in other varieties.[41] As in all cheeses, this breakdown results from coagulating enzymes, indigenous milk proteinases and microbial proteinases among which, in our case, enzymes synthesized by *Penicillium* spp. have a dominant role.

3.2 Effect of Rennet

The action of rennet is quickly detectable in cheese by α_{s1}-casein hydrolysis and the production of α_{s1}-I peptide. Mould-ripened cheeses are no exception: α_{s1}-I peptide is seen in Camembert by electrophoresis after 6 h of draining and the concentration of this peptide increases during ripening.[42] Rapid production of α_{s1}-I peptide has also been observed in blue-veined cheeses.[35] Besides α_{s1}-I, Hewedi and Fox[34] detected other peptides typical of rennet action (α_{s1}-V and α_{s1}-VII) in blue-veined cheese. However, peptides resulting from α_{s1}-casein hydrolysis by *P. roqueforti* proteinases have similar or identical[43,44] electrophoretic mobilities and could also explain the intensification of the α_{s1}-V and α_{s1}-VII bands during ripening. In simulated cheese, Noomen[45] showed that rennet breakdown of casein was optimal at pH 5·0. Inside blue-veined cheese, the pH quickly rises to this value and after one month of ripening reaches 5·5 in Danish Blue

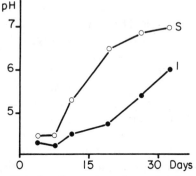

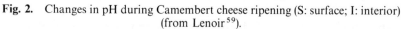

Fig. 2. Changes in pH during Camembert cheese ripening (S: surface; I: interior) (from Lenoir[59]).

cheese[35] or 6·0 in 'bleu d'Auvergne'.[20] The pH in the outer part of Camembert increases more quickly, reaching more than 5·0 after 2 weeks and can attain 7·0 after 4–5 weeks (Fig. 2).[38] Under these conditions, one may suppose that rennet action decreases at the end of ripening when cheese pH has increased. As in other cheeses, β-casein is not attacked by rennet in mould-ripened cheeses or at least this action is not detectable by electrophoresis: β-I (the peptide obtained quickly *in vitro* by rennet hydrolysis of β-casein) has not been observed during Camembert ripening.[42]

3.3   Effect of Milk Proteinases

Milk proteinases are much less active than rennet or microbial enzymes during cheese ripening.[46,47] However, in Camembert, Trieu-Cuot and Gripon[42] found a clear increase in γ-caseins at the end of ripening, showing increased activity of plasmin, the main milk proteinase. This augmented activity, first suggested by Noomen,[48] is not surprising because the pH (about 7·0) of the outer region of Camembert at the end of ripening is not far from the optimum pH of plasmin (about 8·0). At the end of ripening, especially in the outer part of Camembert, this enzyme is probably much more active than in semi-hard cheeses where the pH remains at about 5·0–5·2.

3.4   Effect of Penicillium

Studies on controlled-flora rennet curds, in which *P. roqueforti* (or *P. camemberti*) develops alone with no other micro-organism, have shown and permitted the definition of intensity of the proteolysis caused by these two moulds.[49] After 40 days of ripening, nitrogen soluble at pH 4·6, NPN, and nitrogen soluble in phosphotungstic acid in these curds represented about 50, 30 and 10%, respectively, of the total nitrogen. These values were very much higher than those for the control curds (where only rennet and plasmin were active) and show that there is extensive production of high- and low-molecular weight peptides as well as of free amino acids. These moulds thus have both an endopeptidase and an exopeptidase action. While rennet, plasmin or other flora have an effect, it is clear that *Penicillium* spp. play a major proteolytic role in the mould-ripened cheeses.

The extracellular proteolytic systems of *P. roqueforti* and *P. camemberti* are somewhat similar. They both synthesize a metalloproteinase[50–53] and an aspartate proteinase[54–57] as well as an acid carboxypeptidase[58–60] and an alkaline aminopeptidase.[61,62] Moreover, *P. roqueforti* synthesizes one or more alkaline carboxypeptidases[63] and some strains also produce an alkaline proteinase.[63]

Strains of *P. camemberti* have very similar enzyme potentials. In almost 110 strains studied, Lenoir and Choisy[26] observed that proteolytic enzyme production (measured at pH 6·0) varied only by a factor of 2. In contrast, the levels of proteinases produced by *P. roqueforti* varied greatly from one strain to another.[64,65]

3.4.1 Properties of proteinases

The aspartate proteinases (also named acid proteinases) of *P. roqueforti* and *P. camemberti* have similar properties.[51,55,57] Their pH optima are in the acid range (4 on haemoglobin as substrate and 5·5 on casein as substrate), and they are stable between pH 3·5 and 5·5 (*P. camemberti*) or pH 3·5–6·0 (*P. roqueforti*).

The *P. camemberti* enzyme hydrolyses α_{s1}-casein better than β- and κ-caseins (relative activity ratio, 1:0·7:0·6).[66] The acid proteinases of both species have the same action on β-casein and 3 bonds of the Lys-X type (Lys$_{97}$-Val$_{98}$, Lys$_{99}$-Glu$_{100}$ and Lys$_{29}$-Ile$_{30}$) are cleaved more rapidly than others.[43,67] Of the 3 corresponding N-terminal fragments, β_{ap1}-peptide (Val$_{98}$-Val$_{209}$) has a lower electrophoretic mobility than β-casein and is easily detected in the electrophoretograms of mould-ripened cheeses.

Gripon and Hermier[50] and Lenoir and Auberger[52] also found that the metalloproteinases of *P. roqueforti* and *P. camemberti* had similar properties. Their pH optima are at 5·5–6·0 and they are stable between pH 4·5 and 8·5, which suit the conditions found in mould-ripened cheeses. Their specificity is wide and does not follow a clear rule.[53] *In vitro*, the *P.*

camemberti enzyme cleaves α_{s1}-casein better than β- and κ-caseins (ratios of relative activity, $1:0.4:0.6$).[66] An electrophoretic study[44] showed that the metalloproteinases of both species have similar modes of action on α_{s1}- and β-caseins. Among the peptides of β-casein hydrolysate, β_{mp1}-peptide is clearly seen in the electrophoregrams of mould-ripened cheeses and can be used as a marker for the action of this enzyme *in situ*.[20,42,44] The Lys_{28}-Lys_{29}, Pro_{90}-Glu_{91} and Glu_{100}-Ala_{101} bonds of β-casein are cleaved by the *P. camemberti* enzyme.[44]

Our knowledge of the intracellular endopeptidases of *P. roqueforti* and *P. caseicolum* is very limited. Crude extracts of *P. roqueforti*, probably containing extra- and intracellular enzymes, have an optimum pH of 5.0–6.0.[68,69] Lenoir and Choisy[26] observed an optimum pH of 6.0 for *P. camemberti* extract on casein. Two fractions with pH optima of 6.0 and 6.5 were separated by Takafuji and Yoshioka;[70] they hydrolysed β-casein, giving products with low electrophoretic mobilities.[71]

3.4.2 Action of proteinases in cheese

When the aspartate proteinase of *P. roqueforti* or the metalloproteinase of *P. camemberti* was added to aseptic control curds with no flora,[67,72] the electrophoregrams obtained after ripening were very similar to those of normal cheese, showing that these proteinases play a major role in mould-ripened cheeses. In these control curds, the enzymes very markedly increased the level of pH 4.6-soluble nitrogen as well as NPN but they released no free amino acids.[72]

The evolution of proteolytic activity in curds has been studied during Camembert ripening.[73–75] At the centre of the cheese, this activity is very low and hardly changes during ripening. However, in the outer region, it increases suddenly after 6–7 days of ripening, i.e. when the *Penicillium* begins to grow (Fig. 3). Aspartate proteinase and metalloproteinase are both synthesized and their concentrations are maximal after about 15 days and then decrease slowly.[74,59] These two enzymes are thus fairly stable in cheese.

Trieu-Cuot and Gripon[42] studied the role of these enzymes *in situ* by following electrophoretic changes in the β_{ap1}- and β_{mp1}-peptides which are the respective markers for aspartate proteinase and metalloproteinase. β_{ap1} appeared shortly after *P. camemberti* developed and it intensified regularly during ripening, indicating the continuous action of aspartate proteinase during maturation, although the pH conditions of the curd were not favourable to its action. β_{mp1} decreased after 10–14 days of ripening, suggesting either that the action of metalloproteinase decreased or that

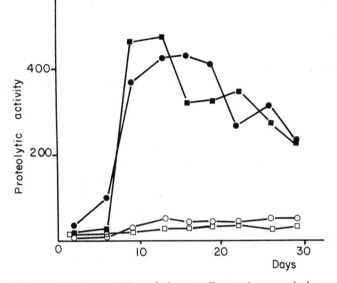

Fig. 3. Changes in the activities of the metalloproteinase and the aspartate proteinase of *P. camemberti* during Camembert cheese ripening (from Lenoir[59]). Aspartate proteinase: ●——● surface; ○——○ interior; metalloproteinase: ■——■ surface; □——□ interior.

β_{mp1} was actively degraded by another proteinase. The fact that the proteolytic activity in the curd is very slow at the centre of Camembert, although it is high at the surface during ripening, suggests that migration of *Penicillium* proteinases in the curd is limited.[73,75] However, β_{ap1} has been detected inside Camembert at a depth of more than 7 mm at the end of ripening;[42] this may be due to the migration of either the aspartate proteinase or β_{ap1}. Lenoir[73] noted that the difference in the degree of proteolysis between the centre and the surface of Camembert was proportionally lower than the difference in proteolytic activity and suggested that the peptides migrated towards the centre of the cheese.

Scanning electron microscopy studies of Camembert cheese[9] show mycelium alterations at the end of ripening, and the action of intracellular proteinases cannot be discarded. However, electrophoregrams of cheese do not show the appearance of new hydrolytic products, and the soluble nitrogen fraction increases little after 20 days of ripening, indicating that intracellular proteinases play a more limited role than extracellular proteinases.

3.4.3 Properties of peptidases

Some trials on controlled-flora curd have shown that *P. roqueforti* and *P. camemberti* can produce large amounts of free amino acids,[49] of the same order of magnitude as those observed in normal cheeses.[34] As mentioned earlier, *P. roqueforti* synthesizes several extracellular exopeptidases. Acid carboxypeptidase[58] is a serine carboxypeptidase with an optimum pH of 3·5. It has broad specificity and releases acidic, basic or hydrophobic amino acids. Alkaline aminopeptidase is a metalloenzyme with an optimum pH of 8·0. It releases apolar amino acids but glycine in the penultimate or N-terminal positions causes low activity.[61] Paquet and Gripon[76] have observed intracellular exopeptidase activities (acid and alkaline carboxypeptidases, alkaline aminopeptidase) and Ichishima *et al.*[77] have characterized an intracellular acid carboxypeptidase with properties similar to the corresponding extracellular enzyme.[58]

P. camemberti also produces several peptidases. The properties of the acid carboxypeptidase studied by Ahiko *et al.*[60] also correspond to those of serine carboxypeptidases. This enzyme reduces the bitterness of a casein hydrolysate[78] by releasing hydrophobic amino acids. Due to their broad specificity, the acid carboxypeptidases of *Penicillium* spp. may clearly contribute to the hydrolysis of the bitter peptides in mould-ripened cheese. Intracellular carboxypeptidase activity with an optimum pH of 6·5,[59] as well as alkaline aminopeptidase activities (intra- and extracellular), are also synthesized by *P. camemberti.*[62]

3.5 Effect of Other Flora

'As in all cheeses, lactic bacteria participate in proteolysis, mainly by producing small peptides and free amino acids. However, the pH optima of the peptidases of these bacteria are usually closer to neutrality than to the pH of cheeses with a mainly lactic flora.[79] The higher pH of mould-ripened cheeses could thus favour their action.

Geotrichum candidum synthesizes extracellular and intracellular proteinases (pH optima: about 6·0).[80] Enzyme production varies greatly from one strain to another.[81,82] Proteolysis by *G. candidum* is difficult to determine but is clearly lower than that of *P. camemberti*; in fact, the proteolytic activity in the outer region of traditional Camembert does not increase during *Geotrichum* growth but only during that of *Penicillium.*[73] Also, *Geotrichum* seeded alone on the surface of the curds caused lower proteolysis than *P. camemberti* (L. Vassal, personal communication).

Yeasts also have proteolytic activity which appears to be uniquely intracellular. Schmidt[83] observed caseinolytic activity with an optimum pH of about 6·0 in 165 strains isolated from Camembert cheese. The intracellular exopeptidases of *Kluyveromyces lactis* (a carboxypeptidase and 3 aminopeptidases) were partially purified and characterized.[84] *B. linens* secretes extracellular proteolytic enzymes: a proteinase has been demonstrated[85] and an aminopeptidase isolated and characterized;[86-88] several intracellular peptidases have been detected.[89] Although this bacterium plays a role in the development of the typical flavour of traditional Camembert cheese, its role in proteolysis at the end of ripening is difficult to determine.

3.6 Amino Acid Breakdown

The various breakdown reactions which amino acids undergo during ripening have been reviewed by Hemme *et al.*[90] Citrulline and ornithine, found in blue-veined cheese and in Camembert,[36,39] result from arginine breakdown, as shown for Gorgonzola.[91] γ-Aminobutylic acid resulting from glutamic acid decarboxylation is found in mould-ripened cheeses.[36,39] Decarboxylation also leads to the production of non-volatile amines. Tyramine is usually observed in higher amounts than tryptamine or histamine.[92] Concentrations of amines in mould-ripened cheeses vary greatly with the sample[93,94] and seem to decrease at the end of ripening.[92] Phenylalanine and tyrosine catabolism by coryneform bacteria isolated from Camembert have been studied by Lee *et al.*[95,96] *B. linens* degrades these amino acids by transamination and cleavage of the benzene ring by 3,4-dihydrophenylacetate-2,3-dioxygenase. This enzyme, as well as aminotransferase, is inducible.[90] Amino acid breakdown in mould-ripened cheeses also leads to the production of volatile compounds such as ammonia, aldehydes, acids, alcohols, amines or other products such as methanethiol resulting from the breakdown of the amino acid side chains (see Section 7).

4. LIPOLYSIS

4.1 Degree of Lipolysis in Cheese

As with proteolysis, lipolysis in mould-ripened cheeses is much more extensive than in other cheeses (Table 1). While the extent of lipolysis should not exceed 2% of the triglycerides in cheeses such as Gouda,

TABLE I

Fat acidity of different cheese varieties

Cheese variety	meq acid/100 g of fat
Gouda	6·14 ± 0·50
Camembert	22·27 ± 13·73
Danish Blue	45·34 ± 14·93
Roquefort	27·55 ± 12·16

Mean values of six samples.
Adapted from Van Belle et al.[98]

Gruyère or Cheddar, it is usually between 5 and 20% in mould-ripened cheeses. Data in the literature vary greatly, probably depending on the degree of ripening. Extensive lipolysis can be attained in mould-ripened cheeses without any rancid taste occurring, probably due to neutralization of fatty acids on elevation of the pH. Anderson and Day[97] found even higher levels of free fatty acids in blue-veined cheese: about 65–100 meq/100 g of fat, i.e. 18–25% of the total fatty acids. Other workers report lower lipolysis in Danish blue (about 45 meq/100 g of fat).[98] The extent of lipolysis in Roquefort is 8–10% of the total fatty acids. Godinho and Fox[99] noted a lower free fatty acid level in the outer part of blue cheese due to higher NaCl concentrations that limited the production of lipases and possibly their activity. Morris et al.[100] noted a regular increase in free fatty acid levels during ripening, while others[99] observed that these levels decreased at the end of ripening.

In Norman Camembert made with raw milk, lipolysis reaches 6–10% of

TABLE II

Relative proportions in Camembert of free fatty acids and of fatty acids in glycerides (expressed as % of total)

Fatty acids	Glycerides	Free fatty acids
4:0 + 6:0 + 8:0	2·8	2·2
10:0 + i 10:0 to 12:0	3·8	3·0
12:0 + i 12:0 to 14:0	4·5	4·7
14:0 + i 14:0 to 16:0	16·1	14·3
16:0 + i 16:0 to 18:0	28·6	23·3
18:0	10·2	7·3
18:1 + 18:2 + 18:3	34·0	45·2

i = sum of intermediate peaks between the indicated fatty acids.
From Kuzdzal and Kuzdzal-Savoie.[101]

total fatty acids[101] but other, probably less typical, samples had lower values of 3–5%.[98] Lipolysis is always highest towards the surface.[102] Most of the free fatty acids arise from lipolysis: short-chain fatty acids, resulting from the breakdown of lactose or some amino acids, represent only 5% of the total free fatty acids.[103] In Camembert, the relative proportions of free fatty acids are different from that of milk triglycerides since the former have a higher concentration of oleic acid[101] (Table II).

4.2 Properties and Effect of Mould Lipases

The essential lipolytic agents in mould-ripened cheeses are *Penicillium* spp. The natural lipase of milk is not very active, even in raw milk cheeses: however, its effect has been shown in blue-veined cheeses made with homogenized milk.[100] Except for *Geotrichum candidum*, micro-organisms other than *P. roqueforti* or *P. camemberti* have very low lipolytic activity in mould-ripened cheeses. The particularly high proportion of free oleic acid in Camembert has been attributed to *G. candidum* lipase[101] which preferentially releases this fatty acid.[104]

Lamberet and Lenoir[105,106] noted that *P. camemberti* produces only one extracellular lipase which has optimal activity on tributyrin at pH 9·0 and 35°C. The production level of this enzyme varies from 1 to 10 (relative scale), depending on the strain.[107] At pH 6·0, this lipase retains 50% of its maximal activity and remains very active between 0 and 20°C. It is more active when calcium ions are present.[105] The production of lipase has been studied during the ripening of raw-milk Camembert:[108] activity appears after 10 days of ripening during or shortly after mycelium growth, is maximal at 16 days and then decreases slightly until the 30th day when it increases again on lysis of mycelia. In 10 cheeses of different origin, the lipase activity in the outer region of the cheeses varied from 1·2 to 4·45 units/g of cheese.

P. roqueforti has been observed to produce 2 lipases, one with an optimum at acid pH values, the other with an optimum in the alkaline pH range.[65,109–111] Several authors[65,109,111,112] report that the alkaline lipase is optimally active at pH 7·5–8·0 but optimum pH values at 9·0–9·5 have also been reported.[110,113] This enzyme still retains 20% of its activity at pH 6·0.[113] The activity of acid lipase is maximal at pH 6·0–6·5.[114,115] The specificities of the 2 enzymes are different, the acid lipase being more active on tricaproin and the alkaline lipase on tributyrin.[113] The activity of both enzymes has been measured in cheese.[116] More acid lipase was synthesized in 6 out of 7 samples. However, in spite of the favourable pH of the cheese, it may not always play the more important role since alkaline lipase has higher activity on milk fat.[113,114] Samples in which alkaline lipase is high may have a slightly piquant taste or soapy aroma.[116] This would reflect the relative activity levels of the 2 lipases[105,114] and probably their different specificities.

5. LACTOSE BREAKDOWN

5.1 Lactose and Lactic Acid Content

The lactic starters used to make Camembert are mainly homofermentative mesophilic streptococci, and lactose breakdown leads mainly to lactic acid production by the hexose diphosphate pathway. Rennet is added to the milk after ripening when the pH is about 6·4. Intense acidification occurs mainly during draining and the pH of the curd when taken from the moulds is about 4·6. The amount of residual lactose in the curd decreases very quickly between 5 and 10 days after processing, i.e. when *P. camemberti* grows; thereafter the lactose level continues to decrease more slowly.[117] After 20–30 days of ripening, the lactose has completely disappeared, this clearance being more rapid on the surface than at the centre of the cheese. Galactose and glucose concentrations in Camembert are very low.[117]

Besides homofermentative streptococci, the lactic flora of Roquefort cheese includes leuconostocs, heterofermentative bacteria which convert lactose into lactic acid, acetic acid, ethanol and CO_2.[14,18] The latter compound causes small openings in the curd that favour the implantation of *P. roqueforti*. In this same cheese, yeasts also metabolize lactose[14,17] and contribute to the formation of openings in the curd.

In mould-ripened cheeses, lactic acid produced by starters is utilised by moulds and yeasts. In Camembert, Berner[118] observed initial L-lactate levels of 2·9% (of dry matter) at the surface and 3·6% at the centre of the cheese. A rapid decrease in these levels between days 5 and 10 of ripening coincides with *Penicillium* growth and the amount of L-lactate in ripened cheese is <0·02%. Puhan and Wanner[119] noted levels of 0·06% on the surface and 0·02% at the centre of ripe Camembert. D-Lactate is present in low amounts[118,120] and has almost disappeared by the end of ripening.[120] Lactic acid breakdown leads to neutralization of the curd; the surface of a traditional Camembert reaches about pH 7·0 at the end of ripening[38] and the pH at the centre is about 6·0 (Fig. 2). The rise in pH in blue-veined cheese is less spectacular than on the surface of Camembert; however, the pH reaches about 6·2 in 'bleu d'Auvergne'[20] or 6·5 in Danish Blue.[35]

5.2 Consequences of pH Increase

This neutralization in cheese plays a considerable role in the ripening process. Due to it, acid-sensitive bacteria, including micrococci and coryneform bacteria, establish on the surface of mould-ripened soft cheese and contribute to their traditional taste qualities. Neutralization also favours the activity of various ripening enzymes whose pH optima are often closer to neutrality than to the acid zone. Furthermore, as we shall see in Section 8, it clearly influences the rheological properties of cheese. Besides these three main results, neutralization of cheese causes the minerals in surface-mould cheeses to migrate. Metche and Fanni[121] and Le Graet *et al.*[122] showed considerable calcium and phosphate migration towards the exterior of Camembert during mould implantation on the surface. The rind of surface-mould cheeses attains high inorganic calcium and phosphorus levels (17 and 9 g/kg, respectively),[122] while the levels of these decrease in the centre. Le Graet *et al.*[122] showed that the high pH of the surface causes the formation of insoluble calcium phosphate, immobilizing this salt on the rind. This is of nutritional interest as far as the mineral supply in surface-mould ripened cheese is concerned, depending on whether the rind is eaten or not, since at the end of ripening, the rind contains about 80% of the calcium and 55% of the phosphorus.[122]

6. OTHER METABOLISMS

Changes in niacin and vitamin B6 levels have been studied during the ripening of blue-veined cheeses. The niacin content increases for the first 6 weeks and then decreases slowly; vitamin B6 concentration increases between the 3rd and 6th month of ripening.[123] In Camembert, the presence of ergosterol, which is a precursor of vitamin D, has been reported. Synthesis is carried out by *P. camemberti* and this substance does not migrate to the interior of the curd.[124]

Like other moulds, *P. roqueforti* and *P. camemberti* can synthesize toxic substances called mycotoxins. Their proportions and presence in cheese have been reviewed.[125-127] *P. roqueforti* synthesizes roquefortine,[28] isofumigaclavine A and B,[128,129] PR-toxin,[130] mycophenolic acid,[131] patuline,[132] penicillic acid[132] and siderophores.[138] *P. camemberti* produces cyclopiazonic acid.[134] Patuline and penicillic acid are not found in cheese[132] nor is PR-toxin which is unstable under curd conditions.[135,136] The fungal metabolites that can be detected in cheese are roquefortine,[137] isofumigaclavine A,[137] mycophenolic acid,[138] sidero-phores[138] and cyclopiazonic acid.[134] Considering the low levels (ppm) and biological activity of these substances, it has been concluded that there is no risk to human health, even if large amounts of cheese are eaten.[139–142]

7. AROMA COMPOUNDS

7.1 Blue-veined Cheeses

Although the nature of the molecules determining the taste of some cheeses is well known, it is often difficult to define the role of one molecular species or a class of molecules in the taste perception of the consumer. Blue-veined cheeses are an exception because it has been shown that methylketones have a key role in the flavour typifying these cheeses. 2-Heptanone and 2-nonanone are the most abundant; 2-pentanone, 2-propanone, 2-undecanone, 2-tridecanone are also present but in lower amounts[143–147] (Table III).

There are wide variations between samples as to total or individual concentrations of methylketones, and it is difficult to produce norms.[144–147] Dartey and Kinsella[148] observed that the concentration of methylketones increases regularly up to day 70 and then decreases. Comparable kinetics have been reported by Sato *et al.*[149]

The mechanism of methylketone formation in blue-veined cheeses has been thoroughly reviewed by Kinsella and Hwang.[150] Methylketones are produced by *P. roqueforti* from fatty acids via the β-oxidation pathway. β-

TABLE III
Methyl ketone content of blue veined cheese

	mg ketone/kg cheese						
	A	*B*	*C*	*D*	*E*	*F*	*G*
2-Propanone	3·4	2·8	3·9	1·7	2·7	2·7	0·0
2-Pentanone	18·4	7·2	20·9	6·5	17·5	19·2	3·6
2-Heptanone	40·8	19·0	71·8	17·9	39·1	69·9	17·6
2-Nonanone	28·0	22·3	88·3	19·8	42·5	78·9	18·9
2-Undecanone	6·4	6·0	29·9	4·9	12·3	6·7	2·4
Total	97·0	57·3	214·8	50·8	114·1	177·4	42·5

Samples A–E: American blue cheese, samples F and G: Roquefort (from Anderson and Day[145]).

ketoacid-CoA, obtained by β-hydroxyacyl CoA dehydrogenation, is deacylated to β-ketoacid by a β-ketoacyl-CoA deacyclase or thiohydrolase. A decarboxylase converts β-ketoacyl into methylketone and CO_2. Mycelium, as well as spores, can produce methylketones.[150,151] Spores oxidize fatty acids of 2–12 carbon atoms; however, octanoic acid is the most rapidly converted substrate. Mycelium oxidizes fatty acids within a wide pH range but the reaction is optimal between pH 5 and 7,[152,153] i.e. at a pH similar to that of ripe cheese. A decarboxylase that converts β-ketododecanoic acid into 2-undecanone has an optimum pH of 6·5–7·0.[150]

There is a positive correlation between the free fatty acid level and the amount of methylketones produced,[65,149,150] and cheeses with limited lipolysis do not have a strong aroma.[150] This might be a result of a great excess of substrate and adding lipases to the curd favours the appearance of methylketones.[154] Addition of fatty acids to a slurry system inhibits lipolysis but increases methylketone concentration.[155] Mycelium physiological stage[156] and pH[151] play a role too. The intensity of *P. roqueforti* development is important; high salt concentrations limit mould growth, retard lipolysis and reduce methylketone production.[99]

The volatile fraction of blue-veined cheeses includes many other compounds besides methylketones (see review of Adda and Dumont[157] Secondary alcohols (2-pentanol, 2-heptanol and 2-nonanol) are produced by *Penicillium* due to methylketone reduction. Their concentrations are lower than those of methylketones but are still appreciable.[145,147] Other alcohols,[145] as well as many esters and aldehydes,[145,146] have also been identified. Jolly and Kosikowski[158] reported the presence of γ-lactones. Ney and Wirotama[159] showed the presence of volatile amines and Spettoli[93] quantified some of these in two samples of Gorgonzola. Fatty acids have been identified by Anderson.[146]

All these data have contributed to the development of formulae for the composition of synthetic blue-veined cheese aroma.[141,160] The production of this aroma by fermentation (*P. roqueforti* culture on a fat-rich culture medium) has also been developed for use in salad dressing or processed cheeses and has been reported in many studies.[161–165]

7.2 Surface-mould Ripened Soft Cheeses

The work of Dumont *et al.*[166,167] and Moinas *et al.*[168–170] has defined the aroma of Camembert and revealed its complexity. Table IV summarizes the composition of the volatile products found.

Methylketones and their corresponding secondary alcohols are the most

TABLE IV
Volatile compounds isolated in Camembert cheese

1-Alkanols	C2, 3, 4, 6, 2-methylpropanol, 3-methylbutanol, oct-1-en-3-ol, 2-phenylethanol
2-Alkanols	C4, 5, 6, 7, 9, 11
Methyl ketones	C4, 5, 6, 7, 8, 9, 10, 11, 12, 13, 15
Aldehydes	C6, 7, 9, 2 and 3-methylbutanal
Esters	C2, 4, 6, 8, 10-ethyl, 2-phenylethylacetate
Phenols	phenol, p-cresol
Lactones	C_9, C_{10}, C_{12}
Sulphur compounds	H_2S, methyl sulphide, methyldisulphide, methanethiol, 2,4-dithiapentane, 3,4-dithiahexane, 2,4,5-trithiahexane 3-methylthio 2,4-dithiapentane, 3-methylthiopropanol
Anisoles	anisole, 4-methylanisole, 2,4-dimethylanisole
Amines	phenylethylamine, $C_{2,3,4}$, diethylamine, isobutylamine, 3-methylbutylamine
Miscellaneous	dimethoxybenzene, isobutylacetamide

From Adda.[174]

abundant neutral compounds in the volatile fraction [166,171] and contribute to the flavour of surface-mould cheeses. The work of Lamberet *et al.*[172] shows that the ability of *P. camemberti* to produce methylketones varies greatly among strains.

Oct-1-en-3-ol plays a particular role because it is responsible for the mushroom note in the characteristic flavour of Camembert.[173] When the level of oct-1-en-3-ol is too high, the aroma is faulty.

Sulphur compounds also play an important part; they cause the garlic note that is clearly present in ripe traditional Camembert. Compounds such as methylsulphide, methyldisulphide and 3-methylthiopropanol, which are present in other cheeses also, give a basic cheesy note, while 2,4-dithiapentane, 2,4,5-trithiahexane and 3-methylthio-2,4-dithiapentane are observed in typical Camembert.[174] Coryneform bacteria are usually thought to be key contributors to the formation of sulphur products in surface-mould cheeses. Strains of *B. linens* isolated from dairy products have been shown to produce methanethiol,[175–178] and these bacteria have a demethiolase which releases methanethiol from methionine. Methanethiol and sulphur compounds are also produced by *P. camemberti*[179] and *Geotrichum candidum*.[180] Several sulphur compounds develop from methanethiol by non-enzymatic reactions.[181]

Substantial amounts of 2-phenylethanol and lower amounts of 2-

phenylethylacetate and 2-phenylethylpropionate are produced in traditional Camembert.[164] 2-Phenylethanol has a pleasant rose-like odour; its maximal concentration is reached after the first week of ripening and then decreases (Roger, Degas and Gripon, unpublished data). Lee and Richard[182] noted that yeasts can produce 2-phenylethanol from phenylalanine, while *G. candidum* and *B. linens* cannot. It is probable that phenylethanol is produced by yeasts that develop at the beginning of ripening. Phenylethanol would be obtained by the breakdown of phenylalanine by the Ehrlich–Neubauer pathway with phenylpyruvate as the intermediate product.[182] The mean detection thresholds of phenylethanol in a curd-type substrate are 7·6 ppm (aroma) and 9 ppm (flavour). The levels of phenylethanol found in cheese are slightly lower but correspond to the most sensitive taster thresholds (Roger *et al.*, unpublished data). This compound may therefore cause the floral note that some tasters can distinguish in traditional Camembert.

N-isobutylacetamide has been identified in Camembert.[183] This compound has a bitter taste which may contribute to bitterness.[173] It may originate from the Val-Gly dipeptide after decarboxylation and deamination. However, the Val-Gly sequence is not found in caseins and the presence of N-isobutylacetamide would imply that a transamination reaction occurs.[181] Another mechanism involving amine acetylation has been proposed.[181]

It must be recalled that ammonia is an important element in the aroma of traditional Camembert and results from the deamination activity of the microbial flora on amino acids. The various elements in the surface flora probably play a role; the action of *G. candidum*[184] and *B. linens* has been emphasized.[90]

Free fatty acids are found in large amounts in the non-volatile fraction (see Section 4). They contribute to the basic flavour of the cheese and are the precursors of methylketones and secondary alcohols.

The effect of milk fat oxidation on Camembert flavour has been studied by adding small amounts of copper to the milk used to make the cheese,[185] but this did not lead to substantial fat oxidation in the curd nor to the appearance of an oxidized taste in ripe cheese.

8. CHANGES IN TEXTURE

The outer part of Camembert undergoes considerable modification of texture and the curd which is firm and brittle at the beginning of ripening,

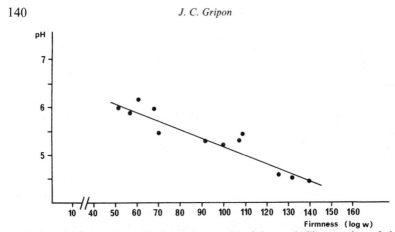

Fig. 4. Camembert firmness in relation to pH of the curd. Cheeses about 3 days old and without *Penicillium* were incubated for 1 h 30 min in an ammoniacal atmosphere. 24 h. later a pH gradient was established and cheese firmness was measured at various distances from the surface by penetrometry. A metal blade was allowed to penetrate in the curd, at a constant speed and perpendicularly to a section of cheese (i.e. parallel to cheese surfaces). The pH of the measured area varied depending on its distance from the surface. Firmness was determined by the logarithm of the work (*w*) necessary to insert the blade to a depth of 5 mm (Monnet *et al.*, unpublished data).

later becomes soft. Softening is visible in a cross-section of cheese and gradually extends towards the centre. The water content of Camembert is about 55% and, if it is too high, the outer part tends to flow when the ripe cheese is cut. These changes are usually attributed to the high level of proteolysis created by *P. camemberti*.[186,187] However, as seen earlier, the diffusion of fungal protease is limited [74,75] and they can affect only the outer few millimetres. Another important change caused by *P. camemberti* and the surface flora is the establishment of a pH gradient from the surface to the centre due to lactic acid consumption and ammonia production. This pH gradient can be simulated by incubating young Camembert (3 days of ripening without *Penicillium* seeding) in an ammoniacal atmosphere. The ammonia dissolves in the curd and, after equilibration, the pH gradient established is expressed by cheese softening; this process is more evident near the surface where the pH is higher (Monnet, Le Bars and Gripon, unpublished data) (Fig. 4). Increasing the pH therefore plays an important role by causing the cheese to soften. This may. be explained by the fact that the pH increase augments the net charge on casein and modifies protein–protein interactions. It also changes protein–water interactions and thus the water sorption capacity of the caseins.[188] Indeed, during ripening, the outer part of Camembert has a higher water content than the centre, in spite of surface evaporation, which is inevitable.[122] According to Noomen,[75] the physico-chemical conditions (water content and pH) in Camembert cannot alone explain softening which could be related to rennet action. Indeed, experimental cheeses, containing no rennet and incubated in an ammoniacal atmosphere do not soften but become hard and springy, while cheese with rennet does soften.[75] The softening of Camembert could thus be explained by two processes: (1) α_{s1}-casein breakdown by rennet and (2) a rise in the pH caused by the surface flora. The importance of rennet action on α_{s1}-casein and of the physico-chemical conditions have also been reported for Meshanger cheese, a soft cheese with no surface flora.[189,190]

Few data are available on the texture of blue-veined cheeses. The degree of mineralization and the dry matter vary (50–58%), depending on the way the cheese is made, and this would explain the various textures of the different varieties. Because of their higher dry matter content, the rise in pH does not lead to softening as for surface-mould cheeses. The modification of blue-veined cheese texture, therefore, mainly results from the extensive proteolysis.

9. CONTROL OF RIPENING

The intensity of the biochemical activity of *P. roqueforti* varies considerably among strains[64] and the choice of strain has a major effect on the quality of blue-veined cheese.[65,149,191] The characteristics of the desired strains also vary from one variety of cheese to another; 'bleu d'Auvergne' requires highly proteolytic strains which have low lipolytic activity, while 'fourme d'Ambert' needs strains with low proteolytic and low lipolytic activities (G. Pradel, personal communication). The control of strain growth is another crucial factor. If mould growth is too extensive or too limited, the aroma is faulty or weak. *P. roqueforti* develops within the curds because it tolerates a low O_2 level and a high CO_2 level.[22,192] Aeration and space for mould growth depend on whether the curd is more or less pierced. When heterofermentative leuconostocs are added to the milk during Roquefort production, CO_2 is produced, causing the formation of spaces which enhance mycelial development.[18]

Salt content, which is particularly high (6–8% of the liquid phase) in blue-veined cheeses, also affects *P. roqueforti* growth. Depending on the strain, such concentrations may retard growth.[193] Prolonging salting causes the rate of proteolysis and lipolysis to decrease.[35,99] Besides acting on *Penicillium*, salting also influences the implantation of micrococci and yeasts of the surface of Roquefort.[19]

The choice of the *P. camemberti* strain is also important in the production of surface-mould soft cheeses. However, the proteolytic activity of the different strains does not vary[26] as much as their lipolytic and fatty acid oxidative activities.[27,172] The choice of a *P. camemberti* strain is also guided by the growth rate, colour, density and height of mycelium which play a part in the appearance and attractiveness of surface mould cheeses.[21]

Salting has a selective effect on the moulds of surface-mould cheeses. Too much salting limits or prevents *G. candidum* growth, while *P. camemberti* growth is much less affected. In whey culture, *P. camemberti* growth is slowed down when 10–15% of salt is present.[23] Inversely, too little salt, combined with insufficient draining, causes *G. candidum* to grow too much and hinders *Penicillium* implantation, giving defective cheeses; this defect is called 'toad skin'. Under-salting may also favour the surface implantation of *Mucor*, altering the appearance of the cheese; this defect is called 'cat hair'. Reducing the water activity by higher salting[23,194] and using a *Penicillium* strain that implants quickly, helps to correct this defect. Salting also influences the activity of *Penicillium* enzymes and at 4% it reduces the degree of proteolysis in Camembert (25 versus 40% in an unsalted control).[195]

The production of surface-mould soft cheeses using milk highly contaminated with psychrotrophic bacteria leads to organoleptic defects. The lipase activity of these bacteria is expressed by increased lipolysis and a rancid taste; bitterness has also been reported.[196]

It is difficult to control the coliform flora of Camembert. Even a low level of coliform contamination of the milk can result in a high multiplication rate later. At the beginning of cheesemaking, there is already some development before the pH has dropped enough. Acidification destroys a large part of this flora, but when the pH rises, the bacteria multiply again, resulting in some cases in high numbers of coliforms in the cheese.[12] To avoid this in pasteurized milk cheese, coliform bacteria should be less than 100 cells/g 3 days after curd making; this can be achieved by taking the necessary hygienic precautions.

As mentioned above, uncontrolled development of *G. candidum* produces defects in the appearance and taste of cheese, even though this mould probably contributes notably to the taste qualities of Camembert. Some strains of *G. candidum* clearly improve the taste and aroma of pasteurized Camembert cheeses. Their controlled growth results in a more typical flavour, close to that of traditional Camembert.[180]

As in all cheeses, acidification plays an essential role by controlling syneresis and the degree of surface mould cheese mineralization. When acidification is too high, the Camembert curd is too dry and brittle and enzyme activities are limited; insufficient acidification results in a cheese that is too moist at the end of ripening. The last 20 years have witnessed an increasing interest in 'stabilized' cheeses. Washing the curd permits a higher pH to be obtained at the end of draining. This gives a less demineralized cheese that seems riper than traditional cheese of the same age. These cheeses made with pasteurized milk have a milder taste and keep better. This could be due to more limited *P. camemberti* activity, perhaps because of the lower levels of available lactose and lactate. Due to their higher pH, these products are more sensitive to coliform bacteria.

An investigation in France by Pelissier *et al.*[197] showed that mould-ripened cheeses are more sensitive to bitterness than other varieties and the intensity of this defect may cause considerable damage. Cheboratev *et al.*[198] have selected strains of *P. roqueforti* for their ability to clear the bitterness of a protein hydrolysate, and they recommend using such strains to avoid the defect in blue-veined cheeses. *P. camemberti* has a crucial role in the appearance of bitterness in Camembert. A too abundant growth of the mycelium can lead to the defect; if *Penicillium* growth is limited by the presence of *G. candidum* or by incubating the cheese in an ammoniacal atmosphere, proteolysis is lower and the defect does not occur.[199] Therefore, this defect could occur when there is too much proteolysis by *Penicillium* proteases. The rennet dose used and its augmentation does not seem to change bitterness, perhaps because the pH of Camembert does not favour the action of coagulating proteinases at the end of ripening.[199] Lactic bacteria and their proteinases have also been reported to affect the occurrence of bitterness: the defect appears when high populations of lactic bacteria are present in the curd; on the other hand, if these populations are decreased (for example, by phages), bitterness does not appear.[200] This seems to be related to the degree of curd acidification since the probability of bitterness is increased if the pH is low at the end of draining (L. Vassal, personal communication). Bitterness might not result directly from high amounts of lactic bacteria but could be related to *Penicillium* whose growth and protease production might be higher in very acid curds.

10. CONCLUSION

The particular characteristics of *P. roqueforti* and *P. camemberti* are expressed in mould-ripened cheese, giving the cheese its characteristic

144   *J. C. Gripon*

appearance and contributing to the development of the rheological and gustative qualities of the cheese. However, the secondary flora contributes to the attainment of traditional quality products. Great progress has been made during the last 15 years in our knowledge of the mechanisms of blue-veined and surface-mould cheese ripening. However, the processes are very complex and no close relationship can yet be seen between the composition and the quality of mould-ripened cheese.

While studies on traditional mould ripened cheeses should not be abandoned, it is to be recalled that more cheese is now being produced in large, automated factories. The good quality of these products must be maintained, taking into account consumer taste which often favours rather mild products. Improving the storage life of surface mould-ripened soft cheese should also make it easier to distribute and to develop its production.

ACKNOWLEDGEMENTS

The author wishes to thank Drs M. J. Desmazeaud, G. Lamberet and L. Vassal for making useful comments and Mrs Alice Daifuku for her assistance during the preparation of this manuscript.

REFERENCES

1. Morris, H. A., *Blue-veined Cheeses*, Pfizer Cheese Monographs, Vol. VII, Pfizer Inc., New York, 1981.
2. Kosikowski, F. In: *Cheese and Fermented Milk Food*, Edwards Brothers, Michigan, p. 317, 1977.
3. Bakalor, S., *Dairy Sci. Abstr.*, 1962, Parts I and II, **24**, 529 and 583.
4. Pernodet, G. In: *Le Fromage* (Ed. A. Eck), Lavoisier, Paris, pp. 229 and 234, 1984.
5. Coghill, D., *Aust. J. Dairy Technol.*, 1979, **34**, 72.
6. Lenoir, J., *Lait*, 1963, **43**, 262.
7. Schmidt, J. L. and Lenoir, J., *Lait*, 1978, **58**, 355.
8. Schmidt, J. L. and Lenoir, J., *Lait*, 1980, **60**, 272.
9. Rousseau, M., *Milchwissenschaft*, 1984, **39**, 129.
10. Richard, J. and Zadi, H., *Lait*, 1983, **63**, 25.
11. Richard, J., *Lait*, 1984, **64**, 496.
12. Mourgues, R., Vassal, L., Auclair, J., Mocquot, G. and Vandeweghe, J., *Lait*, 1977, **57**, 131.
13. Tolle, A., Otte, I., Suhren, G. and Heeschen, W., *Milchwissenchaft*, 1980, **35**, 21.
14. Devoyod, J. J., Bret, G. and Auclair, J., *Lait*, 1968, **48**, 613.

15. Devoyod, J. J., *Lait*, 1970, **50**, 277.
16. Devoyod, J. J. and Bret, G., *Proc. 17th Int. Dairy Congr.*, Munich, 1966, Vol. D, p. 585.
17. Devoyod, J. J. and Sponem, D., *Lait*, 1970, **50**, 524.
18. Devoyod, J. J. and Muller, M., *Lait*, 1969, **43**, 369.
19. Devoyod, J. J., *Lait*, 1969, **49**, 20.
20. Trieu-Cuot, P. and Gripon, J. C., *Lait*, 1983, **63**, 116.
21. Moreau, C., *Lait*, 1979, **59**, 219.
22. Moreau, C., *Lait*, 1980, **60**, 254.
23. Choisy, C., Gueguen, M., Lenoir, J., Schmidt, J. L. and Tourneur, C. In: *Le Fromage* (Ed. A. Eck), Lavoisier, Paris, p. 259, 1984.
24. Sanson, R. A., Eckardt, C. and Orth, R., *Antonie van Leuwenhoek*, 1977, **43**, 341.
25. Pitt, J. I., *The Genus Penicillium and its Teleomorphic States*, Academic Press, New York, 1979.
26. Lenoir, J. and Choisy, C., *Lait*, 1970, **51**, 138.
27. Lamberet, G., *Proc. 18th Int. Dairy Congr.*, Sidney, 1970, Vol. **1F**, 143.
28. Tourneur, C., *Proc. 21st Int. Dairy. Congr.*, Moscow, 1982, Vol. 1, Book I, p. 380.
29. Delespaul, G., Gueguen, M. and Lenoir, J., *Revue Laitière Française*, 1973 (313), 715.
30. Ottogali, G. and Galli, A., *Scienza e Technica lattiero casearia*, 1972, **23**, 363.
31. Carini, S., Kaderavek, G., De Gregori, A. and Ivernizzi, F., *Il Latte*, 1971, **45**, 615.
32. Oterholm, A., *IDF Bulletin*, Vol. 171, 1984.
33. Chapman, H. R. and Sharpe, M. E. In: *Dairy Microbiology* (Ed. R. K. Robinson), Elsevier Applied Science, London, p. 157, 1981.
34. Hewedi, M. M. and Fox, P. F., *Milchwissenschaft*, 1984, **39**, 198.
35. Godinho, M. and Fox, P. F., *Milchwissenschaft*, 1982, **37**, 72.
36. Ismail, A. and Hanson, A. A., *Milchwissenschaft*, 1972, **27**, 556.
37. Kosikowski, F. V. and Dahlberg, A. C., *J. Dairy Sci.*, 1954, **37**, 167.
38. Lenoir, J., *C.R. Acad. Agric.*, 1962, **48**, 160.
39. Do Ngoc, M., Lenoir, J. and Choisy, C., *Revue Laitière Française*, 1971, **288**, 447.
40. Lenoir, J., *Ann. Technol. Agric.*, 1963, **12**, 51.
41. Marcos, A., Esteban, M. A., Leon, F. and Fernandes-Salguero, J., *J. Dairy Sci.*, 1979, **62**, 892.
42. Trieu-Cuot, P. and Gripon, J. C., *J. Dairy Res.*, 1982, **49**, 50.
43. Trieu-Cuot, P., Archieri-Haze, M. J. and Gripon, J. C., *J. Dairy Res.*, 1982, **49**, 487.
44. Trieu-Cuot, P., Archieri-Haze, M. J. and Gripon, J. C., *Lait*, 1982, **62**, 234.
45. Noomen, A., *Neth. Milk Dairy J.*, 1978, **32**, 49.
46. Visser, F. M. W., *Neth. Milk and Dairy J.*, 1977, **31**, 210.
47. Visser, F. M. W. and Groot-Mostert, A. E. A., *Neth. Milk Dairy J.*, 1977, **31**, 247.
48. Noomen, A., *Neth. Milk Dairy J.*, 1978, **32**, 26.
49. Desmazeaud, M. J., Gripon, J. C., Le Bars, D. and Bergere, J. L., *Lait*, 1976, **56**, 379.

50. Gripon, J. C. and Hermier, J., *Biochimie*, 1974, **56**, 1323.
51. Lenoir, J. and Auberger, B., *Lait*, 1977, **57**, 164.
52. Lenoir, J. and Auberger, B., *Lait*, 1977, **57**, 471.
53. Gripon, J. C., Auberger, B. and Lenoir, J., *Int. J. Biochem.*, 1980, **12**, 451.
54. Zevaco, C., Hermier, J. and Gripon, J. C., *Biochimie*, 1973, **55**, 1353.
55. Lenoir, J., Auberger, B. and Gripon, J. C., *Lait*, 1979, **59**, 244.
56. Modler, H. W., Brunner, J. R. and Stine, C. M., *J. Dairy Sci.*, 1974, **57**, 523.
57. Modler, H. W., Brunner, J. R. and Stine, C. M., *J. Dairy Sci.*, 1974, **57**, 528.
58. Gripon, J. C., *Ann. Biol. Anim. Biochem. Biophys.*, 1977, **17**, 283.
59. Lenoir, J., *IDF Bulletin*, Vol. 171, p. 3, 1984.
60. Ahiko, K., Iwasawa, S., Ueda, M. and Miyata, N., Reports of Research Laboratory, Snow Brand Milk Products Co., Vol. 77, p. 127, 1981.
61. Gripon, J. C., *Biochimie*, 1977, **59**, 679.
62. Auberger, B., Bontals, M. and Lenoir, J., *Proc. 21st Int. Dairy Congr.*, Moscow, Vol. 1(2), p. 276, 1982.
63. Gripon, J. C. and Debest, B., *Lait*, 1976, **56**, 423.
64. Fournet, G. P., Thèse, 1971, University of Montpellier, France.
65. Niki, T., Yoshioka, Y. and Ahiko, K., *Proc. 17th Int. Dairy Congr.*, Munich, Vol. D., p. 531, 1966.
66. Lenoir, J. and Auberger, B., *Proc. 21st Int. Dairy Congr.*, Moscow, Vol. 1(2), p. 335, 1982.
67. Le Bars, D. and Gripon, J. C., *J. Dairy Res.*, 1981, **48**, 479.
68. Nishikawa, I., Reports of Research Laboratory, Snow Brand Milk Products Co Ltd, Vol. 36, p. 1, 1957.
69. Imamura, T., *J. Agr. Chem. Soc.*, 1960, **34**, 375.
70. Takafuji, S. and Yoshioka, Y., Reports of Research Laboratory, Snow Brand Milk Products Co. Ltd, **78**, p. 63, 1982.
71. Takafuji, S. and Yoshioka, Y., Reports of Research Laboratory, Snow Brand Milk Products Co. Ltd, **78**, 1982.
72. Gripon, J. C., Desmazeaud, M. J., Le Bars, D. and Bergere, J. L., *J. Dairy Sci.*, 1977, **60**, 1532.
73. Lenoir, J., *Revue Laitière Française*, 1970 (275), 231.
74. Lenoir, J. and Auberger, B., *Proc. 21st Int. Dairy Congr.*, Moscow, Vol. 1(2), p. 336, 1982.
75. Noomen, A., *Neth. Milk Dairy J.*, 1983, **37**, 229.
76. Paquet, J. and Gripon, J. C., *Milchwissenschaft*, 1980, **35**, 72.
77. Ichishima, E., Takeuchi, M., Yamamoto, K., Sano, Y. and Kikuchi, T., *Current Microb.*, 1978, **1**, 95.
78. Ahiko, K., Iwasawa, S., Ueda, M. and Miyata, N., Reports of Research Laboratory, Snow Brand Milk Products Co. Ltd, Vol. 77, p. 135, 1981.
79. Law, B. A. and Kolstad, J., *Antonie van Leeuwenhoek*, 1983, **49**, 225.
80. Gueguen, M. and Lenoir, J., *Lait*, 1976, **56**, 439.
81. Gueguen M. and Lenoir, J., *Lait*, 1975, **55**, 621.
82. Gueguen, M. and Lenoir, J., *Lait*, 1975, **55**, 145.
83. Schmidt, J. L., *Proc. 21st Int. Dairy Congr.*, Moscow, Vol. (12), p. 365, 1982.
84. Desmazeaud, M. J. and Devoyod, J. J., *Ann. Biol. Anim. Biochim. Biophys.*, 1974, **14**, 327.
85. Friedman, M. E., Nelson, W. O. and Wood, W. A., *J. Dairy Sci.*, 1953, **36**, 1124.

86. Foissy, H., *Milchwissenschaft*, 1978, **33**, 221.
87. Foissy, H., *FEMS Microb. Lett.*, 1978, **3**, 207.
88. Foissy, H., *Z. Lebensmitt. Unters. Forsch.*, 1978, **166**, 164.
89. Torgersen, H. and Sorhaug, T., *FEMS Microb. Lett.*, 1978, **4**, 151.
90. Hemme, D., Bouillanne, C., Metro, F. and Desmazeaud, M. J., *Science des Aliments*, 1982, **2**, 113.
91. Cecchi, L. and Resmini, P., *Scienza et Technica Lattiero-Casearia*, 1972, **23**, 389.
92. Colonna, P. and Adda, J., *Lait*, 1976, **56**, 143.
93. Spettoli, P., *Ind. Agr.*, 1971, **9**, 42.
94. Sen, N. P., *J. Food Sci.*, 1969, **34**, 22.
95. Lee, C. W., Lucas, S. and Desmazeaud, M. J., *FEMS Microb. Lett.*, 1985, **26**, 201.
96. Lee, C. W. and Desmazeaud, M. J., *Arch. Microbiol.*, 1985, **140**, 331.
97. Anderson, D. F. and Day, E. A., *J. Dairy Sci.*, 1965, **48**, 248.
98. Van Belle, M., Vervack, W. and Foulon, M., *Lait*, 1978, **58**, 246.
99. Godinho, M. and Fox, P. F., *Milchwissenschaft*, 1981, **36**, 476.
100. Morris, H. A., Jeseski, J. J., Combs, W. B. and Kuramoto, S., *J. Dairy Sci.*, 1963, **46**, 1.
101. Kuzdzal, W. and Kuzdzal-Savoie, S., *Proc. 17th Int. Dairy Congr.*, Munich, Vol. D2, p. 335, 1966.
102. Kuzdzal-Savoie, S., *Qualities plantarum et Materiae Vegetabiles*, 1968, **16**, 312.
103. Kuzdzal-Savoie, S. and Kuzdzal, W., *Techn. Lait.*, 1966, **14**, 17.
104. Marks, T. A., Quinn, J. G., Sampugna, J. and Jensen, R. G., *Lipids*, 1968, **3**, 143.
105. Lamberet, G. and Lenoir, J., *Lait*, 1976, **56**, 622.
106. Lamberet, G. and Lenoir, J., *Lait*, 1976, **56**, 119.
107. Lamberet, G. and Lenoir, J., *Lait*, 1972, **52**, 175.
108. Lamberet, G. and Lopez, M., *Proc. 21st Int. Congr.*, Moscow, Vol. 1(1), p. 499, 1982.
109. Imamura, T. and Kataoka, K., *Jap. J. Zootechn. Sci.*, 1963, **34**, 349.
110. Kman, I. M., Chandan, R. C. and Shahani, K. M., *J. Dairy Sci.*, 1966, **49**, 700.
111. Morris, H. A. and Jezeski, J. J., *J. Dairy Sci.*, 1953, **36**, 1285.
112. Eitenmiller, R. R., Vakil, J. R. and Shahani, K. M., *J. Food Sci.*, 1970, **35**, 130.
113. Menassa, A. and Lamberet, G., *Lait*, 1982, **62**, 32.
114. Lamberet, G. and Menassa, A., *J. Dairy Res.*, 1983, **50**, 459.
115. Lobyreva, L. B. and Marchenkova, A. I., *Mikrobiologiya*, 1981, **50**, 459.
116. Lamberet, G. and Menassa, A., *Lait*, 1983, **63**, 33.
117. Berner, G., *Milchwissenschaft*, 1970, **25**, 275.
118. Berner, G., *Milchwissenschaft*, 1971, **26**, 685.
119. Puhan, Z. and Wanner, E., *Deutsche Molkerei-Zeitung*, 1979, **24**, 874.
120. Markwalder, H. U., *Lebensm. Wiss. u-Technol.*, 1982, **15**, 68.
121. Metche, M. and Fanni, J., *Lait*, 1978, **58**, 336.
122. Le Graet, Y., Lepienne, A., Brule, G. and Ducruet, P., *Lait*, 1983, **63**, 317.
123. Nilson, K. M., *Diss. Abst. Int. B.*, 1967, **28**, 398.
124. Huyghebaert, A. and De Moor, H., *Lait*, 1979, **59**, 464.
125. Scott, P. M., *J. Food Protection*, 1981, **44**, 702.
126. Orth, R. In: *Mycotoxine in Lebensmitteln* (Ed. J. Reiss), Gustav Fischer Verlag, Stuttgart, p. 273, 1981.

127. Sieber, R., *Zeitschrift für Ernährungswissenschaft*, 1978, **17**, 112.
128. Scott, P. M., Merien, M. A. and Polonsky, J. *Experientia*, 1976, **32**, 140.
129. Ohmono, S., Sato, T., Utagawa, T. and Abe, M. *Agr. Biol. Chem.*, 1975, **39**, 1333.
130. Scott, P. M., Kennedy, B. P. C., Harwig, J. and Blanchfield, B. J., *Appl. Environ. Microbiol.*, 1977, **33**, 249.
131. Siriwardana, M. G. and Lafont, P., *J. Dairy Sci.*, 1979, **62**, 1145.
132. Engel, G. and Prokopek, D., *Milchwissenschaft*, 1980, **35**, 218.
133. Ong, S. A. and Neilands, J. B., *J. Agr. Food Chem.*, 1979, **27**, 990.
134. Le Bars, J., *Appl. Environ. Microbiol.*, 1979, **38**, 1052.
135. Scott, P. M. and Kanhere, S. R., *J. Assoc. Off. Anal. Chem.*, 1979, **62**, 141.
136. Piva, M. T., Guiraud, J., Crouzet, J. and Galzy, P., *Lait*, 1976, **56**, 397.
137. Scott, P. M. and Kennedy, B. P. C., *J. Agr. Food Chem.*, 1976, **24**, 865.
138. Engel, G., Von Milczewski, K. E., Prokopek, D. and Teuber, M. *Appl. Environ. Microbiol.*, 1982, **43**, 1034.
139. Scholch, U., Luthy, J. and Schlatter, C., *Milchwissenschaft*, 1984, **39**, 76.
140. Scholch, U., Luthy, J. and Schlatter, C., *Z. für Lebensm. Unters. Forsch.*, 1984, **178**, 351.
141. Franck, H. K., Orth, R., Reichle, G. and Wunder, W., *Milchwissenschaft*, 1975, **30**, 594.
142. Franck, H. K., Orth, R., Ivankovic, S., Kuhlmann, M. and Schmahl, D., *Experientia*, 1977, **33**, 515.
143. Schwartz, D. P. and Boyd, E. N., *J. Dairy Sci.*, 1963, **46**, 1422.
144. Schwartz, D. P. and Parks, O. W., *J. Dairy Sci.*, 1963, **46**, 989.
145. Anderson, D. F. and Day, E. A., *J. Agr. Food Chem.*, 1966, **14**, 241.
146. Anderson, D. F., *Diss. Abstr.*, 1966, **26**(6), 6636.
147. Svensen, A. and Ottestad, E., *Meieriposten*, 1969, **58**, 50, 77.
148. Dartey, C. K. and Kinsella, J. E., *J. Agr. Food Chem.*, 1971, **19**, 771.
149. Sato, M., Honda, T., Yamada, Y., Takada, A. and Kawanami, T., *Proc. 17th Int. Dairy Congr.*, Munich, Vol. D, p. 539, 1966.
150. Kinsella, J. E. and Hwang, D. M., *CRC Crit. Rev. Food Sci. Nutr.*, 1976, **8**, 191.
151. Lawrence, R. C., *J. gen. Microbiol.*, 1966, **44**, 383.
152. Dwivedi, B. K. and Kinsella, J. E., *J. Food Sci.*, 1974, **39**, 83.
153. Lawrence, R. C. and Hawke, J. C., *J. gen. Microb.*, 1968, **51**, 289.
154. Jolly, R. C. and Kosikowski, F. V., *J. Dairy Sci.*, 1975, **58**, 846.
155. King, R. D. and Clegg, G. H., *J. Sci. Food Agric.*, 1979, **30**, 197.
156. Fan, T. Y., Hwang, D. H. and Kinsella, J. E., *J. Agr. Food Chem.*, 1976, **24**, 443.
157. Adda, J. and Dumont, J. P., *Lait*, 1974, **54**, 1.
158. Jolly, R. C. and Kosikowski, F. V., *J. Dairy Sci.*, 1974, **57**, 597.
159. Ney, K. H. and Wirotama, I. P., *Z. Lebensm. Unters. Forsch.*, 1972, **149**, 275.
160. Ney, K. H., Wirotama, I. P. and Freytag, W. G., *British Patent*, 1, 381, 737.
161. Knight, S., *US Patent*, 1963, 3, 100, 153.
162. Watt, J. C. and Nelson, J. H., *US Patent*, 1963, 3, 072, 488.
163. Nelson, J. H., *J. Agr. Food Chem.*, 1970, **18**, 567.
164. Jolly, R. C. and Kosikowski, F. V., *J. Food Sci.*, 1975, **40**, 285.
165. Luksas, A. J., *US Patent*, 1973, 3, 720, 520.
166. Dumont, J. P., Roger, S., Cerf, P. and Adda, J., *Lait*, 1974, **54**, 501.
167. Dumont, J. P., Roger, S. and Adda, J., *Lait*, 1976, **56**, 595.

168. Moinas, M., Groux, M. and Horman, I., *Lait*, 1973, **53**, 601.
169. Moinas, M., Groux, M. and Horman, I., *Lait*, 1975, **55**, 414.
170. Groux, M. and Moinas, M., *Lait*, 1974, **54**, 44.
171. Schwartz, D. P. and Parks, O. W., *J. Dairy Sci.*, 1963, **46**, 1136.
172. Lamberet, G., Auberger, B., Canteri, C. and Lenoir, J., *Revue Laitière Française*, 1982(406), 13.
173. Adda, J., Roger, S. and Dumont, J. P. In: *Flavor of Food and Beverages* (Ed. G. Charalambous and G. E. Inglett), Academic Press, New York, p. 65, 1973.
174. Adda, J. In: *Le Fromage* (Ed. A. Eck), Lavoisier, Paris, p. 330, 1984.
175. Sharpe, M. E., Law, B. A., Phillips, B. A. and Pitcher, D. G., *J. gen. Microbiol.*, 1977, **101**, 345.
176. Law, B. A. and Sharpe, M. E., *J. Dairy Res.*, 1978, **45**, 267.
177. Ferchichi, M., Hemme, D., Nardi, M. and Pamboukjian, N., *J. gen. Microb.*, 1985, **131**, 715.
178. Cuer, A., Dauphin, G., Kergomard, A., Dumont, J. P. and Adda, J., *Appl. Microbiol.*, 1979, **38**, 332.
179. Tsugo, T. and Matsuoka, H., *Proc. 16th Int. Dairy Congr.*, Copenhagen, Vol. IV, p. 385, 1962.
180. Mourgues, R., Bergere, J. L. and Vassal, L., *La Technique Laitière*, 1983(978), 11.
181. Adda, J., Gripon, J. C. and Vassal, L., *Food Chemistry*, 1982, **9**, 115.
182. Lee, C. W. and Richard, J., *J. Dairy Res.*, 1984, **51**, 461.
183. Dumont, J. P. and Adda, J. In: *Progress in Flavor Research* (Ed. D. G. Land and H. E. Nursten), Elsevier Applied Science, London, p. 245, 1978.
184. Greenberg, R. S. and Ledford, R. A., *J. Dairy Res.*, 1979, **62**, 368.
185. Korycka-Dahl, M., Vassal, L., Ribadeau-Dumas, B. and Mocquot, G., *Sciences des aliments*, 1983, **3**, 79.
186. Knoop, A. M. and Peters, K. H., *Milchwissenschaft*, 1971, **26**, 193.
187. Knoop, A. M. and Peters, K. H., *Milchwissenschaft*, 1972, **27**, 153.
188. Ruegg, M. and Blanc, B., *J. Dairy Sci.*, 1976, **59**, 1019.
189. Noomen, A., *Neth. Milk Dairy J.*, 1977, **31**, 75.
190. De Jong, L., *Neth. Milk Dairy J.*, 1977, **31**, 314.
191. Graham, D. M., *J. Dairy Sci.*, 1968, **41**, 719.
192. Golding, N. S., *J. Dairy Sci.*, 1945, **28**, 737.
193. Goldinho, M. and Fox, P. F., *Milchwissenschaft*, 1981, **36**, 205.
194. Hardy, J., *Revue Laitière Française*, 1979(377), 19.
195. Kikuchi, T. and Takafuji, S., *Jap. J. Zootech. Sci.*, 1971, **42**, 276.
196. Dumont, J. P., Delespaul, G., Miguot, B. and Adda, J., *Lait*, 1977, **57**, 619.
197. Pelissier, J. P., Mercier, J. C. and Ribadeau-Dumas, B., *Revue Laitière Française*, 1974(325), 817.
198. Cheboratev, L. N., Bratsilo, T. E. and Rogoja, T. A., *Sovershenstovovanie teckhnologischeskikh protsessov molochnoi promyshlennosti* Tom I Chast'II 1974, 28 (*Dairy Sci. Abst.*, 1976, **38**, 4406).
199. Vassal, L. and Gripon, J. C., *Lait*, 1984, **64**, 397.
200. Martley, F. G., *Lait*, 1975, **55**, 310.

Chapter 5

Bacterial Surface-ripened Cheeses

A. Reps

University of Agriculture and Technology,
Olsztyn, Poland

1. INTRODUCTION

One of the most significant periods in cheese production is the curing
(ripening) process; only a properly conducted ripening process, specific for
a given type of cheese, ensures the production of a high quality product.
During ripening, micro-organisms develop on the surface of cheeses.
Quite often, this phenomenon is undesirable and periodic cleaning or
wrapping of the cheeses with protective coating prevents the growth of
micro-organisms on the surface. This is particularly the case with hard and
semi-hard cheeses ripened internally through the participation of
coagulant, indigenous milk enzymes and of microbial enzymes present
throughout the body of the cheese.

However, a group of cheeses exists for which the development of desirable
micro-organisms on the surface and, in effect, the formation of a viscous,
red-orange (various shades) smear is necessary because it determines the
organoleptic properties of these cheeses. They are soft cheeses, which ripen
from the surface to interior, mainly through the participation of enzymes
secreted by micro-organisms present in the smear.

There is also a group of semi-hard cheeses which ripen through the
combined action of enzymes present inside the cheese and of enzymes
secreted by micro-organisms present in the smear.

Soft smear cheeses are characterized by a rich aromatic, piquant
flavour; semi-hard smear cheeses are milder, with a pleasant, sweetish
flavour.

The curing of cheeses without a smear considerably simplifies the
ripening process and therefore their global production is increasing

markedly. It is significant that the ripening process of non-smear cheeses may be automated, which favours the building of large cheesemaking plants. Ripening of cheeses with the participation of a smear is very laborious and therefore their production is considerably lower than that of internally-ripened cheese varieties. In the case of certain types of cheese, smear is not used intentionally in the ripening process but it should be mentioned that during the ripening of certain types of hard cheeses, the presence of a smear on the surface positively affects their flavour properties.[1-3]

Depending on the production technology and the changes during ripening, the influence of the smear on the organoleptic properties of cheeses may be differentiated as:

—significant, e.g. Tilsiter, Gruyère, Beaufort, Appenzeller;
—of major importance, e.g. Trappist, Munster, Brick, Blue;
—essential, e.g. Romadour, Lederkranz, Saint Paulin.

The most popular soft smear cheeses in Europe are Limburger and Romadour. In the United States, the semi-hard, smear cheese, Brick, is very common. In the Soviet Union, many types of smear cheeses are produced; their organoleptic properties are similar to those of Backstein, a cheese of German origin.

Due to their short ripening period, relatively easy digestibility and high flavour properties, soft and semi-hard smear cheeses deserve attention.

2. FACTORS AFFECTING THE RIPENING PROCESS IN SMEAR CHEESES

A number of factors have an important influence on the more rapid (compared with other types of cheese) ripening process in smear cheeses and on the more intense flavour properties, namely:

—water content;
—size;
—manner of curing;
—development of desirable micro-organisms on the surface of the cheese, i.e. microbiological composition of smear.

2.1 Water Content

The structure, consistency and the course of ripening of smear cheeses, which is the result of the development of a bacterial microflora on a surface, are affected, to a large extent, by the water content of the cheese.

During the manufacture of soft smear cheeses, cutting of the rennet coagulum may be delayed and consequently, the resulting firm curd retains whey well, i.e. has poor syneresis properties. Furthermore, the curd is cut into large particles which also reduces exudation of whey. As a consequence, there is a lot of whey, and as a result, of lactose, in the fresh cheese. The high lactose content favours the development of an acidifying microflora and the accumulation of high concentrations of lactic acid.

The pH of Brick cheese after manufacture is 5–5·2;[4] acidity increases further during the early stages of ripening, reaching a maximum of about pH 5 on the third day after production.[5] The acidity of Limburger cheese is higher and its pH reaches values much lower than 5.[6,7]

The correct water content, which ensures obtaining a product of high quality, is dependent on fat content. For example, in Romadour cheeses with fat contents of 20, 30, 40, 45 and 50% in dry matter (FDM), the water content should be 60·8, 57·8, 53·8, 51·6 and 49·2%, respectively, and in Limburger cheeses with 20 and 40% FDM, it should be 58·8 and 51·7%, respectively. Cheeses with incorrect water contents have an irregular consistency and an atypical, often unclean odour.

The high acidity and high salt level in the surface layer of these cheeses are inhibitory factors to the development of many micro-organisms. The ripening process is inhibited initially and may commence only after neutralization of part of the lactic acid to a level at which the growth of bacteria and the activity of enzymes become possible.

2.2 Size of Cheese

Micro-organisms that develop on the surface of smear cheeses synthesize much more active proteolytic and lipolytic enzymes than bacteria present inside the cheese. These enzymes penetrate the body of the cheese and participate in the ripening process.

Simultaneously, as a result of vital processes of smear micro-organisms, many alkaline products are formed which also diffuse into the cheese, reducing the acidity of the cheese mass and creating conditions favourable for the development of other micro-organisms on the surface of the cheese and also activating enzymatic processes within the cheese.

The influence of the smear on flavour development in the cheese is, therefore, affected by the size of cheese—the bigger the cheese, the smaller is the effect of the smear enzymes. Due to this fact, smear cheeses are of small dimensions in order to ensure a high surface:volume ratio, and as a result a short distance for the penetration of enzymes and metabolic products of smear micro-organisms.

2.3 Curing of Cheeses During Ripening

The method of curing smear cheeses differs from that for other types of cheese. The curing procedure involves the creation of conditions favourable for the optimal development of desirable micro-organisms on the surface of the cheese. The resultant viscous, red-orange smear has a decisive effect upon the course of ripening and on the organoleptic properties of the cheese. The colour of smear is a result of the development of micro-organisms, which form coloured colonies during growth.

Smear cheeses are ripened in rooms with a relative humidity above 95%, although certain types of smear cheese are maintained in a ripening room with a lower humidity for a short period to permit strengthening of the rind. The temperature of ripening is dependent on the type of cheese; for example, for Limburger cheese it is 15–20°C and for Trappist 12–13°C. During curing, the cheeses are inverted frequently and the surfaces massaged with a 2–3% NaCl solution.

On the cheeses after salting and in ripening rooms, on the walls and equipment, there are micro-organisms which may develop on the surfaces of cheeses under favourable conditions. After a few days, a pudding-like coloured bloom appears on the surface of the cheeses and during further ripening it changes colour to red-orange. Smear appears non-uniformly; coloured spots should be uniformly distributed over the whole surface of the cheese and smear should be rubbed into all irregularities on the cheese surface. In order to accelerate the development of smear, a pure culture of the desirable bacteria or 'good' smear collected from ripened cheeses, may be added to the salt solution used to massage the cheese surface.

The time of appearance of the smear and intensity of its development should be noted and followed. Weak or excessive development of smear has a negative effect on cheese quality. If the smear has a whitish colour it means that the cheese has been oversalted and when the smear dries too quickly it indicates that the cheese is under-salted. During incorrect curing, the layer of smear may become too thick which often causes a change of its colour, and simultaneously, beneath the layer of smear, under the anaerobic conditions, putrefaction of the cheese rind may occur. Absence of smear on the surface of cheeses may cause development of undesirable micro-organisms, especially of moulds.

The duration of ripening of smear cheeses depends on the desired intensity of the cheese flavour. Certain cheeses, e.g. Limburger or Brick, are freed of smear after 2–3 weeks and after coating with protective layers, they are transferred to a ripening room at a lower temperature—about 10°C. For example, the ripening period for Limburger, Munster and Brick is 6–8 weeks and for Romadour is 3–4 weeks.

2.4 Microbiological Composition of the Smear

On the basis of studies conducted to date, it is very difficult to answer unequivocally the question: what is the microbiological composition of the smear?

First of all, the micro-organisms found on the surface of cheese may be those which appear in a particular dairy plant. However, the most important factors affecting the composition of the smear microflora are:

—composition of the microflora in the brine and in rooms in which the cheeses are ripened;
—water activity, acidity and salt content in the surface layer of the cheese;
—humidity and temperature in the ripening room;
—rate of growth of the particular groups of micro-organisms;
—symbiosis and anabiosis between the micro-organisms;
—the regularity with which curing is conducted in a particular factory.

During the initial period of ripening, micro-organisms may develop on the surface of the cheese which tolerate the high acidity of the cheese as well as the high salt content in the surface layer of the cheese at that time.

In 1899, Laxa[8] isolated yeasts, lactic acid bacteria, yellow pigment-producing rods and the mould, *Oospora lactis* (now called *Geotrichum candidum*) from Backstein-type cheese. He expressed the opinion that growth of *Geotrichum candidum* on the surface of cheese lowers its acidity, creating favourable conditions for the development of other micro-organisms and that the characteristic odour and flavour of these cheeses is a result of symbiosis between all micro-organisms in the smear.

Kelly[9] examined microbiological changes in smear during the ripening of Limburger cheese in 14 plants. He stated that during the initial period of ripening, yeasts develop on the surface of the cheese, reaching maximal numbers in 4–5 days. From the 10th to 18th day of ripening, the number of yeasts decreased. From the 6th day of ripening, intensive growth of *Bacterium linens* (now *Brevibacterium linens*) was observed. The other micro-organisms, including *Geotrichum candidum*, were sporadically present. He observed that the colour of the smear in various plants may range from red-brownish to orange. The rate of cheese ripening was dependent on the water content, the method of salting and the temperature of ripening.

In further studies, Kelly and Marquardt[6] confirmed that the first micro-organisms which develop on the surface of Limburger cheeses are yeasts and sporadically, small numbers of *Geotrichum candidum*. When the pH of the cheese surface is increased to 5·85 due to the growth of yeasts, the growth of *B. linens*, which also tolerates high NaCl concentrations, is possible (Table I).

Similar results were obtained by Macy and Erekson[10] in their studies on microbiological changes on the surface of Roquefort, Port du Salut, Tilsiter and Limburger, and by Morris *et al.*[11] who examined Minnesota Blue cheese. However, they[10,11] stated that the micro-organisms which developed successively on the surface of cheese following yeasts included not only *Brevibacterium linens* but also micrococci.

Yale[12] isolated 243 bacterial cultures from the surfaces of various smear cheeses. He stated that the dominant micro-organisms in smear were Gram-positive bacteria followed by *Brevibacterium linens*. The quality of

TABLE I

Changes in the microflora of surface smear (from Kelly and Marquardt[6]) (reproduced by permission of the *Journal of Dairy Science*)

Description of cheese	Age (days)	Micro-organisms in surface smear
	1	A few rods evenly scattered
White slime	2	A few yeasts
	3	Few rods, yeasts well distributed
	4	Yeasts; some rods, increasing
	6	Yeasts in masses, fewer rods
Gassy cheese	7	Yeasts more numerous, fewer rods
Good red colour	8	Yeasts same, rods in masses
Gassy cheese	10	Yeasts fewer, rods fewer, *Geotrichum* present
	11	Yeasts few, rods in masses, a few *Geotrichum*
	12	Yeasts fewer and smaller, rods in masses
Ready for storage	13	Yeasts in masses; small, rods in masses
	4 weeks	Yeasts small, rods in masses
	5 weeks	No yeasts, rods in masses
	6 weeks	Yeasts small and numerous, rods in masses
	7 weeks	Yeasts small and few, rods in masses
Ready for market	8 weeks	Yeasts small and few, rods in masses

experimental Limburger cheeses was lower when only *B. linens* was present on the surface than that of commercial cheeses from dairy plants. Similarly, Hartley and Jezeski[13] stated that *B. linens* was not always the dominant micro-organism in smear and its numbers depended on pH and the temperature of cheese ripening. From Blue cheese smear, they isolated 167 pure cultures, 3 of which were classified as *Micrococci*, 41 as *Bacterium erythrogenes* (now *Brevibacterium erythrogenes*) and 8 as *B. linens*. At ripening temperatures of 46–49°F (7·7–9·4°C), *B. erythrogenes* developed intensively on the surface of the cheeses, while at 55–58°F (12·7–14·4°C), *B. linens* predominated.

By controlling the intensity of smear development on the surface of cheeses, it is possible to influence their flavour properties. Langhus *et al.*,[5] when studying the microflora of Brick cheeses, observed that 1–2 days after salting, yeasts began to develop and on the cheese surface they grew intensively until the 3rd–4th day; micrococci then grew to very high numbers and *B. linens* to a lesser extent. Lubert and Frazier[14] isolated 136 yeast cultures and 329 micrococcal cultures from the smear of Brick cheeses. In all cheeses examined, *Micrococcus varians* was present in high numbers followed by *M. caseolyticus* and *M. freudenreichii*. According to the authors, these micrococci play a decisive role in developing the typical flavour of Brick cheese because cheeses containing only *B. linens* in smear did not develop a flavour typical of this cheese.

Mulder *et al.*[15] stated that 90% of the microflora of Limburger cheese was constituted of coryneform bacteria. The dominant group was grey-white bacteria; orange-coloured bacteria constituted 9–24% and micrococci amounted to 3–6% of the total bacterial count (Table II). Accolas *et al.*[1] studied changes in the smear microflora of Gruyère and Beaufort cheeses. In the smear, yeasts, coryneforms (90–95% of the total count), micrococci and Gram-negative Bacilli were present. They also observed the

TABLE II

Occurrence of coryneform bacteria on Limburger cheese surfaces (from Mulder *et al.*[15]) (reproduced by permission of the *Journal of Applied Bacteriology*)

Cheese	Total plate count/g of rind	Coryneform bacteria (%)			Micrococci (%)	Other types (%)
		Orange	Yellow	Grey-white		
Limburger I	1·9 × 10^{10}	9	2	80	3	6
Limburger II	2·6 × 10^{10}	24	3	65	6	2

TABLE III

Total counts and groups of micro-organisms in the surface layer of Limburger cheese during ripening. (from El-Erian[16]) (reproduced by permission of the Redactiecommissie of *Mededelingen Landbouwhogeschool*)

Age of cheese[a]	Total count per gram of scraped surface material	Number of strains examined	Type of organism, as % of the total count						
			Lactic acid bacteria	Yeast	Arthrobacter	B. linens	Other coryneforms	Sarcina	Moulds
Fresh cheese	4.2×10^7	66	100.0	—	—	—	—	—	—
After salting	2.41×10^7	72	19.4	20.8	30.6	15.3	11.1	2.8	—
5 days	1.48×10^8	84	—	100.0	—	—	—	—	—
9 days	4.41×10^8	76	—	52.6	47.4	—	—	—	—
14 days	1.81×10^8	70	—	—	91.4	8.6	—	—	—
20 days	4.70×10^9	68	—	—	80.9	19.1	—	—	—
27 days	4.60×10^9	80	—	—	73.8	26.2	—	—	—
35 days	3.17×10^9	75	—	—	62.7	37.3	—	—	—

[a] The first sample was taken just before salting, the second after salting the cheese in brine overnight.

presence of moulds in the smear of cheeses but the massaging of cheeses does not permit their development.

El-Erian[16] isolated 251 bacterial studies from Limburger cheese and classified them into the *Arthrobacter* group, *Brevibacterium linens* and other coryneforms. On the basis of detailed studies on changes in surface microflora during the ripening of Limburger cheese (Table III), he concluded that fresh cheese contained only lactic bacteria. After salting, the composition of surface microflora of the cheese was the same as that of the brine. After 5 days of ripening, only yeasts were present on the surface of the cheeses but from the 9th day, the number of yeasts decreased while the Arthrobacter-type bacteria became dominant. *Brevibacterium linens* was not observed until as late as the 14th day of ripening but its numbers then

TABLE IV

Effect of light on pigmentation of coryneform bacteria from different cheeses (from Mulder *et al.*[15]) (reproduced by permission of the *Journal of Applied Bacteriology*)

Organism	Source	No. of strains examined	Colour of colonies grown in the	
			Dark	Light
Coryneform bacteria from cheese; grey-white strains	Ed[a], Go, Lei, Limb, Mesh	11	Grey-white	Grey-white; growth reduction in 6 strains
	Go, Mesh	6	Grey-white	Light yellow; growth reduction in 2 strains
	Go, Limb, Mesh	6	Grey-white with pink shade	Grey-white with pink shade; growth reduction in 4 strains
B. linens, cultures 3, 5, 6, 7, 8 and 9	Culture collections	6	Orange	Orange
B. linens, cultures 1 and 2		2	Light cream-yellow	Orange
Orange pigmented strains	Ed, Go, Ke, Limb, Mam, Mesh, Pe, Rom, St.P	13	Orange	Orange
	Ed, Go, He, Ho, Mam, Marv, Mesh, Mu, Rom, St.P, Vach	16	White	Orange; growth reduction in 1 strain
	Go, Ke	3	Light cream-yellow	Orange

[a] Type of cheese: Ed, Edam; Go, Gouda; He, Hervse; Ho, Hohenheim; Ke, Kernhemmer; Lei, Leidse kanter; Limb, Limburger; Mam, Mamirolle; Marv, Marville; Mesh, Meshanger; Mu, Munster; Pe, Pénitent; Rom, Romadour; St.P, St. Paulin; Vach, Vacherin Mont d'Or.

TABLE V

Influence of temperature and pH on the growth of yeasts from Limburger cheese (from Kelly and Marquardt[6]) (reproduced by permission of the *Journal of Dairy Science*)

Culture 65

pH	Incubation period (days)	18°C	25°C	30°C	37°C	45°C
3·5	1	—	—	—	—	—
	2	+	+	—	—	—
	3	++	++	—	—	—
	7	++	++	—	—	—
4·5	1	—	—	—	—	—
	2	++	++	—	—	—
	3	++	++	—	—	—
	7	++	++	—	—	—
5·5	1	—	—	—	—	—
	2	++	+++	—	—	—
	3	++	+++	—	—	—
	7	+	+++	++	—	—

Culture 67

pH	Incubation period (days)	18°C	25°C	30°C	37°C	45°C
3·5	1	—	—	—	—	—
	2	—	—	—	—	—
	3	—	—	—	—	—
	7	+	+	—	—	—
4·5	1	—	—	—	—	—
	2	—	—	—	—	—
	3	—	++	—	—	—
	7	++	++	—	—	—
5·5	1	—	—	—	—	—
	2	—	+	—	—	—
	3	++	++	—	—	—
	7	++	++	++	—	—

Table (a)

pH	Strain					
6·5	1	–	–	–	–	–
	2	–	–	–	+	–
	3	–	–	–	++	++
	7	–	–	++	++	++
7·5	1	–	–	–	–	–
	2	–	–	–	+	–
	3	–	–	–	++	++
	7	–	–	++	++	++
8·5	1	–	–	–	–	–
	2	–	–	–	–	–
	3	–	–	+	+	+
	7	–	–	–	–	–
9·5	1	–	–	–	–	–
	2	–	–	–	–	–
	3	–	–	–	–	–
	7	–	–	–	–	–

Table (b)

pH	Strain					
6·5	1	–	–	–	+	–
	2	–	–	+++	+++	+++
	3	–	–	+++	+++	+++
	7	–	–	+++	+++	+++
7·5	1	–	–	–	+	–
	2	–	–	+++	+++	+++
	3	–	–	+++	+++	+++
	7	–	–	+++	+++	+++
8·5	1	–	–	–	–	–
	2	–	–	+	+	+
	3	–	–	++	++	++
	7	–	–	+	+	+
9·5	1	–	–	–	–	–
	2	–	–	–	–	–
	3	–	–	–	–	–
	7	–	–	–	–	–

– No growth; + first sign of growth; ++ good growth; +++ heavy growth.

increased quickly. He did not mention the presence of moulds on the surface.

The colour of smear on the surface of cheeses is dependent on its microbiological composition. The curing procedure, thickness of the smear layer and exposure to light influence the colour of the smear. The influence of light on pigment synthesis by bacterial strains isolated from many types of cheese is summarized in Table IV.

On the basis of studies conducted to date, one fact appears certain, i.e. that yeasts are the first micro-organisms which develop on the surface of smear cheeses. Subsequently, other micro-organisms, and especially coryneforms of the *Arthrobacter* and *Brevibacterium linens* types, may develop on the surface. Therefore, the composition of the smear microflora is not known exactly. Furthermore, it is observed that the interest of research workers in smear cheeses is rather low at present which is a reflection of the low level of interest in the production of these cheeses.

3. SIGNIFICANCE OF MICRO-ORGANISMS PRESENT IN SMEAR

3.1 Yeasts

Little is known about the role of yeasts in the process of cheese ripening. Previously it was considered that it involved only the lowering of the acidity of the cheese surface which makes the development of other micro-organisms, which tolerate a high salt concentration, possible.

Kelly and Marquardt[6] stated that yeasts isolated from the surface of Limburger cheese (two groups, e.g. cultures 65 and 67 which differed in their growth patterns in a liquid medium) may grow at pH 3·5–8·5 in the presence of 18–20% salt (Table V). Similar results were obtained by Iya and Frazier[17] who stated that Mycoderma yeasts isolated from the surface of Brick cheeses could grow at pH 3–8, in the presence of 15% NaCl. They also observed that yeasts synthesize substances that stimulate the growth of *B. linens.*

Purko et al.[18] confirmed the findings of Burkholder et al.[19] who reported that *B. linens*, isolated from Limburger cheese, requires pantothenic acid for growth. A similar effect on the growth of *B. linens* is exerted by the presence of p-aminobenzoic acid in the medium, and the presence of both these acids is especially favourable (Fig. 1). Purko et al.[20] also showed that several strains of yeasts isolated from Limburger cheese synthesize

TABLE VI
Synthesis of vitamins by yeasts (from Purko *et al.*[20]) (reproduced by permission of the *Journal of Dairy Science*)

Yeast culture	Vitamins present (μg/ml)			
	Pantothenate	Niacin	Riboflavin	Biotin
A	12	20	41	0
B	1	10	19	0
C	15	15	49	0
D	15	45	200	0
E	8	15	52	0
F	9	20	53	0
G	15	19	49	0
H	21	19	47	0
I	20	19	43	0
J	27	10	6	0
K	1	20	32	0
L	26	181	47	0
M	3	18	27	0
N	170	104	33	3
O	35	20	55	0
P	49	17	18	2
Q	15	43	16	0
R	15	13	20	0
S	14	40	12	0
T	13	33	25	0
U	44	36	47	0
V	54	40	53	0
W	10	20	50	0
X	190	104	32	4
Y	10	60	22	0
Z	14	16	20	0
AA	2	57	5	0
AB	5	17	16	0
AC	10	40	13	0

considerable amounts of pantothenic acid, niacin and riboflavin (Table VI). Yeasts isolated from the smear of Brick cheese (two groups differing in proteolytic and lipolytic activities) also synthesize substances that stimulate the growth of *Micrococcus caseolyticus*, *M. freudenreichii* and *M. varians*[14] (Table VII).

However, yeasts also synthesize proteolytic enzymes. The endoproteinases of *Debaryomyces*, and especially of *Trichosporon* yeasts, isolated from the smear of Trappist cheese, hydrolyse casein at pH 5–7,

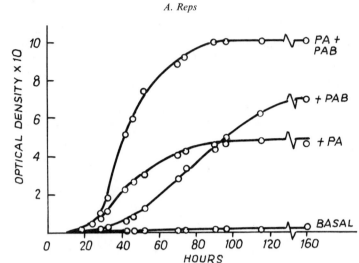

Fig. 1. Growth of *B. linens* with *p*-aminobenzoic acid (PAB) or pantothenic acid (PA) (from Purko *et al.*[18]) (Reproduced by permission of the *Journal of Dairy Science.*)

optimum 5·8,[21] and also degrade polypeptides released from casein by *B. linens* enzymes.[22] According to Szumski and Cone,[21] the fact that during the rapid decrease of yeast numbers on the surface of cheese, the pH of the outer layer is near to the optimum for the activity of the endopeptidases of *Debaryomyces* and *Trichosporon* yeasts, indicates that these yeasts participate in the ripening process. This is confirmed by the fact that the content of free amino acids in the surface layer of Trappist cheese (6·25 mm)

TABLE VII

Effect of autolysates of two film yeast on the growth of micrococci in skim-milk at room temperature (from Lubert and Frazier[14]) (reproduced by permission of the *Journal of Dairy Science*)

Micrococcus	Numbers of micrococci per ml ($\times 1000$)					
	Control		B6 autolyzate		B7 autolyzate	
	0 h	*48 h*	*0 h*	*48 h*	*0 h*	*48 h*
M. caseolyticus 11	280	640 000	190	1 400 000	330	1 300 000
M. caseolyticus 32	6 900	1 100 000	6 700	2 200 000	9 600	1 700 000
M. freudenhreichii 43	10 000	3 800 000	17 000	7 800 000	14 000	6 400 000
M. varians 22	220	490 000	220	1 200 000	190	800 000

TABLE VIII

Average content of free amino acids formed in the surface layer of Trappist cheese during three ripening studies (modified from Ades and Cone[23]) (reproduced by permission of the *Journal of Dairy Science*)

	0 days		7 days		14 days		21 days		28 days		35 days	
	1[a]	2[b]	1	2	1	2	1	2	1	2	1	2
	(μmoles/10 g cheese)											
Lysine	4·29	7·49	9·64	9·42	18·55	13·24	25·30	14·32	24·81	17·28	32·88	25·67
Histidine	0·71	1·40	1·71	1·94	2·20	1·63	2·06	1·44	2·78	1·67	4·82	1·76
Arginine	0·64	2·11	2·15	1·63	11·90	1·60	1·58	1·54	1·79	1·55	2·66	1·25
Aspartic acid	1·48	3·34	3·00	2·53	3·88	3·55	5·17	4·12	6·22	5·13	9·76	5·93
Threonine	Trace	2·00	Trace	Trace	1·03	0·77	1·13	1·03	2·25	1·20	3·74	1·76
Serine	1·26	4·15	5·89	3·95	5·78	3·69	5·25	4·24	7·36	4·92	13·63	6·45
Glutamic acid	3·98	7·66	22·67	15·40	33·25	25·53	42·16	30·30	44·65	29·68	53·30	29·22
Proline	2·52	2·91	20·82	20·98	13·82	16·36	10·45	8·38	10·06	11·71	16·39	12·89
Glycine	0·41	2·52	1·80	1·51	4·13	3·48	5·62	3·72	5·76	3·80	7·88	4·16
Alanine	1·79	6·42	9·34	5·07	12·21	6·59	12·89	8·26	16·18	10·74	22·89	15·43
Cysteine	0·11	0·22	0·43	0·23	0·79	0·30	0·59	0·63	0·92	0·91	1·02	0·91
Valine	1·07	3·50	5·06	3·96	11·85	6·46	16·21	7·81	17·50	9·66	24·82	18·48
Methionine	0·07	0·78	0·65	0·59	1·76	1·38	1·81	1·29	1·82	1·25	2·16	1·73
Isoleucine	0·49	2·53	1·41	1·28	4·30	2·47	5·92	3·07	5·18	3·76	9·89	6·12
Leucine	2·11	5·42	11·28	9·45	21·14	12·70	24·53	15·52	21·19	18·60	37·41	24·51
Tyrosine	0·97	1·27	1·67	2·74	2·72	3·16	2·99	2·42	2·79	2·25	3·18	2·72
Phenylalanine	1·61	3·17	5·56	4·82	10·03	8·80	12·38	8·52	17·38	11·61	16·37	12·08
Total	23·51	56·89	103·08	85·55	159·34	111·71	176·04	116·61	188·64	135·72	262·80	171·07

[a] Control cheeses with a mixed smear microflora.
[b] Pure cultured cheeses containing a *B. linens* on the surface.

was considerably higher when surface yeasts and *B. linens* spp. were present than in cheese on which only *B. linens* was found[23] (Table VIII).

The data presented show that the development of yeasts on the surface of cheese is indispensable for the growth of other smear-forming micro-organisms and consequently affects the cheese ripening process.

3.2 Moulds

The presence of moulds on the surface of smear cheeses seems to be accidental and the correct execution of cheese curing does not permit the development of moulds on the surface of cheese. The most common mould on the surface of smear cheeses is *Geotrichum candidum* at 15–25°C and it is capable of growth at up to 10% NaCl and at high/medium acidity, optimum about pH 4.[24]

Geotrichum candidum synthesizes lipolytic enzymes[24-26] with the activity dependent on strain,[27] acidity and composition of the medium.[28] Synthesis of lipolytic enzymes by *G. candidum* depends on the presence of oxygen; the quantity of water-insoluble fatty acids released from the fat of cream during incubation of *G. candidum* was proportional to the surface area of the cream.[29] The optimum pH for the lipolytic enzymes of *G. candidum* is about 6.[30]

Pulss[31] believed that the proteolytic enzymes of *G. candidum* do not participate in the ripening process, the principal influence of this organism on ripening being in lowering of acidity of the cheese surface. However, the studies of Dłużewski and Bruderer[32] demonstrated that the presence of these moulds on the surface of cheeses affects the increase in the level of water-soluble nitrogenous compounds (Table IX).

That the proteinases of *G. candidum* are capable of hydrolysing α- and β-caseins was confirmed by Chen and Ledford[33] who studied the proteolytic

TABLE IX
Hydrolysis of protein in cheese ripened with and without *Geotrichum candidum* (from Dłużewski and Bruderer[32]) (reproduced by permission of the *Bull. Polon. Acad. Sci.*)

Samples	Soluble nitrogen	Amino nitrogen
	as % of total nitrogen	
Without *G. candidum*	2·4	0·77
With *G. candidum*	8·4	1·93

TABLE X
Proteolytic activity of enzymes from *Geotrichum candidum* (from Gueguen and Lenoir[34]) (reproduced by permission of *Le Lait*)

Strain	Extracellular activity (µg tyrosine/ml/h)	Intracellular activity (mg tyrosine/g/h)
D.49	125	29
G.25	150	28
G.36	70	17
G.59	145	37
G.116	255	20
G.117	95	22
G.410	145	23
G.618	60	17
633	615	40
635	530	39
637	235	32
638	165	19
G.802	215	36
G.812	135	32
G.813	135	41
G.816	205	37
G.817	160	38
G.819	615	69
G.820	205	46
G.821	115	26
G.822	160	23
G.823	110	38
G.824	170	24
G.825	90	32
G.826	95	—
G.827	195	28
G.830	615	55
G.832	215	30

activity of the enzymes from a culture of this mould isolated from the surface of Limburger cheese. Gueguen and Lenoir[34,35] studied the proteolytic activity of many strains of *G. candidum* isolated from surface of many types of cheese. The optimum pH for casein hydrolysis was 5·5–6·0. The proteolytic activities of individual strains were very different; especially large differences between strains were observed during studies on the proteolytic activities of extracellular enzymes (Table X). The authors suggest that the proteolytic activity of particular strains may be a criterion of their suitability for cheesemaking.

Greenberg and Ledford,[36] who examined the proteolytic activity of the intracellular enzymes of strains of G. candidum isolated from the smear of Limburger cheese and from raw milk, stated that these enzymes are capable of deaminating glutamic and aspartic acids; the resulting ammonia decreases the acidity of the medium.

The data presented demonstrate that G. candidum cannot be classified as a component of the microflora of smear cheeses. It may, however, develop on the surface of cheeses simultaneously with yeasts and its presence may have an influence on the cheese ripening process.

3.3 Micrococci

The majority of the authors who have studied the microbiological composition of smear observed the presence of micrococci. Micrococci have been found on the surface and in the interior of many types of cheese but to date, most of the studies have concerned Cheddar cheese[37] and mould-type cheeses.[38]

The addition of starter containing micrococci to a cheese milk affects positively the organoleptic properties of Cheddar cheese.[39] However, it is not the quantity but the type of micrococci that is of practical significance since not all micrococci influence the organoleptic properties of cheese.[40] Micrococci isolated from Cheddar cheese possess considerable lipolytic and proteolytic activities.[41,42] Moreno and Kosikowski[43,44] studied the activity of enzymes from M. freudenreichii, M. caseolyticus and M. candidus on β-casein. Maximum proteolytic activity was found at pH 5·5 and 22°C. They released high amounts of methionine which is the precursor of flavouring substances, and therefore they may contribute to the formation of typical Cheddar cheese flavour.

Lubert and Frazier[14] suggest that certain strains of M. freudenreichii, M. caseolyticus and M. varians present in the smear of Brick cheese are decisive factors in the formation of the typical flavour of this cheese (Table XI). Cheeses, inoculated only with Brevibacterium linens or B. linens and yeasts did not possess the characteristic flavour of Brick cheese. Best results were obtained when the surface of Brick cheese was inoculated with yeasts and a mixture of six strains of micrococci representing the three above species (Table XII).

The results presented show that micrococci may be present in the smear. However, their influence on the ripening process in smear cheeses,

TABLE XI

Effect of adding various micrococci species plus a pair of film yeasts to the surface on the flavour of Brick cheese (from Lubert and Frazier[14]) (reproduced by permission of the *Journal of Dairy Science*)

Micrococcus added[a]	Flavour grade[b]	Total grade	Brick cheese flavour	Description of flavour
Mc 11	4·0	3·7	—	salty, acid, fermented
Mc 32	4·0	3·7	—	salty, sl. bitter, sl. acid, fermented
Control[c]	4·0	3·7	—	salty, acid, fermented
Mc 11	3·0	3·3	—	salty, bitter, acid, yeasty, pleasant
Control	2·3	2·0	—	yeasty, pleasant
Mc 11	3·8	4·0	+	salty, sl. acid, yeasty, sl. fermented
Mc 32	3·2	3·3	+	salty, sl. acid, fermented, glutamic
Mc 58	3·8	3·8	+ +	salty, bitter, acid, glutamic
Mf 15	3·2	3·5	—	salty, sl. acid, yeasty, sl. fermented
Mf 43	3·2	3·3	+ + +	salty, sl. acid, sl. unclean, yeasty
Mv 22	3·8	3·8	+	salty, bitter, sl. acid, yeasty, fermented
Control	3·2	3·5	—	salty, acid, sl. unclean, fermented
Mc 11	2·7	2·8	+ +	salty, sl. acid, sl. yeasty, pleasant
Mc 32	2·6	2·6	+	salty, sl. bitter, sl. yeasty, acetic
Mc 58	2·8	3·8	—	salty, sl. acid, sl. yeasty, sl. unclean
Mf 15	3·0	3·1	—	salty, sl. acid, yeasty, acetic
Mf 43	2·9	2·9	—	salty, sl. acid, yeasty, sl. unclean, fruity
Mv 22	2·7	2·7	—	salty, sl. acid, yeasty, acetic
Control	3·6	3·7	—	salty, acid, yeasty, Limburger, acetic

[a] Cheese previously inoculated with a saline suspension containing both film yeasts B6 and B7.
[b] 1, excellent; 2, desirable; 3, satisfactory; 4, objectionable; 5, very objectionable; 6, not saleable as original cheese.
[c] Control without added micrococci.
Mc = *Micrococcus caseolyticus*; Mf = *Micrococcus freudenreichii*; Mv = *Micrococcus varians*.

especially on the development of their characteristic flavour, requires further study.

3.4 Coryneforms

Studies to date have revealed that the most numerous micro-organisms in smear are coryneform bacteria[1,15,45] from the genus *Arthrobacter* in which (a matter of discussion) *Brevibacterium* spp. are included.[46]

TABLE XII

Effect of adding a mixture of six micrococci species and a pair of film yeasts together to the surface on flavour of Brick cheese (from Lubert and Frazier[14]) (reproduced by permission of the *Journal of Dairy Science*)

	Flavour grade[a]	Total grade	Brick cheese flavour	Description of flavour
Test	4·0	4·0	+	salty, acid, fermented, sl. Limburger
Control[b]	3·2	3·5	—	salty, acid, sl. unclean, yeasty
Test	2·8	3·8	+	salty, acid, yeasty, sl. fermented, sl. Cheddar
Control	3·6	3·7	—	salty, acid, yeasty, Limburger, acetic

[a] See Table XI for numerical grading.
[b] Control without added micrococci.

3.4.1 *Arthrobacter*

Mulder *et al.*[15] isolated 22 strains of *Arthrobacter* from the surface of many types of cheese; they grew, forming grey-white colonies. In the presence of NaCl, they could develop at pH 5·5, i.e. considerably earlier than in the case of *B. linens* (Table XIII).

Arthrobacter organisms appear in high numbers in smear on the surface of Limburger cheese. El-Erian[16] isolated 173 strains of *Arthrobacter* from the smear of this cheese and classified then into 4 groups according to the colour of the colonies formed during growth. He stated that they may grow at high concentrations of salt (Table XIV).

The presence of such high numbers of *Arthrobacter* spp., which are capable of casein hydrolysis,[15,16,38] in smear undoubtedly has an influence on the cheese ripening process. Nevertheless, this problem requires further study.

3.4.2 *Brevibacterium*

The properties of *Brevibacterium linens* are well known.[47] This bacterium appears in high numbers in the smear on cheese surfaces. Mulder *et al.*[15] stated that 40% of cultures isolated from the surfaces of various types of cheese show resemblance to *B. linens*. El-Erian[16] isolated 52 strains from the smear of Limburger cheese and included them in the *B. linens* group.

B. linens affects decisively the colour of smear, giving it an orange or orange-brown colour. Albert *et al.*[48] noticed that the colour of *B. linens* colonies during growth depends on the composition of the medium, age

TABLE XIII

Influence of temperature and pH on the growth of *Brevibacterium linens* (cultures 4 and 56a) (from Kelly and Marquardt[6]) (reproduced by permission of the Redactiecommissie of *Mededelingen Landbouwhogeschool*)

pH	Incubation period (days)	Temperature				
		18°C	25°C	30°C	37°C	45°C
3·5	2	−	−	−	−	−
	3	−	−	−	−	−
4·5	2	−	−	−	−	−
	3	−	−	−	−	−
5·5	2	−	−	−	−	−
	3	−	−	−	−	−
5·85	2		+			
	3		+			
6·0	2		+			
	3		+			
6·5	2	+	+	+	−	−
	3	+ +	+ +	+ +	−	−
7·5	2	+	+	+	−	−
	3	+ +	+ +	+	−	−
8·5	2	+	+	+	−	−
	3	+ +	+ +	+	−	−
9·5	2	+	+	+	−	−
	3	+ +	+ +	+	−	−

− No growth; + poor growth; + + good growth.

of the culture and the presence of oxygen. Mulder *et al.*[15] (Table IV), El-Erian[16] and Crombach[45] observed that some of the strains of *B. linens* examined were capable of synthesizing orange pigment only in the presence of light. El-Erian[16] reported that among 52 strains isolated from the smear of Limburger cheese, 24 strains of *B. linens* did not synthesize orange pigment in darkness. In further studies, EL-Erian and El-Gamal[49] found that among 150 strains of *B. linens* examined, 72 synthesized orange pigment only in the presence of light.

TABLE XIV

Effect of salt on the growth of *Arthrobacter* isolated from cheese (from El-Erian[16]) (reproduced by permission of the *Journal of Applied Bacteriology*)

Colour of colonies	Number of tested strains	Added NaCl, %							
		0	2	4	6	9	12	16	20
		Number of strains growing							
Cream	62	62	62	62	62	62	22	—	—
Grey-white	42	42	42	42	42	42	8	—	—
Red	36	36	36	36	36	36	12	—	—
Greenish-yellow	33	33	33	33	33	33	33	—	—

In spite of the fact that *B. linens* tolerates high NaCl concentrations (Table XV), it may develop on the surface of cheese only when the pH of the cheese is $\geqslant 5.85$[6] (Table XIII).

During growth, *B. linens* synthesizes highly active proteolytic enzymes; it also synthesizes lipases.[50-52] Thomasow[53] observed two maxima in the synthesis of proteolytic enzymes during the growth of *B. linens*. This was

TABLE XV

Effect of salt on the growth of coryneform bacteria from cheese (from Mulder *et al.*[15]) (reproduced by permission of the *Journal of Dairy Science*)

Organism	Growth[a]					
	0	3	5	8	12	15
	(Added salt, %)					
B. linens strain 7	+	+	+	±(+)	0(+)	0(±)
B. linens strain 6	+	+	+	+	0(+)	0
B. linens strain 1[b]	+	+	+	+	±	0
B. linens strain 2[b]	+	+	+	±(+)	0(+)	0(±)
B. linens strain 3	+	+	+	±(+)	±	0(±)
B. linens strain 5	+	+	+	+	0(±)	0(±)
Strain 251⎫ orange isolates	+	+	+	+	+	0(±)
Strain 252⎭ from cheese[b]	+	+	+	+	+	0(±)

[a] Growth was recorded after 7 days, but marks in brackets indicate growth after 31 days: 0, no growth; ±, slight growth; +, normal growth.
[b] Orange in the light only.

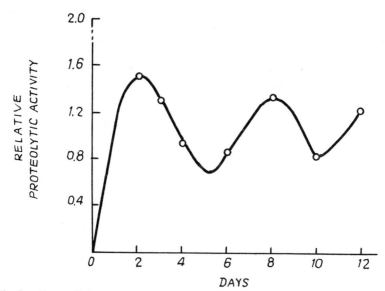

Fig. 2. Extracellular proteolytic activity during growth of *B. linens* (modified from Friedman *et al.*[54]) (Reproduced by permission of the *Journal of Dairy Science.*)

confirmed by the studies of Friedman *et al.*[54] who reported intense synthesis of intracellular enzymes up to the 2nd day and from the 6th to 8th day of growth (Fig. 2). The proteolytic activity of extracellular enzymes was many times higher than that of intracellular enzymes (Table XVI).

Tuckey and Sahasrabudhe[55] reported that the proteinases *B. linens* hydrolyse casein intensively, in contrast to yeasts and starter bacteria, and release high concentrations of amino acids. The presence of metal ions

TABLE XVI
Activity of proteinases from *Brevibacterium linens* (from Friedman *et al.*[54]) (reproduced by permission of the *Journal of Dairy Science*)

Enzyme preparation	12% TCA insoluble casein	12% TCA soluble	
		Polypeptides	Peptides, amino acids
	Δ mg/ml in 6 h		
Extracellular	3·50	1·99	0·44
Cell extract	0·80	0·07	0·03
Extracellular + cell extract	4·00	2·43	0·60

174 A. Reps

TABLE XVII
Amino acids liberated in sterile skim-milk shake cultures, incubated at 60°F (μg/ml) (from Tuckey and Sahasrabudhe[55]) (reproduced by permission of the *Journal of Dairy Science*)

Culture	B. linens 9174	Yeast culture	Starter culture	Starter and rennet extract	Starter and rennet + 2% NaCl
Age (days)	12	39	7	23	52
pH	8·2	7·5	4·45	4·6	4·47
Alanine	184	+	20	37	108
Aspartic acid	765	+	+	−	+
Glutamic acid	298	38	55	48	+
Glycine	344	+	−	−	−
Leucines	411	+	+	73	233
Methionine	285	−	−	+	119
Serine	94	50	−	−	+
Threonine	133	+	14	−	+
Tyrosine	1 500	−	+	+	+
Valine	475	+	+	39	68

+ present; − absent.

positively affects the activity of *B. linens* proteinases[56] (Table XVII). Foissy[57] and Sørhaug[58] observed significant differences in proteolytic activity as well as in the specificity of *B. linens* proteinases.

Tokita and Hosono,[59,60] when cultivating *B. linens*, found the presence of volatile sulphur compounds which determine the characteristic flavour of Limburger cheese and also volatile and non-volatile amines which at low concentrations affect positively the organoleptic properties of cheese.[61]

The above data indicate that the particular strains of *B. linens* or their mixtures present in the smear of cheeses, may participate, with various intensities, in the cheese ripening process.

4. INFLUENCE OF SMEAR ON THE PROCESS OF CHEESE RIPENING

Soft smear cheeses are characterized by rapid ripening and a high degree of proteolysis and lipolysis[16,62−65] which affect, in a decisive way, their consistency and flavour. Many research workers have stated that the development of smear on the surface of cheese has a major influence on the

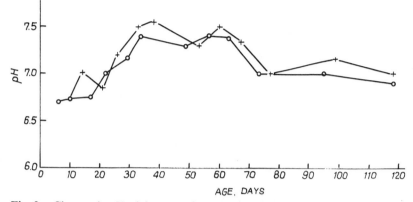

Fig. 3. Changes in pH of the smear from two lots of blue cheeses (from Morris *et al.*[11]) (Reproduced by permission of the *Journal of Dairy Science.*)

course of ripening, especially on the development of the typical rich aroma of these cheeses. The influence of smear on textural changes during ripening is also clearly visible, especially in the case of soft cheese. After cutting Romadur cheese, it may be seen that the consistency of the outer layer of the cheese, to a depth dependent on the duration of ripening, is softer than at the centre of the cheese.

The influence of the smear becomes especially apparent when changes in the concentration of particular components in different layers of cheese are analysed. As it may be seen from Fig. 3, the pH of the smear that develops on Blue cheese increases to 7·5 about the 38th day of ripening and then, from the 60th to the 75th day, decreases to 7 at which it remains during the rest of the ripening period. The pH of the smear is considerably higher than that of the surface and central layers of this cheese (Fig. 4).

Similarly, the pH of the smear of Limburger cheese increases to about 7·5 during the second week of ripening, and then remains at this level. As with Blue cheese, the pH of the smear is considerably higher than that of surface layer of the cheese (Fig. 5). The fact that the pH of the centre layer of smear cheeses is considerably lower than that of the surface layers points to the influence of smear on the cheese-ripening process and its progress from the surface to the interior, i.e. ripening occurs faster in the surface layer of Limburger cheese than at the centre, e.g. the content of free amino acids in the surface layer of the cheese is several times higher than that at the centre (Table XVIII). However, the same free amino acids were present in the surface and centre layers of the cheese.[55]

Ramanauskas,[66] who examined the ripening process in semi-hard smear

TABLE XVIII

Amino acids liberated during the ripening of Limburger cheese (mg/g of cheese) (from Tuckey and Sahasrabudhe [55]) (reproduced by permission of the *Journal of Dairy Science*)

Age (days)	1	11		18		32		46		80		101	
Portion	Whole	Rind	Int.	Rind	Int.	Rind	Int.	Rind	Int.	Rind	Int.	Rind	Int.
pH	4·95	5·25	4·90	5·65	5·0	5·95	5·00	6·2	5·45	7·0	—	7·2	—
Alanine	0·15	0·38	0·13	0·60	0·23	0·39	0·13	0·39	0·29	+	0·80	0·73	
Aspartic acid	+	+	Lost	+	+	+	+	0·32	+	0·80	+	+	
Glutamic acid	0·24	0·47	Lost	1·11	0·21	0·81	0·08	0·62	0·44	1·26	0·96	1·96	
Glycine	−	+	Lost	0·08	+	+	+	0·15	+	0·28	0·14	0·20	
Leucine + Isoleucine	0·19	0·35	0·32	1·39	0·43	1·38	0·50	1·38	1·05	+	2·47	2·42	
Serine	−	+	Lost	0·29	+	0·19	+	0·12	+	0·84	0·20	0·15	
Tyrosine	+	0·52	0·12	0·14	0·19	0·32	0·92	0·58	1·32	+	0·36	0·99	
Valine	0·23	0·28	0·23	0·26	+	0·25	0·16	0·31	0·30	+	0·40	0·71	

Rind—6·3 mm cut from outer surface.
Interior—centre portion.
+ present; − absent.

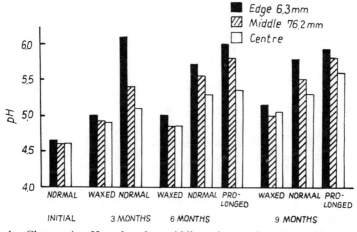

Fig. 4. Changes in pH at the edge, middle and central portions of blue cheeses development (from Morris *et al.*[11]). (Reproduced by permission of the *Journal of Dairy Science.*)

cheeses, also observed that smear effected a more intensive degradation of proteins in the surface layer which contained significantly higher concentrations of free amino acids and volatile fatty acids than the centre layer. The differences increased as the fat content of cheeses was increased and cheeses with a higher fat content had fuller flavour profile.

After 3 and 6 months of ripening, the outer layer of Blue cheeses, ripened

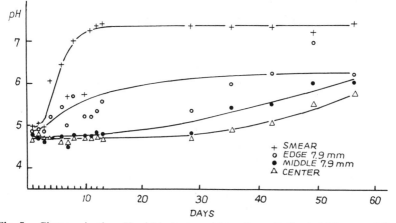

Fig. 5. Changes in the pH of Limburger cheese (from Kelly and Marquardt[6]). (Reproduced by permission of the *Journal of Dairy Science.*)

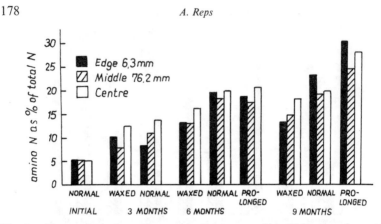

Fig. 6. Changes in amino nitrogen as a percentage of total N in the edge, middle and central portions of blue cheeses that had been waxed (no smear) or had undergone normal or prolonged smear development (from Morris *et al.*[11]) (Reproduced by permission of the *Journal of Dairy Science.*)

for 2 months with some smear, was softer than that of dry-rind cheeses.[11] It had a red-orange colour and a nutty-bitter flavour. No differences were reported between the cheeses in respect of their middle and central layers. The cheese ripened for 4 months with the development of smear had a considerably softer consistency after 6 months of ripening. The centre of cheese was red-orange as a result of the migration of pigment from the surface layer. The central layer was creamy, in contrast to white appearance to the remaining cheeses. This cheese had many organoleptic defects.

After 9 months of ripening, the best quality cheeses were those ripened for 2 months with the participation of smear. According to experts, the best cheeses, characterized by a full, rich aroma, may be obtained only when a smear is developed for 2 months on their surfaces.

In cheeses ripened with a smear, the pH of outer layer was considerably higher than that of the middle and central layers. In cheeses ripening without smear (waxed), the pH of all layers was approximately equal and considerably lower than that of cheeses with smear (Fig. 4). The volatile acidity of the outer layer of smear-ripened cheeses was considerably higher than that of waxed cheeses (no smear). The degree of proteolysis in cheeses with smear was also considerably higher than in waxed cheeses. Nevertheless, the differences in the levels of amino nitrogen between the particular layers of the cheese were not large, which according to the authors, was a result of mould development inside the cheese (Fig. 6).

Similarly, Hartley and Jezeski[13] express the opinion that it is possible to

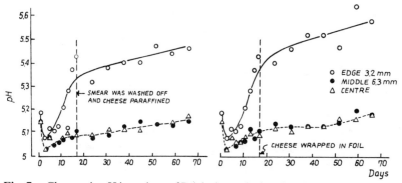

Fig. 7. Changes in pH in regions of Brick cheese during ripening (from Langhus *et al.*[5]). (Reproduced by permission of the *Journal of Dairy Science.*)

affect the intensity of the aroma of Blue cheese by controlling smear development on its surface.

Brick cheese is semi-hard cheese, which ripens uniformly throughout, i.e. after cutting, no layers differing in colour and consistency are observed. Langhus *et al.*,[5] who examined the influence of smear on the ripening of Brick cheese, stated that the increase in the pH of the outer layer from the 3rd day of ripening was a result of smear development. After removal of smear and paraffin-coating of cheeses, a decrease in pH was observed and then, later a considerably slower increase in pH occurred during further ripening at 4·4–7·2°C. The pH values of centre and middle layers were similar. When smear was not removed from the surface of the cheeses, i.e. those which were only wrapped in foil (film), the difference between the pH values of the surface and the inner layers were considerably higher. Cheeses wrapped in film were characterized by a richer aroma than paraffin-coated cheeses (Fig. 7). During ripening, an increase in the level of water-soluble nitrogenous compounds was observed, being intense between the 10th and 17th days of ripening; the rapid increase in the level of these compounds in the outer layer of the cheese was the result of smear development. If the smear was removed, the level of soluble nitrogen in the outer layer was similar to that in other layers. However, the presence of smear did not influence the level of 80% ethanol-soluble nitrogenous compounds. In cheeses wrapped in film, no differences in the levels of soluble nitrogen between the various layers was observed. The more intensive formation of soluble nitrogen was attributed by the authors to a higher temperature (14·4–15·5°C) during further ripening of cheeses after wrapping in film (Fig. 8).

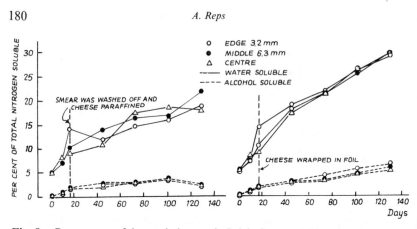

Fig. 8. Percentages of the total nitrogen in Brick cheese soluble in water and 80% alcohol (from Langhus *et al.*[5]). (Reproduced by permission of the *Journal of Dairy Science.*)

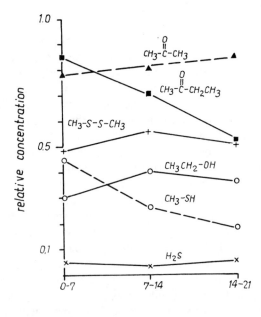

DEPTH FROM EDGE, MM

Fig. 9. Volatile compounds in Limburger cheese at various depths (modified from Parliment *et al.*[69]). (Reproduced by permission of the American Chemical Society.)

TABLE XIX

Nitrogen-containing volatiles in Swiss Gruyère cheese. (from Liardon et al.[71])
(reproduced by permission of Lebensmittel—Wissenschaft & Technologie)

Retention index	Component name/MS[a]	Relative abundance[b]		
		Edge 15 mm	Middle 20 mm	Centre
1095	m/e[c] 112, 86, 83, 71, 58, 42	60	—	—
1122	m/e 113, 98, 72 (2 isomers)	190	—	—
1127		210	—	—
1318	2,5-Dimethylpyrazine	60	2	—
1327	2,6-Dimethylpyrazine	1 000	10	—
1340	Ethylpyrazine (T)	15	—	—
1346	2,3-Dimethylpyrazine	40	3	—
1385	Ethylmethylpyrazine	60	—	—
1405	Trimethylpyrazine	700	15	—
1446	na	70	—	—
1450	na	50	—	—
1456	m/e 112, 71, 42	45	2	—
1460	na	45	—	—
1476	Tetramethylpyrazine	170	10	—
1515	Ethyltrimethylpyrazine	75	3	—
1591	m/e 112, 81, 54, 43	15	—	—
1600	m/e 112, 71, 42 (2 isomers)	160	—	—
1602		85	—	—
1618	m/e 112, 98, 71, 43	30	—	—
1621	m/e 126, 43	80	—	—
1640–1720	m/e 112 or 126	100	—	—
1941	Benzothiazole	12	22	10
2420	Indole	100	7	—

[a] T: tentative identification; na: mass spectrum not available.
[b] Normalized with respect to the abundance of 2,6-dimethylpyrazine in the outer zone sample.
[c] m/e represents international marking typical of the analytical method applied.

The above data show that the influence of smear on proteolysis in Brick cheese is small. However, as stated by the authors, the presence of smear on the surface of cheese has a decisive influence on the development of the specific flavour of the cheese. Flavouring substances, contained in the smear, are absorbed by the cheese. Simultaneously, the intensity of Brick cheese aroma may be regulated by controlling smear development on its surface.

Many studies have been conducted, especially on Limburger cheese, with the aim of explaining the basis of the characteristic aroma of smear cheeses.[67-70] Many chemical compounds which participate in formation of its flavour have been identified. Following examination of the influence of smear on the formation of cheese aroma, Parliment *et al.*[69] concluded that the concentrations of certain compounds which affect the aroma of Limburger cheese were lower at the surface than in the interior of the cheese; only the levels of methyl mercaptan and 2-butanone were higher at the surface (Fig. 9).

Liardan *et al.*[71] studied the aroma profile of Gruyère cheese, ripened with a smear. Among many alkaline volatile compounds present in the surface layer of the cheese, only a few, in small quantities, were present in the centre (middle) layer, and only one was found in the central layer (Table XIX).

The data presented show that micro-organisms contained in the smear influence the cheese ripening process. This influence is different for particular types of cheese, the greatest effect being for soft cheeses but the presence of smear on the surface of semi-hard and hard cheeses has a significant influence on the development of the typical flavour of these cheeses also.

5. CONCLUSIONS

During the ripening of cheese, red-orange, smear-forming micro-organisms may develop on their surfaces. In the case of certain types of cheeses, so-called smear cheeses, this is a favourable phenomenon because it has a decisive influence on the ripening process and in obtaining the specific flavours of these cheeses.

The composition of the smear microflora depends on the microflora of the brine and the rooms in which the cheeses are ripened and on the correctness of the curing procedure.

The first micro-organisms which develop on the surface of cheese are yeasts which tolerate high acidity and high NaCl concentrations. Then, after the acidity has been reduced, coryneforms develop. The red-orange colour of smear is a result of the development of *Brevibacterium linens*. Other micro-organisms may also grow in the surface smear.

The influence of enzymes secreted by micro-organisms in the smear on the cheese ripening process depends on the type of cheese, the composition of the microflora and on the duration of the smear's presence on the surface of the cheese.

Soft smear cheeses ripen with the participation of bacterial enzymes from the smear, from the surface toward the interior of the cheese; the influence of smear enzymes is especially evident in a cross-section of the cheese. In semi-hard cheeses, ripening occurs more uniformly throughout but the presence of smear has a definite influence on the development of a specific flavour in such cheeses also.

REFERENCES

1. Accolas, J. P., Melcion, D. and Vassal, L., *Proc. 20th Int. Dairy Congress, Paris*, p. 762, 1978.
2. Federation International Laitaire, Doc. No. 141, 1981.
3. Mocquot, G., *J. Dairy Res.*, 1979, **46**, 133.
4. Foster, E. M., Garey, J. C. and Frazier, W. C., *J. Dairy Sci.*, 1942, **25**, 313.
5. Langhus, W. L., Price, W. V., Sommer, H. H. and Frazier, W. C., *J. Dairy Sci.*, 1945, **28**, 827.
6. Kelly, C. D. and Marquardt, J. C., *J. Dairy Sci.*, 1939, **22**, 309.
7. Yale, M. W., *New York Agr. Exp. Stn. Tech. Bull.* No. 253, p. 1, 1940.
8. Laxa, O., *Cent. f. Bakt., II Abt.*, 1899, **5**, 755.
9. Kelly, C. D., *J. Dairy Sci.*, 1937, **20**, 239.
10. Macy, H. and Erekson, J. A., *J. Dairy Sci.*, 1937, **20**, 464.
11. Morris, H. A., Combs, W. B. and Coulter, S. T., *J. Dairy Sci.*, 1951, **34**, 209.
12. Yale, M. W., *New York Agr. Exp. Stn, Tech. Bull.* No. 268, p. 1, 1943.
13. Hartley, C. B. and Jezeski, J. J., *J. Dairy Sci.*, 1954, **37**, 436.
14. Lubert, D. J. and Frazier, W. C., *J. Dairy Sci.*, 1955, **38**, 981.
15. Mulder, E. G., Adamse, A. D., Antheunisse, J., Deinema, M. H., Woldendorf, J. W. and Zevenhuizen, L. P. T. M., *J. appl. Bacteriol.*, 1966, **29**, 44.
16. El-Erian, A. F. M., *Meded. Landb. Hogesch., Wageningen*, 1969, **69**(12), 1.
17. Iya, K. K. and Frazier, W. C., *J. Dairy Sci.*, 1949, **32**, 475.
18. Purko, M., Nelson, W. O. and Wood, W. A., *J. Dairy Sci.*, 1951, **34**, 874
19. Burkholder, P. R., Collier, J. and Moyer, D., *Food Res.*, 1943, **8**, 314.
20. Purko, M., Nelson, W. O. and Wood, W. A., *J. Dairy Sci.*, 1951, **34**, 699.
21. Szumski, S. A. and Cone, J., *J. Dairy Sci.*, 1962, **45**, 349.
22. Maginnis, R. L. and Cone, J. F., *J. Dairy Sci.*, 1958, **41**, 706.
23. Ades, G. L. and Cone, J. F., *J. Dairy Sci.*, 1969, **52**, 957.
24. Macy, H. and Gibson, D. L., *J. Dairy Sci.*, 1937, **20**, 447.
25. Tsujisaka, Y., Iwai, M. and Tominaga, Y., *Agr. Biol. Chem.*, 1973, **37**, 1457.
26. Wilcox, J. C., Nelson, W. O. and Wood, W. A., *J. Dairy Sci.*, 1954, **38**, 775.
27. Dłużewski, M., *Bull. Polon. Acad. Sci., Serie des Sci. Biol.*, 1963, **11**, 227.
28. Nelson, W. O., *J. Dairy Sci.*, 1953, **36**, 143.
29. Purko, M. and Nelson, W. O., *J. Dairy Sci.*, 1951, **34**, 477.
30. Nelson, W. O., *J. Dairy Sci.*, 1952, **35**, 455.
31. Pulss, G., *Kieler Milch. Forsch. Ber.*, 1955, **7**, 385.
32. Dłużewski, M. and Bruderer, G., *Bull. Polon. Acad. Sci., Serie des Sci. Biol.*, 1963, **11**, 221.
33. Chen, M. H. and Ledford, R. A., *J. Dairy Sci.*, 1972, **55**, 666.

184   *A. Reps*

34. Gueguen, M. and Lenoir, J., *Le Lait*, 1975, **55**, 145.
35. Gueguen, M. and Lenoir, J., *Le Lait*, 1976, **56**, 439.
36. Greenberg, R. S. and Ledford, R. A., *J. Dairy Sci.*, 1979, **62**, 368.
37. Feagan, J. T. and Dawson, D. J., *Austr. J. Dairy Technol.*, 1959, **14**, 59.
38. Lenoir, J., Federation International Laitaire, Doc. No. 171, 1948.
39. Alford, J. A. and Frazier, W. C., *J. Dairy Sci.*, 1950, **33**, 115.
40. Robertson, P. S. and Pery, K. D., *J. Dairy Res.*, 1961, **28**, 245.
41. Marth, E. H., *J. Dairy Sci.*, 1963, **48**, 869.
42. Nath, K. R. and Ledford, R. A., *J. Dairy Sci.*, 1972, **55**, 1424.
43. Moreno, V. and Kosikowski, F. V., *J. Dairy Sci.*, 1973, **56**, 33.
44. Moreno, V. and Kosikowski, F. V., *J. Dairy Sci.*, 1973, **56**, 39.
45. Crombach, W. H. J., *Antonie de Leeuwenhoek*, 1974, **40**, 361.
46. Holt, J. G. In: *Shorter Bergey's Manual of Determinative Bacteriology*, Williams, Wilkins Co., Baltimore, p. 224, 1977.
47. Boyaval, P. and Desmazeaud, M. J., *Le Lait*, 1983, **63**, 187.
48. Albert, J. O., Long, H. F. and Hammer, B. W., *Iowa Agr. Exp. Stn, Res. Bull.*, No. 328, 1944, p. 235.
49. El-Erian, A. F. M. and El-Gamal, S., *3th Conf. Microbiol.*, Cairo, p. 73, 1975.
50. San Clemente, C. L. and Wadhera, D. V., *Appl. Microbiol.*, 1967, **15**, 110.
51. Dagonneau, H. and Kuzdzal- Savoie, S., *Proc. 20th Int. Dairy Congress*, Paris, p. 594, 1978.
52. Stadhouders, J. and Mulder, W., *Neth. Milk Dairy J.*, 1959, **13**, 291.
53. Thomasow, J. T., *Kieler Milch. Forsch. Ber.*, 1950, **1**, 35.
54. Friedman, M. E., Nelson, W. O. and Wood, W. A., *J. Dairy Sci.*, 1953, **36**, 1124.
55. Tuckey, S. L. and Sahasrabudhe, M. R., *J. Dairy Sci.*, 1957, **40**, 1329.
56. Palo, V. and Bačiková, D., *Proc. 16th Int. Dairy Congress, Copenhagen*, Vol. D, p. 497, 1962.
57. Foissy, H., *Milchwissenschaft*, 1978, **33**, 221.
58. Sørhaug, T., *Milchwissenschaft*, 1981, **36**, 137.
59. Tokita, F. and Hosono, A., *Jap. J. Zootech. Sci.*, 1968, **39**, 127.
60. Tokita, F. and Hosono, A., *Milchwissenschaft*, 1968, **23**, 690.
61. Tsugo, T., Matsuoka, H. and Hirata, H., *Proc. 17th Int. Dairy Congress, München*, Vol. D, p. 275, 1966.
62. Schober, R., Christ, W. and Enkelmann, D., *Milchwissenschaft*, 1957, **14**, 206.
63. Singh, S. and Tuckey, S. L., *J. Dairy Sci.*, 1968, **51**, 942.
64. Tokita, F. and Hosono, A., *Milchwissenschaft*, 1968, **23**, 758.
65. Woo, A. H., Kollodge, S. and Lindsay, R. C., *J. Dairy Sci.*, 1984, **67**, 874.
66. Ramanauskas, R., *Proc. Int. Dairy Congress*, Paris, p. 777, 1978.
67. Dumont, J. P., Degas, Ch. and Adda, J., *Le Lait*, 1976, **56**, 177.
68. Grill, H., Patton, S. and Cone, J. F., *J. Dairy Sci.*, 1966, **49**, 409.
69. Parliment, T. H., Kolor, M. G. and Rizzo, D. J., *J. Agric. Food Chem.*, 1982, **30**, 1006.
70. Simonart, P. and Mayaudon, J., *Neth. Milk Dairy J.*, 1956, **10**, 261.
71. Liardon, R., Bosset, J. O. and Blanc, B., *Lebensm. Wiss. u. Technol.*, 1982, **15**, 143.

Chapter 6

Spanish and Portuguese Cheese Varieties

A. Marcos

Departamento de Tecnología y Bioquímica de los Alimentos,
Universidad de Córdoba, Spain

1. INTRODUCTION

In the context of cheese production in 24 West European countries, Spain occupies an intermediate position and Portugal a relatively low one.[1] Similar to the above seems to be the status of cheesemaking industrialization and level of technological development, as well as the scientific and technical knowledge on the indigenous cheeses of these countries.

In the Iberian Peninsula, as in other Mediterranean lands, herds of sheep are abundant and widely distributed. From ewe's milk are made the most representative cheese varieties of Spain and Portugal, namely 'Queso Manchego', originally made by shepherds in the central plain of La Mancha, and 'Queijo Serra', produced in farmhouses in the Serra da Estrella mountains by curdling milk with extracts from thistle ('cardo') flowers.

Cheesemaking from cow's milk is concentrated in the North of the Peninsula, although insular production (from the Balearic Islands and Azores Archipelago) is also significant. Part of this is sent to their respective Mediterranean and Atlantic mainlands. Goat's milk cheese is made mainly in the South and Southeast of the Peninsula, as well as in the Canary Islands.

Autochthonous cheese varieties of major commercial importance have been subject to industrial manufacture along with other universally-known foreign varieties of Dutch, Swiss and French origin, processed cheeses and several fresh dairy products. Edam cheese, popularly known by Spaniards and Portuguese as 'Bola' cheese due to its spherical shape, is the best seller of the foreign varieties produced in Iberian countries.

185

A. Marcos

Both countries have strong local cheesemaking traditions. Many varieties are still made for consumption on the producing farm or for direct trade at the local markets within their production area. Measures are being taken to save traditional cheesemaking practices and the uniqueness and authenticity of their produce.

2. SPANISH CHEESE VARIETIES

The annual cheese consumption per capita by Spaniards is moderate, about 5 kg in 1981.[2] In that year, total production amounted to almost 174 000 tonnes (Table I), 80% of which was produced industrially. The distribution of cheese types manufactured industrially (in 1980) from milk of different species is shown in Table II. Both tables are included only for orientation purposes; perhaps some figures may be underestimates with respect to farm production (which is difficult to assess) and cheese varieties based on sheep's and goat's milks to which variable proportions of cow's milk are commonly added.[2,3]

Although there are a large number of assorted cheese varieties[4-9] and the country is almost self-sufficient,[2] imports of many cheese varieties are made from several European countries,[2,3,10] mainly to meet the demands of foreign tourists. Cheese exports (ca. 2000 tonnes in 1981) are negligible compared to imports (ca. 20 000 tonnes in 1981).[11] A detailed, prospective market survey on the production, distribution, trade and consumption of cheese in Spain carried out in 1977, concluded that this country was, potentially, one of the most important cheese markets in Western Europe.[3]

TABLE I
Production (tonnes) of Cheese in Spain (1981)[a]

Cheese made from	Industrial production	Farmhouse production	Total production
Cow's milk	100 271	9 368	109 639
Sheep's milk	30 257	14 416	44 673
Goat's milk	8 224	10 863	19 087
Totals	138 752	34 647	173 399

[a] Many cheese varieties are made from mixtures of milks in variable proportions.
Source: Anuario de Estadística Agraria 1982, Ministerio de Agricultura, Pesca y Alimentación, Secretaría General Técnica (provisional data).

TABLE II
Industrial production (tonnes) of cheese types in Spain (1980)[a]

Cheese type	From cow's milk	From sheep's milk	From goat's milk	Total
Fresh	14 621	1 630	3 333	19 584
Soft	2 365	402	463	3 230
Hard, uncooked	41 697	18 238	8 671	68 606
Hard, cooked	5 410	2 312	270	7 992
Blue veined	16	76	—	92
Processed	17 152	—	—	17 152
Special	157	—	—	157

[a] Data collected from 509 cheesemaking plants.
Source: Anuario de Estadística Agraria 1982, Ministerio de Agricultura, Pesca y Alimentación, Secretaría General Técnica.

Essential steps in traditional manufacturing methods for 36 cheese varieties, major characteristics of the cheeses ready for consumption and other general items of information have been collected in a catalogue on Spanish cheeses;[4] the most relevant features of the main varieties have been included in international cheese guides written in (or translated into) English.[8,9] Legal regulations on milk and dairy products have been the subject of a compilation updated to December 1982.[12]

Most of the scientific and technical information available on Iberian dairy products has been obtained during the last two decades by a few research groups.[13] In the following pages, brief reference will be made to those research papers dealing with cheese chemistry, physics and microbiology. Data on the chemical and physical parameters of the most representative varieties with current high rates of consumption, selected from the results of an extensive and systematic analytical project[14] concluded shortly before the preparation of this manuscript, are also included in Tables III-VII.

2.1 Tables of Chemical and Physical Characteristics

Although Volume 1 covers general aspects of cheese chemistry and physics such as the relationship between cheese composition and quality (Chapter 7), cheese rheology (Chapter 8), nutritional aspects of cheese (Chapter 9) and proteinases and proteolysis (Chapter 10), some comments on certain data contained in Tables III–VII seem to be pertinent.

Soluble tyrosine and tryptophan contents of cheeses (included in Table VI)

A. Marcos

TABLE III

Mean chemical composition and metabolizable energy (per 100 g) of some major Spanish cheeses purchased (1982–1984) at large supermarket chains[14]

Cheese variety	Moisture	Fat	Protein	Lactose	Lactic acid	Ash	kcal	M/FFC[a]	F/DM[b]
Cuajada	81·9	4·5	4·5	4·4	0·2	1·3	75	85·8	24·5
Fresco de vaca (fresh from cow's milk)	67·0	17·8	8·3	2·5	0·5	1·3	203	81·2	52·0
Burgos (type)	54·0	24·0	16·0	1·6	0·3	2·7	286	71·0	52·1
Fresco de cabra (fresh from goat's milk)	54·7	21·8	17·4	1·1	0·3	3·4	270	70·1	48·2
Requesón (whey cheese)	74·5	7·3	9·9	2·3	0·5	1·9	113	80·3	27·6
Gallego	46·6	28·0	19·4		1·0	3·5	329	64·7	52·3
Tetilla	39·1	33·3	22·0		1·1	3·8	387	56·3	53·3
San Simón (pear-shaped)	34·0	33·0	27·2		1·7	4·0	406	50·7	50·0
Mahón	31·7	32·6	26·9		1·7	6·8	400	47·0	47·8
Bola	43·6	26·3	23·6		1·1	4·5	331	59·3	46·8
Manchego	37·5	33·6	23·0		1·4	4·6	394	56·6	53·8
Roncal	29·4	38·8	24·7		1·6	4·8	447	48·1	54·9
Idiazábal	33·2	37·8	23·3		1·7	4·0	433	53·2	56·6
Majorero	45·3	23·4	25·2		1·8	5·0	311	59·1	42·6
Cabrales	41·8	32·6	21·5		2·2	5·8	379	62·0	56·0
Azul de oveja (Blue from sheep's milk)	44·0	31·3	20·6		2·0	5·3	363	64·1	55·8
Fundido, graso (processed cheese, 40–45% F/DM)[b]	54·8	18·8	15·0	2·3	1·8	4·7	238	67·4	41·5
Rallado (grated cheese)	31·4	24·4	31·6		2·8	8·0	346	41·2	35·5

[a] M/FFC = g moisture/100 g fat-free cheese.
[b] F/DM = g fat/100 g dry matter.

TABLE IV

Salt, macrominerals and major microminerals (per 100 g) of cheeses from Table III[a]

Cheese variety	NaCl (g)	Ca	P	Na (mg)	K	Mg	Zn	Fe	Cu (μg)	Mn
Cuajada	0·32	146	106	155	315	18	1006	462	63	530
Fresco de vaca (fresh from cow's milk)	0·75	100	170	272	121	8	529	330	43	73
Burgos (type)	0·54	622	385	222	93	21	2417	613	75	167
Fresco de cabra (fresh from goat's milk)	1·51	543	818	480	90	88	2034	398	117	48
Requesón (whey cheese)	0·27	591	329	57	111	21	313	556	56	57
Gallego	1·67	559	394	547	55	16	2316	630	72	65
Tetilla	1·52	597	415	349	39	12	1574	214	34	70
San Simón (pear-shaped)	2·28	632	483	660	73	18	2781	324	67	91
Mahón	4·29	559	478	1274	143	21	3078	388	71	56
Bola	2·22	743	467	649	67	19	2708	736	76	68
Manchego	2·39	685	544	670	80	59	2376	544	102	98
Roncal	2·37	753	534	658	89	22	2895	766	84	122
Idiazábal	1·57	757	522	443	77	21	2491	466	84	107
Majorero	2·14	727	501	878	153	29	1558	634	95	65
Cabrales	3·70	358	379	1067	95	16	2324	500	66	77
Azul de oveja (Blue from sheep's milk)	4·15	368	292	1375	60	19	1977	659	82	75
Fundido, graso (processed cheese, 40–45% F/DM)	1·41	398	648	893	120	11	1485	552	82	66
Rallado (grated cheese)	3·15	724	1068	1875	107	67	2704	1360	160	129

[a] Data obtained by León.[14]

TABLE V

Major esterified fatty acids (per 100 g of total fatty acids) of cheeses from Table III[a]

Cheese variety	4:0	6:0	8:0	10:0	12:0	14:0	14:1	15:0	16:0	16:1	17:0	18:0	18:1	18:2	18:3
Cuajada	3·2	2·6	1·6	3·6	3·5	11·1	1·8	1·4	28·4	3·8	1·0	8·4	23·5	3·2	1·4
Fresco de vaca (fresh from cow's milk)	3·4	2·6	1·5	3·4	3·7	11·4	1·6	1·3	29·8	3·4	1·3	8·4	22·9	2·9	0·9
Burgos (type)	4·3	3·4	2·7	7·2	4·4	11·2	1·1	1·0	26·7	3·1	0·7	8·5	21·1	2·7	1·0
Fresco de cabra (fresh from goat's milk)	4·1	3·0	2·4	7·0	3·9	10·3	1·5	0·9	27·6	3·3	0·5	8·2	22·7	2·7	0·9
Requesón (whey cheese)	3·2	2·7	1·9	5·1	3·8	10·5	1·2	1·2	28·3	3·5	0·8	8·9	23·9	2·4	1·2
Gallego	3·4	2·4	1·4	3·1	3·3	10·9	1·9	1·5	26·8	3·2	1·0	10·4	25·1	2·1	1·5
Tetilla	2·9	2·2	1·3	2·6	3·1	10·7	1·8	1·5	27·2	2·9	1·2	11·7	25·5	1·5	1·7
San Simón (pear-shaped)	2·8	2·5	1·5	3·3	3·6	11·4	2·0	1·4	26·6	3·0	1·2	11·0	24·4	1·6	1·7
Mahón	2·5	2·0	1·3	2·8	3·1	10·4	1·8	1·4	24·6	2·8	1·2	12·1	27·0	2·8	1·8
Bola	3·3	2·8	1·6	3·4	3·6	11·8	2·3	1·8	28·2	4·2	1·5	7·6	22·4	2·5	1·4
Manchego	2·5	2·9	2·9	9·5	5·3	11·6	0·7	0·9	26·5	3·1	1·0	7·8	20·8	1·5	1·3
Roncal	3·0	3·6	3·3	9·5	4·9	10·9	1·1	1·5	21·5	2·9	1·8	8·7	20·7	1·8	2·2
Idiazábal	3·3	3·5	2·8	7·5	4·5	11·5	1·1	1·7	26·6	2·7	1·7	7·3	20·7	1·4	1·2
Majorero	2·3	3·6	4·2	14·1	5·9	10·7	0·2	1·1	24·1	2·2	0·5	5·9	20·0	2·7	0·8
Cabrales	2·0	1·7	1·1	2·4	3·0	9·6	1·1	0·8	32·4	3·1	0·6	9·3	28·6	2·6	1·3
Azul de oveja (Blue from sheep's milk)	1·6	2·3	2·3	7·1	4·0	12·0	1·1	1·3	31·3	1·4	0·6	5·8	22·4	3·7	1·0
Fundido, graso (processed cheese, 40–45% F/DM)	2·8	2·2	1·5	3·4	3·3	10·0	1·8	1·4	28·1	3·0	1·2	10·6	24·2	2·2	1·5
Rallado (grated cheese)	3·3	2·6	1·7	3·9	3·5	10·3	1·5	1·4	26·9	3·0	1·3	10·2	24·3	2·6	1·5

[a] Data obtained by Fernández-Salguero.[14]

Nitrogen distribution in cheeses from Table III

Cheese variety	Nitrogen fractions[a] (per 100 of total N)				Quantitative PAGE[b] (Relative percentages)					UV measurements[c] (mg/100 g cheese)	
	SN	NPN	FN	NH_3N	Pre-α_s-cn	α_s-cn	β-cn	γ-cn	Origin	SN-Tyr	SN-Trp
Cuajada	30·7	13·8	11·4	1·3	6·1	33·0	28·3	27·9	4·6		
Fresco de vaca (fresh from cow's milk)	15·9	9·1	6·1	1·6	1·7	46·3	32·8	14·8	4·3		
Burgos (type)	13·6	4·4	3·1	0·5	2·0	38·4	29·1	24·2	6·2	87	67
Fresco de cabra (fresh from goat's milk)	14·7	5·6	4·4	0·4	4·1	27·0	34·8	28·0	6·1	126	59
Requesón (whey cheese)	21·4	8·0	6·0	1·1							
Gallego	24·5	12·4	7·1	0·8	12·0	20·9	32·8	27·1	7·2	124	130
Tetilla	24·5	11·9	4·5	0·8	12·0	24·0	28·4	28·5	7·1	85	106
San Simón (pear-shaped)	26·6	15·9	5·8	0·8	7·8	25·5	29·1	31·1	6·5	249	173
Mahón	31·1	18·6	7·3	1·4	8·3	23·5	25·7	37·5	3·3	334	160
Bola	24·3	15·7	5·7	0·8	15·4	21·7	27·8	30·9	5·0	108	104
Manchego	25·9	14·4	5·2	1·1	9·0	21·7	38·6	23·6	7·1	161	97
Roncal	26·2	19·6	8·9	2·7	9·9	28·2	34·0	22·7	5·4	322	89
Idiazábal	29·0	20·2	8·6	2·3	6·8	20·0	34·7	32·3	6·0	387	123
Majorero	27·4	15·9	5·5	1·0	15·5	14·2	33·0	33·8	3·3	247	88
Cabrales	58·1	55·4	29·6	10·4	8·1	13·2	8·0	66·4	4·2	440	226
Azul de oveja (Blue from sheep's milk)	56·3	50·0	27·5	10·5	6·0	9·9	16·2	62·0	5·9	333	241
Fundido, graso (processed cheese, 40–45% F/DM)	20·3	13·2	6·9	1·4	4·5	27·0	35·0	27·6	5·8		
Rallado (grated cheese)	16·1	10·4	6·0	1·3	5·2	27·1	34·6	24·6	8·6		

[a] Data obtained by Beltrán de Heredia;[14] N = nitrogen; SN = soluble N; NPN = non-protein N; FN = formol N; NH_3N = ammonia N.

[b] Data obtained by Esteban;[14] PAGE = polyacrylamide gel electrophoresis; cn = casein; Pre-α_s-cn = breakdown products from α_s-cn with greater electrophoretic mobility.

[c] Data obtained by Alcalá;[14] SN-Tyr = tyrosine from SN; SN-Trp = tryptophan from SN.

TABLE VII

Water activity (a_w) and pH of cheeses from Table III and differences between calculated and measured a_w

Cheese variety	Experimental values[a]		Calculated a_w by the equation: Difference from measured a_w		
	pH	a_w	b	c	d
Cuajada	6·38	0·995	+0·003		+0·012
Fresco de vaca (fresh from cow's milk)	4·54	0·985	+0·008		−0·002
Burgos (type)	5·94	0·994	0·000		−0·002
Fresco de cabra (fresh from goat's milk)	6·06	0·984	0·000		0·000
Requesón (whey cheese)	6·57	0·997	+0·001		+0·010
Gallego	5·23	0·967		+0·002	−0·001
Tetilla	5·08	0·956		−0·002	+0·001
San Simón (pear-shaped)	5·04	0·933		+0·007	+0·003
Mahón	4·94	0·881		−0·011	
Bola	5·17	0·957		−0·007	−0·006
Manchego	5·05	0·945		−0·008	−0·004
Roncal	5·10	0·919		−0·010	+0·002
Idiazábal	5·03	0·944		−0·007	−0·002
Majorero	4·88	0·942		+0·004	+0·006
Cabrales	5·67	0·887		+0·012[e]	
Azul de oveja (Blue from sheep's milk)	6·08	0·906		+0·006[e]	+0·022
Fundido, graso (processed cheese, 40–45% F/DM)	5·66	0·966			+0·008
Rallado (grated cheese)	5·20	0·874			

[a] Determined by Alcalá.[14]

[b] $a_w = 1 − 0.033$ NaCl$_M$, where M is the NaCl molality in the total water of the product;[35] this relationship applies to fresh cheese with %$H_2O \leq 40$ and NaCl$_M \geq 1.2$.

[c] $a_w = 1.0234 − 0.007$ g ash/100 g moisture;[36] this relationship applies to natural cheese ripened by bacteria.

[d] $a_w = 0.945 − 0.0056$ (NPN) − 0.0059 (NaCl) − 0.0019 (ash − NaCl) + 0.0105 pH, where concentration units are expressed in g/100 g water; equation from Rüegg and Blanc[28] applicable in the range $a_w > 0.90$.

[e] ...this relationship applies to mould ripened varieties (unpublished data)

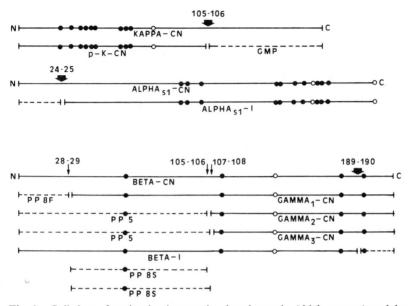

Fig. 1. Splitting of major bovine caseins by chymosin (thick arrows) and by plasmin (thin arrows) to yield insoluble (continuous lines) and soluble (dashed lines) polypeptides. The tyrosinyl (black circles) and tryptophanyl (white circles) residues in the primary structure of the casein molecules and their enzymic cleavage fragments are shown. (For updated nomenclature of caseins and casein fragments released by plasmin see Eigel *et al.*[17]).

are each highly related to soluble nitrogen in Cheddar cheese[15] and have been used as rapid methods for measuring cheese ripening. In assorted cheese varieties it was found [10] that neither soluble tyrosine nor tryptophan is related to α_s-casein hydrolysis but both are highly related to β-casein hydrolysis. Consequently, such values seem to be specific indexes of the type of proteolysis.[16] The relationships for soluble tyrosine are explained on the basis of the primary structure of casein molecules and their most sensitive bonds to chymosin and plasmin,[10,16] as shown in Fig. 1.

Water activity (a_w) and pH of cheeses (see Table VII) are major physical parameters related to the stability and safety of food systems (others are temperature and Eh). The significance of pH is well known and the concept of a_w is not a new one,[18] but the full acknowledgement of its influence on the quality of foods in general[19-28] and cheese in particular[27-30] dates from more recent times. The influence of suboptimal values of both pH and a_w on the growth of spoilage or pathogenic organisms and toxin

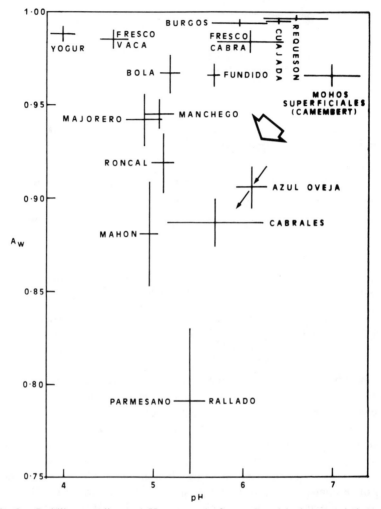

Fig. 2. Stability coordinates (pH versus a_w) of some Spanish cheese varieties and related dairy products. The intercept point of the crosses indicate mean values; their branches indicate standard deviations. The stability and safety of the products increase from higher values towards lower ones as shown by the thick arrow (e.g. as the thin arrows show for 'Azul de oveja' cheese samples in particular).

production, tend to be enhanced when acting concomitantly so that the stability and safety of products mapped in Fig. 2 increases as one or both values decrease, until either a_w or pH reach a *per se* low-enough inhibitory 'upper limit'.

The a_w value of cheeses reported in Table VII were determined by a simplified and improved gravimetric method[14,31,32] based on that of McCune *et al.*[33] In the a_w range 0·98–1·00, the values were calculated by extrapolation; although such an extrapolation is not feasible in the technical modification of Lenart and Flink,[34] our extrapolated values were only slightly underestimated (-2 to $-3 \times 10^{-3} a_w$ units) above $a_w > 0·990$, according to the results of trials carried out on dilute NaCl solutions of known molality (0·3–0·05 M) and a_w (0·990–0·998), as well as on deionized water[14] (similar underestimated results were obtained on milk and other foods with very high a_w subjected to parallel assays by a reference method using a thermocouple psychrometer/nanovolt thermometer system). On the other hand, differences between measured (or extrapolated) values of a_w and those calculated from several predictive equations[28,35,36] are not greater (cf. Table VII) than those found using different measurement techniques or methods (including modern electronic devices).[37–39]

For cheese varieties italicised in the manuscript, average data (of at least 6 samples) are reported in Tables III–VII (standard deviations have been omitted in order to save space).

2.2 Fresh Cheeses and Related Products

Unripe fresh cheeses are those that undergo only partial lactose fermentation yielding lactic acid. All are characterized by high moisture content (and high a_w) and some residual lactose which contributes to their perishability. 'Cuajada' and whey cheese ('requesón') are other fresh and perishable related dairy products made in dairy factories and distributed together with fresh cheeses by refrigerated transport through the same commerical channels.

Cuajada is a traditional farmhouse product made from ewe's milk, whose consumption has increased steadily, so that currently it is produced in dairy plants mainly from cow's milk and is often commercialized in small earthenware containers. According to a recent quality standard,[40] 'cuajada' is the semi-solid product obtained from heat-treated (HTST or UHT) whole milk, skimmed milk or partly skimmed milk, curdled by rennet or other permitted coagulant, without added starter cultures or whey drainage. The finished product must contain at least 15% total dry matter. Because the treated milk and the product are exposed to post-pasteurization contaminants, legal regulations allow the addition of sorbic acid, benzoic acid and their Na and K salts up to a total of 2000 mg/kg, as preservatives. The presence of additives with aromatic structures (in this and other perishable products) interferes with the UV spectrophotometric measurement of soluble tyrosine and tryptophan (cf. Table VI).

Fresh cheese manufactured from pasteurized cow's milk to which suitable starter cultures (Streptococcus lactis and Str. cremoris) are added, is industrially produced in significant amounts (Table II) and commercialized under different trade-marks. Miscellaneous commercial brands found on the market have been analysed (cf. Tables III–VII).

Burgos cheese and Villalón cheese are the major fresh varieties (traditionally made in Castile) from raw sheep's milk; both are similar except for their shape. Burgos (low cylinder) and Villalón (loaf-shaped)-type cheeses are currently factory-made outside their original loci from mixtures of sheep's and cow's milks. The methods available for detecting mixtures of milks used in cheesemaking have been reviewed by Ramos and Juárez.[41] A new approach applicable to fresh cheeses, in which proteolysis is rather limited, may, perhaps, be based on the almost non-overlapping ranges of the α_s/β-casein ratios found by Storry et al.[42] in cow's (1·78–0·95), sheep's (0·98–0·78) and goat's (0·64–0·28) milk; when applied to data (in Tables V and VI) for Burgos-type cheese (made from mixtures of sheep's and cow's milk according to their labels), this procedure worked better than that based on the ranges of the ratios of the C_{12}/C_{10} fatty acids in the milk fats from these species.[43–46] Chemical composition, a_w and pH of Burgos and Villalón varieties have been reported,[47] along with other fresh and ripe cheeses.

Fresh cheese from goat's milk is common everywhere,[48] but mainly in Andalusia, where important varieties such as those from Málaga and Cádiz are eaten both fresh and slightly cured; these varieties have been the subject of some studies[49–52] on chemical and physical characteristics. Pure goat's milk or mixtures of goat's and cow's milks are used in the manufacture of fresh cheeses. Pasteurization of goat's milk is not commonly practised in rural cheesemaking and the fresh product may harbour Brucella melitensis which occasionally causes outbreaks of undulant fever when legal and sanitary measures by veterinarian inspection are evaded. The data in Tables III–VII refer to commercial brands manufactured from pasteurized goat's milk.

Whey cheese or 'requesón' is obtained by heat precipitation of whey proteins in acidic media to yield a soft paste.[12] The whey used as raw material in its manufacture is a by-product from the manufacture of pressed varieties. Whey cheese proteins are those highly nutritive albumins and globulins from milk; only trace amounts (unquantifiable) of residual caseins were electrophoretically detectable in the samples analysed (Table VI). The average percentage of soluble nitrogen in whey cheese was intermediate between those found in cuajada and in fresh cheeses (cf. Table VI). The a_w of whey cheese, however, exceeds those of fresh cheeses and cuajada (cf. Table VII), and even that of fluid milk ($a_w \simeq 0.995$). The higher a_w of whey cheese may be due, perhaps, to the thermal denaturation of the whey proteins that renders them insoluble by reducing protein–water interactions and promoting protein–small ions and protein–protein interactions.

In fresh cheeses (and some other related dairy products), the a_w can be calculated from the NaCl molality in the aqueous phase of the product[35] (see equation in footnote to Table VII) or determined graphically (as shown in Fig. 3A) from two common compositional percentages.[53]

Because salt-in-cheese moisture has become an essential parameter in compositional grading schemes (the other three are moisture-in-non-fat substance = MNFS, fat-in-dry matter = FDM, and pH),[54,55] a suitable equation for calculation of the a_w of salted curds and fresh or young cheese (with salt-in-moisture ≤ 7) is:

$$a_w = 1 - 0.00565 \text{ g NaCl}/100 \text{ g H}_2\text{O}$$

The true a_w may be lower than that calculated by the above procedures (due to the additional a_w-lowering capacities of other low molecular weight solutes), but not higher, as shown in Table VII. All these approaches may be useful in predicting the a_w at any point in the cheese after any period of brining, according to relationships reported by Guinee and Fox[56] on salt /moisture diffusion in cheese during the initial salting period. The author believes that it may be advantageous to use a_w (instead of salt-in-moisture) in grading systems to assess the potential quality (at maturity) of young cheese and suggests the classification of cheeses into categories on the basis of two physical (pH and a_w) and two chemical (MNFS and FDM) parameters. Such a proposed grading system provides improved additional specifications about the storage stability and safety of cheese. Cheap and simple a_w range-finding procedures (e.g. weight changes of samples exposed over saturated salt solutions) allow easy, fast and inexpensive estimation of a_w of sufficient accuracy for routine quality control purposes.

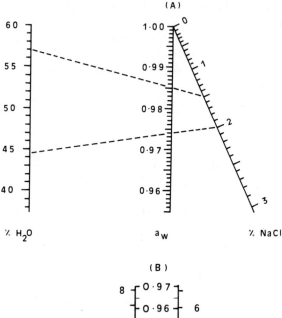

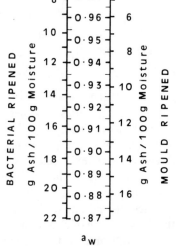

Fig. 3. Nomograph (A) for direct estimation of water activity (a_w) of fresh cheese from percentages of moisture (% H_2O) and salt (% NaCl). Examples: If % $H_2O = 57.0$, and % NaCl = 1·5, then $a_w = 0.985$; if % $H_2O = 44.5$, and % NaCl = 2·0, then $a_w = 0.974$. (Taken from the *J. Dairy Sci.*[53] by courtesy of the *American Dairy Science Association*). Nomograph (B) may be used to estimate a_w's of cheeses ripened by bacteria or mould from ash/moisture quotients (cf. Equations in footnotes to Table VII).

2.3 Bacterial Ripened Cheeses

Cheeses ripened by bacteria constitute the main group, both for quantity and diversity. Varieties within this group comprise those based on cow's, sheep's and goat's milk. Reference will be made to some varieties within each sub-group.

2.3.1 Varieties made from cow's milk

The national production of Dutch-type cheeses, particularly Edam and to a lesser extent Gouda, exceeds the production of all other cheese varieties made from cow's milk.[3] There is also limited production of other foreign varieties such as Cheddar and hard, cooked Swiss-type cheeses such as Emmental and Gruyère (cf. Table II). Some of these varieties (Edam, Cheddar, Emmental) are primarily used as raw materials for processed cheese manufacture. Since there is extensive international research literature on these varieties (cf. Chapters 1–3), studies on domestic Spanish versions are very scarce.

Indigenous cow's milk varieties, made in significant amounts, are those from Galicia and that from Mahón (Minorca).

Descriptions of rural cheesemaking practices traditionally used in Galicia, together with data on chemical composition and counts of some microbial groups in typical varieties (Ulloa, Tetilla, San Simón and Cebrero cheeses) gathered directly from producers and at local markets, were reported by Compairé.[57]

The biochemical and microbiological aspects of *Gallego cheese* (also called Ulloa) were researched by Ordóñez and Burgos.[58–61] They followed proteolysis and the evolution of the major microbial groups during the ripening process of traditionally-made cheeses from raw milk: lactic acid bacteria and enterococci increased steadily during the first few days and stabilized afterwards, while staphylococci and micrococci decreased progressively during maturation.[58] For cheese manufacture from pasteurized milk, they propose the use of a mixture of *Str. lactis*, *Str. cremoris*, *Lactobacillus plantarum* and *Str. faecalis* var. *liquefaciens* as starter, the latter being assumed to play a significant role in the curing process.[59] Free amino acids[60] and a detailed analysis of the lipid composition of curds and cheeses made both from raw and pasteurized milk with the above starter have been reported.[61]

A similar soft variety, also with a washed rind, is *Tetilla cheese*, which takes its name from its similarity of shape to a woman's breast. Its chemical and physico-chemical characteristics[14,47] are virtually identical with those of Gallego cheese (cf. Tables III–VII). The a_w of Ulloa and Tetilla cheeses have been calculated[61] from literature data.[57]

San Simón cheese is a smoked variety now produced industrially in two versions, one with the traditional pear shape (data in Tables III–VII) and a softer one (about 60% moisture on a fat-free basis)[14] with a flat disc shape. Since their moisture content is highly variable (ranging from <20% to >45%), their a_w is closely related both to the moisture content and to the aqueous concentration of ash.[36] The latter relationship (cf. footnote to Table VII) or a nomograph derived from it (see Fig. 3B) may be applied to most natural cheese varieties ripened by bacteria in order to estimate their a_w (cf. Table VII). Both relationships were used by Alcalá et al.[63] to calculate the a_w of San Simón cheese from previously published compositional data.[57]

Mahón cheese takes its name from the capital of Minorca (Balearic Islands) where it is produced; the appelation d'origine was legally recognized in 1980 with a provisional character.[12] Although sold in the natural form, mainly in the Balearic Islands, Catalonia and Madrid, most of the overall production is transformed into processed cheese ('queso fundido'), a fraction of which is presented in powder form as grated cheese ('queso rallado'). Information of the same type as that included in Tables III–VII for natural Mahón cheese (with the exception of the fatty acid composition of lipids) was obtained earlier on natural, processed and grated preparations.[64–67] Natural cheese has some peculiar characteristics (cf. Tables III–VII): low moisture content, high levels of salt, soluble nitrogen, non-protein nitrogen, reduced a_w and an unusual C_{16}/C_{18} ratio, lower than that found in any other cheeses analysed.[14] Ramos et al.[68] followed proteolysis and the microbial flora during ripening in order to identify a suitable specific starter culture for this variety; the results suggest that the starter should contain Str. lactis, Lb. plantarum, Lb. casei and Str. durans in different ratios. Taxonomical studies on yeast[69] and bacterial[70] strains isolated from milk, curd and maturing cheese have been also carried out. Peptides and free amino acids at several ripening stages have been determined recently.[71]

Some compositional, physical and microbiological information has been collected on commercial Bola cheese (Edam ball-shaped).[72–74] Data obtained on Edam cheese and Nata cheese[14] were very similar to those shown in Tables III–VII for Bola cheese.

2.3.2 Varieties made from sheep's milk

The main varieties in this group are hard, uncooked cheeses, manufactured from whole milk, with excellent keeping quality. This group includes the most popular indigenous variety, genuine Manchego cheese and Manchego-type cheeses (whose average yearly production is estimated to be greater than 50 000 tonnes[3]), together with many other varieties, some of which are similar to Manchego.[4]

Manchego cheese takes its name from the La Mancha region, where it was traditionally farmhouse-made from raw sheep's milk from local herds. The manufacture of this highly appreciated type of cheese has spread throughout both Castilian plateaus ('mesetas') in which sheep's milk production is high. The increasing demand for the product throughout the year has led to the inclusion in its manufacture, together with ewe's milk, variable amounts of milks from other species (cow's and/or, to a lesser extent, goat's) giving rise to binary and ternary mixtures. Traditional farmhouse cheesemaking methods are almost at the risk of being superseded by factory production from pasteurized milk. All these events have diversified the genuine product emerging as Manchego-type cheeses. In December 1984, authorities decided on the definitive *appellation d'origine* (AO) 'Queso Manchego' and established its legal regulations.[75]

Some essential requirements for the manufacture and ripening of Manchego cheese with AO are: sheep's milk (from Manchega breed) produced in Albacete, Ciudad Real, Cuenca and Toledo provinces (the chemical composition of the milk from these herds has been published recently[173]); minimum values for milk composition: 6% fat, 4% lactose, 4·5% protein, 0·8% ash, 16·5% total dry matter and methylene blue reduction time 3 h; maximum acidity; 30 Dornic degrees. No heat treatment for 'artesanal' (farmhouse-made) cheese and pasteurization for 'industrial' cheese. Curdling by natural rennet or other permitted coagulant added to milk at 28–32°C for 45–60 min. Cutting into grains 5–10 mm size (stir while heating to 40°C maximum). Moulding and pressing in cylindrical hoops. Wet-salting in NaCl brine (maximum immersion time, 48 h), dry-salting or both. Ripening for at least two months from moulding date in curing rooms at 12–15°C and 75–85% RH, with turning and cleaning (washing) if necessary; store at below 10°C. Packing to commercialize with natural or washed rind; the rind may be coated with wax, inert transparent substances or impregnated with olive oil; the word 'Manchego' and the number of week of manufacture (1–52) must be printed on the cheese.

The cheesemaking process used by a major industrial producer from La Mancha is basically as follows: sheep's milk (with an acidity usually from 20 to 25°D) is cleaned by filtration and centrifugal clarification, cooled to 5°C and stored under agitation for 12–18 h. The refrigerated milk is HTST pasteurized (72–73°C for 20 s), cooled to 33°C and delivered to the vats; during the filling period (about 20 min), a starter culture of mesophilic lactic acid streptococci is added (1% of mixed *Str. lactis*, *Str. cremoris* and *Str. lactis* sub-sp. *diacetylactis* inoculated into Marstar culture media and incubated at 22°C for 20 h to reach an acidity of 160°D). To the milk plus starter mixture are added 10 ml of liquid rennet (strength 1:15 000 according to label) per hectolitre of inoculated milk, to yield a soft curd in 20 min at 29–30°C and then the coagulum is cut into small grains of the size of a pea. The curd particles are stirred in the whey while heating to 37°C over a period of 30 min. After removal of the whey from the vat, the grains pass into a curd strainer and later the strained curd is cut into cubes, each of which is placed in a cylindrical hoop lined with smooth cloth where the curd is moulded and pressed for 2 h. After removal of the cloths, the curds are pressed again for 3 h. The pressed curds are then immersed in a brine bath (18–20% NaCl) at 12–14°C for about 36 h. Fresh salted cheeses are placed in a drying room at 16–18°C and 80% RH where they are kept, with periodic turning, for 10 days, whereupon they are transferred to a curing cellar at 10°C for 2 months and finally to a cold store at 7°C for 10–12 months before distribution and sale.

There are other recipes for manufacture by traditional [4] and industrial [76] methods, e.g. the latter use 2% of a mesophilic culture (*Str. lactis* and *Str. cremoris*) and 0·5% of a thermophilic culture (*Str. thermophilus*) as lactic starter and add calcium chloride and a lipase preparation before renneting.[76]

Manchego cheese may be consumed at several stages of ripening: fresh ('fresco') some days after manufacture, half-cured ('semicurado') after a few weeks, cured ('curado') for 2–3 months, matured for 3–6 months ('viejo') and a year old ('añejo'). Cured cheese may be preserved up to two years by immersion in olive oil ('manchego en aceite'). (Legal regulations do not permit consumption of any cheese type made from raw unpasteurized milk within 2 months of manufacture.[12])

The physical, physico-chemical and microbiological characteristics of the ripe cheese with AO should be: cylindrical shape (18–22 cm diam. × 8–12 cm high; 2–3·5 kg weight) with a hard rind printed with weave markings ('pleitas') on the sides and typically grooved or estriated ('flor') on both flat surfaces, pale yellow in colour or with dark green surface mould growth. The body should be firm and compact, white to ivory-yellow in colour, without holes or with many small ones irregularly distributed; the cheese should have characteristic aroma and flavour, and a pH value of 5·1–5·8. Chemical composition limits are: minimum dry matter, 55%;

minimum fat-in-dry matter, 50%; minimum protein-in-dry matter, 30%; maximum NaCl, 2·3%. Fat indices ranges: refractive index at 40°C, 1·4539–1·4557; Reichert value, 26–32; Pollenske value, 5–8; Kirschner value, 19–27; maximum cholesterol, 98% of the unsaponifiable esterolic fraction. Maximum microbiological limits: 1×10^1 cfu. *Escherichia coli*/g, 1×10^2 cfu *Staphylococcus aureus*/g and the absence of *Salmonella–Shigella* in 25 g.

The chemical and physical data shown in Tables III–VII refer to cheeses manufactured from ewe's milk in La Mancha (*loc. cit.* provinces). For seven other batches of samples of Manchego-type cheeses (made outside the original region or from binary and ternary milk mixtures) that were analysed by Marcos *et al.*,[14] no marked differences were found in most parameters from those reported for Manchego cheese, with the natural exception of 'manchego en aceite', which had a significantly lower moisture content, higher oleic acid percentage, more extensive proteolysis and a lowered a_w. Studies carried out on commercial ripe Manchego cheese deal with gross composition,[47,72] nitrogen compounds,[77–81] free amino acids[82–84] and other flavour substances,[84] tyramine,[85] mineral elements,[86] a_w pH,[87] chemical and physical values of fat and some microbiological indices of hygienic quality.[72]

From a practical point of view, it is obviously important to know the type of milk used as raw material. This problem was faced by Charro *et al.*[88] and more recently by Ramos *et al.*[89,90] The chemical and microbiological aspects of ripening, together with some physical parameters, of cheese batches manufactured from either raw or pasteurized sheep's milk or milk admixtures have been researched. Different chemical and biochemical changes occurring during proteolysis have been followed[16,91–96] as well as fatty acid profiles after various periods of immersion in olive oil.[97] Microbiological research[98–117] deals mainly with the evolution of the major microbial groups during maturation and with the screening of microbial strains isolated from milk, curd and cheese at different curing stages; laboratory culture collections of isolated strains have been used for identification and/or testing their physiological activities and biotechnological suitability for the development of appropriate starter cultures, some of which have been subject to experimental trials. Parallel assays carried out on a semi-industrial scale with a starter culture constituted of *Str. lactis, Lb. casei, Lb. plantarum* and *Leuconostoc lactis* yielded successful results with respect to scores for flavour, texture and overall acceptance.[114–116] The survival of pathogenic organisms during cheese ripening has been also investigated.[118,119]

Roncal cheese, another variety with definitive *appelation d'origine* and subject to legal regulations since 1981,[12] takes its name from the Roncal Valley (Navarre) where it is produced (from December to July) from sheep's milk (Rasa or Lacha breeds) and ripened for at least 4 months. It has a cylindrical shape (8–12 cm high and variable diameter and weight); the rind is hard, thick, coarse, with or without surface moulds, and brown or straw-yellow in colour. The body is hard, with pores but without eyes, white or pale yellow in colour and with a characteristic slightly piquant aroma and flavour. The moisture content must be less than 40% and the fat-in-dry matter $\geq 60\%$. Chemical and physical information on this variety, similar to the data in Tables III, IV, VI and VII, has been reported.[47] The evolution of pH, some chemical parameters, major nitrogen fractions and main microbial groups was followed by Ordóñez *et al.*[120] during the first 3 months of ripening of two farmhouse-made batches; lactic acid bacteria (*Str. lactis, Lb. casei, Lb. plantarum, Leuc. dextranicum* and *Leuc. lactis*) increased markedly during the first days and stabilized afterwards; *Micrococci* (identified species were *M. saprophyticus, M. lactis* and *M. roseus*) and *Staphylococci* decreased slightly; yeast and moulds remained steady throughout maturation and coliform organisms decreased progressively until disappearing. López *et al.*[82] followed the quantitative evolution of several free amino acids during the first few weeks of ripening in research work on the free amino acids in selected cheese varieties.

A smoked, hard variety made from whole sheep's milk of the Lacha breed is *Idiazábal cheese*, traditionally produced in the mountains of the Basque country and Navarre, where it is cured in natural caves for about 1 month. The cheese is cylindrical in shape (16–25 cm diam. × 8–12 cm high; 1–2 kg weight) and has a smooth, shiny, smoked, hard rind. The body is firm, white-yellowish, with few small holes, a 'sui generis' odour and a rather delicate smoky flavour. It can be stored for consumption for up to 1 year. The chemical and physical characteristics of commercial cured cheeses have been reported.[47]

Most of the technical information available on our farmhouse-made varieties from sheep's milk curdled by vegetable rennet (coagulant from *Cynara* spp. thistles) have been obtained by Fernández-Salguero *et al.*[121-130] Two related varieties of Manchego-type cheese are those made in the valleys of Los Pedroches (Córdoba) and La Serena (Badajoz). Proteolysis during the ripening of Pedroches cheese was researched by Fernández-Salguero[121-123] who also measured some chemical and physical parameters of the cured cheeses.[124-126] Compositional and physical characteristics of Serena cheese were also determined[127,131] as well as counts of the major microbial groups.[128] Another variety from Extremadura, produced with thistle rennet near the city of Cáceres, is Torta del Casar cheese, for which composition, major nitrogen fractions, a_w and pH have been reported,[129,130] as well as the fatty acid pattern and additional mineral elements.[14] The microbiological study of this variety was begun with a screening of microbial strains (isolation and identification of lactic acid bacteria, enterococci and yeast spp.).[132] An outstanding feature common to all these varieties is their high percentage of soluble nitrogen (average ranges from 40 to 50% of total nitrogen), closer to those of mould ripened varieties than to bacterial ripened cheese, due to the high proteolytic activity of the plant coagulant relative to its clotting ability (cf. section 3.2).

2.3.3 Varieties made from goat's milk

Several hundred tons of *Majorero cheese* are produced annually on Fuerteventura Island; this cheese, based on goat's milk, is marketed not only in the Canary Archipelago but also on the mainland. Nitrogen fractions, soluble tyrosine and tryptophan, and free amino acids were determined by Barreto[133] and gross composition, salt, calcium, phosphorus, a_w, pH and quantitative electrophoresis by Fernández-Salguero et al.[134]

Chemical and physical information, such as that contained in Tables III–VII, has been published on two farmhouse varieties from goat's milk: Ibores cheese,[135] from the Ibores mountains (province of Cáceres) and Badaya cheese,[136] an acid curd variety from the Badaya mountains (Alava). The latter has unique characteristics and a remarkably high degree of proteolysis that seems to be related to the presence or absence of surface moulds and fine herbs on the rind. Microbiological studies of this unusual variety, the most proteolysed of all goat's cheeses examined, would be interesting.

2.4 Mould-ripened Cheeses

Within this group there are several autochthonous blue-veined varieties from Asturias, such as Cabrales cheese and Gamonedo cheese, traditionally made from mixtures of cow's, sheep's and goat's milk, that are ripened in natural caves and typically presented wrapped in leaves, as well as factory-developed commercial brands of blue cheese, Roquefort-type or imitation, that use sheep's milk as raw material. Surface white mould-ripened varieties, mainly Camembert and Brie, are produced in smaller quantities from cow's milk; there is also a commercial brand of this type manufactured from goat's milk, that has many chemical and physical features common to those of their cow's milk counterparts.[14]

The most genuine and representative of our mould-ripened varieties is *Cabrales cheese*, whose provisional *appellation d'origine* was legally recognized in 1981.[12] The cheesemaking process was described in some detail by Núñez.[137] The raw milk mixture is curdled by rennet without addition of starter cultures or mould spores to milk or curd; the unpressed cheeses are dry-salted and then ripened in cellars of the Picos de Europa mountains for about 3–4 months under natural air currents; the ripe product is sold wrapped in leaves of *Acer pseudoplatanus*, now represented in a proposed label. The biochemistry and microbiology of the ripening process was ignored until 1971, when Burgos *et al.*[138–141] reported that lactobacilli constituted the dominant flora[138] and *Penicillium roqueforti* was the main ripening agent among other isolated moulds;[139] some yeast species were also identified.[140] Sala and Burgos[141] followed the release of individual free amino acids during curing. Further investigations by Núñez *et al.*[137,142–144] deal with changes in internal and surface micro-flora during cheesemaking and naturation,[137] and with the isolation and identification in milk, curd and maturing cheese of strains of lactic acid bacteria,[142] micrococci and staphylococci[143] and yeast and moulds.[144] Juárez *et al.*[145,146] analysed Cabrales with respect to: composition, physical and chemical values of fat, fatty acid patterns, major nitrogen fractions, soluble tyrosine and tryptophan, total free amino acids and casein breakdown in milk, curd and cheeses at three different curing stages. Commercially ripe cheese has also been chemically and physically characterized.[47]

Of the several brands of '*queso Azul de oveja*' (blue cheese from ewe's milk) marketed, the production of one brand exceeds the production of all others. It is made from HTST (72°C for 15 s) pasteurized ewe's milk to which a lactic starter (0·8–1·0%) and an inoculum of *P. roqueforti* spores are added before curdling by rennet (9·25 ml Hansen's liquid rennet per hectolitre); the curd is cut into cubes (2·5 cm) and scalded (31°C for 3 h 10 min); after hooping, the unpressed cheese is dry-salted (for 5 days) and ripened for 4 months (at 7°C and 96–98% RH), being pierced after 2 and 4 weeks of ripening. The finished cheese (cylinder 2·5 kg weight) is packed in aluminium foil and stored at 0°C. The composition of commercial blue cheese from ewe's milk is rather similar to that of Cabrales cheese, except for the fatty acid profile (cf. Tables III–VII).

As shown in Tables III–VII, distinctive features of blue-veined cheeses are, among others (cf. Chapter 4), their high salt content and degree of proteolysis (as well as lipolysis[14]) and, therefore, they have low a_w values due to the high aqueous concentration of NaCl and other low-molecular-weight compounds produced by the activity of fungal enzyme systems. The levels of both soluble nitrogen (which often range from 50 to 75% of total nitrogen) and non-protein nitrogen are high and usually rather similar (sometimes equal). This accounts for the small pool (or lack) of soluble polypeptides (proteoses-peptones), when expressed as a percentage of soluble nitrogen, in comparison to that found during the ripening of most cheese varieties. Both α_s- and β-caseins are highly proteolysed; the hydrolysis of the latter yields greater levels of soluble tyrosine and tryptophan than in cheeses ripened by bacteria, in which α_s-casein breakdown is more extensive than that of β-casein. Electrophoretic patterns of mould-ripened varieties show, as a result, very high relative levels of non-polar (insoluble) polypeptides released from β-casein cleavage by plasmin (cf. Fig. 1), that accumulate in the low mobility (γ-casein) zone (cf. Table VI) because of their resistance to proteinases. Only in over-ripened samples do the electrophoretograms appear devoid of polypeptides stainable with Amido Black and which may be made evident with Coomassie Blue, a dye for which their affinity is much greater. As stated by Hewedi and Fox,[147] other techniques are consequently required for monitoring the advanced stages of proteolysis in mould-ripened varieties.

Surface mould-ripened varieties have, in comparison to internal mould-ripened cheeses, higher moisture contents and fat-in-dry matter levels but lower levels of NaCl and non-protein nitrogen compounds, and, therefore, their a_w (as well as the pH value) is higher[14] (cf. Fig. 2).

An empirical equation for the calculation of a_w from ash-in-cheese moisture, of a similar type as that applied to bacterial-ripened cheeses, has been developed based on data for 50 samples of multinational assorted mould-ripened cheeses. This equation (cf. footnote to Table VII) and the nomograph derived from it (cf. Fig. 3B), fits better to blue-veined cheeses (of lower a_w) than to their surface mould counterparts, in which the differences between measured and calculated a_w values are more significant due to their higher a_w.

3. PORTUGUESE CHEESE VARIETIES

The overall Portuguese cheese production in 1981 amounted to about 40 000 tonnes.[1] That year, cheese imports amounted to 5000 tonnes and

exports to 1000 tonnes.[11] Current production of the major cheese types and
varieties is shown in Table VIII.

Although from a quantitative point of view, the industrial production
of cheese from pasteurized cow's milk, with starter cultures added and
curdled by animal rennet, amount to 60% of total production, the most
representative and genuine cheeses typical of Portugal are those farmhouse
varieties made from raw ewe's milk curdled by plant rennet from 'cardo',

TABLE VIII
Current Portuguese cheese production

Cheese made from[a]	Tonnes per year	Major cheese types and varieties
Cow's milk	ca. 27 000	ca. 24 000 tonnes of Flamengo cheese (Dutch-type), ca. 3 000 tonnes of Ilha (Açores) cheese (Cheddar-type), minor amounts of processed cheeses and others
Sheep's milk	16 000–17 000	mostly Serra cheese and smaller amounts of Serpa, Azeitão, Castelo Branco, Évora, Rabaçal, Tomar cheeses and others
Goat's milk	ca. 1 600	mostly fresh cheeses and Castelo Branco (á Cabreira) cheese

[a] Many cheese varieties are made from mixtures of milks in variable proportions.
Source: Updated information (1984) from the Junta Nacional Dos Productos
Pecuários supplied by courtesy of the Embaixada de Portugal em Madrid.

the most famous of which from the viewpoint of both quality and quantity
is the 'Queijo Serra da Estrella', annual production of which exceeds 13 000
tonnes in its traditional production area.[148] Goat's milk cheese manufacture is a wholly craft activity of low significance.[148,149] Home production
of cheese from ewe's and goat's milk versus industrial production has been
discussed by Vieira de Sá.[150]

Research papers on Portuguese cheese varieties collected by international information services on food science and technology are scarce. The
sheep's milk cheeses, Serra and Serpa, together with the plant coagulant
used in their manufacture, have been the subject of most studies, carried out
mainly by the research and development team of the Departamento de
Tecnologia de Indústrias Alimentares from the Laboratório Nacional de
Engenharia e Tecnologia, at Lisbon.

3.1 Characteristics and Manufacture of Major Cheese Varieties

One of the most comprehensive sources of general information on the domestic cheese varieties is the guide by Carr[8] which includes characteristics and other information on 19 Portuguese varieties. More detailed information and manufacturing methods for the major varieties have been reported by Vieira de Sá and Barbosa.[151] Both sources have been used as the main basis for the compilation of Table IX on some important characteristics of the major indigenous varieties.

3.1.1 Varieties made from cow's milk

Industrial cow's milk cheesemaking is based on the manufacture of foreign varieties, mainly of Dutch-type (Edam and Gouda) known as 'Flamengo' cheese. The production of the Portuguese version of Edam cheese alone, improperly called Bola cheese, accounts for almost 90% of the total production of cow's milk cheese.[151] Other foreign varieties manufactured in minor amounts are Camembert and Emmental, as well as fresh cheese such as Quark and Petit Suisse, and various processed cheeses, most of which use imported cheese as raw material.

In the Azores Islands, there is also, in addition to Flamengo cheese manufacture, significant production of Cheddar-type cheese, generally known on the mainland as 'Ilha' cheese, although such a name applies more properly to the cheese produced in large creameries on São Miguel Island.

The essential principles in the manufacture of *Ilha cheese* are pasteurization of milk, addition of a starter culture and clotting by rennet at about 30°C for 30 min. The curd is cut into small cubes with a vertical harp and afterwards with a horizontal harp; after a brief standing period, cutting is resumed until the curd particles are reduced to the size of a pea and then these are stirred for at least 30 min while the temperature is increased by about 5°C. After cooling to room temperature and removing the whey, the curd is thoroughly mixed with dry salt (about 3%) and filled into large cylindrical hoops which are pressed for 24 h. Maturation is carried out in stores (at 10–12°C and 75–85% RH) over a period of 2–3 months.

São Jorge cheese takes its name from the island in which it is produced from raw milk in small co-operative factories; this cheese is similar to Ilha cheese but has a stronger and more piquant flavour and aroma.

TABLE IX
Some characteristics of major Portuguese cheese varieties [a]

Cheese name	Similar types	Type of milk	Type of consistency	Ripening (weeks)	Weight (kg)	Shape [b]	Interior	Exterior	Flavour and aroma	% Fat-in-dry matter
Mainland varieties										
Serra da Estrella	Unique	Sheep	Soft to semisoft	4–6	1·0–1·7	LC	Creamy, white or pale yellow, no holes or few small ones	Thin, smooth, straw yellow	Delicate, mildly lactic	45–60
Serpa	Serra	Sheep	Soft to semi-soft	6–8	1·7–2·0	LC	Slightly creamy, some holes, white ivory	Smooth, straw yellow, sometimes with dry white or lemon moulds	Strong, piquant, sharp peppery	45
Azeitão	Serra	Sheep	Soft	3–4	0·2–0·3	LC	Creamy, pale straw yellow	Thin, soft, smooth, straw yellow	Mild, slightly sourish	45
Castelo Branco	Serra	Sheep	Semi-hard	3–4	1·0	LC	White, smooth, small holes		Strong, peppery	45
Évora		Sheep	Semi-hard to hard	26–52	0·1	LC	Pale yellow, crumbly	Dark yellow	Very strong, salty	45
Rabaçal		Sheep	Fresh		1·0	TC	White curd	No rind		
Tomar	Serra	Sheep	Semi-hard	2–3	0·03–0·04	LC	Pale, crumbly, small holes	Tough, grey yellow		45
Varieties from the Azores Archipelago										
Ilha	Cheddar	Cow	Hard	8–12	5–10	TC	Firm-bodied, yellow	Hard, dark yellow	Mild to mellow and nutty	45
São Jorge	Cheddar	Cow	Hard	8–12	3·5–7	TC	Crumbly		Strong, piquant	45
Pico		Cow	Soft	3–4	0·5	LC	Creamy	Pale, smooth	Fairly piquant	45

[a] Compiled from Carr,[8] Vieira de Sá and Barbosa[151] and Eekhof-Stork.[9]
[b] Abbreviations: LC = Low Cylinder; TC = Tall Cylinder.

3.1.2 Varieties made from sheep's milk

As stated above, the varieties in this group, farmhouse-made from raw milk and clotted by plant coagulant, such as Serra, Serpa, Azeitão, among other cheeses (cf. Table IX), are the most interesting and typical of the country. Traditional methods used in the farmhouse manufacture of Serra and Serpa cheeses were studied and described by Vieira de Sá *et al.*[151,152]

Serra da Estrella cheese is, internationally, the best-known variety from Portugal. In 1982, a legal standard for the 'Queijo Serra da Estrella' was published in order to define it, to establish its characteristics and to specify the packaging and preservation conditions, including a score for quality evaluation.[153]

This variety is farmhouse-made in the cold season from raw sheep's milk (Bordoleira breed) around the National Park of Serra da Estrella, mainly in villages in the Guarda and Viseu districts. Milk at 25–30°C is clotted by an aqueous extract obtained from cardoon flowers (*Cynara cardunculus* L.). The coagulum is hand-cut and placed into plaited cheese-moulds lined with cloths. After slight pressing for 6–12 h, the cheese is removed from the mould and dry-salted.

The ripening period is at least 1 month and comprises two phases. During the first 15 days the cheeses are turned daily in an atmosphere of very high relative humidity that promotes the development of a yeasty smear, called 'reima', on the surface. In the second phase the cheeses are held in a dry environment to facilitate rind formation; during this period the cheeses are turned every 2 days and the 'reima' is washed off periodically.

The finished product must have a minimum ripening index of 40% soluble N, a moisture content from 61 to 69% on a fat-free basis and a fat-in-dry matter of 45–60%. The mature cheese is a semi-soft type with creamy body ('Serra amaintegado') and has the shape of a low cylinder (15–20 cm diam. × 4–6 cm high). It is stored at 0–5°C and has a maximum shelf-life of 4 months when held at refrigeration temperatures (below 10°C).

The average chemical composition of Serra cheeses, classified as excellent and good, is as follows:[151] 48·8% moisture, 28·8% fat, 19·9% protein, 0·7% lactic acid and 2·6% ash; the percentages of moisture in the fat-free cheese and fat-in-dry matter are 68·5 and 56·2, respectively, the salt content is 2·56%, the ripening index 49·2% soluble N and the pH 5·1.

There is a semi-hard variant, called 'Serra velho', obtained by extending the aging period of 6–12 months.

There are modern cheesemaking factories based on sheep's milk (to which cow's milk is often added) but the manufactured product, although more standardized, is not comparable in quality to the authentic counterpart made by traditional methods.[148]

Serpa cheese, a variety similar to Serra cheese, is made in the Alenteijo region from sheep's raw milk (Merina breed). There are also two versions, one is a soft to semi-soft type, ripened for 6–8 weeks ('Serpa amaintegado'), and the other a hard to very hard type, cured for over 6 months ('Serpa velho').

3.1.3 Varieties made from goat's milk

There is a moderate production of several types of cheeses from goat's milk, generally for consumption in the fresh state. One of the most important is Castelo Branco ('á Cabreira') cheese with its fresh, cured ('amarelo') and piquant variants. Currently, there is a trend to increase the manufacture of pure goat's milk cheese and to this end, selected breeds of goat are being imported.[148]

3.2 Thistle Rennet

The milk coagulant extracted with water from the flowers of cardoons from the genus *Cynara* (mainly *C. cardunculus* L., *C. scolymus* L. and *C. humilis* L.) is used traditionally in the rural manufacture of Serra and many other cheese varieties made from sheep's milk in the Iberian Peninsula.[4,7–9]

Vieira de Sá and Barbosa[154] were the first to obtain scientific knowledge on the milk-clotting ability and proteolytic properties of the *C. cardunculus* extract, and to confirm earlier observations.[155–157] The thistle extract is thermostable like other proteolytic enzymes obtained from vegetable sources, their clotting activity being accelerated by increasing temperature and acidity; it shows a stronger proteolytic activity than animal rennet, but is better than animal rennet for the production of Serra cheese from sheep's milk. However, its high proteolytic activity results in reduced yield and defective flavour and texture when used for the manufacture of Edam and Roquefort cheeses.

New trials on the potential use of the coagulant from *C. cardunculus* as a substitute for animal rennet in the manufacture of Camembert and Gruyère cheeses were made by Barbosa *et al.*;[158] both types of cheese developed a very bitter flavour when thistle rennet was used in their manufacture.

Biochemical research on the enzyme system of the wild thistle, *C. humilis*, was accomplished by Esteban *et al.*[159–164] The petals of the flowers and their aqueous extracts show proteolytic, lipolytic and amylolytic activities;

TABLE X

Kinetic and thermodynamic parameters of the transition state during thermal denaturation of the proteinases from the thistle *Cynara humilis* L., extracted with citric acid (0·1 M) disodium phosphate (0·2 M) (pH = 5·0), buffer, after 15 days of activation at refrigeration temperature[161]

Proteinase:	Thermolabile	Thermostable
% of total milk-clotting activity:	55	45
Kinetic constants		
Reactions rates at 65°C		
D (min)	17·00	43·65
k ($\times 10^2$ min^{-1})	13·55	5·28
$t_{1/2}$ (min)	5·12	13·13
Temperature dependence		
z (°C)	5·5	4·7
E_a (kcal mol^{-1})	96	112
Q_{10}	66	134
Thermodynamic constants		
ΔF_+^+ (cal mol^{-1})	23 978	24 605
ΔH_+^+ (cal mol^{-1})	95 614	111 772
ΔS_+^+ (e.u.)^a	212	258
No. bonds broken^b	19	22

^{a} Entropy units in cal mol^{-1} K^{-1}.
^{b} No. of non-covalent bonds broken on denaturation $= \Delta H_+^+/5\,000$ where the average ΔH_+^+ per bond is assumed to be 5 000 cal mol^{-1}.

the crude fresh extract contains a complex proteinase system; the kinetics of thermal inactivation suggest the occurrence of three independent first-order reactions derived from the inactivation of proteinases with different thermostability ($D_{65°C} = 9·5$, 23·5 and 37·0 min); the proteinases are localized in the petals, probably as zymogens since the milk-clotting activity of the extracts increases with time after extraction. The activated extracts show only two proteinases whose kinetic and thermodynamic parameters after activation at refrigeration temperature are shown in Table X.[161]

In studies on ripened cheeses of two varieties made from sheep's milk curdled by thistle rennet it was found[165-168] that some composition-related factors, such as moisture content, a_w, ash/moisture, NaCl/moisture and others, were not related to the extent of hydrolysis of β-casein but were related to the amounts of residual α_s-casein. The relationships found seem to indicate that, in this type of cheese, there is an inverse influence of solute concentration on the relative rates of hydrolysis of the major caseins, since in Gouda cheese, Creamer[169] observed that the extent of hydrolysis of β-casein increases with increasing moisture content while that of α_{s1}-casein is unaffected, suggesting[170] that low a_w is responsible for the resistance of β-casein to proteolysis; Fox and Walley[171] and Phelan et al.[172] showed that the susceptibility of β-casein to proteolysis is affected more by NaCl concentration than that of α_{s1}-casein, suggesting[172] that the reduced relative susceptibility of β-casein to proteolysis is due to some concentration-dependent physical change in the casein molecule which renders the β-casein inaccessible to proteases, and that the salt concentration appears to influence this change.

ACKNOWLEDGEMENTS

The author is much indebted to the Editor, Professor P. F. Fox, for encouragement, useful suggestions and considerable help in the improvement of the manuscript, I also wish to thank the Comisión Asesora de Investigación Científica y Técnica for the financial support of the research project No. 244/81, my research colleagues for their co-operation in the project, and the Embaixada de Portugal in Spain for information kindly supplied on Portuguese national cheeses.

REFERENCES

1. FAO Production Yearbook, FAO, Rome, 1981.
2. Ministerio de Agricultura, Pesca y Alimentación, Anuario de Estadística Agraria 1982, Secretaría General Técnica, Madrid.
3. Centre Français du Commerce Exterior, Le Marché des Fromages en Espagne, Departement des Etudes de Marché Agricoles et Alimentaires, Paris, 1978.
4. Ministerio de Agricultura, Catálogo de Quesos Españoles, 2nd edn, Servicio de Publicaciones Agrarias, Madrid, 1973.
5. Ministerio de Agricultura, Pesca y Alimentación, Quesos de España, Imprenta del Servicio de Publicaciones Agrarias, Madrid, 1983.
6. Ortega, S., Tabla de Quesos Españoles, Ediciones Poniente, Madrid, 1983.
7. Canut, E. and Navarro, F., Els Fortmatges a Catalunya, Alta Fulla, Barcelona, 1980.
8. Carr, S., The Mitchell Beazley Pocket Guide to Cheese, Mitchell Beazley Publishers, London, 1981.
9. Eekhof-Stork, N., The World Atlas of Cheese, Paddington Press Ltd, London, 1977.
10. Marcos, A., Esteban, M. A., León, F. and Fernández-Salguero, J., J. Dairy Sci., 1979, 62, 892.

11. OECD, *Milk and Milk Products Balances in OECD Countries, 1974–1982*, OECD, Paris, 1984.
12. Ministerio de Agricultura, Pesca y Alimentación, *Recopilación Legislativa Alimentaria*, Capítulo 15.-Leches y derivados, Servicio de Publicaciones Agrarias, Madrid, 1982.
13. Juárez, M. and Núñez, M., *Milchwissenschaft*, 1981, **36**, 523.
14. Marcos, A., Fernández-Salguero, J., Esteban, M. A., León, F., Alcalá, M. and Beltrán de Heredia, F. H., *Quesos Españoles: Tablas de Composición, Valor Nutritivo y estabilidad*, Servicio de Publicaciones de la Universidad, Córdoba, 1985.
15. Vakaleris, D. G. and Price, W. V., *J. Dairy Sci.*, 1959, **42**, 264.
16. Marcos, A. and Mora, M. T., *Arch. Zootecn.*, 1981, **30**, 253.
17. Eigel, W. N., Butler, J. E., Ernstrom, C. A., Farrel, H. M., Harwalkar, V. R., Jenness, R. and Whitney, R. McL., *J. Dairy Sci.*, 1984, **67**, 1599.
18. Scott, W. J., *Adv. Food Res.*, 1957, **7**, 83.
19. Karel, M., *Crit. Rev. Food Technol.*, 1973, **3**, 329.
20. Duckworth, R. B. (Ed.), *Water Relations of Foods*, Academic Press, London, 1975.
21. Davies, R., Birch, G. G. and Parker, K. J. (Eds), *Intermediate Moisture Foods*, Elsevier Applied Science, London, 1976.
22. Troller, J. A. and Christian, J. H. B., *Water Activity and Food*, Academic Press, New York, 1978.
23. Rockland, L. B. and Stewart, G. F. (Eds), *Water Activity: Influences on Food Quality*, Academic Press, New York, 1981.
24. Iglesias, H. A. and Chirife, J., *Handbook of Food Isotherms*, Academic Press, New York, 1982.
25. Jowitt, R., Escher, F., Hallström, B., Meffert, H. F. Th., Spiess, W. E. L. and Vos, G. (Eds), *Physical Properties of Foods*, Elsevier Applied Science, London, Part 1, p. 13, 1983.
26. Labuza, T. P., *Moisture Sorption: Practical Aspects and Use*, American Association of Cereal Chemists, St. Paul, 1984.
27. Rüegg, M. and Blanc, B. In: *Water Activity: Influences on Food Quality* (Eds L. B. Rockland and G. F. Stewart), Academic Press, New York, p. 791, 1981.
28. Rüegg, M. and Blanc, B., Paper presented at the *III International Symposium on the Properties of Water in Food* (ISOPOW III), Beaune, 1983; published in *Properties of Water in Foods* (Eds D. Simatos and J. L. Multon), Martinus Nijhoff Publishers, Dordrecht, p. 603, 1985.
29. Hardy, J. In: *Le Fromage* (Ed. A. Eck), Technique et Documentation Lavoisier, Paris, p. 37, 1984.
30. Choisy, C., Desmazeaud, M., Gripon, J. C., Lamberet, G., Lenoir, J. and Tourneur, C. In: *Le Fromage* (Ed. A. Eck), Technique et Documentation, Lavoisier, Paris, p. 72, 1984.
31. Marcos, A., Beltrán de Heredia, F. H., Alcalá, M., Fernández-Salguero, J., Esteban, M. A., León, F. and Sánz, B., *Alimentaria*, 1982, **134**, 29.
32. Marcos, A., Alcalá, M., Esteban, M. A., Fernández-Salguero, J., León, F., Beltrán de Heredia, F. H. and Sánz, B., *Ind. Láct. Españolas*, 1983, **53–54**, 57.
33. McCune, T. D., Lang, K. W. and Steinberg, M. P., *J. Food Sci.*, 1981, **46**, 1978.
34. Lenart, A. and Flink, J. M., *Lebensm. Wiss. u.-Technol.*, 1983, **16**, 84.

35. Marcos, A., Alcalá, M., León, F., Fernández-Salguero, J. and Esteban, M. A., *J. Dairy Sci.*, 1981, **64**, 622.
36. Marcos, A., Esteban, M. A., Alcalá, M. and Millán, R., *J. Dairy Sci.*, 1983, **66**, 909.
37. Leung, H., Morris, M. H., Sloan, A. E. and Labuza, T. P., *Food Technol.*, 1976, **7**, 42.
38. Labuza, T. P., Kreisman, L. N., Heinz, C. A. and Lewicki, P. P., *J. Food Process. Preserv.*, 1977, **1**, 31.
39. Stamp, J. A., Linscott, S., Lomauro, C. and Labuza, T. P., *J. Food Sci.*, 1984, **49**, 1139.
40. Presidencia del Gobierno, *Boletín Oficial del Estado*, 1983, **153**, 18015.
41. Ramos, M. and Juárez, M., International Dairy Federation, A-Doc 74, 1983.
42. Storry, J. E., Grandison, A. S., Millard, D., Owen, A. J. and Ford, G. D., *J. Dairy Res.*, 1983, **50**, 215.
43. García, R. and Coll, L., *Anal. Bromatol.*, 1976, **28**, 211.
44. Juárez, M., Martinez, I., Méndez, A. and Martín, P. J., *Estudio sobre la Composición de la Leche de Vaca en España*, Instituto de Productos Lácteos, Arganda, Madrid, 1978.
45. García, R., Carballido, A. and Arnáez, M., *Anal. Bromatol.*, 1979, **31**, 227.
46. García, R., Carballido, A. and Arnáez, M., *Anal. Bromatol.*, 1980, **32**, 169.
47. Marcos, A., Millán, R., Esteban, M. A., Alcalá, M. and Fernández-Salguero, J., *J. Dairy Sci.*, 1983, **66**, 2488.
48. Martín-Hernández, M. C., Juárez, M. and Ramos, M., *Alimentación*, 1984, **4**, 61.
49. Millán, R., Alcalá, M., Esteban, M. A. and Marcos, A., *ITEA*, 1982, **1**, 418.
50. Esteban, M. A., Millán, R., Alcalá, M. and Marcos, A., *ITEA*, 1982, **1**, 424.
51. Alcalá, M., Marcos, A., Esteban, M. A. and Marcos, A., *ITEA*, 1982, **1**, 431.
52. Millán, R., Alcalá, M., Esteban, M. A. and Marcos, A., *ITEA*, 1982, **1**, 439.
53. Marcos, A. and Esteban, M. A., *J. Dairy Sci.*, 1982, **65**, 1795.
54. Gilles, J. and Lawrence, R. C., *N.Z. J. Dairy Sci. Technol.*, 1974, **8**, 148.
55. Lawrence, R. C. and Gilles, J., *N.Z. J. Dairy Sci. Technol.*, 1980, **15**, 1.
56. Guinee, T. P. and Fox, P. F., *J. Dairy Res.*, 1983, **50**, 511.
57. Compairé, C., *Fabricación de Quesos en Galicia*, Ed. Comité Nacional Lechero, Madrid, 1966.
58. Ordóñez, J. A. and Burgos, J., *Lait*, 1977, **57**, 150.
59. Burgos, J. and Ordóñez, J. A., *Lait*, 1977, **57**, 278.
60. Ordóñez, J. A. and Burgos, J., *Lait*, 1977, **57**, 416.
61. Burgos, J. and Ordóñez, J. A., *Milchwissenschaft*, 1978, **33**, 555.
62. Esteban, M. A. and Alcalá, M., *Alimentaria*, 1982, **132**, 31.
63. Alcalá, M., Fernández-Salguero, J., Esteban, M. A. and Marcos, A., *Ind. Láct. Españolas*, 1984, **63**, 37.
64. Alcalá, M., Beltrán de Heredia, F. H., Esteban, M. A. and Marcos, A., *Arch. Zootecn.*, 1982, **31**, 131.
65. Alcalá, M., Beltrán de Heredia, F. H., Esteban, M. A. and Marcos, A., *Arch. Zootecn.*, 1982, **31**, 257.
66. Esteban, M. A., Marcos, A., Alcalá, M. and Beltrán de Heredia, F. H., *Arch. Zootecn.*, 1982, **31**, 305.
67. Marcos, A., Esteban, M. A., Alcalá, M. and Beltrán de Heredia, F. H., *Arch. Zootecn.*, 1983, **32**, 17.

68. Ramos, M., Barneto, R., Suárez, J. A. and Iñigo, B., *Chem. Mikrobiol. Technol. Lebensm.*, 1982, **7**, 167.
69. Suárez, J. A. and Iñigo, B., *Chem. Mikrobiol. Technol. Lebensm.*, 1982, **7**, 173.
70. Suárez, J. A., Barneto, R. and Iñigo, B., *Chem. Mikrobiol. Technol. Lebensm.*, 1983, **8**, 52.
71. Polo, C., Ramos, M. and Sánchez, R., *Food Chem.*, 1985, **16**, 85.
72. Juárez, M., Román, M., Martínez, I. and Barros, C., *Alimentaria*, 1972, **9**, 43.
73. Madrid, I., *Ind. Láct. Españolas*, 1980, **21**, 15.
74. Esteban, M A., Marcos, A., Fernández-Salguero, J. and León, F., *Arch. Zootecn.*, 1979, **28**, 301.
75. Ministerio de Agricultura, Pesca y Alimentación, *Boletín Oficial del Estado*, 1985, **5**, 267.
76. Scott, R., *Cheesemaking Practice*, Applied Science Publishers Ltd, London, p. 454, 1981.
77. Marcos, A., Esteban, M. A., Fernández-Salguero, J., Mora, M. T. and Millán, R., *Anal. Bromatol.*, 1976, **28**, 57.
78. Marcos, A., Esteban, M. A., Fernández-Salguero, J., Mora, M. T. and Millán, R., *Anal. Bromatol.*, 1976, **28**, 69.
79. Marcos, A. and Esteban, M. A., *Anal. Bromatol.*, 1976, **28**, 401.
80. Esteban, M. A. and Marcos, A., *Anal. Bromatol.*, 1977, **29**, 35.
81. Marcos, A., Fernández-Salguero, J. and Esteban, M. A., *Arch. Zootecn.*, 1978, **27**, 341.
82. López, P., Sánz, B. and Burgos, J., *Anal. Bromatol.*, 1962, **14**, 221.
83. Marcos, A., Fernández-Salguero, J., Mora, M. T., Esteban, M. A. and León, F., *Arch. Zootecn.*, 1979, **28**, 29.
84. Wirotama, I. P. G., Ney, K. H. and Freytag, W. G., *Z. Lebensm. Unters.-Forsch.*, 1973, **153**, 78.
85. Muñóz, M. H., Rivas, J. C. and Mariné, A., *Anal. Bromatol.*, 1981, **33**, 225.
86. Juárez, M. and Martín-Hernández, M. C., *Rev. Agroquim. Tecnol. Aliment.*, 1983, **23**, 417.
87. Marcos, A., Esteban, M. A. and Fernández-Salguero, J., *Anal. Bromatol.*, 1979, **31**, 91.
88. Charro., A., Simal, J., Creus, J. M. and Trigueros, J., *Anal. Bromatol.*, 1969, **21**, 7.
89. Ramos, M., *Rev. Esp. Lechería*, 1976, **101**, 147.
90. Ramos, M., Martínez, I. and Juárez, M., *J. Dairy Sci.*, 1980, **60**, 870.
91. Ramos, M. and Martínez, I., *Lait*, 1976, **56**, 164.
92. Ordóñez, J. A., Barneto, R. and Ramos, M., *Milchwissenschaft*, 1978, **33**, 609.
93. Mora, M. T. and Marcos, A., *Arch. Zootecn.*, 1981, **30**, 139.
94. Mora, M. T. and Marcos, A., *Arch. Zootecn.*, 1982, **31**, 27.
95. Marcos, A. and Mora, M. T., *Arch. Zootecn.*, 1982, **31**, 115.
96. Ordóñez, J. A. and Burgos, J., *Milchwissenschaft*, 1980, **35**, 69.
97. Juárez, M., Martínez, I. and Ramos, M., *III Congr. Nac. Quin. Agric. Aliment.*, Sevilla, 1980.
98. Román, M., *Lait*, 1975, **55**, 401.
99. Núñez, M. and Martínez-Moreno, J. L., *Anal. INIA*, 1976, **4**, 11.
100. Martínez-Moreno, J. L. and Núñez, M., *Anal. INIA*, 1976, **4**, 33.
101. Ordóñez, J. A., Barneto, R. and Mármol, M. P., *Anal. Bromatol.*, 1978, **30**, 361.
102. Martínez-Moreno, J. L., *Anal. INIA*, 1976, **4**, 41.
103. Núñez, M., *Anal. INIA*, 1976, **4**, 57.

218   A. Marcos

104. Núñez, M., *Anal. INIA*, 1976, **4**, 67.
105. Núñez, M., *Anal. INIA*, 1976, **4**, 75.
106. Martínez-Moreno, J. L., *Anal. INIA*, 1976, **4**, 83.
107. Ortíz, M. J. and Ordóñez, J. A., *Anal. Bromatol.*, 1979, **31**, 11.
108. Martínez-Moreno, J. L., *Anal. INIA*, 1976, **4**, 93.
109. Núñez, M., *Anal. INIA*, 1976, **4**, 103.
110. Núñez, M., *Anal. INIA*, 1976, **4**, 113.
111. Núñez, M., Núñez, J. A., Medina, A. L., García, C. and Rodríguez, M. A., *Anal. INIA*, 1981, **12**, 53.
112. Núñez, M., Martínez-Moreno, J. L. and Medina, A. L., *Anal. INIA*, 1981, **12**, 65.
113. Marcos, A., Esteban, M. A., Espejo, J., Martínez, P. and Muñóz, M. T., *Arch. Zootecn.*, 1977, **26**, 189.
114. Ordóñez, J. A., Barneto, R. and Ramos, M., *Proc. XX Int. Dairy Congr.*, Paris, 1978, Vol. E, p. 573.
115. Barneto, R. and Ordóñez, J. A., *Alimentaria*, 1979, **107**, 39.
116. Ramos, M., Barneto, R. and Ordóñez, J. A., *Milchwissenschaft*, 1981, **36**, 528.
117. Núñez, M., Núñez, J. A. and Medina, A. L., *Milchwissenschaft*, 1982, **37**, 328.
118. Medina, M., Gaya, P. and Núñez, M., *J. Food Prot.*, 1982, **45**, 1091.
119. Gaya, P., Medina, M. and Núñez, M., *J. Food Prot.*, 1983, **46**, 305.
120. Ordóñez, J. A., Masso, J. A., Mármol, M. P. and Ramos, M., *Lait*, 1980, **60**, 283.
121. Fernández-Salguero, J., *Anal. Bromatol.*, 1978, **30**, 123.
122. Fernández-Salguero, J., *Anal. Bromatol.*, 1978, **30**, 131.
123. Fernández-Salguero, J., *Anal. Bromatol.*, 1978, **30**, 136.
124. Fernández-Salguero, J., Esteban, M. A. and Marcos, A., *Trab. Cient. Univ. Córdoba*, 1977, **7**, 1.
125. Fernández-Salguero, J. and Marcos, A., *Trab. Cient. Univ. Córdoba*, 1977, **13**, 1.
126. Marcos, A., Esteban, M. A. and Fernández-Salguero, J., *Trab. Cient. Univ. Córdoba*, 1977, **15**, 1.
127. Fernández-Salguero, J., Barreto, J. D. and Marsilla, B. A., *Arch. Zootecn.*, 1978, **27**, 365.
128. Martínez, P. and Fernández-Salguero, J., *Arch. Zootecn.*, 1978, **27**, 93.
129. Fernández-Salguero, J., Ruíz, J. and Marcos, A., *Rev. Agroquím. Tecnol. Aliment.*, 1984, **24**, 383.
130. Ruíz, J., Fernández-Salguero, J., Esteban, M. A. and Marcos, A., *Arch. Zootecn.*, 1984, **33**, 301.
131. Marsilla, B. A., *Arch. Zootecn.*, 1979, **28**, 255.
132. Suárez, J. A., Barneto, R. and Iñigo, B., *Ind. Láct. Españolas*, 1984, **67**, 25.
133. Barreto, J. D., *Arch. Zootecn.*, 1979, **28**, 287.
134. Fernández-Salguero, J., Barreto, J. D. and Marsilla, B. A., *Alimentaria*, 1981, **119**, 71.
135. Marcos, A., Fernández-Salguero, J., Esteban, M. A., León, F., Alcalá, M. and Beltrán de Heredia, F. H., *Ind. Láct. Españolas*, 1984, **64**, 15.
136. Marcos, A., Fernández-Salguero, J., Esteban, M. A., León, F., Alcalá, M. and Beltrán de Heredia, F. H., *Ind. Láct. Españolas*, 1984, **65-66**, 21.
137. Núñez, M., *J. Dairy Res.*, 1978, **45**, 501.
138. Burgos, J., López, A. and Sala, F. J., *Anal. Fac. Vet. León*, 1971, **17**, 109.

139. Sala, F. J., Burgos, J. and Ordóñez, J. A., *Anal. Fac. Vet. León*, 1971, **17**, 115.
140. Sala, F. J. and Burgos, J., *Anal. Bromatol.*, 1972, **24**, 83.
141. Sala, F. J. and Burgos, J., *Anal. Bromatol.*, 1972, **24**, 61.
142. Núñez, M. and Medina, M., *Lait*, 1979, **59**, 497.
143. Núñez, M. and Medina, M., *Lait*, 1980, **60**, 171.
144. Núñez, M., Medina, M., Gaya, P. and Dias-Amado, C., *Litt*, 1981, **61**, 62.
145. Juárez, M., Alonso, L. and Ramos, M., *Rev. Agroquím. Tecnol. Aliment.*, 1983, **23**, 541.
146. Alonso, L., Juárez, M. and Ramos, M., *Proc. Euro. Food Chem. II*, Rome, p. 437, 1983.
147. Hewedi, M. M. and Fox, P. F., *Milchwissenschaft*, 1984, **39**, 198.
148. International Dairy Federation Bulletin, Doc. 158, 1983.
149. International Dairy Federation, *Ewe's and Goat's Milk. Results of question-naire 2779/A*, 1980.
150. Vieira de Sá, F. In: *Production and Utilization of Goat's and Ewe's Milk*, IDF Bulletin, Doc. 158, p. 66, 1983.
151. Vieira de Sá, F. and Barbosa, M., *Ind. Láct. Españolas*, 1982, **45**, 39.
152. Vieira de Sá, F., Reis Machado, B., Rafael Pinto, O. P., Vicente da Cruz, I. M., Dias Carneiro, M. J., Antunes Barbosa, M. M. and Costa Reis, M. M., *INII. Quimica e Biologia* No. 6, Lisboa, 1970.
153. Norma Portuguesa, *Queijo Serra da Estrella: Definição, características, acondicionamento e conservação*, NP-1922, 1982.
154. Vieira de Sá, F. and Barbosa, M., *J. Dairy Res.*, 1972, **39**, 335.
155. Christen, C. and Virasoro, E., *Lait*, 1935, **15**, 354.
156. Christen, C. and Virasoro, E., *Lait*, 1935, **15**, 496.
157. Pereira de Matos, A. A. and Vieira de Sá, F., *Boletim Pecuário*, 1948, **16**, 6.
158. Barbosa, M., Valles, E., Vassal, L. and Mocquot, G., *Lait*, 1976, **54**, 1.
159. Serrano, E. and Marcos, A., *Arch. Zootecn.*, 1980, **29**, 11.
160. Martínez, E. and Esteban, M. A., *Arch. Zootecn.*, 1980, **29**, 107.
161. Marcos, A., Esteban, M. A., Martínez, E., Alcalá, M. and Fernández-Salguero, J., *Arch. Zootecn.*, 1980, **29**, 283.
162. Cabezas, L., Esteban, M. A. and Marcos, A., *Alimentaria*, 1981, **128**, 17.
163. Marcos, A., Cabezas, L. and Esteban, M. A., *Alimentaria*, 1982, **129**, 33.
164. Esteban, M. A., Marcos, A. and Cabezas, L., *Alimentaria*, 1982, **130**, 19.
165. Marcos, A., Esteban, M. A. and Fernández-Salguero, J., *Arch. Zootecn.*, 1976, **25**, 73.
166. Marcos, A., Fernández-Salguero, J. and Esteban, M. A., *Anal. Bromatol.*, 1978, **30**, 314.
167. Marcos, A., Esteban, M. A. and Fernández-Salguero, J., *Arch. Zootecn.*, 1978, **27**, 285.
168. Marcos, A., Fernández-Salguero, J., Esteban, M. A. and León, F., *J. Dairy Sci.*, 1979, **62**, 392.
169. Creamer, L. K., *N.Z. J. Dairy Sci. Technol.*, 1970, **5**, 152.
170. Creamer, L. K., *N.Z. J. Dairy Sci. Technol.*, 1971, **6**, 91.
171. Fox, P. F. and Walley, B. F., *J. Dairy Res.*, 1971, **38**, 165.
172. Phelan, J. A., Guinee, J. and Fox, P. F., *J. Dairy Res.*, 1973, **40**, 105.
173. Juárez, M., Ramos, M., Goicoecha, A. and Jiménez-Pérez, S., *Chem. Mikrobiol. Technol. Lebensm.*, 1984, **8**, 143.

Chapter 7

Italian Cheeses

P. F. Fox and T. P. Guinee

*Department of Dairy and Food Chemistry,
University College, Cork, Ireland*

1. INTRODUCTION

While Italy may not be ranked among the leading dairying countries of the world, at least relative to its size, its cheese industry is of the highest order. It is in many respects unique, with a history of at least 2500 years. To cite Reinbold[1] 'Like Italian art, architecture, music and literature, Italian cheese is a product of an ancient culture. Cheese graced the banquet tables of the Caesars, served as rations for the conquering Roman armies, and, today is part of traditional dishes'.

Today, Italy has a greater range of cheese varieties than any other country with the exception of France, and two Italian cheeses, Gorgonzola and Parmesan, rank among the most famous international cheese varieties. While Roquefort and Stilton may challenge Gorgonzola as the prime blue-mould cheese, Parmesan is at the forefront of grating cheeses. Italy is also the principal producer of that rather unique family of cheeses—the *Pasta filata* or stretched curd cheeses—of which Provolone, Caciocavallo and Mozzarella are the best known members. Italy is probably also unique in that milks from four species, cow, sheep, goat and buffalo, are used commercially for cheese production. In fact the animal species from which the milk is obtained is often included in the name of some Italian cheeses: pecarino (ewe), caprino (goat), vacchino (cow).

The level of cheese production in Italy, 637 000 tonnes in 1982,[2] is the third largest in Europe after France and West Germany (Table I). A higher proportion (44%) of milk production is converted into cheese in Italy than in any other major dairying country but even at this level, local supply is inadequate to meet the demand and Italy is currently the largest cheese

221

TABLE I
Cheese production in Europe, 1982 (Ref. 2)

Country	Milk production ('000 tonnes)				% Total milk production		% Milk utilized for cheese			Total cheese production	Cheese exported	Cheese imported	Used domestically
	Cow's milk	Goat's milk	Sheep's milk	Total	Retained on farms	Delivered to dairies	Retained on farms	Delivered to dairies	Total milk		('000 tonnes)		
Germany	25 759	22	—	25 781	8	92	—	14	12	839	261	256	830
France	32 901	440	1 086	34 427	25	75	2	29	22	1 195	249	63	1 008
Italy	10 770	124	593	11 487	27	73	21	51	44	637	36	267	868
Netherlands	12 708	—	—	12 708	3	97	22	26	26	492	317	35	207
Belgium	4 102	—	—	4 102	25	75	—	7	5	54	32	101	123
Luxembourg	299	—	—	299	9	91	—	—	—	—	—	—	—
United Kingdom	18 455	—	—	18 455	14	86	9	14	14	244	34	130	349
Irish Republic	5 680	—	—	5 680	14	86	—	12	10	56	44	4	13
Denmark	5 358	—	—	5 358	6	94	—	28	26	245	198	7	56
Greece[a]	841	551	784	2 176	58	42	29	54	39	—	—	—	—

[a] 1981.

importer in the world (Table I). A small percentage (~ 6%) of Italian cheese production is exported, mainly to the US.

Resulting from the large numbers of Italian emigrants to the US and to a lesser extent, Australia, Argentina and Brazil, some of the principal Italian cheese varieties, especially Parmesan, Romano and Mozzarella, have become international varieties. The second largest producer of Italian cheese is the US, which in 1979 produced 421 356 tonnes, equivalent to 74% of that produced in Italy in the same year.[3] Other factors which have contributed to the spread of Italian cheeses are the increasing popularity of Italian dishes, notably pizza pie and spaghetti which has created an international demand for Mozzarella-type and Parmesan-type cheeses, respectively, and the large imports of cheese into Italy, some of which are of Italian-types produced in neighbouring European countries.

Cheesemaking in Italy is concentrated in the fertile Po valley where the principal Italian varieties Parmesan (Grana), Asiago, Swiss-type cheeses, Gorgonzola, Taleggio, Fontina and Bel Paese are manufactured on a large scale. The Pasta filata types were, traditionally, made principally in southern Italy and Sicily, frequently from buffalo milk, while Romano-type cheeses were made in the regions around Rome and in Sardinia. However, today the manufacture of the Pasta filata and Romano types is not restricted to their locality of origin.

2. CLASSIFICATION OF ITALIAN CHEESES

According to Breed,[4] there are several hundred varieties of Italian cheese. Walter and Hargrove[5] list 77, excluding synonyms; Schulz and Sydow[6] list 22 varieties and the Associazione Italiana Lattierio Casearia[7] list 17. Reinbold[1] lists 43 varieties (although some differ only in milk type or origin) which he classifies into 8 families (not including Ricotto), based on moisture content (very hard, hard, semi-soft and soft) and the principal (distinctive) ripening agent. Classification of Italian cheeses is complicated by the use of different names for the same or very similar cheeses in different regions, and by qualifications based on the species from which the milk is obtained and even the season when the cheese is produced, e.g. Romano. Many varieties are consumed after different degrees of ripening, e.g. as table cheeses after 2–4 months but may be used as grating (low moisture) cheeses if ripened for a longer period, e.g. 12 months; it is therefore impossible to classify many cheeses on the basis of moisture content.

Using a modification of the scheme employed by Reinbold,[1] the 77 varieties listed by Walter and Hargrove[5] are classified in Table II.

TABLE II
Classification of Italian cheeses (listed by Walter and Hargrove[5])

1. *Very hard/hard*[a]
   Asiago (old, grating; also medium and fresh variants which may be used as table cheeses)
   Parmesan-types: Parmesan (or Grana); Bagozzo (also known as Bagzo, Bresciano); Emiliano; Grana Lombardo; Grana Reggiano; Lodigiano; Parmigiano; Modena; Monte; Veneto (like Asiago)
   Romano-types: Romano; Romanello (little Romano); Sardo (Sardo Romano); Fiori Sardo (ewe's milk); Pepato (Siciliano Pepato, flavoured with peppers)
   Bra
   Calcagno (ewe's milk, i.e. pecorino)
   Nostrale (Formaggio Duro)
   Raschera (probably the same as Nostrale)
   Toscanello (ewe's)

2. *Pasta filata*
   (a) *ripened*: Caciocavallo; Caciocavallo Siciliano; Casigiolu (also called Panedda or Pera di Vacca, made in Sardinia); Provolone (pear-shaped, 4–6 kg; if made up in small cylindrical forms, it is called various names e.g. Provoletti, Provolotini, Provoloncini); Incanestrato (Pecorina Incanestrato; Pasta filata as made in Sicily but may be made by Romano process in US); Mogocchino (Sicily; cow's, goat's or ewe's milk); Manteca or Manteche (butter enclosed in a large 'bag' made of Pasta filata cheese; also called butirro, burriello, burino, buro); Moliterno (also Pecorino Moliterno if made from ewe's milk); Cartonese (ewe's milk seasoned with peppers); Salami (large Provolone-type); Foggiano (ewe's milk)
   (b) *fresh*: Mozzarella, Provatura, Provole, Scamorze (or Scarmorze), Trecce

3. *Swiss-type*
   Asin (few large eyes, also whitish surface mould growth); Salmistra (variant of Asin ripened in special brine for 2–3 months); Bitto (small eyes); Fontina (Gruyère-type usually ewe's milk, but also cow's milk); Montasio; Rayon; Sbrinza (Sbrinz or Spalen; Swiss-type cheese; no eyes or only small eyes; may be used as a grating cheese when fully ripened)

4. *Blue mould*
   Castelmagno; Gorgonzola; Moncenisio; Pannarone (also known as Stracchino di Gorgonzola; Gorgonzola-type but without blue veining)

5. *Bacterial surface ripened*
   Bel Paese (a group of cheeses including Königskäse; Bella Alpina, Bella Milano, Bel Piano Lombardo, Bel Piemonte Fior d'Alpe, Savoia, Vittoria; members of this group were developed ~1900); Cacio Fiore (Caciotta); Crescenza (Carsenza; Stracchino Cresenzo; Crescenza Lombardi); Milano (also known as Fresco, Quardo or Stracchino Quartirolo); Raviggiolo; Robbiole; Robbiolini; Taleggio   *(continued)*

TABLE II—*contd.*

6. *Fresh, soft*
Bernarde; Formagella (goat's or sheep's milk, made in Alpine regions); Formaggini (small cheese; name applied to several types of small Italian cheeses, e.g. Formaggini di Lecco; usually consumed fresh but may be ripened); Formaggini di Montepellier (made with rennet paste containing white wine, thistle blossoms and flavourings); Fresa (cooked cheese made in Sardinia from cow's milk); Mascarpone (soft cream cheese); Nostrale (Formaggio Tenero); Ricotta

7. *Miscellaneous*[b]
Borelli (buffalo milk)
Chiavari (sour-milk cheese)
Mozarinelli (cow or buffalo milk)
Scanno (ewe's milk, cheese dipped in solution of ferric oxide—black colour)

---

[a] These have not been separated because moisture content varies with age and many of these cheese varieties may be very hard, hard or even semi-soft depending on age at consumption.
[b] These varieties are listed by Walter and Hargrove[5] but insufficient information is supplied to permit their classification.

Burkhalter[8] lists 14 Italian varieties: Asiago, Caciocavallo, Fiore Sardo, Fontina, Gorgonzola, Grana Padona, Montasio, Parmigiano-Reggiano, Pecorino Romano, Pecorino Siciliano, Pressato, Provolone, Ragusano, Taleggio (surprisingly Mozzarella is not listed as an Italian variety; Pressato which is not listed by Walter and Hargrove,[5] is an Asiago-type cheese[9]). Simon[9] states that Ragusano is a Caciocavallo-type cheese and also gives slightly different names for some of the varieties listed in Table II.

2.1 Parmesan, Romano and Pasta Filata Cheeses

While there are individual characteristics, the Swiss-type, Blue and bacterial surface-ripened Italian varieties are members of larger international families which have been reviewed in Chapters 3, 4 and 5, respectively. In this chapter, only the 'characteristic' Italian groups: Pasta filata-types, Parmesan and Romano are considered.

Manufacturing procedures for these 3 families of cheese are described by Reinbold,[1] Walter and Hargrove,[5] Kosikowski[10] and Scott.[11] Studies on the manufacture of a fast-ripening Romano-type cheese are described by Mattick *et al.*[12]—the manufacturing protocol described in this study differs appreciably from the more 'traditional' methods, e.g. *S. lactis*, with or without *L. acidophilus*, was used as starter and indigenous milk lipase,

TABLE III
Manufacturing protocol for hard Italian cheeses[a]

	Romano (Pecorino Romano)	Grana/Parmesan	Provolone	Mozzarella
Type of milk	Cow (sheep)	Cow	Cow	Cow (traditionally buffalo)
% fat in milk	2·0–2·2	1·8–2·5	3·5	1·6–3·0
Pasteurization	Raw but now usually pasteurized	Raw but now usually pasteurized	Raw but now usually pasteurized	Usually pasteurized
Starter	L. bulgaricus or similar rod starter; S. thermophilus	L. bulgaricus S. thermophilus	S. thermophilus Lactobacillus spp.	S. thermophilus Lactobacillus spp.
Rennet	(1) Rennet paste or (2) Rennet extract + PGE[a] or rennet paste	(1) Rennet paste or (2) Rennet extract + PGE or rennet paste	(1) Rennet paste or (2) Rennet extract + PGE or rennet paste	Rennet extract
Cut size	~1 cm	0·5 cm	0·7 cm	1·5 cm
Setting temp (°C)	32	32–35	32	32
Cooking temp (°C)	45–46	51–54	40–45	40–42
Acidity at draining (%)	0·2	0·17–0·19	0·2	0·19

	Cylindrical; diam: 20 cm height: 14–21 cm weight: 6–22 kg	Cylindrical; diam: 35–46 cm height: 18–33 cm weight: 24–40 kg	Various shapes and sizes (spheres, pear-shaped, salami shapes) 0.5–100 kg	Loaves
Shape, size, dimensions	Cylindrical; diam: 20 cm height: 14–21 cm weight: 6–22 kg	Cylindrical; diam: 35–46 cm height: 18–33 cm weight: 24–40 kg	Various shapes and sizes (spheres, pear-shaped, salami shapes) 0.5–100 kg	Loaves
Salting	Brining, 24% NaCl, 3–4 days; dry salted, 30–60 days	Brining, 24% NaCl, 15 days	Brining, 24% NaCl, 1–3 days, depending on size	Brining, 15% NaCl, 1 h; 24% NaCl, 1–3 days depending on size
Ripening: Temp (°C)	7–10 75–85% RH	10–15	13; 4–5	Consumed fresh
Duration	5–12 mth	2–4 yrs	2–12 mth	Consumed fresh
Traditional packaging	None; wash surface with brine	Surface oiling	Wash; oil or wax	
Composition: % FDM	≤38 [PR ≤36]	32–35	≤44 [≤45 (US)]	~40 [≤38 pizza, Can]
% H₂O	>34 [PR >33]	30–34	>38 [>45 (US)]	>52 [>48 pizza, Can]
Pressing	No external pressure; double stacking	10–20 psi overnight		Piling process very similar to cheddaring

a Compiled from Refs 1, 5, 10, 11.
PGE = Pregastric esterase; PR = Pecorino Romano; US = US standard; Can = Canadian standard.

fungal lipase or pancreatic lipase was used as lipolytic agent rather than the more traditional pregastric esterase, purified or as a rennet paste; the fungal and pancreatic lipases gave unsatisfactory flavours.

The manufacture of Mozzarella cheese by 'conventional' methods was described by Kosikowski,[13] while Breene *et al.*[14] described a direct acidification method using lactic, acetic or hydrochloric acids for the manufacture of Pizza cheese which had good stretching properties at ~pH 5·6, i.e. slightly higher than the optimum stretching pH of conventional Mozzarella (5·3–5·4). (The term 'Pizza' cheese is sometimes applied to low-moisture (48 versus 56%) Mozzarella and has somewhat better sliceability).

While the procedure described by the above authors differ in detail, all agree on the general principles; an attempt is made to summarize these in Table III.

There are obviously many similarities in the manufacturing protocol for the 4 cheeses—the procedures for Provolone and Mozzarella are almost identical and the latter might be regarded as an unripened version of the former. Not surprisingly, the general properties of Romano and Grana are quite similar: while both may be consumed as table cheeses when young, both assume a granular texture when mature and when the moisture content decreases to <35%, both are used mainly as grating cheeses. Because of the stretching process, the texture of Provolone is rather flaky and the flavour is quite mild compared with Grana and Romano, partly because it is normally matured for a shorter period and undoubtedly the heat treatment prior to stretching inactivates most bacteria and enzymes in the curd, although information on this appears to be lacking. Creamer[15] showed that on mixing curd at 20–22°C with twice its weight of water at 85°C, the temperature of the curd 1 cm beneath the surface reached 68–72°C while the temperature of the homogeneous mass after kneading was 55°C. He showed that rennet was inactivated if the curd was heated to temperatures >65°C but indigenous milk proteinase (plasmin) was not inactivated on heating at up to 85°C for 5 min.

2.2 Mozzarella

As far as the properties of the finished cheeses are concerned, Mozzarella is the odd man out of this group and will be discussed separately. Burkhalter[8] has classified Mozzarella as a semi-soft/semi-hard cheese whereas the other three were classified as hard or very hard. It is used mainly as a filling in pizza pie, lasagne and other Italian dishes. In pizza pie, which has enjoyed very rapid growth in popularity in North America and throughout Europe over the past 20–30 years, the principal prerequisites for good quality Mozzarella are stretchability and melt-down characteristics. Optimum stretchability of Mozzarella is obtained at pH 5·2–5·4 for biologically acidified cheese or pH 5·6 for chemically acidified curd.[14] Curd for stretching is heated in water at 74°C and the temperature of the curd reaches 58°C.[10,14] Procedures for assessing the melt-down properties of cheese are described by Breene *et al.*,[14] Kosikowski,[10] and Arnott *et al.*;[16] a comparison of these and other methods was reported by Park *et al.*[17]

The level of proteolysis in Mozzarella cheese is quite low. Creamer[15] showed that in 12-week-old samples of Mozzarella (which is older than the normal age at consumption), Gouda and Cheddar, the percentages of total N soluble at pH 4·5 were 7·3, 20 and 15·5, respectively, and in 12% TCA were 2·4, 13·9 and 10·3, respectively. Gel electrophoresis showed that the level of residual α_{s1}-casein in Mozzarella was greater than that in Cheddar (lowest) and Gouda, presumably due to the thermal inactivation of rennet during stretching, although the level of α_{s1}-I-casein (produced from α_{s1}-casein by rennet) was intermediate between Cheddar and Gouda. The formation of γ-caseins was greatest in Gouda and least in Cheddar, which probably reflects the rate of acidification in the 3 cheeses (Cheddar, Mozzarella, Gouda) and the pH at draining since the level of plasmin in cheese curd depends on this.[18]

These findings were confirmed and extended by Di Matteo *et al.*[19] who studied proteolysis in Mozzarella cheese by the formation of non-protein N, pH 4·6-soluble N and by electrophoresis. They showed the almost complete breakdown of α_{s1}-casein to α_{s1}-I and α_{s1}-II, indicating that some rennet activity survives the kneading and stretching process; however, compared to other cheese varieties, the extent of proteolysis in Mozzarella is very limited. Considerable levels of γ-caseins were apparent in all samples studied. Little lipolysis occurs in Mozzarella (Tables IV and V).

Mozzarella with a very white colour is preferred by users. Because of its high carotene content, Mozzarella made from cow's milk has a yellowish colour. Several methods are available to reduce the intensity of the colour of cow's milk Mozzarella, e.g. bleaching with benzoyl peroxide, homogenization (both of which adversely affect the stretching and melting properties of the cheese and the former may also cause development of oxidized off-flavours), use of blue or green food dyes to mask the yellow colour or titanium oxide (0·02–0·05%) which Kosikowski and Brown[20] recommend.

TABLE IV

Free fatty acid (FFA) compositions and flavours of Mozzarella cheeses during aging (Ref. 42) (reproduced by permission of the Journal of Dairy Science)

Sample number	Aging time (days) at 7°C	FFA concentration (ppm)								Flavour
		$C_{4:0}$	$C_{6:0}$	$C_{8:0}$	$C_{10:0}$	$C_{12:0}$	$C_{14:0}$	$C_{16:0}$	C_{18} congeners	
1	63[a]	16	5	13	154	20	78	175	151	Mild, milky, tart, slightly bitter
	83	12	9	24	115	16	15	80	66	Lacks flavour, slightly sulphury
	111	49	11	10	150	92	53	135	131	Mild, milky
2	63[a]	24	5	9	64	31	39	171	236	Mild, milky
	83	32	14	7	171	13	33	116	101	
	111	53	3	31	55	32	52	106	73	Lacks flavour, slightly bitter
3	58[a]	29	4	6	13	10	32	58	88	Milky, aged, tart, clean
	78	10	7	24	54	45	27	64	46	
	106	70	1	13	23	6	35	74	72	Very aged, sharp flavour
4	61[a]	23	5	9	5	14	24	73	101	Milky, tart, aged
	81	19	11	10	87	29	54	92	119	
	109	19	1	12	9	16	40	56	51	Very aged, sharp flavour

[a] Age of cheese upon receipt of and initiation of experimental aging.

TABLE V

Free fatty acid (FFA) compositions and flavours of retail samples of Italian cheese varieties (Ref. 42) (reproduced by permission of the *Journal of Dairy Science*)

Cheese variety	Sample code	Concentration of FFA (ppm)								Flavour
		$C_{4:0}$	$C_{6:0}$	$C_{8:0}$	$C_{10:0}$	$C_{12:0}$	$C_{14:0}$	$C_{16:0}$	C_{18} congeners	
Provolone	A	376	162	45	259	83	104	245	258	Lacks full flavour, coarse
	B	386	139	56	94	114	198	352	388	Tart, coarse, lacks full flavour
	C	782	308	81	172	122	120	199	334	Very balanced FFA flavour
	D	1 892	1 062	284	718	446	496	890	1 019	Very strongly rancid, soapy
Parmesan	A[a]	140	106	84	158	181	684	1 750	1 890	Full, blended mild FFA flavour
	B	502	174	98	223	163	368	621	662	Strong flavour, lacks balance
Romano	A	1 756	843	328	942	428	448	785	1 224	Full blended flavour, smooth
	B	2 680	1 478	607	1 350	1 006	1 063	1 857	2 748	Pronounced coarse flavour
	C[a]	5 508	2 814	1 061	2 074	1 902	2 581	4 796	4 424	Very strong butyric, soapy
Mozzarella[b]	A	48	0	6	10	26	72	147	156	Bland, flat, milky
	B	54	7	1	120	12	27	76	66	Mild, milky, tart

[a] Grated cheese.
[b] Mozzarella samples A and B were made from whole and part skim-milk, respectively.

As a bland unripened cheese, Mozzarella is particularly amenable to production by direct acidification methods. Mozzarella (Pizza) cheese with satisfactory flavour, colour, elasticity and melt-down properties was produced from whole or partly skimmed milk, usually homogenized, acidified to pH 5·6 at 5°C with lactic, acetic or hydrochloric acid by Breene et al.[21] Continuous agitation of milk during coagulation to give irregularly-shaped curd particles from acidified milk also yields satisfactory Pizza cheese.[22] This modification should greatly facilitate methods of curd production. (Quarne et al.[23] reported higher losses of fat during moulding and stretching from cheese made by this method than by traditional starter or 'quiescent' direct acidification methods.) Acidification with lactic acid tends to give high moisture cheese while HCl and H_3PO_4 yield cheese of equal quality although the latter gives better retention of calcium in the curd with consequently higher yields.[24] This was confirmed by Quarne et al.[25] who also concluded that porcine pepsin or fungal rennet gave better quality cheese than calf rennet. Keller et al.,[26] taking various characteristics of the cheese into consideration, also confirmed the advantages of H_3PO_4 and concluded that polyvalent organic acids generally gave poor results. Bitterness may be a problem in cheese set at low pH values but may be overcome by reducing the amount of rennet used.[27]

Satisfactory Mozzarella cheese has been manufactured from reconstituted skim-milk powder[28] and Demott[29] has described the manufacture of a Mozzarella-like cheese from recombined skim-milk powder and cream by direct acidification.

A considerable proportion of 'Pizza' cheese is now made from acid or rennet casein (cheese analogues); these products are included with processed cheeses in Chapter 11.

The potential of milk concentrated by ultrafiltration (UF) in cheese manufacture has received considerable attention in recent years. Mozzarella cheese made directly from UF retentate had poor melt-down characteristics but diafiltration of the retentate yielded a very satisfactory product.[30]

2.2.1 Microstructure and rheological properties

The rheological properties of Mozzarella cheese are probably its most important functional property, particularly its meltability and stretchability. These rheological properties are influenced by composition, especially pH, and by the kneading process to which the curd is subjected and which gives stretched Mozzarella and Provolone cheeses a distinctly fibrous microstructure.[31]

Among 11 varieties of cheese examined by Chen *et al.*,[32] Mozzarella had a relatively low value for hardness but had the highest value for elasticity and among the highest for cohesiveness, adhesiveness, chewiness and gumminess. Provolone had a relatively high value for cohesiveness, intermediate values for adhesiveness, chewiness and gumminess and low values for hardness and elasticity. Of the 11 varieties, Parmesan was at the upper or lower extreme for most of the parameters studied: it had the highest values for hardness, adhesiveness, gumminess and chewiness and lowest or second lowest for elasticity and cohesiveness.

The effects of compression ratio on the mechanical properties of some cheese varieties, including Mozzarella, were studied by Imoto *et al.*;[33] at any particular compression ratio, Mozzarella showed a lower compression force and adhesive force and a higher work ratio and recovered height than several samples of Cheddar and was in fact very similar to Muenster. Freezing and thawing of Mozzarella cheese did not significantly affect compression force at 50% compression, firmness, cohesiveness or maximum blending distance; increasing the salt content of the cheese increased the firmness and force at 50% compression but decreased cohesiveness and maximum blending distance.[34]

The 'flowability' of melted Mozzarella cheese has been evaluated by capillary rheometry.[35] This type of rheometer appears to be satisfactory for molten Mozzarella but not for other types of cheese in which slippage and other effects play a dominant role. The influence of cheese composition and ripening and manufacturing variables on the rheological behaviour of molten Mozzarella by this method do not appear to have been investigated. Measurements of this type should provide more objective data than the melting tests described above.[10,14,16,17]

3. RIPENING OF HARD ITALIAN CHEESES

The hard Italian varieties are surface salted, usually by a combination of brine and dry-salting, according to Kosikowski[10] for up to 30–60 days. Therefore, there is a decreasing NaCl gradient from the surface to the centre of the cheese and a consequent moisture gradient in the opposite direction. The diffusion of NaCl during the salting of Parmesan cheese has been studied by Resmini *et al.*[36] and of Romano-type cheese by Guinee and Fox.[37] These gradients persist for a very considerable period after salting, as shown for Romano-type cheese by Guinee and Fox.[38] Consequently, ripening in these cheeses will show zonal variation, as influenced by salt and moisture concentrations.

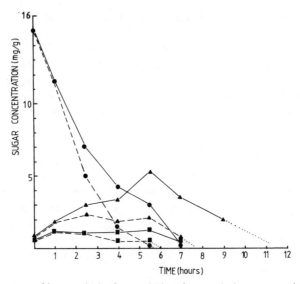

Fig. 1. Changes of lactose (●), glucose (■), galactose (▲) concentrations in the external (– – –) and internal (———) parts of Parmigiano cheese (Ref. 39).

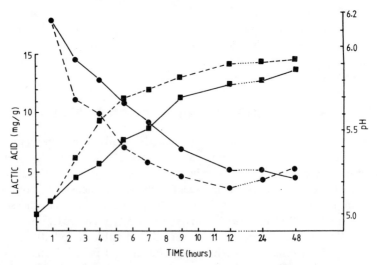

Fig. 2. Changes of pH (●) and lactic acid concentration (■) in the external (– – –) and internal (———) parts of Parmigiano cheese (Ref. 39).

3.1 Lactose Metabolism

Lactic acid fermentation in Parmigiano Reggiano cheese during the first 48 h after manufacture was studied by Mora *et al.*[39] The results showed that the growth of thermophilic lactic acid bacteria and lactose hydrolysis depended mainly on the rate at which the curd cooled after removal from the cheese vat. The temperature at the centre of the cheeses, which were of standard size and dimensions, remained $> 50°C$ for ~ 10 h (the curd was at $55°C$ at hooping) while the exterior of the cheese decreased to $\sim 42°C$ in 2 h. Consequently, bacterial growth commenced earlier and was more intense in the exterior than in the interior of the cheese and this affected sugar metabolism and acidity development (Figs. 1 and 2). After 48 h, bacterial numbers, pH and lactate concentration had not attained equal values throughout the cheese and the authors suggest that these differences may affect cheese subsequent ripening.

3.2 Lipolysis

The ripening of most cheese is accompanied by a low level of lipolysis but extensive lipolysis occurs in the hard Italian varieties (Romano, Parmesan and Provolone) and in blue-veined cheeses. In the latter, lipolysis is due mainly to the action of lipases secreted by *P. roqueforti*, although indigenous milk lipase may also contribute, especially in raw milk cheese.

The hard Italian cheeses are probably unique in that an exogenous lipase is a normal additive. Romano, Provolone and Parmesan have a sharp, peppery 'piccante' flavour primarily due to relatively high levels of short-chain fatty acids, especially butyric.[40-42] The desirable 'piccante' flavour so characteristic of these cheeses is due to the action of pregastric esterase (PGE) activity in rennet pastes, which are still used in Italy as the source of both coagulant (proteinase) and lipolytic agent in cheese manufacture.[43] Early attempts in the USA to produce Italian cheeses with characteristic flavours were largely unsuccessful. Comparison of the cheesemaking technique in Italy with that in the US showed that a rennet paste was used in the former whereas a rennet extract was used in the US. Rennet pastes are prepared by macerating the engorged stomachs, including contents (curdled milk), of young calves, kid goats or lambs which are slaughtered immediately after suckling or pail-feeding (the stomachs and contents are held for ~ 60 days prior to macerating(S. Ferris, personal communication)) whereas commercial animal rennet extracts are prepared from empty, washed vells.[43] Pregastric esterase, the physiological role of which is to aid in the digestion of fat by young animals with limited pancreatic lipase, is secreted during suckling and is carried into the stomach with the ingested milk. The existence of lipolytic activity in pig salivary gland extracts was recognized in 1916[44] and the secretion of an oral lipase by calves was confirmed by Wise *et al.*[45] It is now known that PGE is secreted by at least 13 species, including kid goats and lambs.[43] Pertinent literature on the factors affecting secretion and activity of PGE has been reviewed comprehensively by Nelson *et al.*[43]

While PGE has not been isolated in homogeneous form, much attention has been focussed on the characterization of partially purified PGE preparations from the calf, kid and lamb. Richardson and Nelson[46] showed that calf PGE hydrolyses soluble triacetin at a slightly higher rate than emulsified triacetin and Nelson *et al.*[43] suggested that crude calf PGE contains both lipase and esterase activities. In fact, it appears that commercial PGE preparations contain several lipolytic enzymes with similar molecular weights and electrophoretic mobilities in polyacrylamide gels[47,48] but with different temperature and pH optima.[46,49]

Harper and Gould,[49] who analysed rennet pastes and commercial PGE preparations from calf, kid and lamb for lipolytic activity on milk fat, identified multiple lipase systems in each. Calf PGE contained 3 lipases with pH optima at 5·3, 6·1 and 7·5; kid PGE also contained 3 lipases with pH optima at 5·5, 6·2 and 8·6, while lamb PGE preparation showed 2 pH optima, i.e. at 5·9 and 6·6. The temperature optima, at pH 5·3, for lipolysis ranged from 29 to 35°C for the various preparations; rennet pastes had a broader and higher optimum temperature range than the PGE preparations from the corresponding animal source. In a comparative study, Richardson and Nelson[46] assayed commercial PGE preparations from calf, kid and lamb for lipolytic activity on emulsified tributyrin and on milk fat at pH 5·5. Similar results were obtained on both substrates: pH optima were observed at 5·3–5·5, with minor peaks at pH 8·5 and 8·7 for calf and kid preparations, respectively; different preparations were optimally active at 42–45°C, and the enzymes were most stable at pH 5·5. While the discrepancies between the results of Harper and Gould[49] and Richardson and Nelson[46] may be due to differences in assay conditions and/or the enzyme complement of the various preparations resulting from differences in manufacturing procedures, it is clear that characterization of PGE preparations requires further attention.

Pregastric esterase preparations preferentially hydrolyse short chain fatty acids from milk fat[50–53] and from simple synthetic[51] and mixed triglycerides.[52,54] Although lamb, calf and kid PGE's exhibit specificity for butyric acid and other short chain fatty acids, the 3 esterases differ in the ratios of short-chain:long-chain free fatty acids produced.[41,51] Calf PGE preferentially hydrolyses fatty acids esterified to the Sn-3 position of glycerol[43] which explains the relatively high rate of release of butyric acid from milk fat in which 90% of the butyric acid is attached at the Sn-3 position. Calf PGE does not hydrolyse monobutyrin and hydrolyses dibutyrin very slowly relative to tributyrin.[46] It was suggested that PGE preparations should be supplemented with additional lipolytic enzymes, such as pancreatic lipase (which is capable of hydrolysing tri-, di- and monobutyrins at approximately equal rates), to progress lipolysis in Italian cheeses beyond the release of fatty acids from triglycerides.[46] Lamb, kid and calf PGE preparations are most soluble, and hence most active, in 0·30–0·50 M-NaCl.[46]

The identification and partial characterization of a gastric lipase from cleaned, washed abomasal tissue of lamb (also present in the gastric tissues of calves and kid goats) was reported by Richardson *et al.*[55] A combination of calf gastric lipase and goat PGE gave Cheddar and Provolone cheeses a flavour superior to those made using the PGE preparation alone. The absence of gastric lipase in commercial rennet extracts was explained on the basis of the low solubility of the enzyme in the brine solutions (10% (w/w) NaCl) normally used for extraction of gastric tissues. However, the secretion of a lipase indigenous to the stomach wall is doubted by Nelson *et al.*[43] who suggested that 'gastric' lipase is of oral origin.

Connoisseurs of Italian cheese claim that rennet pastes give cheeses flavours special to those made using PGE preparations; hence, some traditional manufacturers continue to use rennet paste perhaps along with PGE preparations.[10,40] The superiority of rennet pastes may be due to the presence of enzymes other than PGE and the normal gastric proteinases (and possibly gastric lipase). Such enzymes could be of microbial origin since considerable bacterial growth probably occurs during the aging period (up to 60 days) prior to maceration of the stomachs.

The use of rennet pastes, which are considered unhygienic products, is not permitted in some countries and has been replaced by PGE preparations. The first commercial PGE preparation (a liquid extract of calf oral tissue) was introduced to the US Italian cheesemaking industry in 1946 by Farnham who was granted a patent in 1950 for the preparation of PGE extracts and their use in the cheese industry; liquid extracts were superseded by powdered preparations which were first used in 1952. Today, PGE preparations are used world-wide for controlled flavour production of Italian and other cheese varieties.

Harper and Gould[56] investigated flavour development in commercial Romano and Provolone cheeses, selected to include those made with either rennet extract, rennet pastes from calves, kids or lambs, or PGE preparations from kids or calves. Cheeses made with either commercial rennet extracts or purified rennet pastes did not develop satisfactory flavour whereas cheeses made with either non-purified pastes or PGE preparations developed characteristic piccante flavours. In a similar study, Harper and Long[50] determined the free fatty acids (FFA) and free amino acids (FAA) in a range of commercial Provolone cheeses of different ages made with either purified or non-purified rennet pastes or commercial PGE preparations. The FFA and FAA levels exhibited wide variations in cheeses of the same age. Butyric acid was the only FFA definitely related to the type of enzyme preparation used and to the desirable 'piccante' flavour of Provolone cheese. Aged Provolone cheeses made with purified rennet pastes had lower characteristic scores and lower butyric acid contents (0·18–0·5 mg/g cheese solids) than those made with crude rennet paste (1·7–2·8 mg butyric acid/g cheese solids). While the concentration of total FAA was not related to either the type of enzyme preparation used or to the intensity of the characteristic flavour, increasing concentrations of some amino acids (glutamic acid, alanine, valine and aspartic acid) were paralleled by an increase in the characteristic piccante flavour. The ratio of free butyric acid to free glutamic acid in cheese which exhibited the characteristic piccante flavour was 1:2; however, threshold values for butyric acid (1·0 mg/g cheese solids) and glutamic acid (2·0 mg/g cheese solids) had to be reached before the piccante flavour was evident. The intensity of the desired flavour increased with increasing concentration of these acids in the desired ratio. These results were essentially confirmed by Long and Harper[57] who also showed [58] that a kid PGE preparation gave higher concentrations of butyric acid in Romano and Provolone cheeses than a calf PGE preparation. The development of the desired flavour was related to the concentrations of both butyric acid and glutamic acid in Provolone cheese but only to butyric acid levels in Romano cheese.

There is a direct relationship between the flavour intensity of commercial Provolone and Romano cheeses and butyric acid content but the relationship between flavour desirability and butyric acid concentration is more variable.[41] Flavour desirability was influenced mainly by the relative proportions of the various free fatty acids but there is no standard flavour of Italian cheeses which is particularly acceptable to all segments of the population. While connoisseurs of Italian cheeses prefer sharp piccante cheese with a high flavour intensity and butyric acid content, the typical

TABLE VI

Free fatty acid (FFA) compositions and flavours of Provolone cheeses during aging (Ref. 42) (reproduced by permission of the *Journal of Dairy Science*)

Sample number	Aging time (days) at		FFA concentration (ppm)								Flavour
	2°C	7°C	$C_{4:0}$	$C_{6:0}$	$C_{8:0}$	$C_{10:0}$	$C_{12:0}$	$C_{14:0}$	$C_{16:0}$	C_{18} congeners	
1A	62[a]	—	267	124	40	77	49	93	185	249	Mild, balanced FFA flavour
	123	—	520	206	51	115	87	105	180	242	Lacks full flavour, imbalanced
	213	—	589	268	81	238	128	152	272	296	Slightly soapy, imbalanced, C_6-like
1B	—	123	674	266	64	130	94	83	166	208	Balanced flavour
	—	213	413	235	113	177	144	140	267	230	Sharp, blended FFA
2A	53[a]	—	389	170	66	136	127	289	550	612	Mild, balanced FFA flavour, smoky
	114	—	576	236	79	142	150	218	290	354	Full, balanced FFA flavour
	204	—	533	326	109	241	236	328	525	327	Full, balanced flavour
2B	—	114	722	265	84	224	184	239	457	457	Pronounced smooth flavour, smoky
3A	—	204	807	316	106	261	229	415	661	384	Soapy, not desirable flavour
	52[a]	—	822	373	111	227	194	267	493	932	Coarse FFA flavour, soapy
	102	—	916	371	115	239	207	257	430	791	—
	232	—	1 293	446	154	273	227	290	567	964	Strong FFA flavour, butyric dominates
3B	—	102	1 067	432	116	234	200	308	510	904	—
	—	232	1 069	427	165	318	261	364	694	1 448	Very strong FFA flavour, soapy, bitter

[a] Age of cheese upon receipt and initiation of experimental aging.

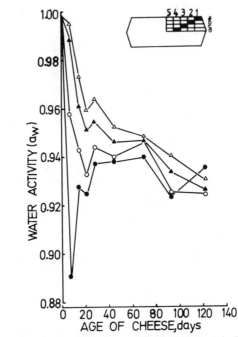

Fig. 3. Changes in water activity (a_w) at selected locations in Romano-type cheese during ripening: A[1] (●), B[2] (○), C[3] (▲), D[4] (△) (see inset for sampling locations).

young consumer in the US prefers cheeses with intermediate flavour intensities and butyric acid contents.[40] Since the specificities of PGE preparations from different sources vary,[40,49–51] it should be possible to select lipase preparations for the production of cheeses 'tailor-made' to suit the tastes of different consumer segments.

Woo and Lindsay[42] suggest that minor branched-chain free fatty acids that occur in milk fat and which have lower flavour thresholds than the straight-chain analogues and possess sharp 'goaty' flavours, may contribute to the piccante flavour of Parmesan cheese. The decreases in the concentrations of some of the major free fatty acids in Romano cheese during advanced ripening[42] suggest the formation of methyl ketones, via oxidation of free fatty acids which are major flavour compounds in Blue cheese (cf. Chapter 4).

The concentrations of the major free fatty acids in the principal Italian cheeses on retail scale in the US are shown in Tables V–VIII.

As indicated previously, salt and moisture concentrations, and hence water activity, in hard Italian cheeses vary throughout the cheese;

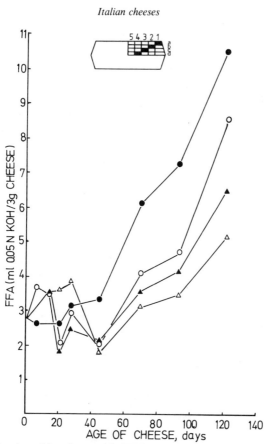

Fig. 4. Production of free fatty acids (FFA) at selected locations in Romano-type cheese during ripening: A^1 (●), B^2 (○), C^3 (▲), D^4 (△) (see inset for sampling locations).

consequently lipolysis varies. A further variable arises from the development of a surface microflora since these cheeses are not normally packaged to prevent this.

The data in Fig. 3 show the changes in a_w at selected locations (surface and interior) in Romano-type cheeses during ripening.[59] Water activity is very low in the surface region initially but as NaCl diffuses inwards, a_w in the surface region increases and that at the interior locations decreases. Because the cheese is not wrapped, evaporation of water results in a general decrease in a_w during the later stages of ripening, the extent and timing of this decrease being influenced by cheese composition and the relative humidity of the environment.

P. F. Fox and T. P. Guinee

TABLE VII

Free fatty acid (FFA) compositions and flavours of Parmesan cheeses during aging (Ref. 42) (reproduced by permission of the *Journal of Dairy Science*)

Sample number	Aging time (days) at 7°C	FFA concentration (ppm)								Flavour
		$C_{4:0}$	$C_{6:0}$	$C_{8:0}$	$C_{10:0}$	$C_{12:0}$	$C_{14:0}$	$C_{16:0}$	C_{18} congeners	
1	69[a]	536	170	80	372	237	477	714	444	Lacks flavour balance, not sharp
	134	840	223	90	277	258	432	728	803	Strong butyric, imbalanced
	245	974	218	116	449	301	496	846	1 136	Butyric, lacks balance, FFA, dominates
2	174[a]	77	25	30	124	57	185	382	316	Mild, flavour not developed
	239	165	28	34	99	72	158	396	489	Mild but blended
	350	184	28	32	96	64	175	410	820	Balanced FFA, lacks flavour strength
3	542[a]	161	64	44	95	88	299	699	489	Full sharp, piccante flavour, nutty
	607	176	71	44	82	97	255	662	1 233	Blended, sharp, piccante flavour
	718	172	48	44	107	107	225	565	1 033	Full flavoured, nutty, musky, sharp

[a] Age of cheese upon receipt and initiation of experimental aging.

Changes in free fatty acid (FFA) levels at the same locations are shown in Fig. 4. FFA levels in the outer sample (A^1) were lowest during the first 15 days of ripening, undoubtedly due to the low a_w in this region during this period. After a slight initial increase, FFA levels in the interior of the cheese decreased to a minimum at ~ 40 days and then increased to the end of ripening. The level of FFA in the surface zone began to increase earlier and at a faster rate than in the interior and there was a decreasing FFA concentration gradient from the surface to the centre of the cheese from the 40th day to the end of ripening (120 days). Guinee[59] suggested that this gradient may have been due to the secretion of lipases by the surface microflora and their slow inward diffusion or to the inward diffusion of FFA from the surface to the centre; the former was considered unlikely due to the very slow diffusion of enzymes in cheese even in high moisture cheeses.[60,61] The diffusion of butanoic acid in cheese is much slower than that of NaCl but diffusion does occur;[60] the diffusion of longer chain fatty acids does not appear to have been investigated. It is also possible that up to a certain concentration, NaCl stimulates PGE activity. Presumably due to the metabolic activity of the surface microflora, the pH in the surface zone of the cheese increased sooner and faster than that in the interior (Fig. 5), with a decreasing pH gradient from the surface to the centre, and this would promote the activity of PGE in the outer regions of the cheese since PGE has pH optima at 5·8–6·2 and at $\sim 8·5$.[49]

The FFA profiles in surface and interior samples are summarized in Table IX; greatest differences were in the longer chain acids. This supports the view that surface microbial lipases may have been responsible since PGE has a high specificity for short-chain acids on the Sn-3 position of glycerol.[43,51]

The suitability of lipases other than rennet paste or PGE for Italian cheese has been assessed. Mattick *et al.*[12] reported that satisfactory Romano cheese could be made from homogenized milk, relying on the indigenous milk lipase for lipolysis. They also reported that Rohm and Haas lipase A (source not given) was acceptable although the cheese had a soapy flavour initially and became fruity on prolonged ripening and the flavour, at best, was not typical of Romano cheese. Pancreatic lipase was not satisfactory; in addition to a strong soapy flavour, which intensified with age, the cheese developed a bitter flavour, presumably due to proteolysis. Salvadori[62] produced satisfactory Romano cheese using lipases produced by bacteria isolated from the abomasa of lambs.

Mucor miehei secretes a lipase that is reported to give satisfactory Fontina and Romano cheeses although this enzyme must be used at five

TABLE VIII

Free fatty acid (FFA) compositions and flavours of Romano cheeses during aging (reproduced by permission of the *Journal of Dairy Science*)

Sample number	Aging time (days) at $7°C$	FFA concentration (ppm)								Flavour
		$C_{4:0}$	$C_{6:0}$	$C_{8:0}$	$C_{10:0}$	$C_{12:0}$	$C_{14:0}$	$C_{16:0}$	C_{18} congeners	
1	71[a]	3034	1454	377	1264	694	576	1138	1118	Flavour not well blended, strong butyric
	128	3027	1416	421	1188	761	775	1245	1272	Imbalanced, butyric dominates, goaty
2	218	2683	1372	474	874	981	1115	1767	1285	Not blended, strong FFA flavour
	232[a,b]	3339	1475	453	944	837	694	1402	1115	Strong, fairly blended FFA flavour
	290	3043	1428	429	1009	690	778	1306	1843	Strong, balanced, piquant
	380	2151	1267	452	1016	907	1423	2057	2287	Strong, blended, FFA flavour

[a] Age of cheese upon receipt and initiation of experimental aging.
[b] Approximate age of cheese upon receipt.

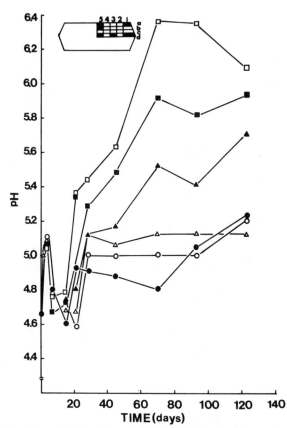

Fig. 5. pH changes at selected locations in Romano type cheese during ripening: A[1] (□), A[5] (■), B[5] (△), D[1] (▲), D[3] (●), D[5] (○). Shaded areas in inset indicate sample locations.

times the lipolytic activity of PGE to obtain satisfactory Romano cheese.[63] *M. miehei* lipase has been characterized[64] and is commercially available as 'Piccantase'. The lipases secreted by selected strains of *P. roqueforti* and *P. candidum* are considered to be potentially useful for the manufacture of Italian and other cheese varieties.[65]

3.3 Methyl Ketones in Grana Cheese

Carbonyl compounds, which are strongly aromatic and sapid, make a significant contribution to the flavour of many cheese varieties[66] and

TABLE IX

Free fatty acid profile of commercial Romano-type cheese (made with crude kid rennet paste extract) during ripening

Age of cheese (days)	Sample location	Free fatty acid concentration (mg/kg cheese)												
	Surface (S) Interior (I)	C_4	C_6	C_8	C_{10}	C_{12}	C_{14}	$C_{14:1}$	$C16$	$C_{16:1}$	$C_{18:0}$	$C_{18:1}$	$C_{18:2}$	$C_{18:3}$
0		147	80	46	62	67	134	23	375	57	153	543	69	24
30	S	373	185	102	138	138	277	52	542	87	184	820	82	41
	I	512	224	118	146	142	256	52	508	80	182	770	79	42
74	S	894	410	305	450	554	1468	321	4093	683	1143	8668	603	281
	I	836	333	139	189	174	284	81	545	92	196	905	85	59
120	S	1450	569	203	358	322	497	135	900	135	298	1335	157	67
	I	1502	600	217	366	321	468	132	841	127	277	1298	150	66

TABLE X

Compositional data for mature commercial Romano-type cheeses (Ref. 68)

Origin	pH	Moisture (%)	NaCl (%)	g NaCl per 100 g H_2O	Fat (%)	Protein (%)	% total N soluble at pH 4·6	% total N soluble in 12% TCA
Ambrose (1)	5·10	31·6	2·53	8·02	29·32	30·00	28·70	23·29
Irish (2)	4·93	34·5	4·97	14·41	32·10	25·80	19·36	16·81
Belgian (3)	5·10	33·1	4·97	15·01	26·38	30·98	21·98	18·75
French (4)	4·98	30·3	3·94	13·01	28·02	32·73	16·70	18·32
Italian (5)	4·90	29·8	4·10	13·76	28·66	32·43	18·94	18·68

methyl ketones make a particularly high contribution to the flavour of Blue cheeses (see Chapter 4). The total concentrations of methyl ketones in Grana cheese are quite low, $0.075\ \mu M/g$ fat, compared with those in Blue ($19.14\ \mu M/g$), Roquefort ($5.18\ \mu M/g$) and even Cheddar ($0.24\ \mu M/g$).[67] The proportions of all methyl ketones, except C_3, in Grana were similar to the proportions of the β-keto acids in the cheese fat, suggesting the spontaneous formation of methyl ketones from β-keto acids in Grana cheese.

3.4 Proteolysis

In contrast to lipolysis, the level of proteolysis which occurs in hard Italian cheeses is roughly similar to that in other hard/semi-hard internal bacterially ripened cheeses. Undoubtedly, the low moisture content, relatively high salt content and the absence of a fungal microflora (except perhaps for slight surface growth) are responsible for this. Therefore, the principal proteolytic agents in the mass of the cheese are coagulant, microbial proteinases (mainly from thermophilic lactic acid bacteria, which are more proteolytic than their mesophilic counterparts) and indigenous milk proteinase. A study of proteolysis in Romano-type cheese has recently been completed.[59,68]

3.5 Gel Electrophoresis

Polyacrylamide gel electrophoretograms of 5 samples of Romano-type cheese (of different national origin) from the Italian market are shown in Fig. 6; there were considerable differences in the proteolysis patterns of the 5 samples. As with other hard/semi-hard internal bacterially-ripened cheeses, β-casein had undergone little proteolysis by rennet (only trace amounts of β-I casein were apparent) but quite high concentrations of γ-casein were present in 2 of the samples (1 and 3), indicating considerable plasmin activity. This might suggest a high pH although this was not apparent for the mature cheese (Table X). Alternatively, it may be due to a high pH at drainage for these samples since the level of plasmin in cheese curd appears to be related to the pH at drainage.[18,69]

In comparison with mature Cheddar or Gouda, α_{s1}-casein had undergone relatively little proteolysis: a high level of α_{s1}-casein remained unhydrolysed in all samples with very high levels in some samples; the primary degradation products of α_{s1}-casein, α_{s1}-I and α_{s1}-II, were apparent in all samples. Although the ages of the cheeses were unknown (except for

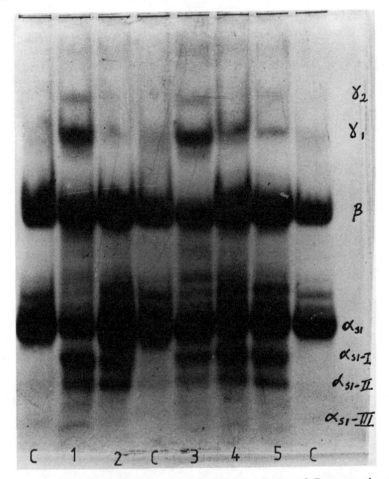

Fig. 6. Gel electrophoretograms of commercial samples of Romano cheese (unknown age) of different national origins obtained on the Italian market. 1: Ambrose; 2: Irish; 3: Belgian; 4: French; 5: Italian; C = sodium caseinate.

sample 2 which was about 3 months, and which had undergone the lowest level of proteolysis of the 5 samples), it appears that rennet, which is the principal primary proteolytic agent for α_{s1}-casein, is not very active in these cheeses. This is confirmed by the slight increases which were observed in the levels of α_{s1}-I and α_{s1}-II in interior samples from Irish-made Romano-type cheese over a 122 d ripening period (Fig. 7); only slightly more proteolysis occurred in a surface sample.

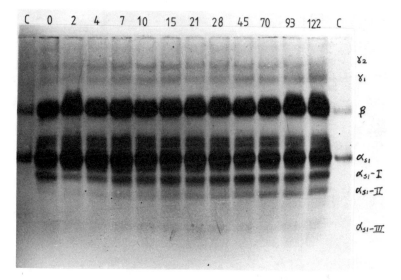

Fig. 7. Gel electrophoretogram of samples from an internal location of Romano cheese after 0–122 days ripening. C = sodium caseinate.

3.6 Soluble Nitrogen

The levels of pH 4·6-soluble N and 12% TCA-soluble N in the 5 commercial Romano samples referred to previously are included in Table X. Possibly the most striking feature of these data is that the level of 12% TCA-soluble N was nearly as high as that soluble at pH 4·6. Since pH 4·6-soluble N is produced principally by rennet while starter and non-starter bacterial enzymes are principally responsible for the formation of 12% TCA-soluble N,[70] these data support the view, expressed above, that rennet is not very active in these cheeses, but once soluble peptides have been formed by rennet, bacterial peptidases hydrolyse them relatively rapidly.

As was the case for lipolysis, considerable zonal variations in proteolysis also occurred in Romano-type cheeses.[68] During the first 30 days, the formation of pH 4·6-soluble N and 12% TCA-soluble N was greater in the surface regions of the cheeses than in the interior (Figs. 8, 9, respectively) but from 40 days onwards, proteolysis was considerably more extensive in the surface samples. Undoubtedly, the slower initial rate of proteolysis in the surface samples was due to the high initial salt concentrations in these regions; there was in fact a fairly good negative correlation between the salt-in-moisture concentration and the level of pH 4·6-soluble N in the

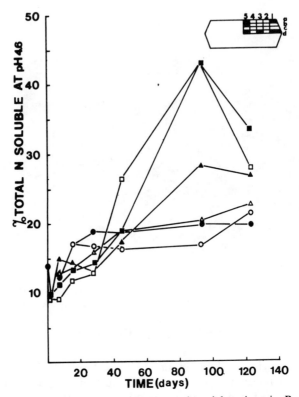

Fig. 8. Formation of pH 4·6-soluble N at selected locations in Romano-type cheese during ripening: A^1 (□), A^5 (■), B^5 (△), D^1 (▲), D^3 (●), D^5 (○). Shaded areas in inset indicate sample locations (Ref. 68).

15-day old cheeses (Fig. 10). Presumably the inward diffusion of NaCl improves the environment for proteolysis in the outer regions during the latter stages of ripening and proteases secreted by surface microflora may also contribute. The wide zonal differences in pH (Fig. 5) also suggest the involvement of a surface microflora. Indeed, in a second experiment in which the cheeses were vacuum packed at 35 days to prevent development of a surface microflora, proteolysis was more extensive in the interior than in the exterior of the cheeses at all stages throughout a 120-day ripening period.

The nature of the proteolysis which occurred at surface and interior locations were studied in detail by Guinee.[59] The levels of water-soluble and pH 4·6-soluble N were very nearly similar at various locations in the

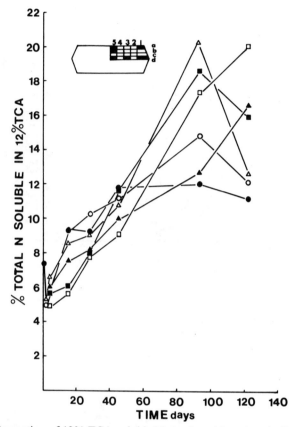

Fig. 9. Formation of 12% TCA-soluble N at selected locations in Romano-type cheese during ripening: A[1] (□), A[5] (■), B[5] (△), D[1] (▲), D[3] (●), D[5] (○). Shaded areas in inset indicate sample locations (Ref. 68).

cheese throughout ripening (Fig. 11). Approximately 50% of the WSN was soluble in 12% TCA but the levels of 70% ethanol-soluble N were much lower and the differences between the inner and outer samples were much less than those indicated by the other criteria. The levels of 5% PTA-soluble N remained very low at both sampling locations throughout ripening, indicating the formation of only very low levels of free amino acids. Nitrogen fractions from interior and exterior locations were analysed by gel filtration, thin layer chromatography, high voltage paper electrophoresis and SDS gel electrophoresis;[59] qualitatively, no major differences were apparent between the samples but large quantitative differences were

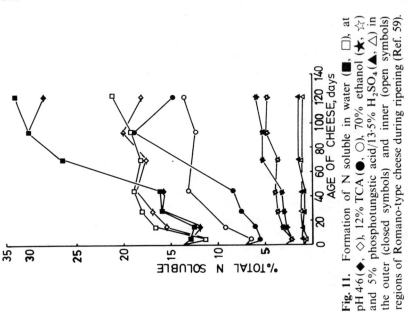

Fig. 11. Formation of N soluble in water (■, □), at pH 4·6 (◆, ◇), 12% TCA (●, ○), 70% ethanol (★, ☆) and 5% phosphotungstic acid/13·5% H₂SO₄ (▲, △) in the outer (closed symbols) and inner (open symbols) regions of Romano-type cheese during ripening (Ref. 59).

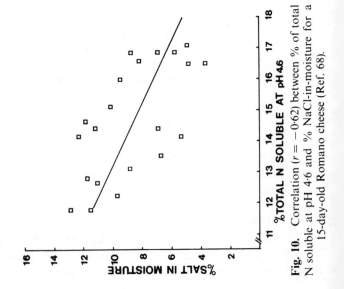

Fig. 10. Correlation ($r = -0.62$) between % of total N soluble at pH 4·6 and % NaCl-in-moisture for a 15-day-old Romano cheese (Ref. 68).

observed. The free amino acid profiles in Romano and Provolone cheeses was studied by Harper and Long[50] and Long and Harper.[57,58]

REFERENCES

1. Reinbold, G. W., *Italian Cheese Varieties*, Pfizer Cheese Monographs, Vol. 1, New York, 1963.
2. Milk Marketing Board (UK), *Dairy Facts and Figures, 1983*, Thames Ditton, Surrey, UK, 1984.
3. Ferris, S., *Italian Cheese—the U.S. Experience and Future Trends*, 9th Marschall International Dairying Symposium, 1980.
4. Breed, R. S., *Milk Plant Monthly*, 1945, **35**(4), 22.
5. Walter, H. E. and Hargrove, R. C., *Cheeses of the World*, U.S. Department of Agriculture, Dover Publications Inc., New York, 1972.
6. Schulz, M. E. and Sydow, G., *Handbook der Veroffenlichungen uber Kase*, Verlag Hans Carl, Nurnberg, 1955.
7. Associazione Italiana Lattiero Casearia, *Milk and Italian Dairy Products*, Comitato Italiano Latte e Derivati, Milano, 1959.
8. Burkhalter, G., *Catalogue of Cheeses*, International Dairy Federation, Document 141, Brussels, 1981.
9. Simon, A. L., *Cheeses of the World*, Faber and Faber, London, 1956.
10. Kosikowski, F. V., *Cheese and Fermented Milk Foods*, Edwards Bros Inc., Ann Arbor, Michigan, 1977.
11. Scott, R., *Cheesemaking Practice*, 2nd Edn, Elsevier Applied Science, London, 1986.
12. Mattick, J. F., Dahle, C. D. and Watrous, G. H., Romano-type Grating Cheese Bulletin 537, Pennsylvania State College, 1951.
13. Kosikowski, F. V., *J. Dairy Sci.*, 1951, **34**, 641.
14. Breene, W. M., Price, W. V. and Ernstrom, C. A., *J. Dairy Sci.*, 1964, **47**, 1173.
15. Creamer, L. K., *N.Z. J. Dairy Sci. Technol.*, 1976, **11**, 130.
16. Arnott, D. R., Morris, H. A. and Combs, W. B., *J. Dairy Sci.*, 1957, **40**, 957.
17. Park, J., Rosenau, J. R. and Peleg, M., *J. Food Sci.*, 1984, **49**, 1158.
18. Richardson, B. C. and Pearce, K. N., *N.Z. J. Dairy Sci. Technol.*, 1981, **16**, 209.
19. Di Matteo, M., Chiovitti, G. and Addeo, F., *Scienza Technica Lattiero-Casearia*, 1982, **32**, 197.
20. Kosikowski, F. V. and Brown, D. P., *J. Dairy Sci.*, 1969, **52**, 968.
21. Breene, W. M., Price, W. V. and Ernstrom, C. A., *J. Dairy Sci.*, 1964, **47**, 840.
22. Larson, W. A., Olson, N. F., Ernstrom, C. A. and Breene, W. M., *J. Dairy Sci.*, 1967, **50**, 1711.
23. Quarne, E. L., Larson, W. A. and Olson, N. F., *J. Dairy Sci.*, 1968, **51**, 527.
24. Shehata, A. E., Olson, N. F. and Richardson, T., *J. Dairy Sci.*, 1967, **50**, 824.
25. Quarne, E. L., Larson, W. A. and Olson, N. F., *J. Dairy Sci.*, 1968, **51**, 848.
26. Keller, B., Olson, N. F. and Richardson, T., *J. Dairy Sci.*, 1974, **57**, 174.
27. Micketts, R. and Olson, N. F., *J. Dairy Sci.*, 1974, **57**, 273.

28. Flanagan, J. F., Thompson, M. P., Brower, D. P. and Gyuricsek, D. M., *Cult. Dairy Prod. J.*, 1978, **13**(4), 24.
29. Demott, B. J., *J. Dairy Sci.*, 1983, **66**, 2501.
30. Covacevich, H. R. and Kosikowski, F. V., *J. Dairy Sci.*, 1978, **61**, 701.
31. Kalab, M., *Milchwissenschaft*, 1977, **32**, 449.
32. Chen, A. H., Larkin, J. W., Clarke, C. J. and Irwin, W. E., *J. Dairy Sci.*, 1979, **62**, 901.
33. Imoto, E. M., Lee, C.-H. and Rha, C., *J. Food Sci.*, 1979, **44**, 343.
34. Carvantes, M. A., Lund, D. B. and Olson, N. F., *J. Dairy Sci.*, 1983, **66**, 204.
35. Smith, C. E., Rosenau, J. R. and Peleg, M., *J. Food Sci.*, 1980, **45**, 1142.
36. Resmini, P., Volonterio, G., Annibaldi, S. and Ferri, G., *Scienza e Tecnia Lattiero-Casearia*, 1974, **25**, 149.
37. Guinee, T. P. and Fox, P. F., *J. Dairy Res.*, 1983, **50**, 511.
38. Guinee, T. P. and Fox, P. F., *Ir. J. Food Sci. Technol.*, 1983, **7**, 119.
39. Mora, R., Nanni, M. and Panari, G., *Scienza e Tecnica Lattiero-Casearia*, 1984, **35**, 20.
40. Neelakantan, S., Shahani, K. M. and Arnold, R. G., *Food Prod. Dev.*, 1971, **5**(7), 52.
41. Arnold, R. G., Shahani, K. M. and Dwivedi, B. K., *J. Dairy Sci.*, 1975, **58**, 1127.
42. Woo, A. H. and Lindsay, R. C., *J. Dairy Sci.*, 1984, **67**, 960.
43. Nelson, J. H., Jensen, R. G. and Pitas, R. E., *J. Dairy Sci.*, 1977, **60**, 327.
44. Porter, A. E., *Biochem. J.*, 1916, **10**, 523.
45. Wise, G. H., Miller, P. G. and Anderson, G. W., *J. Dairy Sci.*, 1940, **23**, 997.
46. Richardson, G. H. and Nelson, J. H., *J. Dairy Sci.*, 1967, **50**, 1061.
47. Ramsey, H. A., *J. Dairy Sci.*, 1962, **45**, 1479.
48. Lee, H. J., Olson, N. F. and Ryan, D. J., *J. Dairy Sci.*, 1980, **63**, 1834.
49. Harper, W. J. and Gould, I. A., *J. Dairy Sci.*, 1955, **38**, 87.
50. Harper, W. J. and Long, J. E., *J. Dairy Sci.*, 1956, **39**, 46.
51. Harper, W. J., *J. Dairy Sci.*, 1957, **40**, 556.
52. Jensen, R. G. and Sampugna, J., *J. Dairy Sci.*, 1964, **47**, 664.
53. Siewert, K. L. and Otterby, O. E., *J. Dairy Sci.*, 1968, **51**, 1305.
54. Pitas, R. E. and Jensen, R. G., *J. Dairy Sci.*, 1970, **53**, 1083.
55. Richardson, G. H., Nelson, J. H. and Farnham, M. G., *J. Dairy Sci.*, 1971, **54**, 643.
56. Harper, W. J. and Gould, I. A., *Butter, Cheese, Milk Prod. J.*, 1952, **43**(8), 22, 44, 46.
57. Long, J. E. and Harper, W. J., *J. Dairy Sci.*, 1956, **39**, 138.
58. Long, J. E. and Harper, W. J., *J. Dairy Sci.*, 1956, **39**, 245.
59. Guinee, T. P., Ph.D. thesis, National University of Ireland, Dublin, 1985.
60. Lee, H. J., Olson, N. F. and Lund, D. B., *J. Dairy Sci.*, 1980, **63**, 513.
61. Noomen, A., *Neth. Milk Dairy J.*, 1983, **37**, 229.
62. Salvadori, P., *Latte*, 1961, **35**, 177.
63. Peppler, H. J., Dooley, J. G. and Huang, H. T., *J. Dairy Sci.*, 1976, **59**, 859.
64. Moskowitz, G. J., Shen, T., West, I. R., Cassaigne, R. and Feldman, L. I., *J. Dairy Sci.*, 1977, **60**, 1260.
65. Kornacki, K., Stepaniak, L., Adamiec, I., Grabska, J. and Wrona, K., *Milchwissenschaft*, 1979, **34**, 340.
66. Adda, J., Gripon, J. C. and Vassal, L., *Food Chemistry*, 1982, **9**, 115.

67. Piergiovanni, L. and Volonterio, G., *L'Industria del Latte*, 1977, **13**, 31.
68. Guinee, T. P. and Fox, P. F., *Ir. J. Food Sci. Technol.*, 1984, **8**, 105.
69. Lawrence, R. C., Gilles, J. and Creamer, L. K., *N. Z. J. Dairy Sci. Technol.*, 1983, **18**, 175.
70. O'Keeffe, A. M., Fox, P. F. and Daly, C., *J. Dairy Res.*, 1978, **45**, 465.

Chapter 8

Mediterranean Cheese Varieties: Ripened Cheese Varieties Native to the Balkan Countries

Marijana Carić

Faculty of Technology, University of Novi Sad, Yugoslavia

1. KASHKAVAL

1.1 General Characteristics

One of the most popular hard cheeses in Balkan countries, dating back to the 11th and 12th centuries, is Kashkaval, which was first brought to Bulgaria by nomadic tribes from the East. Nowadays, it is produced in an area stretching from southern USSR (Crimea, South Ukraine, the Caucasus) and Turkey, through Greece, Bulgaria, Romania, Yugoslavia, Albania and Hungary to Italy, Algeria, Tunisia, Egypt and Morocco. Although there are many varieties of Kashkaval cheese due to certain differences in some operations in their production, there are today three essentially distinct technological processes for Kashkaval production: Balkan (native to Balkan countries), Russian, which is very similar to the first, and Italian. According to differences in language and production, there are the following Kashkaval cheese varieties in Balkan countries and in the southern USSR: Kaškaval Balkan, Kaškaval Preslav, Kaškaval Vitoša (Bulgaria), Kačkavalj (Yugoslavia), Kačkaval, Kačekavalo (USSR), Τυρος καοερλον (Greece), Košer (Turkey, Albania) and Cascaval Dobrogen (Romania).[1,2] It is also given different names according to the production district, e.g. Pirdop in Bulgaria, Epir in Greece, or Sarplaninski and Pirotski Kashkaval in Yugoslavia.[3]

Kashkaval is manufactured from cow's, sheep's, goat's or mixed milk, raw or pasteurized. For example, in Bulgaria, Kaškaval Preslav is produced from mixed milk, Kaškaval Balkan is produced from sheep's milk, while

TABLE I
Average composition of Kashkaval cheese

Type of Kashkaval	Fat (%)	Total solids (%)	Total protein (%)	Salt (%)	Ash (%)	pH	Author
Bulgaria	30·0	60·14	19·60	4·01	5·69	5·0	Kosikowski[5]
Greece	33·88	66·36	25·14	2·17	4·38	5·13	Kosikowski[5]
Yugoslavia	27–32	60–65	—	2–3·5	—	4·9–5	Pejić[2]

Kaškaval Vitoša is produced from cow's milk; in Yugoslavia, Kačkavalj is produced from sheep's, cow's or mixed milk, and in Romania, Cascaval Dobrogen is produced from sheep's milk only.

The typical form of Kashkaval is flat, cylindrical, with a smooth, amber coloured rind; the typical size is: 30 cm diameter, 10–13 cm height and 7–8 kg weight.[4] Average composition is shown in Table I.[2,5]

1.2 Unique Features of the Manufacturing Procedure

Different parameters in Kashkaval technology have been investigated by numerous authors.[3–32] The main characteristics of Kashkaval cheese technology are that it consists of two independent stages: (1) production of the curd, and (2) heat treatment of ripe curd by soaking it in hot water. The operations in the process are as follows: renneting → cutting → fresh curd forming (with low heat treatment: 38–40°C) → curd ripening (cheddaring) → slicing → texturing (heat treatment) → forming → salting → ripening.

The unique feature of all Kashkaval varieties is texturing (soaking the curd in salt water: 12–18% NaCl at 72–75°C for 35–50 s),[1] which has a pasteurizing effect that encourages correct fermentation and ripening,[2,6] thus resulting in high quality cheese with good keeping qualities. Šutić[6] found no *Escherichia coli* or other coliform bacteria in textured curd, although these were present in the curd after cheddaring. The inclusion of the above operation enables production in hot climates and has the further advantage that milk with high acidity can be used as raw material for cheese production.[7] Antonova *et al.*[8] produced high quality Kaškaval Balkan and Kaškaval Vitoša using 2 bacterial enzyme preparations from *Bacillus mesentericus* instead of calf rennet; the experimental cheeses had the same physico-chemical properties, taste and texture as the controls, even after 12 months storage.

Specific technology, together with texturing, yields Kashkaval cheese with a characteristic structure, i.e. pliable, elastic, laminar, very close with visible layers and occasional slits, but no gas holes. Although Kashkaval was originally hand-formed, nowadays the production of this cheese (second stage, in particular), is mostly mechanized, the equipment used for the various operations having a significant influence on the cheese structure. The development of cheese structure by the different types of mechanized cheddaring equipment used was thoroughly investigated by Kalab *et al.*[9] and Lowrie *et al.*[10] The microstructure of Kashkaval at different production steps is shown in Fig. 1.

Texturing has physico-chemical as well as microbiological and structural consequences: partial protein denaturation, removal of a significant quantity of water-soluble substances and fat, and a decrease in the water content of ripe curd have been observed during this operation.[11-14] On the basis of its textural and compositional characteristics, Kashkaval can be successfully frozen, in the form of ripe curd or salted cheese.[15-18]

Possible differences between numerous Kashkaval modifications arise from the fact that its technology may be subjected to many variations in respect to: curd composition, added cultures, degree of curd ripening and heat treatment temperatures.[6,13]

1.3 Ripening Changes

Ripening of Kashkaval takes place at a temperature of 12–16°C and a humidity of 85% RH, for two months.[1,2] Its shelf-life is 10–18 months at 2–4°C. In the production of Kashkaval cheese, a culture containing: *Str. thermophilus*, *Str. lactis*, *Str. diacetylactis*, *Leuc. dextranicum* (*Str. paracitrovorus*), *L. bulgaricus*, *L. helveticus* and *L. casei* (mixed starter) is added (0.1–0.5%).[1,11,19] The following combinations are usual: *L. helveticus*, *Str. thermophilus*; or *Str. lactis*, *Str. diacetylactis*, *Str. thermophilus*, *L. casei*, or *Str. lactis*, *Str. thermophilus*, *L. casei*, *L. bulgaricus*.[1]

The changes in cheese components, particularly proteolysis, start during curd fermentation (cheddaring), which Pejić[20] and Djordjević[21] characterize as a first stage of the ripening process. According to Pejić,[20] the extent of ripening in this stage is 25% from the total ripening in the Balkan procedure, 33% in the Russian and even 46% in the Italian procedure, leaving 75%, 67% and 54% of ripening, respectively, after forming and salting of the cheese. During cheddaring, lactic acid fermentation takes place, with an increase of acidity to pH = 5·4–5·5 (or 150–170°T) when sheep's milk is used, and pH = 5·2–5·3 (or 170–190°T) when cow's milk is

Marijana Carić

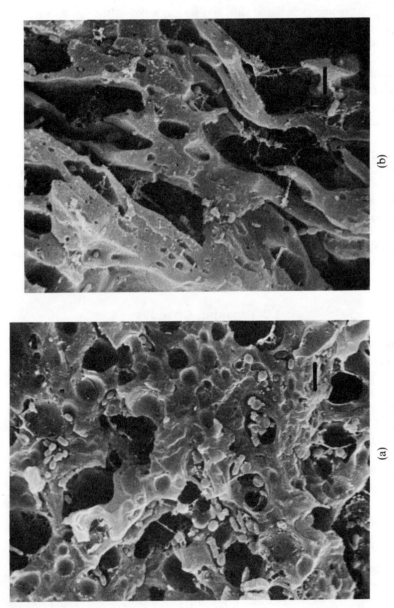

Fig. 1. Microstructure of Kashkaval cheese at different production steps: (a) ripe curd showing bacteria aggregated in nests; (b) textured curd with protein matrix having uniform orientation (bar = 3 μm; courtesy of M.Kaláb).

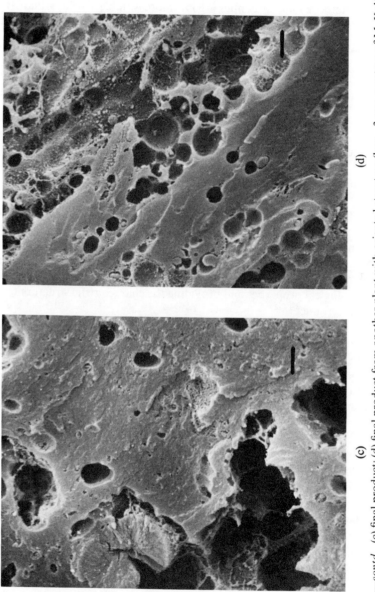

(c)

(d)

Fig. 1—*contd.* (c) final product; (d) final product from another plant with oriented structure (bar = 3 μm; courtesy of M. Kaláb).

used.[1] This leads to an increase in the concentration of soluble calcium (the curd after cheddaring contains 53% more soluble calcium than fresh curd[12]) and the formation of monocalcium paracaseinate according to the following reaction:[22]

$$2 NH_2R(COO)_6Ca_3 + 10 C_3H_6O_3 \Rightarrow$$

Calcium paracaseinate   Lactic acid

$$(NH_2R(COOH)_5COO)_2Ca + 5 Ca(C_3H_5O_3)_2$$

Monocalcium paracaseinate   Calcium lactate

Monocalcium paracaseinate nitrogen in the ripe curd amounts to 1·73%, which is 48·7% of the total nitrogen and 3·6 times higher than at the beginning of cheddaring, or 1·6 times higher than in Cheddar cheese at the beginning of pressing. This is due to the difference in manufacturing procedure between these two cheeses: in Kashkaval manufacture, the curd is subjected to a heat treatment and its plastic properties must be developed without pressing.[21]

Monocalcium paracaseinate is responsible for the ability of the ripe curd to be stretched as fine, long, ductile threads when heated, thus influencing the rheological properties and providing the characteristic structure to the finished product.[11,21]

Both lactic acid producing bacteria and the acid produced by them inhibit the growth of many species of micro-organisms that can cause defects in the finished cheese (gas-forming, proteolytic, lipolytic, etc.).[23]

Ripening processes continue in the formed and salted cheese. Since this stage of ripening occurs after the curd has been textured at high temperatures, which inactivate the added culture, the ripening process is slow and not very intensive.

Proteinases in dairy technology have been reviewed by Fox[24] and proteolysis of cheese proteins during ripening by Grappin *et al.*[25] and in Chapter 10, Volume 1, of this text. Marcos *et al.*[26] investigated the electrophoretic patterns of proteins in 34 different varieties of European cheeses after ripening. A detailed electrophoretic study of proteins during Kashkaval ripening (90 days) was carried out by Alrubai.[27] The (polyacrylamide gel) electrophoretic patterns obtained were quantitatively evaluated and the results are presented in Table II. Then number and quantities of protein fractions evidently differ from those for similar cheese types (e.g. Cheddar).[27] Law[28] and Law and Wigmore[29] succeeded in accelerating cheese ripening by the addition of a bacterial neutral proteinase to the curd. Working with Cheddar cheese, the authors[28,29]

TABLE II

Changes in the relative proportions of casein fractions in Kashkaval cheese during ripening[27]

Ripening (days)	α_s-Casein				β-Casein	κ-Casein[a]			para-κ-Casein		
	α_{s_1}	$\alpha_{s_{1-1}}$	$\alpha_{s_{1-11}}$	Total α_s		I	II	Total κ	I	II	Total para-κ
1	39·10	15·79	—	54·89	22·81	—	—	11·03	—	—	11·28
15	23·78	29·26	—	53·04	21·96	—	—	—	18·07	6·93	25·00
30	15·28	11·36	15·12	41·76	17·59	11·68	16·13	27·81	—	—	12·83
45	13·26	17·36	15·91	46·53	25·08	3·86	14·47	18·33	6·75	3·32	10·07
60	23·19	17·04	—	40·23	26·50	8·78	15·50	24·29	6·87	2·12	8·99
75	24·38	14·63	—	39·01	25·52	5·91	16·01	21·92	8·67	4·88	13·55
90	17·26	10·81	—	28·07	18·79	13·21	21·38	34·59	12·23	6·32	18·55

[a] This protein is referred to as κ-casein in Ref. 27 but it appears likely that the protein in question is γ- or γ-like casein.

obtained about a 20% increase in the level of proteolysis in 2 months with the typical flavour intensity of a 4-month-old untreated cheese.

In Kashkaval cheese production, the concentration of water-soluble N compounds increases slowly during ripening (Table III) and a high monocalcium paracaseinate content, which is specific for this type of cheese, is retained even after advanced ripening.[21,22]

Djordjević[21] has shown (Table IV) a significant increase in monocalcium paracaseinate content during the first month of ripening, reaching a maximum at the beginning of the second month (40 days). At this stage,

TABLE III

Changes in water soluble N as percentage of total N in Kashkaval cheese during ripening[22]

Ripening (days)	Water soluble N (% of total N)
0	4·13
30	10·64
60	12·61
90	13·74
120	15·35
150	16·76
180	17·53
270	20·65
550	30·64

TABLE IV
Dynamics of monocalcium paracaseinate during Kashkaval cheese ripening[21]

Monocalcium paracaseinate	Ripening (months)								
	0	1	2	3	4	5	6	9	18
Monocalcium paracaseinate N (%)	1·56	2·99	3·23	3·14	3·19	3·24	3·28	2·97	2·60
Monocalcium paracaseinate N as % of the total N	41·48	76·71	78·67	74·89	74·46	74·90	75·00	64·79	50·76
Monocalcium paracaseinate N as % of the insoluble N	43·27	83·81	90·50	86·53	87·75	89·54	90·64	81·22	73·47

TABLE V
Free amino acid composition in ripened Kashkaval cheese[27]

Amino acid	Free amino acid (as % of total amino acids)
Lys	17·75
His	0·33
Try	0·42
Arg	0·08
Asp	1·57
Thr + Ser	8·87
Glu	21·22
Pro	6·03
Gly	1·73
Ala	2·53
Cys	0·69
Val	7·26
Met	1·86
Ile	5·05
Leu	18·21
Tyr	0·56
Phe	5·84

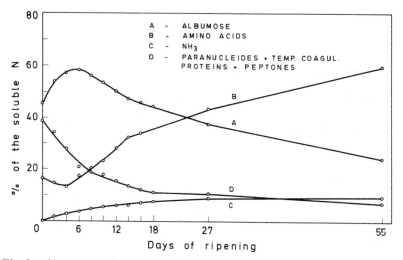

Fig. 2. Changes in the different water-soluble N fractions during ripening; albumose-fraction coagulating on addition of $ZnSO_4$: paranucleides-fraction coagulating on addition of 1% HCl (not entirely defined by Van Slyke).[7,22]

monocalcium paracaseinate nitrogen represents $\sim 81\%$ of the total and $\sim 92\%$ of the insoluble nitrogen in this cheese. Later, the absolute amount remains nearly constant up to 6 months, with a slight decrease afterwards. The author has discussed the advantages of this in detail elsewhere.[22] Proteolysis during the ripening of Kashkaval cheese is shown in Fig. 2.[22]

The free amino acid profile in Kashkaval cheese has been investigated by Alrubai[27] at the end of the ripening period (Table V); glutamic acid was present in the highest concentration followed by leucine and lysine. Only a low level of lipolysis occurs in Kashkaval during ripening due mainly to the destruction of lipolytic micro-organisms during milk pasteurization, leaving only lipases from thermoresistant bacteria.[30] Volatile lower fatty acids, including butyric, caproic, caprylic and capric are detectable.[23] However, an increase in the free fatty acids level in the cheese mass has been observed during ageing, which gives a certain piquancy to the taste of the cheese.[6]

As early as 1905, Van Slyke (cf. Ref. 20) stated the importance of the degree of lactose hydrolysis and noticed the correlation between pH (or acidity) and general cheese quality, including structure. Hydrolysis of lactose (lactic acid fermentation) occurs through different stages of Kashkaval production, reaching its maximum at the end of ripening:

pH $= 4.8$, compared to pH $= 4.9$ for cheese made by the Russian, or pH $= 5.2$ by the Italian methods.[20]

1.4 Quality Defects

The following important quality defects in Kashkaval cheese are encountered: (a) red or yellowish rind, due to growth of the moulds *Oidium crustacea* (red) or *Oidium sulfurea* (yellow); (b) dirty white rind, caused by salt-resistant moulds, yeasts and bacteria, which also produce off-flavours (strong, bitter); (c) development of mites, *Tyroglyphus longior* or *Tyroglyphus siro*, on the rind due to low humidity; (d) late blown curd with gas holes can arise, caused by sporeforming anaerobic bacteria and followed by a sweet and butyric acid taste (early blown curd caused by coliform bacteria is prevented by heat treatment of the curd); (e) oxidative degradation of fat to ketones, which arises from mould growth on the rind; (f) hard and dry curd, caused by incorrect, prolonged cheddaring (too much calcium removed).[1,4,19]

2. WHITE BRINED (PICKLED) CHEESE

White brined (pickled) cheese is a widespread cheese group produced in hot countries and there are many varieties: Feta (Greece), Bjalo salamureno sirene (Bulgaria), Beli sir u kriškama (Yugoslavia), Teleme (Romania), Lori, Imeretinskii, Limanskii, Osetinskii (USSR),[33-37] Domiati (Egypt), Brinza (Israel), Queso Blanco (South and Central America). White brined cheese is suitable for hot climates as it is actually stored in a concentrated brine (4 to 10–16% NaCl).[19,38] At temperatures lower than 8°C, it can be preserved for more than 3 months,[19,39,40] even up to 15 months, depending on storage temperature.[31]

Originally, it was manufactured by shepherds from sheep's, goat's or buffalo's milk, but nowadays cow's and mixed milks are used also, and the production takes place in modern mechanized or automated plants. However, certain differences in the technological processes used for the mentioned varieties are evident.

A common feature of white brined cheese technology is that ripening occurs in brine and lasts from a few weeks up to 2 months. Some of the varieties are produced from milk salted prior to renneting, and some from unsalted milk.[38] Specific parameters in the production schedules of white brined cheese varieties have been extensively studied.[33-36]

TABLE VI
Free fatty acid concentrations in Feta cheese samples (mg/kg)[43]

Acid	Bulgarian	Romanian	Greek	Australian	
				Sample A	Sample B
C_2	604	673	639	411	41
C_3	12	—	19	—	—
C_4	50	35	521	17	470
C_6	26	19	292	12	219
C_8	14	6	146	10	76

Different mixed cultures, including thermophilic and/or mesophilic microflora, are used in white brined cheese production. The main flavour characteristics are acidity and saltiness. Obretenov et al.[41] showed that the total volatile fatty acid content of white brined cheese was 1226 mg/kg of which 89% was acetic acid, while Dilanyan and Magak'yan[42] found 1181 mg/kg, of which 88% was acetic acid, showing a degree of fat lipolysis. A group of authors from the CSIRO Division of Food Research[43] have recently carried out the comprehensive investigation of the fat, headspace volatiles and free fatty acid content of Feta cheeses of different origin, using gas chromatography and mass spectrometry. The results (Table VI) show that acetic acid (C_2) was the major acid present: the levels of butyric (C_4), caproic (C_6) and caprylic (C_8) acids were low. The differences in the free fatty acid concentrations found by various authors may be related either to the techniques used for the distillation and extraction, or connected with the formation of acetic acid due to lactate fermentation (through pyruvic acid).[44]

Proteolysis in white brined cheese has not been studied much. Magak'yan (cf. Ref. 45) found that the free amino acid content of a white brined cheese variety (Chanakh) increased to a maximum during ripening and then decreased, since the amino acids diffused into the brine. The author concluded that the main difference compared to other cheese groups was the predominance of di-*n*-butylamine, being about 20% of the total amine content, which could influence the characteristic flavour of white brined cheese. Polychroniadou and Vlachos[46] investigated the free amino acid, as well as total amino acid composition, of another white brined cheese variety (Teleme) at different stages of ripening by ion-exchange column chromatography. The accumulation of free amino acids (leucine in the highest amounts followed by phenylalanine, lysine and valine) was

TABLE VII
Average composition of white brined cheese

Type of white brined cheese	Fat-in-dry matter (%)	Dry matter (%)	Total protein (%)	NaCl (%)	pH or acidity	Reference
Feta (Greece)	48·52	46·37	—	5·05	4·3–4·4	Veinoglou *et al.*[40]
Bjalo Salamureno	27–31	40–42	10–12	3–4	290–320 (°T)	Dimov *et al.*[1]
Sirene (Bulgaria)	43–45	42–44	16–18	2–3	280–300 (°T)	
Beli sir u kriškama (Yugoslavia)	45–50	52–56	—	3–5	—	Šipka and Zonji (cf. Ref. 4)
	47·78	45·56	19·19	2·22	252 (°T)	Carić *et al.*[59]

accompanied by the development of a characteristic taste. Manolkidis *et al.*[47] estimated the rate and extent of proteolysis by the level of soluble N formed during ripening of Teleme cheese, and Alichanidis *et al.*[51] studied the proteolysis in Feta cheese.

The size and shape of this white, rindless cheese group vary, but the typical form is square, $10 \times 10 \times 10 \, cm^3$, with a weight of about 1 kg.[38] It has a white, firm texture, with no gas holes (only mechanical openings in the curd). The average chemical composition is presented in Table VII.

Most defects in white brined cheese are caused by coliform bacteria, in spite of the high acidity of the curd.[19] Yankov and Denkov[48] stated that slime in the brine caused by *L. plantarum* and/or *L. casei* could be prevented by maintaining the pH of the brine below 4·0 and the salt concentration over 8%.

2.1 Feta

Feta is one of the most popular, international, white brined cheeses made in many southern European and Middle Eastern countries: Greece, Yugoslavia, Bulgaria, Turkey, Egypt, Israel, but recently also in Denmark, United States, Canada and some other Western countries.[5,38,49,50] It was first made in the Greek mountains by the ancient Greeks. Today, Feta, produced from sheep's milk, is the most widely consumed cheese in Greece.[39,40]

Compared to other white brined cheese varieties, Feta has a softer consistency with a piquant, salty flavour. Different mixed cultures are used in the manufacture of Feta: *Str. thermophilus. Str. lactis* or *L. bulgaricus, Str. thermophilus,*[39,40] or *Str. lactis, Str. cremoris.*[19]

The technology and characteristics of Feta cheese manufacture have been studied extensively recently,[43,45,49-54] partly due to the possibility of introducing new technology based on ultrafiltration in its production. The manufacture and ripening of Feta are also discussed in Chapter 9 (Volume 2).

2.2 Bjalo Salamureno Sirene (White Brined Cheese)

Bjalo Salamureno Sirene (Belo Salamureno Sirene or Bjalo Sirene or, simply, Sirene) is a very popular variety of white brined cheese in Bulgaria. Bjalo Salamureno Sirene has all the characteristics of the group, with a consistency that is neither too hard, nor too soft and a slightly salty and acid flavour. A culture composed of *Str. lactis* and *L. casei* is used in its manufacture.[1,4,19] Continuous attempts are being made to improve the technology, which is partly mechanized, and the quality of this widespread cheese of Bulgaria.[1,55-57]

Contamination with *Micrococci*, yeasts or moulds could cause colour changes. A reddish colour could also be the consequence of dosing animals with phenolthiazine. An atypical, sticky consistency is a defect due to *B. viscosium*, and an excessively hard consistency is caused by oversalting (Jotov, cf. Ref. 4).

2.3 Beli Sir U Kriškama

Beli sir u kriškama (the name means white cheese in slices) is produced in Yugoslavia, under the names Srpski, Travnički, Sjenički, Sremski cheese, etc. It is manufactured from sheep's, cow's or mixed milks, and has all the typical characteristics of white brined cheese. A mixed culture, composed of *Str. lactis* and *L. casei* is usually used.[19,38] Šutić *et al.*[58] have produced the white brined cheese, Sremski, using a mixed culture and ripened in vacuum-packed foils. The same cheese variety was successfully produced on an industrial scale using chymosin and pepsin as coagulants.[59] Other authors have also investigated the technology and quality of Travnički-type cheese.[60,61]

3. OTHER BALKAN CHEESE VARIETIES

3.1 Kefalotyri (Greece)

Kefalotyri is a hard, salty Greek cheese, made exclusively of sheep's or goat's milk.[2,4,19,67] It is also known as: Pindos cheese, Skyros cheese,

Vouscos cheese or Xynotiro[4] according to the district of manufacture. Kefalotyri has a flat cylindrical shape, 30 cm diameter, 12 cm height and 5–10 kg weight.[19] It has a high dry matter content, a firm texture with small gas holes and bigger slit holes. Its flavour is strong, piquant and salty. No starter is used in its manufacture. Average composition is: fat, 28·25%; total solids, 65·81%; total protein, 24·76%; salt, 4·77%; ash, 4·60%; and pH, 5·15.[5]

3.2 Rossiiskii (USSR)

Rossiiskii cheese is a hard cheese, made of cow's milk, with a hard, dry rind, a plastic consistency and irregular openings in the structure.[68,69] It has a slight acid flavour and aroma. Its weight is 10·5–18·0 kg, with 57% dry matter and a minimum of 50% fat-in-dry matter.

The technology of Rossiiskii cheese was developed in USSR starting on the basis of Cheddar cheese technology, without cheddaring.[70] During further development, Rossiiskii acquired the characteristics of Dutch cheeses, so it was recently described as a Russian variety of Dutch-type cheese by Shiler *et al.*[71] The significant feature of its manufacture is a low curd heating temperature. The optimal composition of the finished product is: 60–61% dry matter, 1·3–1·8% NaCl and pH = 5·3–5·5.[64] A mixed culture composed of *Str. lactis, Str. diacetylactis* and *Leuc. dextranicum* is used in its manufacture.[68,70,72]

Numerous investigations[68–80] on Rossiiskii cheese have been carried out in order to understand different physico-chemical and biochemical correlations during cheese processing and ripening and to improve and mechanize the technology for its production.

3.3 Sovetskii (USSR)

Sovetskii cheese belongs to the Emmentaler group of cheeses of which it is a modification; the differences in technology are mainly due to mechanization. The size and shape of this variety are also changed compared to original Emmentaler: it is a square block, 50 × 20 × 18 cm³, weight 12–18 kg. Sovetskii cheese has an elastic texture with eyes (about 1 cm diameter), due to the growth of *Propionibacterium shermanni*, and a milky, sweet flavour and aroma.

The culture used in its production is mixed and contains *Str. lactis, Str. diacetylactis, Str. paracitrovorus, L. helveticus, L. lactis, L. casei,* and *P. shermanii.*[81] This type of cheese has become very popular in USSR since it was officially established in 1931 and many scientific centres have investigated different parameters in its technology (acceleration of ripening, biochemical and microbiological processes during ripening, kind of coating, etc.).[81-87] Various improvements in Sovetskii cheese manufacture were reviewed recently by Ostroumov.[88]

3.4 Paški (Yugoslavia)

Paški cheese means 'cheese from Pag', which is the name of the Adriatic island where it is produced. It is a hard cheese made from sheep's milk with characteristics typical of Parmesan, but its technology is more similar to that used for Dutch cheeses. The ripening period is about 2–3 months, possibly longer. Paški cheese has a flat cylindrical shape, 18–22 cm diameter, 7–8 cm height and 2–4 kg weight.[2] It has a high dry matter content and a firm, compact texture, with no holes. Its flavour is surprisingly piquant. No starter is used in its manufacture. Average composition is: fat, 36%; total solids, 66·2%; salt, 2·9%; acidity, 1·5%.[89]

3.5 Somborski (Yugoslavia)

Somborski cheese is a type of soft cheese with characteristics between those of white cheese and Trappist. It originates from Sombor, a city in Vojvodina and was originally made only from sheep's milk. It is very popular in Yugoslavia, although recently it is produced also from mixed, or cow's milk. The specific feature of its manufacture is that all operations after curd forming, i.e. salting, pressing, ripening, take place in wooden buckets. It has a soft, pasty body, with small gas holes and a slightly piquant flavour.[2]

The starter used in Somborski cheese manufacture consists of *Str. thermophilus* and *L. bulgaricus*. Average composition is: fat, 26·00%; total solids, 45·87%, total protein, 17·32%; salt, 2·32%; titratable acidity, 152·10°T.[90]

3.6 Chavdar (Bulgaria)

Chavdar is a soft cheese, produced in Bulgaria from cow's milk. It has a flat cylindrical shape, 20 cm diameter, 8 cm height, and 2 kg weight. Chavdar has a homogeneous, creamy consistency, with small irregular holes, or without holes. Its flavour is specific, pleasant and acidic. A culture containing *Str. lactis* and *Str. cremoris* is used in Chavdar manufacture. Average composition is: fat, 25%; total solids, 50%; salt, 2·5–3·5%.[1]

4. MISCELLANEOUS CHEESE VARIETIES

Besides the cheese varieties described, which are native to all Balkan countries and the southern USSR, many other cheeses are produced in the same area [2,4,69,91] which have either local importance, or are counterparts of well-known western cheese groups. Since 80% of the total cheese production in Bulgaria is white brined cheese (Bjalo Salamureno Sirene)[1] and in Greece, 75% is Feta,[4] and bearing in mind that there is also a significant production of Kashkaval (especially in Bulgaria), the quantities of other cheese varieties produced in those countries are rather small.

Some of the ripened cheeses which originated in, are produced in and are popular only in certain Balkan countries, besides those described, are:

(a) Bulgaria:[1]
    Bezsalamureno Bjalo Sirene (means: unbrined white cheese);
(b) Greece:[4]
    Kasseri (hard);
    Manur (hard cheese made of whey protein);
(c) USSR:
    Kostromskii (hard);[92-94]
    Ukrainskii (hard);[95]
    Donskoi Kazachii (semi-hard);
    Karpatskii (hard);[96]
    Suluguni (hard);[97-100]
(d) Yugoslavia:[2,38]
    Selam (hard);
    Njeguški (hard);
    Krčki (hard).

The most widely produced and popular counterparts of well-known western cheese varieties in Balkan countries are: Parmesan (Greece, Yugoslavia); Cheddar (Bulgaria, Yugoslavia, USSR); Gruyère (Greece); Emmental (Bulgaria, Yugoslavia, USSR); Dutch types (Gouda, Edam) (Bulgaria, Yugoslavia, USSR); Trappist (Bulgaria, Yugoslavia); Roquefort, Gorgonzola (Bulgaria, Yugoslavia, USSR); Kamamber (Yugoslavia).

ACKNOWLEDGEMENTS

The author wishes to thank Dr J. Djordjević for providing most of the references on Kashkaval and useful comments. Thanks is due to Dr Z. Puhan for kind help in supplying important references, to Dr A. Kozev for providing helpful references on Bulgarian cheese varieties, and to Dr E. Alichanidis for supplying references on Greek cheese varieties. Appreciation is expressed to Dr M. Kaláb for his unpublished electron micrographs of Kashkaval and help in their interpretation. Thanks are extended to the author's co-workers: Mr D. Gavarić, Mr S. Milanović, Dipl. Ing. L. J. Kulić and Mrs Z. Kosovac, Dairy Department, Faculty of Technology, Novi Sad, for their kind assistance in technical elaboration of numerous references.

REFERENCES

1. Dimov, N., Kirov, N., Čomakov, H., Georgiev, I., Peičevski, I., Kožev, A., Denkov, C., Mineva, P., Petrova, N. and Konfortob, A., *Handbook for Dairy Technology*, Zemizdat, Sofia, pp. 175, 176, 203, 1984 (in Bulgarian).
2. Pejić, O. M., *Dairy Technology, Vol. 2, Technology of Milk Products*, Naučna knjiga, Beograd, pp. 155, 175, 217, 1956.
3. Pejič, O., *Godišnjak Polj. fak., Zemun.*, 1951, **3**, 141.
4. Mair-Waldburg, H., *Cheese Handbook, Cheeses of the World from A-Z*, Volkswirtschaftlicher Verlag GmbH, Kempten, pp. 303, 544, 549, 1974.
5. Kosikowski, F. V., *Cheese and Fermented Milk Foods*, 2nd edn, F. V. Kosikowski and Associates, Brooktondale, New York, p. 690, 1982.
6. Šutić, M., Ph.D. thesis, Faculty of Agriculture, Beograd University, Beograd, 1966.
7. Djordjević, J., Private communication.
8. Antonova, T., Stefanova-Kondratenko, M., Bodurska, T., Manafova, N., Daov, T. and Nikoevska, T., *Acta Microbiologica Bulgarica*, 1984, **14**, 85.
9. Kaláb, M., Lowrie, J. R. and Nichols, D., *J. Dairy Sci.*, 1982, **65**, 1117.
10. Lowrie, J. R., Kaláb, M. and Nichols, D., *J. Dairy Sci.*, 1982, **65**, 1122.
11. Djordjević, J., Ph.D. thesis, Faculty of Agriculture, Beograd University, Beograd, 1960.
12. Djordjević, J., *Arh. Polj. Nauka*, 1971, **24**, 105.
13. Djordjević, J., *Mlekarstvo*, 1974, **24**, 54.
14. Stefanović, R., Ph.D. thesis, Faculty of Agriculture, Beograd University, Beograd, 1961,
15. Pejić, O., Djordjević, K., Stefanović, R. and Živković, Ž., *Zbornik radova Polj. fak.*, Beograd, 1964, **12**, 374.
16. Pejić, O., Djordjević, J. and Stefanović, R., *Hrana i ishrana*, 1965, **6**, 361.
17. Pejić, O., Djordjević, J. and Stefanović, R., *J. Sci. Agric. Res.*, 1966, **19**, 64.
18. Stefanović, R. and Djordjević, J., *Zbornik radova Polj. fak.*, Beograd, 1965, **13**, 407.
19. Scott, R., *Cheesemaking Practice*, Elsevier Applied Science, London, pp. 272, 437, 447, 1981.
20. Pejić, O., *Arh. Polj. nauka*, 1954, **7**, 17.
21. Djordjević, J., *Proc. 16th Int. Dairy Congress*, Copenhagen, 1962, Vol. B, p. 490.

22. Djordjević, J., Kashkaval, Authorized postgraduate lectures, Faculty of Agriculture, Sarajevo, 1972.
23. Robinson, R. K., *Dairy Microbiology*, Vol. 2, *The Microbiology of Milk Products*, Elsevier Applied Science, London, pp. 179, 183, 1981.
24. Fox, P. F., *Neth. Milk Dairy J.*, 1981, **35**, 233.
25. Grappin, R., Rank, T. C. and Olson, N. F., *J. Dairy Sci.*, 1985, **68**, 531.
26. Marcos, A., Esteban, M. A., León, F. and Fernández-Salguero, J., *J. Dairy Sci.*, 1979, **62**, 892.
27. Alrubai, A., Ph.D. thesis, Faculty of Agriculture, Beograd University, Beograd, 1979.
28. Law, B. A., *Dairy Industries Int.*, 1980, **45** (5), 15.
29. Law, B. A. and Wigmore, A., *J. Dairy Res.*, 1982, **49**, 137.
30. Klimovskii, I. I., *Biochemical and Microbiological Fundamentals of Cheese Technology*, Pishchevaja promishlenost, Moskva, p. 162, 1966 (in Russian).
31. Kožev, A., *Molochnaja promishlenost*, 1972, **33**, 40.
32. Kožev, A., *Izv. Nauchnoizsled. Inst. Mlechna Promsht.*, *Vidin*, 1970, **4**, 137.
33. Dzobadze, K., *Molochnaja promishlenost*, 1965, **4**, 34.
34. Lomsadze, R. N., Mamatelashvili, G. S., Purceladze, N. G., Demurishvili, L. I. and Mandzavidze, N. P., *Molochnaja promishlenost*, 1976, **12**, 13.
35. Martirojan, A. A., Magakjan, A. T. and Karasheninin, P. F., *Molochnaja promishlenost*, 1975, **1**, 21.
36. Hikalo, L. and Tadulev, B., *Molochnaja promishelnost*, 1964, **9**, 26.
37. Ramazanov, I. U., *Molochnaja promishlenost*, 1979, **9**, 15.
38. Slanovec, T., *Cheese Technology*, ČPZ Kmečki glas, Ljubljana, p. 141, 1982.
39. Veinoglou, B., Voyatzoglou, E. and Anifantakis, E., *Mjekarstvo*, 1978, **28**, 30.
40. Veinoglou, B. C., Boyazoglu, E. S. and Kotouza, E. D., *Dairy Industries Int.*, 1979, **44** (10), 29.
41. Obretenov, T., Dimitroff, D. and Obretenova, M., *Milchwissenschaft*, 1978, **33**, 545.
42. Dilanyan, Z. K. and Magak'yan, D. T., *Proc. 20th Int. Dairy Congress*, Paris, 1978, p. 295.
43. Horwood, J. F., Lloyd, G. T. and Stark, W., *Austr. J. Dairy Technol.*, 1981, **36**, 34.
44. Webb, B. H. and Johnson, A. H., *Fundamentals of Dairy Chemistry*, The AVI Publishing Company, Inc., Westport, p. 687, 1965.
45. Lloyd, G. T. and Ramshaw, E. H., *Austr. J. Dairy Technol.*, 1979, **34**, 180.
46. Polychroniadou, A. and Vlachos, J., *Le Lait*, 1979, **59**, 234.
47. Manolkidis, C., Polychroniadou, A. and Alichanidis, E., *Le Lait*, 1970, **50**, 128.
48. Yankov, Y. and Denkov, T., *Izv. Nauchnoizsled. Inst.*, *Mlechna Promsht. Vidin*, 1972, **6**, 103.
49. Hansen, R., *Nordeuropaeik mejeri-tidsskrift*, 1980, **6**, 149.
50. Hansen, R., *Nordeuropaeik mejeri-tidsskrift*, 1977, **9**, 304.
51. Alichanidis, E., Anifantakis, E. M., Polychroniadou, A. and Nanou, M., *J. Dairy Res.*, 1984, **51**, 141.
52. Smietana, Z., Zuraw, J., Kaoka, E. and Poznanski, S., *Technologia Zywnoshci*, 1983, **18**, 55.

53. Carić, M., Gavarić, D., Milanović, S., Kulić, Lj., Popov, B., Cvetkov, D. and Kosovac, Z., *Investigations of the Usage of Ultrafiltration in Dairy Technology*, Faculty of Technology, Dairy Department, Novi Sad, p. 17, 1985.
54. Goncharov, A. I., Konanihin, A. V. and Tabachnikov, V. P., *Molochnaja promishlenost*, 1977, **12**, 14.
55. Baltadzhieva, M., Kyurkchiev, I. and Denkov, T. S., *Khranitelna promishlenost*, 1984, **33**, 14.
56. Baltadzhieva, M. A., Andreev, A. F., Sanechev, I. H., Todorov, T. L. and Minkov, T. H., *Swiss Patent*, 1983, CH 635 985 A5.
57. Stefanova-Kondratenko, M., Antonova, T., Bodurska, I., Manafova, N., Daov, T. and Nikoevska, T., *Acta Microbiologica Bulgarica*, 1984, **14**, 92.
58. Šutić, M., Obradović, D., Pavlović, Ž., Marinković, L. and Birovljev, V., *Mljekarstvo*, 1985, **35**, 99.
59. Carić, M., Milanović, S., Gavarić, D. and Španović, A., *Zbornik radova, Tehn. fak.*, Novi Sad, 1979, **10**, 29.
60. Dozet, N., Stanišić, M., Bijeljac, S. and Perović, M., *Mljekarstvo*, 1983, **33**, 132.
61. Dozet, N., Stanišić, M. and Bijeljac, S., *Mljekarstvo*, 1978, **28**, 78.
62. Renner, E. and Ömeroglu, S., *Milchwissenschaft*, 1981, **36**, 334.
63. Tekinsen, O. C., *Ankara Üniversitesi Veteriner Fakültesi Dergisi*, 1983, **30**, 449.
64. Tekinsen, O. C. and Celik, C., *Ankara Üniversitesi Veteriner Fakültesi Dergisi*, 1983, **30**, 54.
65. Rakshy, S. E. and Attia, I., *Alexandria J. Agric. Res.*, 1979, **2**, 355.
66. Rakshy, S. E. and Attia, I., *Alexandria J. Agric. Res.*, 1979, **2**, 359.
67. Kristensen, J. M. B., *Maelkeritidende*, 1983, **96**, 7.
68. Ivanova, E., *Molochnaja promishlenost*, 1964, **30**, 43.
69. IDF Catalogue of Cheeses, Int. Dairy Federation, Doc. 141, Brussels, 1981.
70. Nikolaev, A., *Molochnaja promishlenost*, 1961, **27**, 22.
71. Shiler, G. G., Nebert, V. K., Alekseev, V. N., Morozov, V. A. and Volodin, V. I., *Molochnaja promishlenost*, 1980, **46**, 8.
72. Nikolaev, A., *Molochnaja promishlenost*, 1961, **27**, 31.
73. Nikolaev, A. and Sharov, S. D., *Molochnaja promishlenost*, 1971, **37**, 7.
74. Dilanyan, Z. H. and Doiljnicin, G. V., *Molochnaja promishlenost*, 1970, **36**, 18.
75. Golovnya, R. V., Zuravleva, I. L., Mironov, G. A. and Abdullina, R. M., *Molochnaja promishlenost*, 1970, **36**, 8.
76. Zelenii, N. P., *Molochnaja promishlenost*, 1970, **36**, 40.
77. Lakomova, L. I., Sokolova, Z. C., Snezko, P. G., Doncova, E. P., Shiler, G. G. and Saharov, S. D., *Molochnaja promishlenost*, 1973, **39**, 15.
78. Nosenko, V. P., Dolynicih, F. G., Davidovskii, A. V., Bershadskii, O. L., Doiljnicjih, G. V. and Shiler, G. G., *Molochnaja promishlenost*, 1976, **42**, 34.
79. Eliseev, O. M. and Chasov, F. V., *Sbornik nauchnykh trudov. Tekhnologiya a tekhnika syrodeliya, Moskva*, 1982, **97**, 21.
80. Golovkov, V. P., Konchakovskii, G. A. and Schneider, L., *Sbornik nauchnykh trudov. Tekhnologiya i tekhnika syrodeliya, Moskva*, 1982, **98**, 28.
81. Klimovskij, I., Alekseeva, K. and Chekalova, K., *Molochnaja promishlenost*, 1965, **31**, 16.
82. Matveeva, E. K. and Andreev, A. N., *Molochnaja promishlenost*, 1981, **46**, 11.
83. Ostroumov, L. A., Gudkov, A. V. and Babuškina, V. A., *Molochnaja promishlenost*, 1974, **40**, 18.

84. Gudkov, A. V., Anishcenko, I. P., Ostroumov, L. A. and Alekseeva, M. A., *Molochnaja promishlenost*, 1980, **46**, 13.
85. Dilanyan, Z., Andreev, A. N., Ostroumov, L. A. and Umanskii, M. C., *Molochnaja promishlenost*, 1972, **38**, 11.
86. Bovikina, V. S., *Molochnaja promishlenost*, 1969, **35**, 13.
87. Dilanyan, Z., Hachatpyan, V., Karagulyan, M. and Jugunyan, G., *Molochnaja promishlenost*, 1962, **28**, 24.
88. Ostroumov, L. A., *Molochnaja promishlenost*, 1981, **46**, 13.
89. Markeš, M., Rubeša, M., Bašić, V., Koludrović, B., Stojak, Lj. and Lešić, Lj., *Mljekarstvo*, 1979, **29**, 26.
90. Carić, M., Milanović, S., Gavarić, D. and Litvai, V., *Zbornik radova, Tehn. fak.*, *Novi Sad*, 1983, **14**, 7.
91. Courtine, R. J., *Larousse des Fromages*, Librarie Larousse, Paris, 1973.
92. Umanskii, M. C., Kozlova, G. A. and Kamenskaj, G. A., *Molochnaja promishlenost*, 1980, **46**, 21.
93. Nikolaev, Am. M. and Saharov, D. S., *Molochnaja promishlenost*, 171, **37**, 13.
94. Tetereva, L. I. and Tolkačev, A. N., *Molochnaja promishlenost*, 1984, **50**, 12.
95. Shulezko, V. F., *Molochnaja promishlenost*, 1971, **37**, 8.
96. Fedin, F. A., Popova, T. V. and Jankovskii, D. S., *Molochnaja promishlenost*, 1984, **50**, 34.
97. Dzobadze, K., *Molochnaja promishlenost*, 1962, **28**, 42.
98. Dilanyan, Z. H. and Piranishvili, A. V., *Molochnaja promishlenost*, 1971, **37**, 23.
99. Piranshvili, A. V., *Molochnaja promishlenost*, 1975, **41**, 28.
100. Mamatelashvili, G. C., Lomsadze, R. N., Kurashvili, I. F. and Melik-Saakov, A. Z., *Molochnaja promishlenost*, 1975, **41**, 23.

Chapter 9

Domiati and Feta Type Cheeses

M. H. Abd El-Salam

Laboratory of Food Technology and Dairying, National Research Centre, Dokki, Cairo, Egypt

1. INTRODUCTION

Manufacture of pickled cheeses in Egypt has been dated to the First Dynasty (3200 BC). Earthenware cheese pots were found in the tomb of 'Hor Aha' at S'aqqara.[1]

Traditionally, the manufacture of pickled cheese varieties was limited to the Mediterranean basin and the Balkans. Possibly, these cheese varieties share the same origin, with various modifications to suit local conditions and needs. Pickled cheeses are of great importance in warm climates: under these conditions, the shelf-life of milk is short and cheese deteriorates before it ripens. Storage in pickle (usually salted whey) becomes one of the inevitable practices necessary for cheese preservation. The pickling practice constitutes the main difference between this group and those cheese varieties produced in colder zones. Production of pickled cheeses was limited for centuries to small-scale production which rendered it difficult to standardize the technological properties and composition of these cheese varieties. Evolution of large-scale production of pickled cheeses in their native countries greatly improved and defined their characteristics. Nowadays, pickled cheeses are gaining popularity, international recognition and new markets all over the world. Their production has been extended to new countries: e.g. Denmark, UK, USA, Australia, New Zealand and Ireland. Also, standardized and advanced technologies have been adopted in their production, including mechanization and ultra-filtration techniques.[2] More than one-third of cheese now produced in Denmark is Feta cheese.[2]

TABLE I
Technological differences between some pickled cheese varieties

Description	Feta[10]	Teleme(a)[11]	Bulgarian white[12]	Brinza[13]	Domiati[14]
1. Type of milk	ewe's or cow's milk				Cow or buffalo or mixture containing 8–15% NaCl
2. Heat treatment	Optional	Optional	—	66–68°C/10–15 min	Optional
3. Starter used	2% Str. lactis + Str. cremoris	2% Str. lactis + L. casei (2:1)	2% Str. lactis + Str. cremoris (2:1)	2% Str. lactis + Str. cremoris (5:2) or L. bulgaricus + Str. thermophilus	Optional
4. Ripening time of milk	2 h	2 h		1 h at 33°C (0·2% acidity)	—
5. Rennet used	Rennet paste or calf rennet (3 g) + lipase (4 g)/100 kg	Calf rennet (3 g/100 kg)	Calf rennet (3 g/100 kg)	Calf rennet (3 g/100 kg)	Calf rennet (5 g/100 kg)
6. Renneting time	60 min	60 min	60 min	60–75 min	150–180 min
7. Cutting	2 cm cubes	2 cm cubes			
8. Ladling	Into hoops, successive turning for 8 h	Into hoops, successive turning	Without cutting, pressing	For 60 min with successive cutting and pressing	In wooden frames/24 h with pressing
9. Salting	Dry salting the top surfaces for 3 days	In brine/24 h	In brine at 12°C/12 h	In brine at 6–8°C/24 h	—
10. Pickling	Wash with water, packed in barrels with 10% brine	In cans using sour whey (L. helveticus + Str. thermophilus) 10% salt	Plastic cartons, sour whey 0·36% acidity, 8–12% salt	In tins using salted whey (heated to 85°C)	In tins (17 kg) using salted whey from the same cheese
11. Storage temperature	5°C	5°C	6–8°C	6–8°C	Room temperature

Many studies in the literature describe the manufacture, composition, quality and ripening of pickled cheeses. Although pickled cheeses share the practice of storage in pickle for extended periods, they are quite different in several aspects, including the type of milk used and manufacturing and storage conditions. Most varieties within this group of cheeses are stored in sealed containers under almost anaerobic conditions, but some are stored in gas-permeable containers, i.e. barrels, which affects biochemical changes during ripening.

A few efforts [3,4] have been made to review work done on specific pickled cheese varieties but no attempt has been made to compile data on these cheeses in a systematic and comparative manner. This chapter deals with this topic.

2. CLASSIFICATION OF PICKLED CHEESES

There is no well-defined, clear classification of pickled cheeses. Confusion usually arises from the lack of such classification as can be observed from the published work on pickled cheeses. Sometimes, the cheese nomenclature does not fit the described procedure for cheese manufacture [5,6] and in many cases, cheeses are described as white pickled cheeses, a general terminology which can apply to all the pickled cheeses. Pickled cheese varieties can be classified as follows (country of origin is given in parentheses).

2.1 Soft Cheese (Moisture Content 55–65%)

2.1.1 Acid coagulation
Mish (Egypt). It is made from naturally fermented milk remaining after gravity separation of sour cream. Salt is sprinkled on the coagulum and the curd is ladled onto cheese mats, cut into suitable pieces and pickled in earthenware containers for more than one year.[7]

2.1.2 Rennet coagulation
The manufacturing conditions for the principal types of rennet-coagulated soft cheeses are summarized in Table I; they may be sub-classified based on the method of salting:

Salting of cheese curd (Feta type)
—Feta (Greece)
—Bulgarian white (Bulgaria)

—Teleme(a) (Greece, Romania)
—Brinza (Bulgaria, USSR)
—Chanakh (USSR)
—Salamoura (Turkey)
—Istamboli (Turkey)
—Akaawi (Syria)

Salting of cheese milk (Domiati type)
—Domiati (Egypt)
—Danie (Egypt), a variant of Domiati cheese made from sheeps' milk.[8]

2.2 Semi-hard Cheeses (Moisture Content 45–55%)

—Halomi (Cyprus)[9]
—Medafara, Magdola, Shinkalish (Syria, Sudan)
—Arab (Iraq)[15]
—Baladi, Montanian (Lebanon).[15]

Data on cheese varieties other than those in class 2.1.2 are scarce; they are produced on a small scale and they are of limited importance. Therefore, this chapter will deal solely with cheese varieties falling in class 2.1.2. To avoid confusion from names given to local varieties which more or less fall into the same category as one of the two sub-classes of this group, we shall refer in this discussion to Domiati and Feta type cheeses to represent the two major categories of rennet-coagulated pickled soft cheeses.

3. ROLE OF SODIUM CHLORIDE IN PICKLED CHEESES

One of the characteristic features of pickled cheeses is their high salt contents and storage for long periods in brine (salted water or whey). Therefore, NaCl has a definite role in determining the chemical, physical and biochemical changes in these cheeses. The chemical changes which occur in the colloidal system of milk and in cheese proteins on addition of NaCl can be summarized as follows.

3.1 Exchange of Colloidal Calcium for Sodium in Milk

Addition of NaCl to milk solubilizes part of the colloidal calcium.[16,17] The amount of calcium released increases with the amount of NaCl added up to

4 g/100 ml and there is no noticeable change thereafter.[17] In buffalo's and cow's milk, about 23–25% of the colloidal calcium can be solubilized by addition of NaCl but only 10% in the case of goat's milk, indicating species differences in exchangeability of the colloidal calcium.

3.2 Disaggregation and Dispersion of the Colloidal Phase of Milk

Addition of NaCl (1 M) to milk or casein micelles of variable size in simulated milk ultrafiltrate[18–20] decreases their turbidity and decreases the average micellar size in addition to non-preferentially solubilizing some of the individual caseins. According to the model proposed by Schmidt,[21] the colloidal calcium phosphate linking micelle sub-units is unevenly distributed and the outer layer of the sub-units is not firmly attached to the core aggregates. Treatment with NaCl seems to remove the surface layer of the micelle sub-units rendering these sub-micelles soluble and releasing their colloidal calcium.

Treatment of casein micelles with NaCl increases particle dispersion.[22] This leads to a decrease in the rate of casein particle aggregation during rennet coagulation and a decrease in the stability of the structural elements of the coagulum,[23] reducing thixotropic characteristics and the intensity of syneresis. Therefore, in Domiati cheesemaking, curd is ladled into frames without cutting due to the fragility of the curd from salted milk. The rennet coagulation times of cow's, buffalo's, goat's and sheep's milks increase with the amount of NaCl added up to 7·5–10% and decrease slightly with further increases in added salt.[24]

Besides its effect on the colloidal state of milk, NaCl affects the action of the coagulant; calf rennet is less affected by the addition of NaCl to milk than *Mucor miehei* protease.[25]

Addition of NaCl to milk increases its titratable acidity up to 5% NaCl beyond which the acidity remains constant.[24] This has been attributed to a base exchange reaction of Na^+ for free NH_3^+ groups in casein micelles, liberating H^+.[26]

3.3 Interaction between Sodium Chloride and Milk and Cheese Proteins

The interaction between NaCl and the proteins of milk and cheese is evident from several studies using various conditions and techniques.[27–29] Adsorption and desorption isotherms for NaCl, paracasein and their mixtures show that the components do not behave independently but more like paracasein, indicating interaction between NaCl and proteins.[29] The amount of NaCl which interacts with milk proteins increases with the concentration of added salt and decreases as the water activity (a_w) increases.[29] The binding of NaCl to paracasein reaches a maximum when the water binding capacity of the protein is maximal.[22] Salt seems to play a major role in regulating cheese consistency.[30] As a result of the interaction of NaCl with paracasein, the amount of strongly-bound moisture decreases.[30] Increasing the amount of weakly-bound moisture causes an increase in firmness but decreases the elasticity and plasticity of cheese.[30] Geurts et al.[31] hypothesized that the degree of NaCl interaction with paracasein depends on pH, [NaCl] and [Ca^{2+}].

3.4 Solubilization of the Paracaseinate–Phosphate Complex

The effect of NaCl or NaCl and lactic acid on simulated soft cheese models[32] or on the paracaseinate–phosphate complex shows the release of significant quantities of calcium phosphate and relatively small quantities of calcium paracaseinate when shaken with dilute NaCl solution. Aqueous solutions containing large quantities of NaCl attack both phosphate and paracaseinate with equal severity and a more extensive release of Ca and inorganic P occurs when lactic acid is added to extracting solutions. Moneib[32] reported that maximum peptidization was obtained when using NaCl concentrations between 3 and 5% within the pH range 5·3–5·6. At pH 5 or less, NaCl has only a very small effect on the amount of nitrogen dissolved.

4. CHANGES IN CHEESES DURING PICKLING

4.1 General Composition

Extensive data are found in the literature concerning the moisture, fat, salt, pH and acidity of pickled soft cheeses. Several interacting variables affect the general composition and acid development in pickled cheeses. No attempt has been made to cover all these variables, but the most important ones are considered.

4.1.1 Cheese type
Keeping other variables almost constant, differences in the pH, acidity, moisture and salt contents of Domiati and Feta type cheese reflect

TABLE II
General composition of Domiati and Feta type cheeses made from cow's milk and
stored at room temperature (about 20°C)

	Domiati[34]		Feta[36]	
	Fresh	*3 months*	*Fresh*	*3 months*
Moisture (%)	65·5	54·0	54·5	48·8
Fat in DM (%)	36·6	47·5		
Salt in water (%)	10·6	11·8	3·7	14·4
Acidity (%)	0·27	2·16	0·85	0·45
pH	6·06[a]	3·30[a]	4·97	5·00

[a] Ref. 41; DM, dry matter.

differences in processing steps.[34–40] Fresh Domiati cheese is characterized
by higher pH, moisture, and salt contents and a lower acidity than fresh
Feta type cheeses (Table II).

These differences are due mainly to the salting step. The direct addition of
salt to milk before renneting ensures even distribution of salt in fresh
Domiati cheese and controls fermentation processes, even before milk
clotting. It also affects the water retention in the curd. Using dry salting or
salting in brine solutions, as practised in the manufacture of Feta type
cheeses, more time is required for salt penetration of the curd and
attainment of salt equilibrium throughout the block of cheese. This allows
time for rapid acid development, leading to increased water exudation from
the curd and a lower moisture content in fresh Feta type cheeses.

The pH of pickled Domiati cheese[35,41] is much lower and the acidity is
much higher, than in Feta type cheeses.[10,36,42] This arises from two factors:
firstly, because of its relatively high moisture content, fresh Domiati cheese
retains more lactose than Feta type cheese (Table III); secondly, the whey
used in pickling Domiati cheese is a rich source of lactose for bacterial
fermentation within the cheese through diffusion. El-Abd *et al.*[43] used
different mixtures of salted whey and brine of the same salt content as pickle
for Domiati cheese; reduction of the amount of whey in the pickle reduced
acid development in the cheese.[43]

Carbohydrates are found in Domiati cheese even after 6 months of
storage; these were identified as lactose and galactose but glucose was not
detected in 6-month-old cheese.[44] It seems that in Domiati cheese, lactose
fermentation proceeds until the developed acidity terminates the growth of
the cheese microflora. However, the available lactose (lactose in cheese and

TABLE III
Changes in carbohydrate content of Domiati and Feta type cheeses
during storage (as lactose, %)

Storage period (days)	Domiati		Feta[42]
	Ref. 35	Ref. 41	
Fresh	3·50		0·82–1·36
15	3·40	2·09	
30	2·85	1·84	
120	1·65		
180		0·54	

pickle) is more than the cheese microflora can utilize, which explains the high residual lactose content in cheese throughout the storage period. In the first step of fermentation, lactose is hydrolysed to glucose and galactose but the cheese microflora selectively utilize glucose with the accumulation of galactose in a similar manner to that reported in yoghurt[45] and Swiss cheese. However, quantitative studies are needed to verify this point. The high salt content of Domiati cheese overcomes the sweet taste of the residual sugars in the cheese. This does not exclude the possible contribution of carbohydrates to the taste of Domiati cheese, especially of fresh cheese. Feta type cheese contains much less lactose than Domiati cheese[42] and it disappears within 1 month of storage. The identified microflora in Domiati cheese[45,47] are mainly homofermentative, indicating that lactose fermentation yields primarily lactic acid. In a sample of Feta cheese, about 90% of the lactic acid was present in the D form.[48]

4.1.2 Storage temperature

Cold storage usually decreases the rate of biochemical changes in Domiati cheese as apparent from the lower acidity and higher pH than cheese stored at room temperature.[34,37] Also, the moisture content of cheese increases during the early storage period at low temperatures due to increased swelling of the cheese proteins at the relatively high pH of the fresh cheese. The increase in cheese moisture arises from absorption of the pickle. Advanced storage at low temperature is accompanied by an increase in acidity but at a slower rate than in cheese stored at higher temperatures (Table IV). In Feta type cheese stored at low temperatures the increase in cheese moisture content has not been observed during the early storage period but it does occur during advanced storage when the pH increases again.[36] Differences in the fat content of cheeses stored at different temperatures are also obvious.

4.1.3 Storage period

The composition of Domiati cheese changes continuously during storage.[35,37,49] The maximum rate of change in cheese composition occurs during the 1st month of storage which coincides with the maximum growth of the cheese microflora:[46,47] changes occur at slower rates thereafter. Usually, the moisture content and pH of cheese decrease while the fat content and acidity increase during storage. The increase in cheese fat content is due to the continuous losses of soluble degradation products of the solids-not-fat of cheese into the pickle.[35,37,50,51] Changes in the gross composition of Feta type cheeses during storage are less pronounced than those in Domiati cheese.[38,39,52]

4.1.4 Salt content

Variable levels of salt are usually added to the milk in Domiati cheesemaking depending on season and quality of the milk. The higher the percentage of salt added to milk, the higher the moisture content of the cheese, either fresh or pickled (Table V).[53] A high salt content weakens the cheese curd and it retains more moisture. Also, a high salt content retards acid development in Domiati cheese during pickling. On the other hand, Feta type cheese stored in brine with high salt content has a lower moisture content than cheeses stored in less concentrated brines.[36]

4.1.5 Heat treatment of milk and use of reconstituted and recombined milks

Pasteurization of cheese milk has little effect on the gross composition of pickled soft cheeses.[37,47,54] A slight increase in moisture content and a decrease in acid development are apparent in pickled cheeses made from pasteurized milk. The use of reconstituted or recombined milks for pickled soft cheeses decreases the moisture content of the cheese.[42,55,56] However, raising the reconstitution ratio, i.e. total solids content of cheese milk, increases the moisture content in pickled soft cheeses.[57–59]

4.1.6 Ultrafiltration

Feta type cheeses are produced now on an industrial scale by ultrafiltration (UF) techniques[2] and the manufacture of Domiati cheese by ultrafiltration has been described.[60–62] The moisture contents of these cheeses are usually higher and the fat contents are lower than those of cheeses made by traditional techniques[60,61,63] due to the high water holding capacity of whey proteins retained in UF cheeses (Table VI).

It is evident from the foregoing that the changes in the gross composition of Domiati cheese during storage are more pronounced than those

TABLE IV
General composition of Domiati and Feta cheeses made from cow's milk as affected by storage temperature

	Domiati[34]					Feta[36]				
	Fresh	Stored at				Fresh	Stored at			
		8 ± 2°C		20 ± 5°C			5°C		20°C	
		1 month	3 months	1 month	3 months		1 month	3 months	1 month	3 months
Moisture (%)	65·5	66·8	68·2	57·8	55·4	54·5	52·8	55·3	48·5	48·8
Fat in DM (%)	36·6	35·1	32·9	43·6	46·2					
Salt in water (%)	10·6	9·9	10·8	11·7	11·9	3·7	13·6	14·3	13·8	19·4
Acidity (%)	0·27	0·40	0·56	1·63	2·16					

TABLE V
General composition of Domiati cheese as affected by the level of NaCl added to the milk[52]

| | 8% NaCl | | 10% NaCl | | 12% NaCl | | 15% NaCl | |
	Fresh	3 months	Fresh	3 months	Fresh	3 months	Fresh	3 months
Moisture (%)	58·6	51·4	59·5	52·2	60·9	54·5	61·7	55·8
Fat in DM (%)	34·6	49·7	35·0	48·2	32·8	48·7	31·8	45·5
Acidity (%)	0·27	2·24	0·24	2·02	0·21	1·42	0·11	1·00

TABLE VI
General composition of Domiati and Feta type cheeses made by ultrafiltration techniques

	Domiati[60]		Feta type[63]	
	Fresh	*1 month*	*Fresh*	*1 month*
Moisture (%)	64·21	61·97	61·30	52·20
Fat in DM (%)	50·01	53·38		50·0
Acidity (%)	0·29	1·92		1·40
pH	6·7	4·5	4·79	4·21
Salt in water (%)	7·2	6·4		4·68

occurring in Feta type cheeses. The determining factor is the higher developed acidity which arises from the higher level of lactose retained in Domiati cheese and the higher storage temperature.

The role of developed acidity in determining the changes in gross composition of pickled Domiati cheese has been realized from the analysis of cheese with added preservative that inhibited acid development.[64] The acidity developed brings the pH of the cheese close to the isoelectric point of caseinate and partially solubilizes the colloidal calcium which leads to shrinkage of the cheese matrix and exudation of cheese serum into pickle.[65] This phenomenon is of practical importance as the weight losses of Domiati cheese during storage (about 30% of fresh weight) arise mainly from exudation of cheese serum as a result of the developed acidity. The role of NaCl in determining the changes in the gross composition of pickled cheeses can be attributed mainly to its effect on the rate of acid development in the cheese.

4.2 Proteolysis

Pickled cheeses undergo continuous proteolysis during storage in pickle. This was manifested in earlier studies by determining soluble nitrogen fractions and recently by the use of more elaborate analytical methods.

Studies on factors affecting proteolysis in Domiati cheese, as followed by determining nitrogen fractions, reveal:

(1) Proteolysis is usually slowed down by low-temperature storage,[34,37] heat treatment of cheese milk,[37,47,49,54] H_2O_2-catalase treatment of milk[66,67] and the use of dried milks in cheese manufacture.[56]

(2) Cheese from cow's milk shows more rapid proteolysis than that

from buffalo milk[34] which reflects differences in the rates of proteolysis of casein fractions of these two species.[68-70]

(3) Increasing the salt content in cheese slightly decreases proteolysis in Domiati cheese.[37,56]

(4) Homogenization slightly increases proteolysis.[35]

(5) Addition of whey proteins,[71] phosphate and citrate,[72,73] and capsicum tincture (ethanol extract of paprika)[74-76] enhance proteolysis in Domiati cheese.

(6) Manufacture of cheese by ultrafiltration techniques[60,77] and by direct acidification[78] increase proteolysis.

(7) The use of milk clotting enzymes other than calf rennet,[79-85] modifies proteolysis in Domiati cheese.

(8) The use of different types and concentrations of cheese starters in Domiati cheese manufacture makes only a limited contribution to proteolysis[84] due to the high salt content of the cheese. However, use of salt-tolerant strains[85] enhances proteolysis.

Changes in the nitrogen fractions of Feta type cheese during storage[30,39,40,42,52,84,86] follow, qualitatively, the same trend as in Domiati cheese. However, it is difficult to compare the results obtained with these two types of pickled cheeses and even in the same type of cheese. There are wide differences in the raw materials used, ingredients added in manufacture, storage conditions and methods of analysis; in some cases essential information is not included.

Generally, the reported data on the nitrogen fractions of pickled cheese during storage can be summarized as follows:

(1) The total nitrogen content of the cheeses gradually decreases while the soluble nitrogen fractions increase continuously during storage, indicating continuous proteolysis. Transfer of degradation products to the pickling solution by diffusion explains the decrease in total N during storage.

(2) The contribution of the cheese microflora to proteolysis is evident from studies on different factors affecting the activity of cheese microflora as measured by the formation of water soluble nitrogen.

(3) The use of different milk clotting enzymes in cheese manufacture modifies protein hydrolysis in pickled cheese, indicating their contribution to proteolysis in these cheeses.

The use of electrophoretic and chromatographic techniques in cheese analysis gives a better insight into changes in individual protein fractions during storage.[36,52,88-90] The milk clotting enzymes contribute much to the level of proteolysis in pickled cheeses. This is due to the high retention of milk clotting enzymes in cheese curd of high moisture content, and to storage of the cheese in salted whey which contains residual clotting enzymes used in milk coagulation. Also in Domiati cheese, a higher enzyme concentration is used in milk coagulation than for most cheese varieties. The changes in the proteins of Domiati cheese are not identical to those observed in Telemea cheese. In Domiati cheese, α_{s1}-casein is hydrolysed rapidly, while β-casein resists hydrolysis.[84,89] The β-casein of Feta cheese made from ewe's milk[52] also resists hydrolysis, while α_{s1}-casein is hydrolysed rapidly. Mansour and Alais[36] showed that the para-κ-casein in Syrian white pickled cheese (Feta type) from cow's milk resists hydrolysis throughout the storage period. This pattern of changes arises from the action of rennet on cheese proteins as affected by salt content.[91] The high salt content of pickled cheeses and high storage temperature in the case of Domiati cheese, enhance polymerization of β-casein and render it less susceptible to rennet action.[91] The use of milk clotting enzymes other than calf rennet alters the degradation pattern of cheese proteins.[52,79,81]

A number of fast- and slow-moving degradation products are apparent in the electropherogram of proteins from pickled cheeses. The breakdown products with mobilities higher than α_{s1}-casein are comparable to those formed by action of chymosin on α_{s1}-casein while the slow-moving fractions are comparable to γ-caseins produced from β-casein by the action of indigenous milk proteinases (plasmin).[92] The β/α_{s1}-casein ratio in Domiati cheese increases continuously during storage[84] and, after extended storage, the water-insoluble cheese proteins are made up mainly of β-casein, which may explain the soft body and texture of ripened Domiati cheese.[93] The use of different starters in Domiati cheese manufacture has only a slight effect on the electrophoretic pattern of the cheese proteins,[84] which indicates that bacterial proteinases are of limited significance to proteolysis as measured by these methods.

The levels of soluble nitrogenous constituents in Domiati cheese seem to be higher than in Feta type cheeses, though this cannot be stated definitively due to wide variations in the experimental variables reported in the literature. However, the high storage temperature may encourage the growth and activity of the microflora of Domiati cheese, resulting in the formation of higher levels of soluble degradation products. Analysis of the soluble nitrogenous constituents of Domiati cheese by gel chromatography[88] shows that they are mainly low molecular weight compounds (amino acids and small peptides). The HPLC patterns of cheese proteins

TABLE VII
Concentration (mg/g) of free amino acids in some pickled cheeses

Amino acid	Domiati[a][95]		Feta[b][52]		
	Range	Average	Fresh 1	60	120 days
Asp	0·07–0·176	0·123	0·027	0·187	0·235
Thr	0·21–0·535	0·373	0·015	0·131	0·649
Ser	0·399–0·683	0·541	0·07	0·363	0·774
Glu	0·32–0·337	0·329	0·026	0·105	0·08
Gly	0·13–0·373	0·253	0·089	0·094	0·248
Pro	0·055–0·066	0·061	0·061	0·382	0·837
Ala	0·244–1·10	0·673	0·031	0·310	1·065
Cys	trace–0·204	0·102	—	0·017	0·155
Val	0·328–0·848	0·588	0·051	0·616	1·258
Met	0·360–0·481	0·421	0·048	0·159	0·343
Ile	0·160–0·655	0·408	0·017	0·244	0·614
Leu	0·804–1·302	1·053	0·058	1·675	2·898
Tyr	0·23–0·270	0·251	0·030	0·169	0·154
Phe	0·480–0·654	0·567	0·028	0·823	1·274
Lys	0·589–0·721	0·655	0·051	1·313	1·077
His	0·07–0·112	0·091	0·014	0·069	0·097
Try	0·648–0·832	0·740	0·024	0·146	0·163
Arg	—	—	0·072	0·124	0·023
Orn	0·345–0·418	0·382			
γ-AB	0·455–0·655	0·555			
Ammonia	3·32–4·83	4·08			

[a] Random market samples (18 samples).
[b] From sheep's milk using calf rennet as coagulant.
γ-AB; γ-aminobutyric acid.

from fresh and 4-month-old Domiati cheese (Fig. 1)[94] show that the proteins of fresh cheese consist of two major fractions with a small number and low concentration of peptides. On the other hand, the number and concentration of peptides increase during storage with a noticeable decrease in the concentration of one of the original protein fractions.

Comparison of the free amino acid profile in Domiati cheese[95] with those of cow and buffalo caseins reveals (Table VII) a marked reduction in the concentration of glutamic acid which is accompanied by the formation of γ-amino butyric acid through a deamination reaction. Also, arginine is almost absent with the appearance of ornithine. The stored cheese has a high concentration of ammonia, which indicates the significance of deamination reactions occurring in Domiati cheese and which contribute

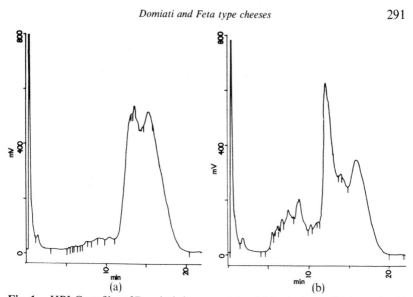

Fig. 1. HPLC profiles of Domiati cheese proteins: (a) fresh cheese, (b) 4 month-old pickled cheese.[94]

to flavour development in this type of cheese. The NH_3 content of pickle brine increased 18-fold during the 12-week storage of Bulgarian white soft cheese.[96] The pattern of free amino acids in Feta cheese from ewe's milk[52] is similar but not identical to that of Domiati cheese. One of the similarities between the amino acid patterns of these two varieties is the low glutamic acid content, indicating that deamination of glutamic acid is a common event in pickled cheeses. The amino acid patterns of Feta and white Bulgarian pickled cheeses were similar, both containing 14–19 amino acids but the contents of individual amino acids were significantly higher in Feta cheese throughout a 6-month ripening period.[97] Lower concentrations of free amino acids were reported in Telemea cheese (Feta type), probably due to the method of sample preparation for analysis.[11]

The formation of volatile amines in Chanakh (Feta type) cheese showed[98] the formation of more than 35 compounds during storage, of which the following were identified: diethylamine, dimethylamine, trimethylamine, triethylamine, isopropylamine, *n*-propylamine, di-*n*-propylamine, tri-*n*-propylamine, isobutylamine, di-*n*-butylamine, isoamylamine, diisoamylamine, pyrrolidine, piperidine, *n*-methylpiperidine, *n*-ethylpiperidine, pyridine, β-picoline or γ-picoline, 2,4-dimethylpyridine, 2,6-dimethyl ethylpyridine and 4-ethylpyridine. Di-*n*-butylamine represents ~ 20% of the total volatile amines in this cheese,[98] suggesting that this

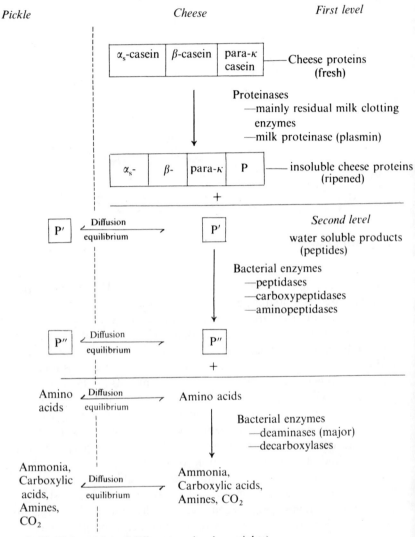

P, P′, P″ (peptides of different molecular weights)

Fig. 2.   Proteolysis in pickled cheeses.

amine could be of some significance to the flavour of pickled cheeses. On the other hand, the tyramine content of Turkish pickled soft cheese (Feta type) is less than other cheese varieties,[99] which supports the view that deamination and not decarboxylation is a major pathway for amino acid catabolism in pickled cheeses.

To conclude, proteins of pickled cheese varieties undergo three levels of proteolysis, as illustrated in Fig. 2. The soluble products from the different levels of proteolysis diffuse into the pickling solution which is in equilibrium with the cheese. Removal of the degradation products from the cheese allows the enzymatic reactions to continue throughout the storage period.

4.3 Lipolysis and Development of Free Fatty Acids

The literature on Domiati cheese contains voluminous data on total volatile acidity as a measure of the formation of volatile fatty acids during pickling as affected by different processing conditions. Most of these data are expressed as ml alkali used in their titration. Acetic acid constitutes the major part of the volatile fatty acids in this type of cheese.[100] The reported values for total volatile fatty acids for Domiati cheese were recalculated as percentage acetic acid in cheese (Table VIII).

Most of the changes occur during the first 15–30 days of storage which coincide with maximum bacterial growth.[47,76] The high concentration of total volatile fatty acids in pickled Domiati cheese would contribute significantly to the total acidity of this type of cheese. Lloyd and Ramshaw[4]

TABLE VIII
Development of volatile fatty acids in Domiati cheese made from buffalo milk during storage (as percentage acetic acid)

Coagulant	Ripening period (days)				
	Fresh	15	30	60	90
Rennet[a]	0·073	0·150	0·158	0·173	0·179
M. pusillus protease	0·073	0·121	0·142	0·184	0·219
Calf rennet[b]	0·034	0·089	0·107	0·109	0·111
Bovine pepsin[b]	0·044	0·092	0·097	0·107	0·109
M. miehei protease[b]	0·052	0·084	0·105	0·108	0·111
E. parasitica protease[b]	0·029	0·078	0·107	0·118	0·120

[a] Ref. 81.
[b] Ref. 79.

TABLE IX
Free fatty acid contents of Domiati and Feta cheeses

Description	Acetic acid	Propionic acid	Butyric acid	Valeric and higher
		(mmole/100 g cheese)		
Domiati cheese[100]				
Raw buffalo milk—fresh	0·74	0·30	0·10	0·06
Raw buffalo milk—2 months	2·06	1·22	0·28	0·29
Raw buffalo milk—4 months	2·30	1·40	0·80	0·86
Raw cow's milk—4 months	2·06	1·30	0·82	0·78
Raw skim milk—fresh	0·66	0·32	—	0·04
Raw skim milk—4 months	2·24	1·28	0·04	0·53
Pasteurized buffalo milk—4 months	1·34	0·73	0·28	0·29
Pasteurized buffalo milk—4 months	1·30	0·71	0·25	0·25
Pasteurized skim milk—4 months	1·24	0·78	0·02	0·20
Feta cheese[102]				
Raw cow's milk, *Str. lactis*				
—5 months	1·97	0·36	0·066	1·01
Pasteurized cow's milk, *Str. lactis*				
—5 months	1·32	0·19	0·084	0·83
Pasteurized cow's milk, *Str. lactis, L. acidophilus* (1:3),				
lipase KL —5 months	1·56	0·67	0·74	2·27

reported that the typical value for volatile fatty acids (VFA) in Bulgarian Feta cheese is 1220 mg/kg, of which 89% was acetic acid. Dilanyan and Magakyan[98] found 1181 mg/kg of total VFA, of which 85% was acetic acid, in Chanakh (Feta type) cheese. The reported values for VFA in Feta and Domiati type cheeses are in good agreement and deviations from this general conclusion reflect factors affecting the biochemical changes in cheese during pickling. Miadenov[101] reported that fat breakdown increases with an increase in storage temperature or a decrease in brine strength; however, changes in cheese stored at 3–5°C were slow and independent of brine concentration.

Determination of different fatty acids in Domiati cheese[100] shows that acetic acid represents the highest percentage of volatile acidity, while butyric, valeric and higher acids are present in smaller quantities during early storage (Table IX). Data for Domiati cheese with different fat contents indicate that butyric acid arises from fat hydrolysis.[100] This suggests that the bacterial lipases or lipases in commercial preparations of milk clotting

TABLE X
Free fatty acids in Feta cheese samples (mg/kg)[103]

	Bulgarian	Romanian	Greek	Australian	
				A	B
C_2	604	673	659	411	41
C_3	12	—	19	—	—
C_4	50	35	521	17	470
C_6	26	19	292	12	219
C_8	14	6	146	10	76

enzymes are responsible for lipolysis in Domiati cheese. The contribution of free fatty acids to flavour development in Feta cheese has been realized from analysis of market samples of different origin and flavour intensities,[103] as shown in Table X. Typical Feta cheese is characterized by a rancid flavour and extensive and distinctive lipolysis that can be attributed to the use of rennet paste from lambs and kid goats in cheese manufacture. The use of commercial calf rennet extract produces Feta cheese with limited lipolysis and lacking the typical sharp flavour of Feta cheese.[102,104] Addition of pregastric lipases from kid lambs and goats to Feta cheese made from pasteurized milk induces the development of typical Feta like flavour.[102] On the other hand, Alichanidis et al.[52] reported lipolysis in Feta cheese made using calf and microbial rennet substitutes. The use of ewe's milk may also enhance the development of higher levels of short chain fatty acids than cow's milk.[105] It is more likely that the enzyme preparation used in cheese manufacture, rather than differences in pH and salting method, as suggested previously,[102] affects the volatile fatty acid pattern of pickled cheeses. Addition of small amounts of pregastric lipases during Domiati cheese manufacture from reconstituted milk enhanced volatile fatty acid development, but a high lipase activity induced an unacceptable rancid flavour in this type of cheese.[106]

Obretenow et al.[107] showed that the concentrations of C_2–C_5 fatty acids in the pickle were higher than in the cheese while the reverse was found in the case of C_6 and C_8 fatty acids due to differences in their solubilities in aqueous solution and in cheese fat.

Analysis of glycerides from pickled Domiati cheese after different storage periods[108] clearly indicates lipolysis during storage. The partial glyceride content of 4-month-old cheese made from unhomogenized milk was comparable to those of 1-month-old cheese made with added lipase (4 g/100 kg). Homogenization influenced the distribution but not the total

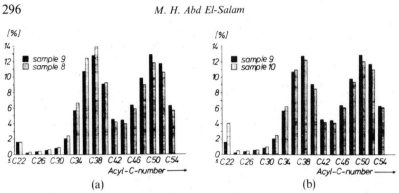

Fig. 3. Glyceride composition of 4-month-old Domiati cheeses: (a) Sample 9, unhomogenized; sample 8, homogenized; (b) sample 10, homogenized with added lipase (4 g/100 kg) (Ref. 108).

proportion of partial glycerides (Fig. 3). The considerably larger surface area of fat globules in homogenized milk allows the lipase to hydrolyse preferentially short chain triglycerides on the globule surface with the formation of monoglycerides and short chain diglycerides. Lipolysis, followed by determining the monoglyceride content, in Syrian white pickled cheese (Feta type) was marked in cheeses stored at 10–20°C but lipolysis was limited at 5°C. Also, increasing the salt content in the brine had a limited effect on lipolysis in this type of cheese. Prodanski and Dzhordzhorowa[105] showed that development of volatile acids and diglycerides was greater in cheese from ewe's than from cow's milk.

Lipolysis in pickled cheeses is, therefore, evident from the different studies cited. However, the lipases responsible for fat hydrolysis in pickled cheeses can originate from the following sources.

(1) Direct addition of pregastric lipases, recommended in some reports to induce the desirable rancidity in Feta cheese.[102]

(2) Lipases in milk clotting enzyme preparations. These lipases are reported to be responsible for the wide variation in lipolysis observed even in the same type of cheese due to differences in concentration and specificities of contaminating lipases. The use of rennet paste from kid goats and lambs produces cheese with high contents of C_4–C_8 fatty acids, since the lipases present preferentially release short chain fatty acids.

(3) Milk lipase.

(4) Bacterial lipases.

The last two sources may be significant in cheeses made from raw milk.

Conclusive evidence for the contribution of lipases from the different sources to lipolysis in pickled cheeses is lacking.

Various studies indicate the importance of acetic acid as a major constituent of volatile flavour and as a flavour determinant in pickled cheeses.[102,103] Nevertheless, the metabolic origin of acetic acid during cheese ripening is still uncertain. Acetic acid can be produced from citrate, lactose and amino acids,[109] and it is very probable that more than one fermentation pathway contributes to the acetic acid content of cheese. It is likely that during the initial stages of pickling, acetic acid arises primarily from lactate fermentation. During the later stages of ripening, acetic acid as well as other short chain volatile fatty acids arises also from oxidative deamination of amino acids by lactic acid bacteria.[110]

4.4 Volatile Flavour Compounds

Apart from the volatile fatty acids, little has been reported on the volatile compounds in pickled cheeses. Dimitrov *et al.*,[111] using steam distillation and GLC, identified several volatile constituents in Feta cheese, including *n*-alkanals and acroline. In Cheddar cheese, acroline arises from the metabolism of methionine with the appearance of methional as a flavour constituent. However, the latter compound was not identified by Dimitrov *et al.*[111] Therefore, the presence and origin of acroline in pickled cheeses is questioned and it was not detected by headspace techniques.[103] Analysis of the volatiles of Bulgarian, Romanian and Greek Feta cheeses[103] by headspace techniques showed that they are qualitatively similar. They contain relatively large quantities of ethanol, *n*-propanol, butan-2-ol, methyl-propan-1-ol, toluene and ethyl butyrate. The presence of high concentrations of alcohols may be due to the presence of several species of yeast in Feta cheese[112] able to ferment lactose to ethanol and carbon dioxide. Australian Feta cheese, however, contains only low concentrations of volatile substances and exhibits headspace volatile profiles different from those of Bulgarian, Romanian and Greek Feta cheeses.

In Domiati cheese, the concentrations of total acidic and neutral carbonyls increase during storage, and the addition of capsicum tincture (ethanol extract of paprika, 0·1–0·3%), stimulates the production of these compounds.[113]

4.5 Vitamin Content

Data on this subject are scarce; the only report is that of Sabry and Guerrant,[114] who found that almost all the vitamin A content of milk was retained in Domiati cheese and that it was stable during storage. On the other hand, variable percentages of thiamine, riboflavin and niacin were retained in fresh cheese and the concentration of these decreased throughout pickling in soldered tins (anaerobic conditions). The levels of riboflavin and niacin in Domiati cheese pickled under aerobic conditions tend to increase during storage, indicating that the microflora occurring under these conditions are able to synthesize these two nutritional factors.

4.6 Changes in the Composition of Pickle

It is unlikely that significant fermentation occurs in pickle during cheese storage due to its high salt content. However, the composition of the pickle changes continuously during storage as a result of chemical and biochemical changes occurring in cheese and diffusion of soluble constituents between cheese and pickle. The changes in the composition of pickle are controlled by the following:

(1)   Composition of fresh cheese and pickle (brine or salted whey).
(2)   Rate and extent of biochemical changes in the cheese. These in turn are controlled primarily by the salt contents of the cheese and pickle, temperature of storage and heat treatment of the milk used in cheesemaking.
(3)   The ratio of cheese to pickle. Practically, the cheese/pickle ratio is in the order of 5–6:1. However, reported studies did not mention this point or other ratios were used. Therefore, care must be taken in the interpretation of the reported results.

In Domiati cheese stored at room temperature, the volume of pickle (salted whey) increased significantly during the first month of storage (12·5%) but changed much less during subsequent storage.[65] Besides, cheese loses 17·4% of the cheese solids during the first month and about 70% of these losses appear in the pickle;[65] a further 5·9% of cheese solids are lost after a further 2 months of storage. This is attributed to partial exudation of cheese serum into pickle due to acid development and shrinkage of the cheese matrix. The reverse occurs during storage of Domiati cheese at low temperatures,[37,65] i.e. a decrease in the volume of pickle during the early storage period through increased swelling of cheese proteins and an increase in the moisture content of the cheese, but further storage is accompanied by an increase in pickle volume and changes in its composition.

The concentration of nitrogenous compounds in cheese pickle increases

TABLE XI

Changes in total and non-protein N in pickle from Feta type cheese stored at different temperatures (g/litre)[85]

Storage period (days)	Using 15% brine				Using 18% brine			
	5°C		20°C		5°C		20°C	
	TN	NPN	TN	NPN	TN	NPN	TN	NPN
1	0·07	0·06 (85·7)[a]	0·17	0·14 (82·3)[a]	0·10	0·09 (90·0)[a]	0·19	0·15 (79·0)[a]
15	0·25	0·21	0·52	0·43	0·45	0·41	0·85	0·78
60	0·86	0·70	1·53	1·40	1·15	1·05	1·98	1·75
120	1·10	1·00 (90·9)[a]	2·53	2·32 (91·7)[a]	1·45	1·32 (91·0)[a]	3·12	3·01 (96·5)[a]

[a] NPN as percentage of total N.

continuously during storage. In Feta type cheese stored in salted brine solutions at different temperatures, most of the total N in pickle is non-protein N. It increases throughout storage due to cheese proteolysis and diffusion of soluble constituents into the pickle, the rate and extent of this increase are dependent on storage temperature (Table XI). The same has been also found in Domiati cheese pickle (Table XII).

The mineral composition, other than NaCl, of pickle also changes during storage of Feta type cheese,[115] reaching almost a steady state after 60–90 days; the Ca content of pickle increases slightly with increases in the salt content in pickle (Table XIII). It has been estimated that 1 kg of Feta cheese discharges the amounts of minerals into pickle shown in Table XIV during

TABLE XII

Changes in the total N content (%) of Domiati cheese pickle as affected by cheese salt content, storage temperature and homgenization

Storage period (days)	% NaCl[a]			Storage[a]		Homogenization[b]	
	7	10	13	20 ± 5°C	8–10°C	Used	Not used
Fresh	0·172	0·173	0·147	0·173	0·173	0·145	0·146
15						0·164	0·156
30	0·419	0·411	0·407	0·411	0·416	0·217	0·201
120	0·512	0·555	0·461	0·555	0·472	0·311	0·303

[a] Ref. 119.
[b] Ref. 20.

TABLE XIII
Changes in the mineral content (g/litre) of pickle from Feta cheese stored at different
temperatures[85]

Storage period (days)	5°C					20°C				
	NaCl	Ca	P	K	Mg	NaCl	Ca	P	K	Mg
				Using 18% brine						
0	180·0	0·06	—	0·1	—	180	0·06	—	0·10	—
15	165·2	0·95	0·30	0·48	0·06	158·2	1·12	0·44	0·60	0·06
60	156·3	1·25	0·51	0·50	—	155·2	1·42	0·60	0·65	—
120	151·8	1·35	0·55	0·51	—	155·5	1·43	0·61	0·63	—
				Using 15% brine						
15	139·8	0·83	0·28	0·48	0·06	135·4	1·07	0·38	0·58	0·06
120	120·5	1·25	0·50	0·52	—	123·1	1·38	0·60	0·62	—

4 months of storage. The same has been found for Domiati cheese.[35] The
Ca and P contents increased to a steady state after 2 months of storage and
this coincides with changes in pH and acidity (Table XV). Addition of
disodium phosphate to milk for Domiati cheese production[116] decreases
the amount of Ca released during pickling. The Ca:P ratio in the pickle is in
the order of 2·3–2·5:1, indicating that both calcium phosphate and
paracasein-bound calcium are released by developed acidity. Increasing the
concentration of NaCl in pickle and the storage temperature increases the
release of Ca and P into the pickle. It seems that the release of Ca and P into
pickle is related to the solubility constants of calcium phosphate and
calcium lactate in pickle as affected by ionic strength, temperature and pH.

TABLE XIV
Amount of some minerals (g) removed in pickle from 1 kg of Feta cheese after 4
months of storage[85]

NaCl% in brine	Storage temperature (°C)	Ca	P	K	Mg
15	5	2·5	1·00	1·04	0·12
	10	2·62	1·12	1·20	0·12
	20	2·76	1·20	1·24	0·12
18	5	2·70	1·10	1·02	0·12
	10	2·68	1·10	1·12	0·12
	20	2·86	1·22	1·26	0·12

TABLE XV

Changes in calcium and inorganic phosphorus contents of Domiati cheese pickle
(g/litre)

Storage period (days)	Homogenized[a] Ca	Homogenized[a] P	Unhomogenized[a] Ca	Unhomogenized[a] P	Added disodium phosphate[b] 0·0% Ca	0·2% Ca	0·4% Ca	0·8% Ca
Fresh	0·87	0·32	0·70	0·30	0·64	0·63	0·55	0·48
15	1·80	0·72	1·91	0·83	1·94	1·68	1·53	1·26
30	1·99	0·80	2·24	0·80	2·33	2·09	1·82	1·46
60	2·46	0·94	2·55	0·99	2·79	2·42	2·18	1·84
90	2·65	1·03	2·65	0·97	2·46	2·18	2·04	1·55
120	2·47	1·03	2·69	1·07				

[a] Ref. 35.
[b] Ref. 116.

Therefore, Ca and P are removed from cheese into pickle until the latter becomes saturated with respect to the salts of these two elements. It is of interest to note that the amount of Ca and P released from Domiati and Feta type cheeses are similar, being in the order of 25–30% of the contents of Ca and P in the cheese.[35,115]

The K content of pickle reaches a maximum after 15 days of storage and the high values of this element in pickle indicate that most of the potassium in cheese is released into the pickle.[115]

The whey used as a pickle for Domiati cheese contains a small amount of fat that increases slightly as the amount of salt added to milk prior to cheesemaking and the severity of the heat treatment of milk are increased, both of which weaken the cheese matrix and increase fat losses in whey.[37] However, the fat content of pickle changes very little during storage.

Changes in the NaCl content of pickle depend on the ratio of its content in the pickle and cheese serum. An equilibrium in NaCl distribution between pickle and cheese serum occurs rapidly during the early days of storage. Equilibria also occur in the distributions of lactose and lactate as measured by developed acidity. The pickle of Domiati cheese usually contains significant amounts of lactose after 4 months of storage.[35]

4.7 Structure

Electron microscopic examination of ultra-thin sections from Domiati cheese[117,118] indicate that the internal structure of fresh cheese is composed of a framework of spherical casein aggregates held by bridges and enclosing fat (Fig. 4). On storage in pickle, the casein aggregates dissociate into smaller spherical particles forming a loose structure (Fig. 5). Additional proof of changes occurring in the microstructure of Domiati cheese during storage has been obtained by scanning electron microscopy.[119] It has been pointed out that the high salt content of this type of cheese has little effect on the morphological characteristics of cheese.[119] The only comparative study on the microstructure of Domiati and Feta type cheeses is that of Knoop *et al.*[118] The casein aggregates in Domiati cheese are smaller than those in Feta type cheese (Figs 4 and 5). It is evident that fat globules in the two types of cheese are unlikely to change during storage. The main differences in the protein matrices of the two cheeses can be explained by differences in pH. The major caseins have isoelectric points near 4·5, which is close to the pH of fresh Feta cheese. At their isoelectric points, the caseins form compact aggregates. In contrast, in fresh Domiati cheese, with a high pH ($>5·8$), the casein molecules have a net negative charge and while hydrophobic interactions persist, the ionic interactions change from attractions between protein molecules to repulsions. Thus, the tight protein aggregates absorb water, partly to solvate the unneutralized ionic charges. Besides, the partial exchange of Na^+ for Ca^{2+} in fresh Domiati cheese weakens the tight interaction in casein aggregates.

The pH of Feta cheese remains more or less unchanged during storage and therefore the compact structure of the casein aggregates is retained. With advanced storage, the pH of Domiati cheese ($<4·0$) is on the acid side of the isoelectric point of the casein components, thus retaining repulsive ionic forces in the cheese matrix, a factor responsible for the loose structure of Domiati cheese. Another factor that may be responsible for the loose structure of Domiati cheese is the fast disintegration of the casein aggregates in Domiati cheese which has been attributed to the higher phosphatase activity in raw milk used in Domiati cheese manufacture.[118]

The microstructure of Feta type cheese from whole dried milk[42] is markedly different from that made from fresh milk. In fresh samples the main characteristic difference is the strong interaction between casein and fat globules which is a result of homogenization employed during the manufacture of dried whole milk. After 2 months of storage, the protein matrix of cheese from raw milk is characterized by a very uniform distribution of small protein particles with the occasional occurrence of small areas (0·1–0·2 μm in diam.) of whey free of protein particles. In contrast, cheeses made from reconstituted milk show a less homogeneous distribution of protein particles. The relatively loose and porous structure

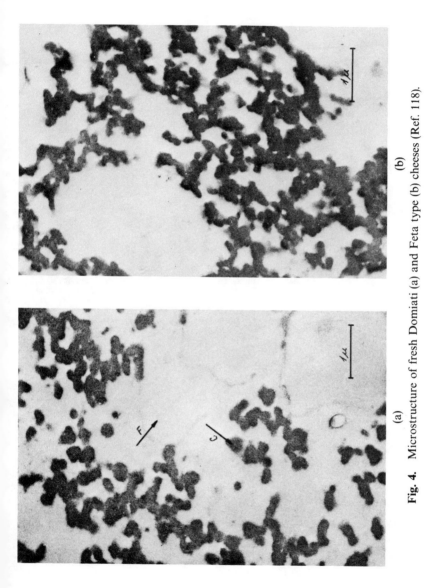

(b)

(a)

Fig. 4. Microstructure of fresh Domiati (a) and Feta type (b) cheeses (Ref. 118).

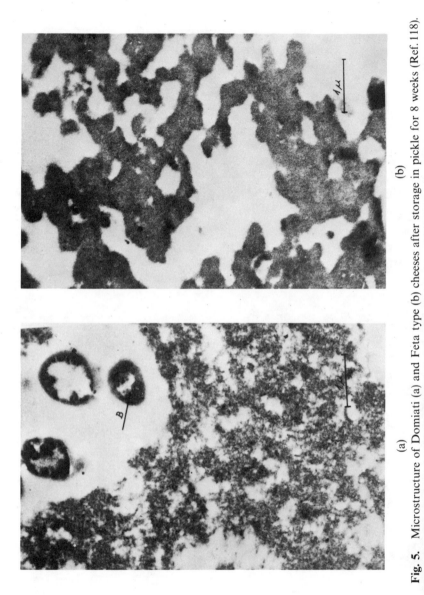

(b)

(a)

Fig. 5.   Microstructure of Domiati (a) and Feta type (b) cheeses after storage in pickle for 8 weeks (Ref. 118).

of the protein matrix of cheese made from reconstituted milk is due to structural changes of the protein during the drying process.

Generally, the changes in the protein matrix of pickled cheeses during storage are responsible for the smooth body of the ripened cheese. These changes are likely to arise from two factors. The first is the partial loss of Ca bridges in the cheese matrix into the pickle.[35,115] The second factor is the continuous proteolysis of α_{s1}-casein. α_{s1}-Casein can interact strongly with two or possibly more casein molecules (either α_{s1}- or β-casein) and can thus be linked into a protein network.[93] Consequently, if the α_{s1}-casein molecules are cleaved so that they lose their ability to act as a link in the protein network, then the network disintegrates. This model explains why cleavage of α_{s1}-casein in pickled cheeses causes a loose structure. In this respect, the changes in the rheological properties of Cheddar cheese are closely related to the hydrolysis of α_{s1}-casein.[93]

4.8 Defects

Incidence of early blowing may be considered the major defect in pickled cheeses, particularly in those made from raw milk. It is characterized by the formation of gas holes in the cheese, a spongy texture and blowing of the tins. This defect arises from two factors.

4.8.1 Gas-forming micro-organisms
The presence of coliform bacteria in cheese, particularly *Aerobacter aerogenes*, was reported to be responsible for blown tins of pickled Domiati cheese.[120] Addition of NaCl at more than 9% to milk prevents this defect in Domiati cheese.[120] It is of interest to note that cheese made from buffalo's milk is less susceptible to this defect than that from cow's milk and gas formation is more obvious in skim-milk cheeses than in full-fat cheeses.

Blowing of pickled Feta type cheese made from ewe's milk[121] may be caused by yeasts if the cheese is too sweet when packed into tins, i.e. has a high lactose content. Nielsen[122] identified *Lactobacillus brevis* as the causative organism for gas production in canned Feta cheese made from UF milk. Gas production was reduced but not prevented at 10% NaCl.

4.8.2 Electrolytic corrosion
The tendency of Domiati cheese packed in tins to blow, especially in summer, is primarily due to electrolytic corrosion by two factors: (1) NaCl, (2) developed acidity.[123] Incubation of tin-plated strips with salted whey from blown cans at 33 and 12°C confirmed this hypothesis.

306   *M. H. Abd El-Salam*

REFERENCES

1. Zaky, A. and Iskander, Z., *Annales de Services des Antiquités de l' Egypte*, 1943, **41**, 295.
2. Hansen, R., *Nordeuropaeisk Mejeri-Tidsskrift*, 1977, **43**, 304.
3. Abd El-Salam, M. H., El-Shibiny, S. and Fahmi, A. H., *N.Z. J. Dairy Sci. Technol.*, 1976, **11**, 57.
4. Lloyd, D. G. T. and Ramshaw, E. H., *Aust. J. Dairy Technol.*, 1979, **34**, 180.
5. Abou Donia, S. A., *Indian J. Dairy Sci.*, 1981, **34**, 136.
6. Mashaly, R. I., Abou Donia, S. A. and El-Soda, M., *Indian J. Dairy Sci.*, 1983, **36**, 93.
7. El-Gendy, S. M., *J. Food Prot.*, 1983, **46**, 358.
8. Sirry, I. and Rakshy, S. D., *Indian J. Dairy Sci.*, 1954, **8**, 9.
9. Anifantakis, E. M. and Kaminarides, S. E., *Aust. J. Dairy Technol.*, 1983, **38**, 29.
10. Anon., *Dairy Ice Cream Field*, 1969, 61.
11. Buruiana, L. M. and Farag, S. I., *Egyptian J. Dairy Sci.*, 1983, **11**, 53.
12. Davis, J. G., *Cheese, Vol. III, Manufacturing Methods*, Churchill Livingstone, Edinburgh, London, New York, 1976.
13. Youssef, A. M., Salama, F. A., Ismail, A. A. and Salem, S. A., *Egyptian J. Dairy Sci.*, 1982, **10**, 81.
14. Fahmi, A. H. and Sharara, H. A., *J. Dairy Res.*, 1950, **17**, 312.
15. FAO, *Food Composition Tables for the Near East*, Food & Agric. Organization, United Nations, Rome, 1982.
16. Sharara, H. A., *Indian J. Dairy Sci.*, 1958, **11**, 175.
17. Puri, B. R. and Parkash, S., *J. Dairy Sci.*, 1965, **48**, 611.
18. Abd El-Salam, M. H., Osman, Y. M. and Nagmoush, M. R., *Egyptian J. Dairy Sci.*, 1978, **6**, 9.
19. Saito, Z. and Hoirose, M., *Bull. Faculty Agric. Hirosaki Univ.*, Japan, 1972, No. 18, 35.
20. Saito, Z., Igarashi, Y. and Nakasato, H., *Bull. Faculty Agric. Hirosaki Univ.*, Japan, 1972, No. 18, 22.
21. Schmidt, D. G. In: *Developments in Dairy Chemistry, Vol. I, Proteins* (Ed. P. F. Fox), Elsevier Applied Science, London, pp. 61–86, 1982.
22. Pestskas, D. and Ramanauskas, R., *Proc. XIX Int. Dairy Congr.*, New Delhi, 1974, Vol. B5, p. 169.
23. Sirry, I. and Shipe, W. F., *J. Dairy Sci.*, 1958, **41**, 204.
24. Abd El-Hamid, L. B., Amer, S. N. and Zedan, A. N., *Egyptian J. Dairy Sci.*, 1981, **9**, 137.
25. Ibrahim, M. K. E., Amer, S. N. and El-Abd, M. M., *Egyptian J. Dairy Sci.*, 1973, **1**, 127.
26. Ling, E. R., *A Text Book of Dairy Chemistry, Vol. 1, Theoretical*, 3rd edn, Chapman & Hall, London, pp. 1–140, 1963.
27. Gal, S. and Bankay, D., *J. Food Sci.*, 1971, **36**, 800.
28. Gal, S. and Hunziker, M., *Makromol. Chem.*, 1977, **178**, 1535.
29. Hardy, J. J. and Steinberg, M. P., *J. Food Sci.*, 1984, **49**, 127.
30. Ramanaskas, R., *Proc. XX Int. Dairy Congr.*, Paris, 1978, Vol. E, p. 265.
31. Geurts, T. J., Walstra, P. and Mulder, H., *Neth. Milk Dairy J.*, 1974, **28**, 46.

32. Moneib, A. F., Ph.D. thesis, Meded. Landrouw, Wageningen, The Netherlands, 1962.
33. Ling, E. R., *J. Dairy Res.*, 1966, **33**, 151.
34. Dawood, A. E., M.Sc. thesis, Cairo University, Cairo, Egypt, 1964.
35. Ahmed, N. S., Abd El-Salam, M. H. and El-Shibiny, S., *Indian J. Dairy Sci.*, 1972, **25**, 246.
36. Mansour, A. and Alais, C., *Le Lait*, 1972, **52**, 515.
37. Teama, Z. Y., Ph.D. thesis, Ain-Shams University, Cairo, Egypt, 1967.
38. Veinoglou, B. C., Boyazoglu, E. S. and Kotouza, E. D., *Dairy Ind. Int.*, 1979, **44**(10), 29.
39. Veinoglou, B. C., Boyazoglu, E. S. and Kotouza, E. D., *Dairy Ind. Int.*, 1980, **45**(8), 11.
40. Rakshy, S. E. and Attia, I., *Alexandria J. Agric. Res.*, 1979, **27**, 359.
41. Tawab, G. A. and El-Koussy, L. A., *Egyptian J. Dairy Sci.*, 1975, **3**, 85.
42. Omar, M. M. and Buchheim, W., *Food Microstructure*, 1983, **2**, 43.
43. El-Abd, M. M., Ibrahim, M. K. E., Amer, S. N. and Mostafa, S., *Egyptian J. Dairy Sci.*, 1975, **3**, 195.
44. Abd El-Salam, M. H., unpublished data.
45. Goodenough, E. R. and Kleyn, D. H., *J. Dairy Sci.*, 1976, **59**, 45.
46. Shehata, A. E., Magdoub, N., Fayed, E. O. and Hofi, A. A., *Egyptian J. Dairy Sci.*, 1984, **12**, 47.
47. Naguib, M. M., El-Sadek, G. M. and Naguib, Kh., *Egyptian J. Dairy Sci.*, 1974, **2**, 55.
48. Thomas, T. D. and Crow, V. L., *N.Z. J. Dairy Sci. Technol.*, 1983, **18**, 131.
49. El-Koussy, L. A., Ph.D. thesis, Ain-Shams University, Cairo, Egypt, 1966.
50. Sharara, H. A., *Indian J. Dairy Sci.*, 1959, **12**, 77.
51. Sharara, H. A., *Agric. Res. Rev.*, 1961, **39**, 168.
52. Alichanidis, E., Anifantakis, E. M., Polychorniadou, A. and Nanou, M., *J. Dairy Res.*, 1984, **51**, 141.
53. Gewaily, E. M., M.Sc. thesis, Ain-Shams University, Cairo, Egypt, 1968.
54. Sharara, H. A., *Alexandria J. Agric. Res.*, 1962, **10**, 127.
55. El-Safty, M. S., M.Sc. thesis, Ain-Shams University, Cairo, Egypt, 1969.
56. Hagrass, A. B., M.Sc. thesis, Ain-Shams University, Cairo, Egypt, 1971.
57. Abd El-Salam, M. H., El-Abd, M. M., Nagmoush, M. R. and Saleem, R. M., *Egyptian J. Dairy Sci.*, 1978, **6**, 221.
58. Abd El-Salam, M. H., Saleem, R. M. and Nagmoush, M. R., *Egyptian J. Dairy Sci.*, 1978, **6**, 187.
59. Moneib, A. F., Abo El-Heiba, A., Al-Khamy, A. F., El-Shibiny, S. and Abd El-Salam, M. H., *Egyptian J. Dairy Sci.*, 1981, **9**, 37.
60. Abd El-Salam, M. H., El-Shibiny, S., Ahmed, N. S. and Ismail, A. A., *Egyptian J. Dairy Sci.*, 1981, **9**, 151.
61. Abd El-Salam, M. H. and El-Shibiny, S., *Asian J. Dairy Res.*, 1982, **1**, 187.
62. Abd El-Salam, M. H., El-Shibiny, S., El-Koussy, L. and Haggag, H. F., *Egyptian J. Dairy Sci.*, 1982, **10**, 237.
63. Veinoglou, B. C. and Boyazoglu, E. S., *J. Soc. Dairy Technol.*, 1982, **35**, 54.
64. El-Shibiny, S., Abd El-Salam, M. H. and Ahmed, N. S., *Milchwissenschaft*, 1972, **27**, 217.
65. Hamed, M. G., M.Sc. thesis, Ain-Shams University, Cairo, Egypt, 1955.

308   M. H. Abd El-Salam

66. Khalafalla, S., El-Sadek, G. M., Shehata, A. and El-Magdoub, M., *Egyptian J. Dairy Sci.*, 1973, **1**, 163.
67. Sirry, I. and Kosikowski, F. V., *Proc. XV Int. Dairy Congr.*, London, 1959, Vol. 2, p. 812.
68. Ganguli, N. C., Prabhakaran, R. J. V. and Iya, K. K., *J. Dairy Sci.*, 1964, **47**, 13.
69. Abd El-Salam, M. H. and El-Shibiny, S., *J. Dairy Sci.*, 1977, **60**, 1519.
70. El-Shibiny, S. and Abd El-Salam, M. H., *J. Dairy Res.*, 1976, **43**, 448.
71. El-Shibiny, S., Abd El-Salam, M. H. and Ahmed, N. S., *Egyptian J. Dairy Sci.*, 1973, **1**, 56.
72. Abd El-Salam, M. H. and El-Shibiny, S., *Egyptian J. Food Sci.*, 1973, **1**, 225.
73. Ahmed, N. S., Abd El-Salam, M. H. and El-Shibiny, S., *Sudan J. Food Sci. Technol.*, 1973, **5**, 18.
74. Ismail, A. A., El-Hifnawi, M. and Sirry, I., *J. Dairy Sci.*, 1972, **55**, 1220.
75. Kamaley, K. M., M.Sc. thesis, El-Monoufia University, Shebein El-Kom, Egypt, 1978.
76. Shehata, A. E., Magdoub, M. N., Fayed, E. O. and Hofi, A. A., *Ann. Agric. Sci.*, Ain-Shams University, 1983, **28**, 737.
77. El-Shibiny, S., El-Koussy, L. A., Girgis, E. A. and Mehanna, N., *Egyptian J. Dairy Sci.*, 1983, **11**, 215.
78. Askar, A. A., Gaafar, R. H., Magdoub, M. N. and Shehata, A. E., *Egyptian J. Dairy Sci.*, 1982, **10**, 73.
79. Abdou, S., Ghita, I. and El-Shibiny, S., *Egyptian J. Dairy Sci.*, 1976, **4**, 147.
80. Edelsten, O., Hamdy, A. and El-Koussy, L. A., Yearbook Royal Veterinary and Agricultural University, Copenhagen, p. 201, 1969.
81. El-Safty, M. S. and El-Shibiny, S., *Egyptian J. Dairy Sci.*, 1980, **8**, 41.
82. Hamdy, A., *Proc. XVIII Int. Dairy Congr.*, Sydney, 1970, Vol. IE, p. 350.
83. Hamdy, A., *Indian J. Dairy Sci.*, 1972, **25**, 73.
84. Abd El-Salam, M. H., El-Shibiny, S. and Mehanna, N., *Egyptian J. Dairy Sci.*, 1983, **11**, 291.
85. Mehanna, N. M., El-Shibiny, S. and Abd El-Salam, M. H., *Egyptian J. Dairy Sci.*, 1983, **11**, 167.
86. Ismail, A. A., Youssef, A. M., Salama, F. A. and Salem, S. A., *Egyptian J. Dairy Sci.*, 1982, **10**, 253.
87. Nagmoush, M. R., El-Koussy, L. A., Ghita, E. I. and El-Kenawi, M. M., *Proc. 2nd Egyptian Conf. Dairy Sci.*, Cairo, 1983, 3M.
88. Abd El-Salam, M. H. and El-Shibiny, S., *J. Dairy Res.*, 1972, **39**, 219.
89. El-Shibiny, S. and Abd El-Salam, M. H., *Milchwissenschaft*, 1976, **31**, 80.
90. El-Shibiny, S. and Abd El-Salam, M. H., *Egyptian J. Dairy Sci.*, 1974, **2**, 168.
91. Fox, P. F. and Walley, B. F., *J. Dairy Res.*, 1971, **38**, 165.
92. Eigel, E. N., *Int. J. Biochem.*, 1977, **8**, 187.
93. Creamer, L. K. and Olson, N. F., *J. Food Sci.*, 1982, **47**, 631.
94. El-Erian, A. F. H., Farag, A. H. and El-Gendy, S. M., *Agric. Res. Rev.*, 1974, **52**, 190.
95. Pfeil, R. and Abd El-Salam, M. H., unpublished data.
96. Zikovic, Z., *Arch. Poljoper Nnaue*, 1963, **16**, 92.
97. Prodanski, P., *Khranit Prom*, 1962, **11**, 21.
98. Dilanyan, Z. Ch. and Magakyan, D. T., *Proc. XX Int. Dairy Congr.*, Paris, 1978, Vol. 1E, p. 295.

99. Kayaalp, S. O., Renda, N., Kayamakralan, S. and Ozer, A., *Toxic. appl. Pharmac.*, 1970, **16**, 459.
100. El-Shibiny, S., Abd El-Baky, A. A., Farahat, S. M., Mahran, G. A. and Hofi, A. A., *Milchwissenschaft*, 1974, **29**, 666.
101. Miadenov, M., *Nanchni Trudove Vissh Veterinaromeditsinski Institut*, 1970, **22**, 531. Cited from *Dairy Sci. Abstr.*, 1973, **35**, 2665.
102. Efthymiou, C. C. and Mattick, J. F., *J. Dairy Sci.*, 1964, **47**, 593.
103. Horwood, J. F., Lloyd, G. T. and Stark, W., *Austr. J. Dairy Technol.*, 1981, **36**, 34.
104. Efthymiou, C. C., *J. Dairy Sci.*, 1967, **50**, 20.
105. Prodanski, P. G. and Dzhordzhorowa, O. D., *Milchwissenschaft*, 1969, **24**, 734.
106. Abd El-Salam, M. H., El-Shibiny, S., Moneib, A. F., Abo El-Heiba, A. and Al-Khamy, A. F., *Egyptian J. Dairy Sci.*, 1981, **9**, 143.
107. Obretenow, T., Dimitroff, D. and Obretenowa, M., *Milchwissenschaft*, 1978, **33**, 545.
108. Precht, D. and Abd El-Salam, M. H., *Milchwissenschaft*, in press.
109. Fryer, T. F., *Dairy Sci. Abstr.*, 1969, **31**, 471.
110. Nakae, T. and Elliot, J. A., *J. Dairy Sci.*, 1965, **48**, 293.
111. Dimitrov, D., Obretenow, T. and Obretenow, M., *Nanchni Tr. Vissh Inst. Khranit. Vkusova, Promst Rovdiiv*, 1976, **23**, 185.
112. Georgautas, St., *Milchwissenschaft*, 1979, **34**, 24.
113. Magdoub, M. N., Shehata, A. E., Fayed, E. O. and Hofi, A. A., *Ann. Agric. Sci.*, Ain-Shams University, 1983, **28**, 761.
114. Sabry, Z. I. and Guerrant, N. B., *J. Dairy Sci.*, 1958, **41**, 925.
115. Mansour, A. and Alais, C., *Le Lait*, 1972, **52**, 642.
116. El-Shibiny, S., Ahmed, N. S. and Abd El-Salam, M. H., *Egyptian J. Food Sci.*, 1973, **1**, 107.
117. Abd El-Salam, M. H. and El-Shibiny, S., *J. Dairy Res.*, 1973, **40**, 113.
118. Knoop, A. M., Omar, M. and Peters, K. H., *Milchwissenschaft*, 1976, **30**, 745.
119. Kerr, T. J., Washam, C. J., Evans, A. L. and Todd, R. L., *J. Food Prot.*, 1981, **44**, 496.
120. Hegazi, F. Z. M., M.Sc. thesis, University of Assiut, Assiut, Egypt, 1972.
121. Kiss, E., Eross, E. and Markus, P., *Proc. XVII Int. Dairy Congr.*, Munchen, 1966, Vol. D, p. 143.
122. Nielsen, E. W., *2nd Egyptian Conf. Dairy Sci. Technol.*, Cairo, 1983, 11 M.
123. Abo-Elnaga, I. G., *Milchwissenschaft*, 1968, **23**, 198.

Chapter 10

Some Non-European Cheese Varieties

P. F. Fox

*Department of Dairy and Food Chemistry,
University College, Cork, Ireland*

1. INTRODUCTION

The chemistry, biochemistry and microbiology of the principal international cheese varieties (families) have been described in the preceding nine chapters. With the exception of Domiati, all these cheese varieties are of European origin; indeed Domiati has its close counterparts in southeastern Europe. Although not all European cheese varieties belong to one of the above families, most are generally similar to one of the principal varieties. As indicated in Table II, Chapter 1, Volume 1, little cheese is produced in Latin America, Africa or Asia, at least by European and North American standards. However, a number of cheeses, in small quantities, are produced in these regions and it was considered worthwhile describing some of them, which are produced by rather interesting methods. Most of these cheeses are produced on a very small scale, frequently on farmsteads, and there is very little scientific information available on most of them; some are produced by rennet coagulation, others by acid precipitation so that the general principles of coagulation, described previously, apply. In many cases, defined starters are not used so that acid production, by indigenous microflora or whey from previous batches, is probably rather variable.

2. ASIA

2.1 India

Cheese production in India is quite limited, which is perhaps surprising for a country with a relatively strong dairying tradition. There is an interesting contrast between the methods used in Egypt and India for preserving milk as concentrated products; in the former, extensive use is made of coagulation (rennet or acid) and salt for preservation whereas in India, concentration by boiling, frequently with the addition of sugar, is widespread.

No production data for India are listed by the FAO[1] but the IDF[2] gives production at 700 tonnes in 1977 and 1000 tonnes in 1980; processed cheeses, Gouda and Cheddar, in that order, appear to be the most popular varieties and there are no imports or exports of cheese. S. Singh (personal communication) confirms this but he reports that Cottage, Cream and Mozzarella are also produced. There are apparently only two indigenous cheese varieties (S. Singh): Chhana, a sour milk cheese made from cow's milk, and Panir (Surati, Bandal (West Bengal): Decca is a variant produced in Pakistan), which is a fresh rennet curd cheese made from cow's or buffalo's milk. The manufacture of these cheeses is described in some detail by De[3] and briefly by Walter and Hargrove[4] and by Davis,[5] who also mentions a Burnese cheese, Deinge, made from curd prepared by boiling buttermilk from ghee (it appears to be rather like Ricotta or Anari).

Panir is normally made from standardized milk (casein:fat = 0·7), inoculated with $\sim$0·5% lactic starter and renneted ($\sim$7 ml/100 litres) at $\sim$35°C. The rennet gel is cut but the curds are not cooked. NaCl at $\sim$2·5% of the weight of milk is added to the curd/whey mixture and stirred in; the curd/whey is then placed in moulds and allowed to drain without pressing, but with turning, for $\sim$2 h. The cheese is then sliced into pieces of the desired size, ready for consumption; shelf-life is usually 2–3 days. Traditionally, the uncut gel is ladled into wicker baskets, salt being sprinkled between successive layers. The typical composition of Panir is: $\sim$71% moisture, $\sim$13% fat.

Chhana (called paneer in some localities) is the acid coagulum of boiled hot whole milk; lactic or citric acids or acid whey is usually used. It may be produced on a very small, farmstead scale or on a commercial, fairly highly mechanized basis. The typical composition is: moisture, $\sim$53%; fat, $\sim$25%; protein, $\sim$17%; lactose, $\sim$2%; ash, $\sim$2%. It is widely used in the preparation of several indigenous sweetmeat and cooked vegetable dishes.

Two fermented milk products, Dahi and Srikhand, are widely produced in India. The former is a cultured buttermilk-type (sweet) or yoghurt-type (sour) product, depending on the culture used; it may also be used as an intermediate in the manufacture of indigenous butter (makkan) or ghee. It is estimated that >40% of total milk production in India is converted into Dahi. There is also a sweetened version of Dahi (known by various names, e.g. misti dahi, hal dahi or payodhi) for the manufacture of which $\sim 6.5\%$ sucrose is added to the milk before fermentation.

Srikhand appears to be more like a fresh cheese than a fermented milk product. Dahi is partly strained through cloth to yield a solid product called Chakka ($\sim 63\%$ H_2O, $\sim 15\%$ fat, 0.8% lactic acid) which is mixed with the desired amount of sucrose to produce Srikhand. The latter may be further desiccated in an open pan to make Srikhand Wadi ($\sim 6.5\%$ H_2O, $\sim 7.5\%$ fat, $\sim 7.5\%$ protein, $\sim 16\%$ lactose, $\sim 63\%$ sucrose).

2.2 Afghanistan and Nepal

Kosikowski[38] includes photographs of cheese manufacture and marketing in these countries but no further information is given; very brief summaries of cheeses from this region are also given by Scott.[45]

2.3 The Philippines

The Philippines are not listed by the FAO.[1] Dr C. L. Dawide (personal communication) estimates that cheese production in the Philippines is ~ 100 tonnes p.a., made in the provinces of Lyzon and the Visayan Islands. The cheese is made on a farmstead scale from buffalo's, cow's or goat's milk or mixtures of these by coagulation with rennet, vinegar or a mixture of these. Only fresh, soft cheeses are made which are generally called 'Kesong Puti' (also Queso; Keso; Kesiyo; Kesilyo; white cheese). Sometimes the cheeses are ripened for a few days and fried. Efforts are being made at the University of the Philippines, Los Banos, to expand cheese production and to introduce new varieties.

2.4 China

FAO[1] indicated that $\sim 20\,000$ tonnes of cheese were produced in China in 1982. However, Mr J. C. McCarthy (personal communication), who has visited China on a few occasions recently, is aware of only very small-scale production of an Edam type called Long Giang, mainly for local consumption.

2.5 Japan

Japan has no indigenous cheese industry but since the 1950s has become a significant cheese producing and consuming country; Cheddar, Edam,

Gouda and Mozzarella are preferred and mild cheeses are most popular. Domestic production in 1982 was 71 506 tonnes.[1] Total consumption in 1979 was 93 000 tonnes.[2] (Domestic production in 1980 was ~66 000 tonnes[1] so that imports amount to ~27 000 tonnes.)

3. AFRICA

Total recorded cheese production in Africa in 1982 was 389 054 tonnes, of which Egypt produced 258 839 tonnes; South Africa (34 715 tonnes) and Sudan (58 271 tonnes) are the only other significant producers.[1]

In South Africa, the cheeses are exclusively of European origin: Cheddar, Gouda, processed and all other types represent 49, 42, 4 and 5%, respectively, of total production.[2]

3.1 Egypt

Four principal indigenous types of cheese are produced in Egypt: Domiati (the most popular cheese in Egypt is a highly salted variety and is considered in detail in Chapter 9); Cephalotyre 'Ras' cheese, which is a hard, bacterially-ripened cheese; Karish (Kareish), a fresh, relatively low-salt variety; and Kishk, which may not be properly classified as a cheese but is nevertheless produced by a rather interesting method.[6,7] Brinza, a highly salted Feta type cheese of Russian origin, and small amounts of Kashkaval are also produced; these varieties are reviewed in Chapters 8 and 9, respectively.

Kishk is produced from the fermented milk, Laban Khad, or its partially dehydrated variant, Laban Zeer (dehydrated during storage in porous earthenware jars through which water evaporates). Laban Khad is produced by fermenting milk in skin bags; after the milk has coagulated, the bags are shaken to coalesce the fat which is removed, leaving behind Laban Khad. Apparently, rennet may be used to coagulate the milk in cold weather.

Kishk is manufactured by mixing two, three or more parts of Laban Khad or Laban Zeer with one part of wheat flour or par-boiled wheat and the mixture boiled and then sun-dried. The product is non-hygroscopic and may be stored in open jars for 1–2 years without deterioration. The composition appears to be quite variable: 9–13% moisture, 2–12% fat, 9–24% protein, 31–65% carbohydrate and 6–10% ash.

Karish is a soft acid cheese, apparently made only on farmsteads. It is made either from Laban Khad (i.e. fermented buttermilk) or from sour defatted milk, Laban Rayed. The latter is prepared from fresh whole milk placed in earthenware jars and left undisturbed; the fat rises to the surface and the partly skimmed milk beneath sours. After 24–36 h, the cream layer is skimmed off and the clotted, skimmed milk (Laban Rayed) is poured on to reed mats or into small cheese moulds. After a few hours, the ends of the mat are tied and some whey squeezed out; the pressed curd is permitted to drain further and the squeezing process repeated until the desired texture is obtained; the curd is then cut into pieces and salted. Increased demand has led to the commercial production of Karish cheese which, under such conditions, is frequently made from pasteurized and/or homogenized milk or reconstituted milk using *L. bulgaricus* as starter and usually with rennet (3 ml/100 kg) rather than acid as coagulant. The approximate composition of Karish cheese is: 31% total solids, 17% protein, 6% fat and 4·5% NaCl.

3.1.1 Cephalotyre 'Ras' cheese

Cephalotyre cheese, apparently of Greek origin (Kefalotyri) and known in Egypt as Ras, is the most popular hard cheese in Egypt. El-Erian *et al.*[8] concluded that the microflora of ripe Kashkaval (Cashkaval) and Ras cheeses are very similar. However, Kashkaval and Kefalotyri are Pasta filata type cheeses whereas Cephalotyre 'Ras' is not. In this review, Kashkaval and Ras are treated as separate varieties and the former is covered under Balkan cheeses where it is a major variety. Ras is also known as Romy (Romi) and a variety called Memphis is similar, if not identical. However, Naghmoush *et al.*,[9] in a study on starter selection for Memphis cheese manufacture, gives the impression that Memphis and Ras are distinct varieties.

Although an M.Sc. thesis (Tawab, 1963) was written on the manufacture of Ras cheese, the first published account on the subject appears to be that of Hofi *et al.*[10] and this appears to be the method used by most subsequent investigators although manufacturing procedures used in Egypt are not standardized. The manufacturing procedure described by Hofi *et al.*[10] is generally similar to that for Gouda except that the curd is cooked to 44°C in 15 min and held at this temperature for 30 min; a further difference is that Ras curd is salted in two stages: after cooking, the whey is drained off to the level of the curd and salt at 1–2% of the weight of the original milk added to the curd, mixed and held for 15 min; the curd is then hooped and pressed overnight and the cheeses further salted by surface application of dry salt

P. F. Fox

TABLE I

Analytical data for Cephalotyre 'Ras' cheese (from Ref. 10)

Age	Moisture (%)	Fat (%)	Dry matter (%)	pH	Salt (%)	Dry matter (%)	Protein				Lactose (%)	Volatile fatty acids (%)
							Total (%)	Dry matter (%)	Soluble (%)	Soluble protein coef. (%)		
Raw milk												
1 day	39·03	34·00	50·57	4·97	0·74	1·21	21·35	35·02	0·90	4·36	0·4	58·68
2 week	34·70	36·70	56·20	4·90	1·18	1·81	22·62	34·62	2·30	10·17	0·2	66·13
1 month	33·77	37·88	57·20	4·90	1·76	2·66	23·87	36·04	3·10	12·99	0·2	75·58
2 month	32·84	38·08	56·70	4·83	2·25	3·35	21·66	36·72	3·60	14·00	0·15	167·08
3 month	31·92	38·36	56·31	5·05	2·28	3·35	26·25	38·56	4·50	17·14	0·1	190·36
6 month	30·03	39·26	56·11	5·03	2·03	2·90	27·18	38·85	5·30	19·50	0·1	222·44
Pasteurized milk												
1 day	45·46	29·75	53·13	5·50	1·06	1·94	22·36	41·00	0·67	3·09	0·5	47·74
2 week	40·78	31·25	52·14	5·32	1·73	2·92	24·66	41·64	1·59	6·08	0·3	48·73
1 month	38·17	32·93	52·19	5·25	2·51	4·06	26·49	42·84	2·80	10·57	0·2	51·71
2 month	37·15	33·83	52·30	5·23	2·80	4·58	26·97	42·91	3·00	11·12	0·2	51·20
3 month	34·95	34·57	51·87	5·25	2·61	4·01	28·16	43·29	3·60	12·78	0·2	55·69
6 month	34·20	34·90	52·37	5·53	2·89	4·39	28·95	44·00	4·50	15·54	0·15	62·65

for up to 12 days. The cheese is normally ripened at 15–18°C for 4–6 months, during which extensive proteolysis and lipolysis occur. The cheese is not normally waxed or otherwise packaged, so considerable moisture loss occurs through the rind.

A considerable amount of information has been accumulated on various aspects of the ripening of Ras cheese. Data from Hofi *et al.*[10] on some of the gross changes occurring during the ripening of Ras cheese made from raw or pasteurized milk are summarized in Table I; changes, especially lipolysis, were considerably more extensive in the raw milk cheese during ripening. Formation of pH 4·6-soluble N, NPN, free amino acid profiles and volatile fatty acids in Ras cheeses made using calf rennet or pepsins or microbial rennet substitutes have been reported.[11–13] Four main classes of carbonyl compounds were identified in mature Ras cheese: four methyl ketones, four alkanals, three 2-enals and two 2,4-dienals; pentanone, pentanal, 2-heptanal and 2,4-undecadienal were the principal carbonyls.[14] No evidence was presented on the significance of the carbonyls to Ras cheese flavour but it was assumed that they are significant contributors.

A surprising amount of activity has been directed toward accelerating the ripening of Ras cheese and a variety of approaches have been employed, e.g. addition of hydrolysed casein or whey protein,[15] inactive dry yeast or yeast hydrolysate,[16] trace elements,[17–19] ripened cheese slurries (30°C for 7 days),[20] autolysed starter,[21] animal or fungal proteinases and lipases.[22–27] There appears to be general agreement that ripening may be accelerated and flavour intensified by all the above methods although some techniques led to off-flavours on extended ripening. The influence of coating materials on compositional changes and ripening reactions in Ras cheese have been studied.[28,29]

Because of the shortage of fresh milk in Egypt, which has a very rapidly increasing population, it is not surprising that there has been quite a lot of interest in the manufacture of Ras cheese from reconstituted skim-milk powder plus cream or butter oil. While the product appears to be acceptable, it is inferior to that made from fresh milk and ripens more slowly.[30–33] There is also an interest in using soybean milk to extend cow or buffalo milk; use of up to 20% soy milk gives satisfactory results and is reported to improve the quantity of Ras or Cheddar cheeses made from buffalo's milk but quality deteriorated on addition of >30% of soy milk.[34] An alternative approach towards extending the available milk supply is the manufacture of processed cheese foods incorporating non-cheese ingredients. Shehata *et al.*[35] report the successful manufacture of such a product based on Ras cheese and skim-milk powder.

3.1.2 Mish (M. M. Hewedi, personal communication and Ref. 7)

Mish is a rather interesting, popular and apparently unique Egyptian cheese product. It is used as a savoury or appetizer by better-off people but it is also used by the poor and in rural areas as a significant source of dietary protein. Mish is a pickling medium in which Karish cheese is stored for ripening; Karish cheese, after ripening in Mish, is called 'Mish cheese'.

Although details of Mish manufacture vary depending upon the available ingredients, the general principles of its manufacture are roughly similar and may be summarized as follows:

1. The daily production of Laban Khad is collected and preserved by adding salt.
2. Mourta, the non-fat product from ghee manufacture, is added to and blended with the Laban Khad.
3. The mixture is concentrated by heating until it becomes viscous (pasty) and a reddish-brown colour develops (this colour is transferred to the cheese during pickling).
4. When required, this paste is diluted with whey or Laban Rayeb or Laban Khad and some Mish from a previous batch (as starter), flavourants and colouring materials added.
5. This mixture, 'primary Mish', is used as a pickling solution for 'Karish cheese' in earthenware jars, 'Ballas'. The flavouring and colouring materials vary according to their availability but the most common flavourings are 'Murta', cinnamon, chilli and pepper, and the colouring agents are saffron and annato.

During ripening, the *Streptococci* spp. die and *Lactobacilli* and sporeformers become predominant. Total solids increase due to the

TABLE II
Chemical composition of Mish

	Minimum %	Maximum %
Moisture	54·76	75·68
Total solids	24·32	35·24
Fat	0·5	4·6
Protein	6·95	13·13
Ash	11·13	19·79
Calcium	0·229	0·403
Phosphorus	0·180	0·215
NaCl	~12% (average)	

disintegration of small pieces of cheese but the extent of the increase depends on the original cheese and Mish composition and ripening conditions as influenced by time and temperature.

Due to the wide variation of factors which influence the changes during ripening, Mish shows considerable variation in chemical composition (Table II).

The chemical and microbiological changes which occur in Mish cheese during ripening lead to the development of a typical and desirable flavour, which is a combination of Cheddar and Roquefort type flavour and a characteristic aroma of butyric and caproic acids (cf. Ref. 7 for further references on Mish cheese).

3.1.3 Artificial Mish

Mish is usually made without any particular or defined specification and this results in a wide variation in composition. The following are procedures by which it is possible to produce Mish with a unique or standard specification and with a typical desirable flavour.

1. By mixing minced ripened hard cheese with milk or whey at an appropriate ratio; the flavouring.and colouring agents to be added as previously described.
2. By mixing fresh cheese with whey or milk and adding 'old cheese flavour' to give the typical taste of Mish. The rest of the ingredients are as above.
3. By mixing yoghurt and adding 'old cheese flavour' (ripened cheese flavour), salt, spices and colouring materials as above.

3.2 Sudan

Although some cheeses of European origin are made in Sudan, the principal, if not the only, indigenous cheese is Karish, similar to that made in neighbouring Egypt.

3.3 Other African Countries

FAO data[1] indicate that cheese production in Africa, excluding Egypt, Sudan and South Africa, amounts to 37 129 tonnes. Enquiries by the author to various individuals in several African countries indicated that most of this production is represented by European varieties; this agrees with the

TABLE III
Composition of Ayib cheese

Constituent	g/100 g
Water	71·5–76·6 (73·7)
Protein	12·5–16·9 (15·2)
Fat	4·7–11·1 (6·4)
Carbohydrate	2·6–3·6 (2·9)
Ash	0·8–2·5 (1·2)
Calcium	0·08–0·13 (0·11)
Phosphorus	0·18–0·22 (0·20)

Source: Ethiopian Nutrition Institute.

conclusions of Davis.[5] Indigenous fermented milks are produced in many African countries and in some cases these may be drained to yield forms of fresh curd; in some cases, the curds are dried.

Apparently, the only indigenous cheese produced in Ethiopia is Ayib, a by-product of butter manufacture (O'Mahony, F., personal communication). Surplus milk is accumulated each day and allowed to ripen naturally. When sufficient milk has accumulated, it is churned; the acidity of the milk varies between 0·85 and 1·1%. The butter is removed and the skim-milk (buttermilk) heated slowly to 35–40°C; coagulation of protein and residual fat occurs in 20–40 min, depending on the acidity of the milk and the heating temperature. The mixture is held at 35–40°C for some time to complete coagulation; it is then allowed to cool and the whey and curd separated. The practice of smoking dairy utensils imparts a smoky flavour to the cheese which has a short shelf-life because of its high moisture content (Table III).

Dairying is a traditional practice among the nomadic Fulani tribes of Nigeria, many of whom are now settled or semi-settled. The systems of cattle-rearing and dairying among these tribes are described by Waters-Bayer.[36] Milk provides ~10% of the energy requirements of settled Fulani and somewhat more of their protein requirements. However, little cheese is produced, the principal dairy products being butter (and sometimes ghee) and 'nono', a skimmed soured milk. Nono is most commonly used as a mixture with 'fura', balls of cooked millet flour spiced with pepper or ginger. Full-cream sour milk (Kindirmo) is also produced and sold usually as a mixture with 'Dambou' (a loose cooked cereal, usually millet).

A soft, white unripened cheese (wara or awara; similar to wagashi and chuku made by other Nigerian tribes) is also made in central Nigeria in the wet season when milk yields are relatively high. Whole fresh milk is heated in a pot over an open fire until the milk almost reaches the boiling point; some sour skim-milk is added (1:6 ratio). When the curds have formed the mixture is placed in a shallow basket to drain, with turning, for about 24 h. The drained cheese is cut into cubes (10–15 g) and fried in palm oil. The cheese is usually sold at local markets and is dipped in a chilli pepper sauce before eating (A. Waters-Bayer, personal communication).

A drier form of a similar cheese, 'Chukumara', is made in northern Nigeria and Niger from cow's milk but more commonly from camel's milk. The cheese, which has a fairly tough texture, is transported and stored in one piece from which portions are broken off and eaten as it is or, more commonly, after frying (A. Waters-Bayer, personal communication).

In the Katsina area of northern Nigeria, a cheese, Dakashi, is made by heating colostrum to the point of coagulation. No additions are made, before or after heating, and the curds are not drained (A. Waters-Bayer, personal communication).

Cheesemaking in the Ahaggar region of southern Algeria was described by Gast *et al.*[37] In this mountainous desert region, two types of cheese are produced by nomadic peoples from goat's milk: a rennet-coagulated cheese (Tikammarin) from whole goat milk (92–93% solids, 42–44% FDM, 34–37% protein in DM, 0·5% NaCl) and a sour-milk cheese (Aoules) produced from naturally-soured milk from which most of the fat has been removed for butter production (composition 87–92% TS; 11–20% FDM; 48–56% protein in DM; 1–1·5% NaCl). Both cheeses are very small, 15–90 g, and are air/sun-dried. A similar type of rennet cheese is produced in Niger.

Walter and Hargrove[4] mention what appears to be a basically similar cheese, Toureg, which is made by Berber tribes from the Barbary states to Lake Chad. Skim-milk is coagulated by animal rennet or by a rennet preparation from the leaves of the Korourou tree. The soft curd is dipped onto mats in very thin layers and when firm enough to retain its shape is dried in the sun or near a fire; it becomes very hard and dry and is not salted.

Kosikowski[38] states that nomads in Saudi Arabia, Syria and Morocco also produce small rennet-type cheeses which are infused with herbs and sun-dried. He also states that the Masai tribesmen of Kenya and Tanzania, who herd large numbers of zebu cattle and consume large quantities of milk, have not developed a cheese-making tradition and cites the experience of an unidentified FAO expert in Dahamey where an indigenous cheese with the flavour and consistency of Edam cheese is produced.

4. MIDDLE EAST

4.1 Syria

According to Abou Donia and Abdel Kader,[39] most cheese in Syria is produced by women in the home from sheep's milk. They list four types of indigenous cheeses: Hallonm (a soft cheese) and three hard varieties, Mesanarah, Medaffarah and Shankalish, the manufacture and composition of which are described below. Walter and Hargrove[4] list Labneh as a sour milk cheese of major importance in Syria. However, Labneh is usually regarded as a concentrated yoghurt rather than a cheese; obviously, the dividing lines are blurred. The preparation and characteristics of various forms of concentrated yoghurts are described by Tamine and Robinson.[40]

4.1.1 Mesanarah

Whole sheep's milk is renneted for 4 h; the coagulum is placed in cheesecloth bags and left to drain for 8 h. The drained curd is cut into small pieces (3 × 3 × 2 cm), sprinkled with dry salt and held for 18–24 h. The curd pieces are then scalded by boiling in brine (10%) for 5 min during which much fat is lost. Nigella grains are pressed into the hot pieces of curd which are then immersed in saturated brine at room temperature for 1 week. The salted, spiced cheese pieces are removed from the brine and sun-dried for 2–3 days prior to storage in tight containers. The cheese pieces are soaked in water for 24 h before consumption.

4.1.2 Medaffarah

Whole sheep's milk is coagulated with rennet and the coagulum drained as for Mesanarah. The drained coagulum is cut into large pieces and pressed until sufficient acidity has developed (as judged by stretchability after heating a sample to 75°C). When the curd is sufficiently acid, it is cut into small pieces (3 × 3 × 3 cm), warmed in water at 75°C for 3 min and kneaded and pulled to form 'cords', three of which are braided into a tress which is cut into pieces ∼8 cm long. The cheese tresses are immersed in saturated brine for ∼1 week and then sun-dried for 2–3 days. Obviously, this is a Pasta-filata type cheese.

4.1.3 Shankalish

This cheese, which is also produced in Jordan, is made from renneted partially-skimmed milk (gravity creaming and skimming). The coagulum is drained in cheesecloth bags for 24 h and the curd then salted at a rate of

TABLE IV
Chemical composition of Mesanarah, Medaffarah and Shankalish cheeses (Ref. 39)

Constituent	Mesanarah	Medaffarah	Shankalish
pH	5·2	5·0	4·5
Moisture (%)	26·6	28·6	30·2
Fat (% in dry matter)	26·2	27·1	17·7
Protein (%)	34·3	35·6	46·6
Ash (%)	6·9	7·0	7·0
NaCl (%)	5·6	5·6	5·5

~7% and spiced with thyme, aniseed, paprika, nigella and cumin. The salted, spiced curd is kneaded into balls, 3–4 cm in diameter, which are ripened in dark moist rooms for ~1 month, after which a sharp flavour has developed. The cheeses are then cleaned and either stored by immersion in olive oil or sun-dried for 2–3 days, both of which arrest ripening.

The microflora and composition (Table IV) of samples of the three cheeses after ripening are reported by Abou Donia and Abdel Kader[39] but no further information on ripening appears to be available. Apparently, no starters are used for any of the cheeses; presumably fermentation is performed by indigenous micro-organisms and is probably variable.

The authors note that the composition of these cheeses is similar to those of other primitive varieties produced in several countries in Asia, Africa, Spain and Portugal as reported by Davis.[5]

4.2 Saudi Arabia

Abou Donia[41] claims the first reported study of Ekt cheese produced by peoples in the Saudi Arabian desert and also in surrounding countries— Kuwait, Iraq, Jordan and Yemen.

Ekt is traditionally produced from sheep's milk which is boiled for ~30 min to evaporate some of the water. The heated milk is cooled to ~45°C and inoculated with a small piece of cheese or curd and left for 4–6 h. The coagulated milk is put into a goat-skin churn and agitated to produce buttermilk and butter, which is removed. The curdled buttermilk is ladled out of the 'churn' and individual ladle-fulls placed on pieces of special matting and drained for ~10 h. The drained pieces of curd are kneaded by hand and placed on fennel mats from which they absorb some aroma. The curd mass is broken into small pieces (2–3 × 1–2 × 0·5 cm) and sun-dried for 2–3 days and later in the shade to the desired degree of dryness. Before consumption, the pieces of dried cheese are reduced to a powder which is dispersed at ~20% in cold water and fermented (nature of fermentation not described).

The microflora of the cheese is reported[41] and the average chemical composition is: pH = 4·2; % moisture = 11·0; % fat-in-dry matter = 15; % protein = 49; % ash = 4·5; % NaCl = 1·2.

4.3 North Yemen

A very brief report on Taizz cheese, made only in the town of Taizz, North Yemen, was made by El-Erian *et al.*;[42] development of a successful standard manufacturing procedure was claimed but details of this or of the normal method were not given. The commercial and modified cheeses contained 32·2 and 31·5% moisture, respectively.

4.4 Iraq

Awshari, the principal cheese in northern Iraq, is produced on a farmyard scale from a mixture of sheep's and goat's milk in the proportions available. The manufacture, composition and characteristics of this cheese have been described by Dalaly *et al.*[43] The milk, directly after milking, is coagulated using a home-produced rennet extract (prepared by extracting a mixture of dried lamb's stomach, sugar, alum, black pepper, zingibel and cloves with a 5% NaCl brine). The coagulum is cut, NaCl is added to ~1% and the mixture is heated to 45°C with stirring for ~15 min. The whey is drained off and the curd transferred to long muslin bags which are continuously pressed by hand. As the curd accumulates at one end of the sack, the sack is twisted to compress the curd into a sphere. The drained whey is collected for making 'Jagi'.

Dry salt is rubbed on the surface of the cheeses twice daily for 4 days. The cheeses are then placed in sheep or goat skins, a measured amount of dry salt added, the skins closed and stored in a cool place for 3 weeks. Expressed whey is drained off, further salt is added and ripening continued for a further 6 weeks with intermittent whey removal.

After 60–70 days, the cheeses, which have become very hard, are transferred to a dry skin in which the spaces between the cheeses are filled with Jagi. The cheeses are stored thus for at least 2 weeks and perhaps for as long as 6 months. Old cheeses may be very hard and it is common practice

TABLE V
Composition of Awshari cheese (5 samples)[a]

Moisture (%)	37·55–47·19
Fat (%)	21·6–33·80
Total N (%)	3·42–4·06
Soluble N (%)	0·51–0·71
Amino acid N (%)	0·30–0·50
Acidity of cheese	0·49–2·12
pH	5·15–6·28
Acid value of fat	4·49–16·27
Total volatile acids	73–124
Salt (%)	2·62–4·14
Salt in moisture (%)	5·55–10·89

[a] From Ref. 43; the author comments that the cheeses may have been soaked in water and hence some of the soluble constituents may have been removed.

to soak them in water for 2–7 days, after which the surface of the cheeses are coated with Jagi and stored in clean dry skins.

Jagi is prepared by either of two methods:

1. Fresh milk (~5%) is added to whey collected from cheese manufacture the previous day, and the mixture heated at 70–90°C until the milk and whey proteins precipitate. The precipitate is recovered by filtration and mixed with diced garlic or kurrat in the proportion of 5:1.

2. The buttermilk obtained on churning sour milk is boiled on a direct flame; the curd which forms is skimmed off and mixed with wild herbs (garlic, onion, dry roses) and salt.

The mature cheese has a sharp peppery, sometimes rancid flavour, a hard, rather brittle texture with some cracks and mechanical openings. The viable bacterial counts in five commercial samples were very low, ranging from 450 to 1220 cfu/g; the microflora was mixed, consisting of streptococci, micrococci, lactobacilli and sporeforms. The chemical composition is variable; the range of composition for five commercial samples analysed by Dalaly *et al.*[43] are shown in Table V. The composition of Jagi is shown in Table VI.

The composition (Table VII) of farmers' soft cheese, produced on farms in Iraq, was described by Saleem *et al.*[44] It is not stated whether the cheese was produced by acid or rennet coagulation. The cheese is sold fresh,

TABLE VI
Composition of Jagi[43]

	I	II
Moisture (%)	48·25	49·09
Fat (%)	8·42	13·45
Total protein (%)	31·98	24·81
Soluble N (%)	0·896	0·868
Amino acid N (%)	0·868	0·840
Acidity (%)	2·34	1·33
Total volatile acids	118	40
pH	5·65	5·85
Salt (%)	3·71	5·09

usually with added herbs, especially garlic, and is frequently referred to as garlic cheese.

Davis[5] does not mention Awshari but includes brief descriptions of 'Roos' and 'Meria', the method of manufacture for which appears to be somewhat similar to that of Awshari, although no mention is made of the use of Jagi. He also mentions a fresh acid cheese, Biza or Fajy.

4.5 Iran

FAO[1] statistics indicate that cheese production in Iran was 105 123 tonnes in 1982 but Kosikowski[38] reports a figure of nearly twice that for pickled white cheese, Lightvan, the manufacture of which he describes in some detail. Lightvan cheese, which is made principally in small village factories, mainly from sheep's milk, is essentially similar to Feta or Bulgarian white

TABLE VII
Chemical composition of Iraq white
soft cheese[44]

Moisture (%)	46·69–60·54
Fat (%)	20·25–28·25
Acidity (%)	0·52–1·85
pH	5·30–4·40
Total N (%)	2·75–3·33
Soluble N (%)	0·16–0·40
Lactose (%)	0·50–0·95
Ash (%)	1·61–4·60
NaCl (%)	0·13–2·83
Herbs (%)	1·48–2·68

cheeses which are described in Chapters 8 and 9. Iran has recently become a major importer of Feta type cheese from European countries.

4.6 Israel

Consumption of cheese in Israel is well up to European standards at ~14 kg/caput[46] (see Table III, Chapter 1, Volume 1); fresh cheeses at 10·6 kg/caput represent the majority of the cheese consumed. According to Davis,[5] most of the hard cheeses produced in Israel are European types, e.g. Edam, Emmental, Provolone, Kashkaval, Blue, Bel Paese, Brinza (Feta type).

4.7 Turkey

According to Davis,[5] an estimated 40 000 tonnes of cheese are produced annually in Turkey but FAO[1] gives a value of ~130 000 tonnes for 1982. The principal cheeses are of the Feta type, e.g. Teleme (Telemea), which have been described previously. Davis[5] mentions some other Turkish varieties but little technical information is provided.

4.8 Cyprus

Although normally considered to be within the European cultural sphere, Cyprus is classified as an Asian country by the FAO and it suits my purpose to classify it as such since a rather unique cheese, Halloumi, is produced only there. The manufacture of Halloumi (Fig. 1) is described by Davis,[5] Scott[45] and Anifantakis and Kaminarides.[49] The unique features of its manufacture are: (1) after separation of the curds, the whey is heated to 80–90°C (depending on acidity) to coagulate the whey proteins which are recovered and used in the manufacture of Anari, a cheese generally similar to Ricotta; (2) the deproteinized whey is maintained at 90–95°C and to it are added pieces (10 × 10 × 3 cm) of pressed curd which are held for ~30 min. The cooked curds are not stretched, as in Pasta filata type cheeses, but are drained, cooled and sprinkled with salt (~5%). The cheese is then ready for consumption or it may be packed in cans submerged in brined whey.

The composition of commercial Halloumi cheese is quite variable (Table VIII) (cf. Ref. 49). The microbiology and biochemistry of the ripening of this cheese, which appears to be a hybrid between the high-salted Feta varieties and the Pasta filata varieties, both families being common in the Middle East, have received little attention to date; only recently have

TABLE VIII

Composition of Halloumi cheese made from sheep's milk and of Halloumi cheese from the Cyprus market (mean of 13 and 17 observations respectively) (from Ref. 49)

Components	Halloumi from sheep's milk			Halloumi from the Cyprus market		
	Mean	Values range	Standard deviation	Mean	Values range	Standard deviation
Moisture (%)	42·15	39·04–43·64	1·39	42·53	35·46–48·56	3·75
Fat (%)	27·85	26·25–29·25	1·76	25·57	20·00–29·50	3·14
Fat in dry matter (%)	48·09	46·10–49·99	1·95	44·52	37·95–50·48	3·98
Protein (total N% × 6·38)	23·71	21·95–25·02	1·02	24·46	20·86–30·45	2·28
Protein in dry matter (%)	41·02	39·22–44·26	2·37	42·53	40·11–48·62	2·30
Soluble protein (%) (soluble N% × 6·38)	0·76	0·64–0·89	—	1·15	0·83–1·55	1·14
NaCl (%)	1·44	1·05–2·05	0·28	3·54	2·31–5·65	0·91
pH	5·86	5·30–6·10	0·22	—	—	—

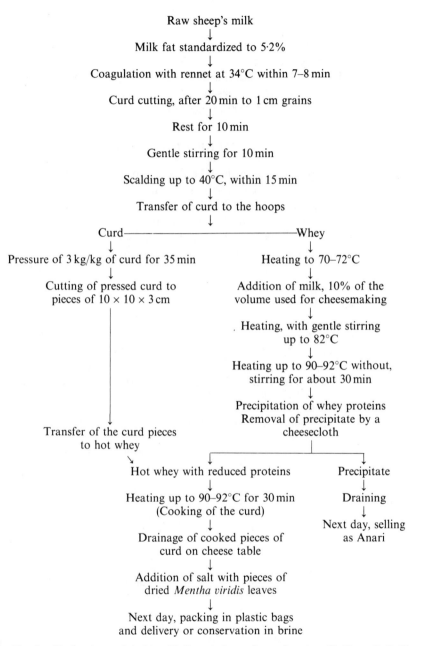

Raw sheep's milk
↓
Milk fat standardized to 5·2%
↓
Coagulation with rennet at 34°C within 7–8 min
↓
Curd cutting, after 20 min to 1 cm grains
↓
Rest for 10 min
↓
Gentle stirring for 10 min
↓
Scalding up to 40°C, within 15 min
↓
Transfer of curd to the hoops
↓

Curd —————————————————— Whey

Curd	Whey
Pressure of 3 kg/kg of curd for 35 min	Heating to 70–72°C
Cutting of pressed curd to pieces of 10 × 10 × 3 cm	Addition of milk, 10% of the volume used for cheesemaking
	Heating, with gentle stirring up to 82°C
	Heating up to 90–92°C without, stirring for about 30 min
	Precipitation of whey proteins Removal of precipitate by a cheesecloth
Transfer of the curd pieces to hot whey	

Hot whey with reduced proteins   Precipitate
↓   ↓
Heating up to 90–92°C for 30 min   Draining
(Cooking of the curd)   ↓
↓   Next day, selling
Drainage of cooked pieces of   as Anari
curd on cheese table
↓
Addition of salt with pieces of
dried *Mentha viridis* leaves
↓
Next day, packing in plastic bags
and delivery or conservation in brine

Fig. 1. Technology of making Halloumi cheese from sheep's milk (from Ref. 49) (reproduced by permission of the *Australian Journal of Dairy Technology*).

studies on this variety been initiated by E. Anifantakis and colleagues of the Agricultural College of Athens.[47-50] Obviously, exposure to very high temperatures kills most micro-organisms and inactivates enzymes so that it is likely that only limited changes occur during ripening. Total cheese production in Cyprus is ~13 000 tonnes p.a.[1]

5. LATIN AMERICAN CHEESES

Recorded cheese production in the whole of Latin America was 524 229 tonnes in 1982 (Table IX). Considering the size of the population, this production is very small compared with many European countries, e.g. the Netherlands (485 000 tonnes; 16 M people), Denmark (245 700 tonnes, 5 M people) or France (1 190 000 tonnes; 60 M people). External trade in cheese is also very small: imports ~59 000 tonnes and exports ~26 000 tonnes. However, Argentina is a very significant cheese producer and is second only to the USA in the entire American continent.

According to Kosikowski,[51] many of the cheeses produced in Latin America are of European origin, mainly Gouda, Romano, Mozzarella, Ricotta and Manchego. Local names are given to many of the cheeses even though their characteristics and manufacturing procedures are similar to those of their European counterparts, e.g. Oaxaca (also called Asadero) of Mexico and Chiclosa of El-Salvador are similar to Mozzarella. Differences

TABLE IX
Cheese production, tonnes, in Latin America, 1982 (Ref. 1)

Central America		South America	
Costa Rica	5 734	Argentina	233 300
Cuba	9 391	Bolivia	7 375
Dominican Republic	1 650	Brazil	59 080
El Salvador	17 614	Chile	22 700
Guatemala	15 082	Columbia	46 500
Haiti	1 700	Ecuador	12 791
Honduras	8 223	Peru	32 740
Jamaica	—	Suriname	—
Mexico	99 421	Uruguay	15 000
Nicaragua	7 508	Venezuela	28 000
Panama	420		
	166 743		457 486
Total	624 229		

TABLE X
Names of some native Latin American cheeses

Anejo	Queso d'Autin	Queso de Puna
Asadero	Queso de Apoyo	Queso de la Tierra
Chihüahua	Queso de Bagaces	Queso del País
Goya (like Asiago)	Queso de Bola	Queso Descremado
Guayana	Queso de Cavallo	Queso Enchilado
Hand	Queso de Cincho	Queso Estera
Minas Freschal	Queso de Crema	Queso Fresco
Minas Gerais	Queso de Hoja	Queso Huloso
Panela	Queso de Mano	Queso Llanero
Patagras (like Gouda)	Queso de Maracay	Queso Metida
Queljo Prato (like Gouda)	Queso de Matera	Queso Oaxaca
Queso Andino	Queso de Perija	Requejão
Queso Blanco	Queso de Prensa	Yearly

Compiled from Refs 4 and 51.

relate principally to composition and properties of the milk and the scale and conditions of manufacture. It is doubtful whether any of the cheeses produced in Latin America are indigenous in the strict sense since they have been introduced by European settlers; as far as I can ascertain via enquiry from a number of personal contacts, there is no evidence that the indigenous population made cheese. Kosikowski[51] lists 24 'indigenous varieties' (Table X), of which Queso Blanco is the most important; Walter and Hargrove[4] list a further 15 names not mentioned by Kosikowski.[51] Queso Blanco (white cheese) is a generic name and includes both rennet and acid cheeses; both of these are usually consumed fresh (Queso Fresco) but they may also be pressed and ripened when different names are applied (e.g. Queso Presna). In Puerto Rico, where it is also known as Queso del País, Queso Blanco is usually produced by adding food-grade acid (acetic, citric, vinegar or citrus juice) to hot milk. The basic procedures described by Kosikowski[51] for acid and rennet coagulated Queso Blanco are summarized in Figs 2–4. A number of Central and South American cheeses, including some hard cheeses, are also described by Davis.[5]

Kosikowski[51] and W. L. Dunkley (personal communication) comment on the problem of classifying Latin American cheeses and on the need for such a classification scheme as an aid to trade. They also comment on the range of technological sophistication used in cheese manufacture—while most cheese is produced on farmsteads or in very small primitive factories, there are also several modern highly mechanized factories, especially in Argentina.

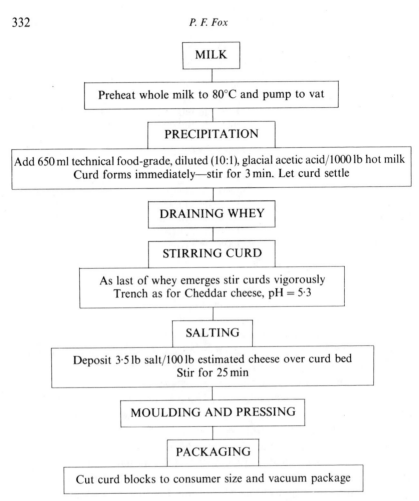

Fig. 2. Manufacture protocol for Queso Blanco—Queso Del País using acetic acid (Ref. 51).

As indicated earlier, most of the cheese in Latin America is consumed fresh. I have no information on the microbiological and chemical changes which occur during the maturation of those cheeses that are ripened. One of the exceptions is Tafi cheese which is produced in the Tafi Valley in the Tucuman province of Argentina. This is a rennet cheese made on a farmstead level from whole raw milk to which whey from the previous day's manufacture is added as 'ferment'. The milk is renneted at 30–31°C; 2 h after addition of rennet and starter, the gel is cut and the curd/whey cooked

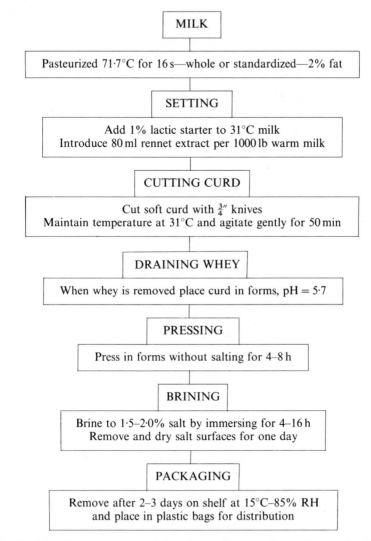

MILK

Pasteurized 71·7°C for 16 s—whole or standardized—2% fat

SETTING

Add 1% lactic starter to 31°C milk
Introduce 80 ml rennet extract per 1000 lb warm milk

CUTTING CURD

Cut soft curd with $\frac{3}{4}''$ knives
Maintain temperature at 31°C and agitate gently for 50 min

DRAINING WHEY

When whey is removed place curd in forms, pH = 5·7

PRESSING

Press in forms without salting for 4–8 h

BRINING

Brine to 1·5–2·0% salt by immersing for 4–16 h
Remove and dry salt surfaces for one day

PACKAGING

Remove after 2–3 days on shelf at 15°C–85% RH
and place in plastic bags for distribution

Fig. 3. Manufacturing protocol for Queso Blanco—Queso Fresco (in Brazil known as Minas Gerais—Freschal) using rennet (Ref. 51).

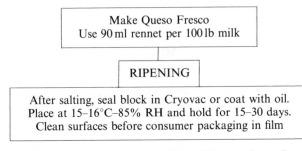

Fig. 4. Manufacture protocol for ripened Queso Blanco—Queso Prensa (in Brazil known as Minas Gerais—Curado) (Ref. 51).

to 39–40°C for ~3 h, when part of the whey is drained off and the curd salted. The salted curd is placed in cylindrical metal moulds and pressed for 14–16 h. The cheese (1–1·25 kg) has a smooth, close-knit body, a maximum of 50% moisture and a minimum of 35% fat. The cheese is ripened for at least 60 days at ~22°C and acquires a surface fungal microflora (G. S. de Giori, personal communication).

Some of the compositional and microbiological changes which occur in this cheese during ripening were described by de Giori *et al.*[52] The microflora of the cheesemilk and whey starter have been classified by de Giori *et al.*[53,54] There is no information on the biochemical changes during ripening (de Giori, personal communication).

6. EPILOGUE

This chapter is obviously very incomplete. It is very difficult to obtain information on non-European cheese varieties since only limited published data are available and much of it is rather superficial compared with that on the major European varieties. Some of the information contained in this chapter was obtained from personal contacts and the assistance of these is acknowledged. If your favourite cheese has been omitted or if you have any information on cheeses not included in this chapter, or further information on those that are included, please write to me so that a revised, more complete version may be published at some time in the future.

Although it is incomplete, it is hoped that this chapter will serve to stimulate interest in non-European cheeses and I look forward to hearing from you.

ACKNOWLEDGEMENTS

I wish to acknowledge the assistance of Dr W. L. Dunkley, Dr F. V. Kosikowski, Dr E. M. Anifantakis, Dr G. S. de Giori, Dr D. K. Dalaly, Dr A. Waters-Bayer, Dr C. L. Dawide, Dr S. Singh and Dr M. M. Hewedi.

REFERENCES

1. FAO, *Production Yearbook*, Vol. 36, p. 247, 1982.
2. IDF, *The World Market for Cheese*, International Dairy Federation, Brussels, Doc. 146, 1982.
3. De, S., *Outline of Dairy Technology*, Oxford University Press, Delhi, p. 382, 1980.
4. Walter, H. E. and Hargrove, R. E., *Cheeses of the World*, Dover Publications Inc., New York, 1972.
5. Davis, J. G., *Cheese, Vol. III, Manufacturing Methods*, Churchill Livingstone, Edinburgh, 1976.
6. Abou Donia, S. A., *N.Z. J. Dairy Sci. Technol.*, 1984, **19**, 7.
7. El-Gendy, S. M., *J. Food Prot.*, 1983, **46**, 358.
8. El-Erian, A. F., Nour, M. A. and Shalaby, S. O., *Egyptian J. Dairy Sci.*, 1976, **4**, 91.
9. Naghmoush, M. R., Mewtally, M. M., Abou-Dawood, A. E., Naguib, M. M. and Ali, A. A., *Egyptian J. Dairy Sci.*, 1979, **7**, 117.
10. Hofi, A. A., Youssef, E. H., Ghoneim, M. A. and Tawab, G. A., *J. Dairy Sci.*, 1970, **53**, 1207.
11. Khorshid, M. A., El-Safty, M. S., Abdel El-Hamed, L. B. and Hamdy, A. M., *Egyptian J. Dairy Sci.*, 1975, **3**, 127.
12. Mabran, G. A., El-Safty, M. S., Abdel-Hamed, L. B. and Khorshid, M. A., *Egyptian J. Dairy Sci.*, 1976, **4**, 13.
13. El-Batawy, M. A., Amer, S. N., Naghmoush, M. R., Fahmi, A. H. and Shibiny, S., *Egyptian J. Dairy Sci.*, 1981, **9**, 27.
14. Osman, Y. M., *Egyptian J. Food Sci.*, 1979, **7**, 77.
15. Hofi, A. A., Mahran, G. A., Ashour, M. Z., Khorshid, M. A. and Faharat, S., *Egyptian J. Dairy Sci.*, 1973, **1**, 79.
16. Abd El-Rahman, N. R., Sultan, N. E. and Abd El-Kader, A. E., *Ann. Agric. Sci. Moshtohar*, 1981, **16**, 45.
17. Abd El-Salam, M. H., Rifaat, I. A., Hofi, A. A. and Mahran, G. A., *Egyptian J. Dairy Sci.*, 1973, **1**, 171.
18. Hofi, A. A., Mahran, G. A., Abd El-Salam, M. H. and Rifaat, I. D., *Egyptian J. Dairy Sci.*, 1973, **1**, 33.
19. Hofi, A. A., Mahran, G. A., Abd El-Salam, M. H. and Rifaat, I. D., *Egyptian J. Dairy Sci.*, 1973, **1**, 47.
20. Abdel-Baky, A. A., El-Fak, A. M., Rabie, A. M. and El-Neshewy, A. A., *J. Food Prot.*, 1982, **45**, 894.
21. Nassib, T. A., *Assiut. J. Agric. Sci.*, 1974, **5**, 123.

22. El-Shibiny, S., Soliman, M. A., El-Bagoury, E., Gad, A. and Abd El-Salam, M. H., *J. Dairy Res.*, 1978, **45**, 497.
23. El-Shibiny, S., Mohamed, A. A., El-Dean, H. F., Ayad, E. and Abd El-Salam, M. H., *Egyptian J. Dairy Sci.*, 1979, **7**, 141.
24. Abd El-Salam, M. H., El-Shibiny, S., El-Baboury, E., Ayad, E. and Fahmy, N., *J. Dairy Res.*, 1978, **45**, 491.
25. Abd El-Salam, M. H., Mohamed, A. A., Ayad, E., Fahmy, N. and El-Shibiny, S., *Egyptian J. Dairy Sci.*, 1979, **7**, 63.
26. Soliman, M. A., El-Shibiny, S., Mohamed, A. A. and Abd El-Salam, M. H., *Egyptian J. Dairy Sci.*, 1980, **8**, 49.
27. Nasr, M., *Egyptian J. Dairy Sci.*, 1983, **11**, 309.
28. Abdel-Hamid, L. B., Dawood, A. H., Abdou, S. M., Yousef, A. M. E. and Sherif, R. M., *Egyptian J. Dairy Sci.*, 1977, **5**, 181.
29. Abdou, S. M., Abd El-Hamid, L. B., Dawood, A. H. M., Yousef, A. M. and Mahran, G. A., *Egyptian J. Dairy Sci.*, 1977, **5**, 191.
30. Omar, M. M. and Ashour, M. M., *Food Chem.*, 1982, **8**, 33.
31. Hagrass, A. E. A., El-Ghandour, M. A., Hammad, Y. A. and Hofi, A. A., *Egyptian J. Dairy Sci.*, 1983, **11**, 271.
32. Hofi, A. A., El-Ghandour, M. A., Hammad, Y. A. and Hagrass, A. E. A., *Egyptian J. Dairy Sci.*, 1983, **11**, 77.
33. El-Ghandour, M. A., Hagrass, A. E. A., Hammad, Y. A. and Hofi, A. A., *Egyptian J. Dairy Sci.*, 1983, **11**, 87.
34. El-Safty, M. S. and Mehanna, N., *Egyptian J. Dairy Sci.*, 1979, **5**, 55.
35. Shehata, A. E., Magdoub, M. N. I., Gouda, A. and Hofi, A. A., *Egyptian J. Dairy Sci.*, 1982, **10**, 225.
36. Waters-Bayer, A., Paper 2C, Agricultural Administration Unit, Overseas Development Institute, London, 1985.
37. Gast, M., Maubois, J.-L. and Adda, J., Le Lait et les Products Laitiers en Ahaggar, Mem. Centre Recherches Anthropologiques, Prehistoriques et Ethnographiques, XIV Arts et Metiers Graphiques, Paris, 1969.
38. Kosikowski, F. V., *Cheese and Fermented Milk Foods*, Edward Brothers Inc., Ann Arbor, Michigan, USA, 1982.
39. Abou Donia, Y. A. and Abdel Kader, Y. I., *Egyptian J. Dairy Sci.*, 1979, **7**, 221.
40. Tamine, A. Y. and Robinson, R. K., *Yoghurt: Science and Technology*, Pergamon Press, Oxford, 1985.
41. Abou Donia, S. A., *Egyptian J. Dairy Sci.*, 1978, **6**, 49.
42. El-Erian, A. F. M., Moneib, A. F. and Dalloul, S. M., *2nd Arab Conference for Food Science and Technology*, Riyad University Press, p. 50, 1979.
43. Dalaly, B. K., Abdel Mottaleb, L. and Farag, M. C., *Dairy Ind. Int.*, 1976, **41**(3), 80.
44. Saleem, R. M., Mohammed, F. O. and Abdel Mottaleb, L., *Mesopotamia J. Agric.*, 1980, **15**, 101.
45. Scott, R., *Cheesemaking Practice*, 2nd edn, Elsevier Applied Science, London, 1986.
46. International Dairy Federation, Doc. 160, 1983.
47. Anifantakis, E. M. and Kaminarides, S. E., *Agric. Res.*, 1981, **5**, 441.
48. Anifantakis, E. M. and Kaminarides, S. E., *Agric. Res.*, 1982, **6**, 119.
49. Anifantakis, E. M. and Kaminarides, S. E., *Aust. J. Dairy Technol.*, 1983, **38**, 29.

50. Kaminarides, S. E., Anifantakis, E. and Likas, D., *J. National Dairy Board of Greece*, 1984, **3**, 5.
51. Kosikowski, F. V., *Proc. 1st Biennial Marschall International Cheese Conference*, Madison, Wisconsin, 1979, p. 591.
52. de Giori, G. S., de Valdez, G. F., de Ruiz Holgado, A. P. and Oliver, G., *J. Food Prot.*, 1983, **46**, 518.
53. de Giori, G. S., de Valdez, G. F., de Ruiz Holgado, A. P. and Oliver, G., *Microbiol. Alim. Nutr.*, 1984, **2**, 233.
54. de Giori, G. S., de Valdez, G. F., de Ruiz Holgado, A. P. and Oliver, G., *Microbiol. Alim. Nutr.*, 1985, **3**, 167.

Chapter 11

Processed Cheese Products

Marijana Carić

Faculty of Technology, University of Novi Sad, Yugoslavia

Miloslav Kaláb

Food Research Centre, Agriculture Canada,
Ottawa, Ontario, Canada

1. INTRODUCTION: GENERAL CHARACTERISTICS

Processed cheese is produced by blending shredded natural cheeses of different types and degrees of maturity with emulsifying agents, and by heating the blend under partial vacuum with constant agitation until a homogeneous mass is obtained. Besides natural cheeses, other dairy and non-dairy ingredients may be included in the blend.

Initially, processed cheese was manufactured without an emulsifying agent; the first attempt was as early as 1895, but only after the introduction of citrates and especially phosphates as emulsifying agents did the industrial production of processed cheeses become feasible. The idea of processing was first meant to make use of natural cheeses which otherwise would be difficult or impossible to utilize, e.g. cheeses with mechanical deformations, localized moulds, trimmings produced during cheese formation, pressing, packaging, etc. Later, the assortment was greatly expanded due to numerous possible combinations of various types of cheese and the inclusion of other dairy and non-dairy components which make it possible to produce processed cheeses differing in consistency, flavour, size and shape.

The principal advantages of processed cheeses compared to natural cheeses are:

—reduced refrigeration costs during storage and transport, which are especially important in hot climates;

339

TABLE I

Some characteristics of processed cheese types

Type of product	Ingredients	Cooking temperatures (°C)	Composition	pH	Reference
Processed cheese block	Natural cheese, emulsifiers NaCl, colouring	71–80	Moisture and fat contents correspond to the legal limits for natural cheese	5·6–5·8	Kosikowski[1]
		80–85		5·4–5·6	Meyer[3]
		74–85	≤45% moisture	5·4–5·7	Thomas[2]
Processed cheese food	Same as above plus optional ingredients such as milk, skim-milk, whey, cream, albumin, skim-milk cheese; organic acids	79–85	≤44% moisture, <23% fat	5·2–5·6	Kosikowski[1]
Processed cheese spread	Same as processed cheese food plus gums for water retention	88–91	≥44% and ≤60% moisture	5·2	Kosikowski[1]
		85–98		5·7–5·9	Meyer[3]
		90–95	≤55% moisture	5·8–6·0	Thomas[2]
Processed cheese analogue	Sodium caseinate, calcium caseinate, suitable vegetable fats (soya-bean, coconut), emulsifying agent, salt, artificial flavour	As for processed cheese food	As for processed cheese food	5·8–5·9	Kosikowski[1]

—better keeping quality with less apparent changes during prolonged storage;
—great diversity of type and intensity of flavour, e.g. from mild to sharp native cheese flavour or specific spices;
—adjustable packaging for various usage, economical and imaginative;
—suitability for home use as well as for snack restaurants, e.g. in cheeseburgers, hot sandwiches, spreads and dips for fast foods.

Processed cheeses are characterized essentially by composition, water content and consistency; according to these criteria, three main groups may be distinguished: processed cheese blocks, processed cheese foods and processed cheese spreads (Table I). In addition, a further group of processed cheese products should be mentioned, i.e. processed cheese analogues which are usually based on vegetable fat–casein blends.

2. PROCESSING: PRINCIPLES AND TECHNIQUES

The manufacturing procedure for processed cheese consists of operations carried out in the following order: Selection of natural cheese → computation of the ingredients → blending → shredding → addition of emulsifying agent → (thermal) processing → homogenization (optional) → packaging → cooling → storage.

2.1 Selection of Natural Cheese

Proper selection of natural cheese is of the utmost importance for the successful production of processed cheese. In some countries, processed cheeses manufactured from only one variety of cheese of different degrees of maturity are very popular, e.g. processed Cheddar in the UK and Australia; Cheddar, Gruyère and Mozzarella in USA and Canada; Emmental in Western Europe. More frequently, processed cheeses are produced from a mix of various natural cheese types. Criteria for cheese selection are: type, flavour, maturity, consistency, texture and acidity. Since it is possible to correct certain physical properties by skilful blending, some defective cheeses can be used in processed cheese manufacture. Natural cheeses with microbial defects should not be selected for processing; spore-forming, gas-producing and pathogenic bacteria are particularly hazardous. However, proper selection of good quality natural cheeses is not, by itself, a guarantee that the processed cheese will have the desired high quality.

2.2 Computation of Ingredients

Computation of the ingredients is conducted on the basis of established fat and dry matter contents of the natural cheese components. Formulation of the material balance of fat and dry matter, including all blend constituents, added water and condensate from live steam used during processing, must be made in such a way as to yield a finished product with the desired composition. Additional adjustments of fat and dry matter are possible, if necessary, before processing is completed.

2.3 Blending

This operation is strongly influenced by the desired characteristics of the final product. According to Thomas,[2] there is a general formulation for processed cheese (block-type): 70–75% of mild cheese and 25–30% of semi-mature or mature cheese. For the production of processed cheese in slices, where a high content of elastic, intact (unhydrolysed) protein is necessary, this ratio is changed to 30–40% young cheese, 50–60% mild cheese and only 10% mature cheese. Kosikowski[1] suggests a similar blend composition: 55% young cheese, 35% medium aged and 10% aged cheese, in order to obtain optimum firmness and slicing qualities.

The main advantages of a high content of young cheese in the blend are[2] reduced raw material costs and the possibility of using cheeses with poor curing properties immediately after manufacture and the formation of a stable emulsion with high water-binding capacity, a firm body and good slicing properties. However, there are certain disadvantages also, such as the production of a tasteless cheese which may have a so-called emulsifier off-flavour, excessive swelling, a tendency to harden during storage and the presence of small air bubbles developed due to the high viscosity of the blend.

A high content of extra-mature cheese in the blend has certain advantages,[2] e.g. development of a full flavour, good flow properties and high melting index; however, disadvantages include a sharp flavour, low emulsion stability and a soft consistency.

Most cheeses with rind are trimmed, i.e. the rind with a thin surface layer of cheese is removed, mechanically or manually.

In addition to natural cheeses, various other dairy and non-dairy ingredients are used in the production of processed cheese spreads and processed cheese foods, as shown in Table II. Since the quality of the final product is influenced considerably by all the components present in the blend, the non-cheese components must also fulfil certain qualitative and quantitative requirements. The most frequently used non-cheese ingredients are skim-milk powder, casein–whey protein coprecipitates, various whey products and milk fat products (Table II).

Skim-milk powder improves the spreadability and stability of processed cheese, but, if used in quantities exceeding 12% of the total mass, it may adversely affect the consistency or may remain undissolved. However, skim-milk powder may be reconstituted first, its casein precipitated by citric acid or proteolytic enzymes and the resulting curd added to the blend.[2] In order to avoid discoloration of processed cheese due to the Maillard reaction, attention must be paid to the total lactose content, which should be less than 6% in the final product.

Milk protein coprecipitates, if added to the blend, increase the stability of the cheese emulsion, improve the physical characteristics of the final product and even act as an emulsifying agent. Their emulsifying capacity is so high that it is possible, in their presence, to reduce the amount of emulsifying salt used. This is important particularly for dietary and special food products where limitation of the sodium content may be desirable. Milk protein coprecipitates should not exceed 5% in processed cheeses.[5]

Although ordinary whey powder is the most common whey product used in processed cheeses, whey protein products with lower mineral and lactose contents are preferable because they yield processed cheeses with better flavours.

All milk fat ingredients (Table II) used to adjust the fat content of the processed cheese to the desired level must be of high quality and be free from off-flavours.

Numerous investigations have recently been carried out in order to develop new processed cheese blends which have improved characteristics and/or which can be produced at a lower cost. A group of Egyptian workers[6] has produced processed cheese spreads with good spreadability by partially substituting calcium caseinate for natural cheese in the blend. Although full replacement, with cheese flavour added, failed to yield a spread with good characteristics, partial replacement improved spreadability. A significant improvement in spreadability was obtained using a blend consisting of 6–8% skim-milk powder, 5–7% calcium caseinate, 15% mature Cheddar cheese, 14% butter oil and 3% emulsifying agent.

Production of a cheese base for the manufacture of processed cheese by ultrafiltration and diafiltration of whole milk at 50°C was developed and patented in the Federal Republic of Germany.[7] The retentate (40% dry

TABLE II

Ingredients used in the manufacture of processed cheese[4] (reproduced by permission of Scanning Electron Microscopy Inc.)

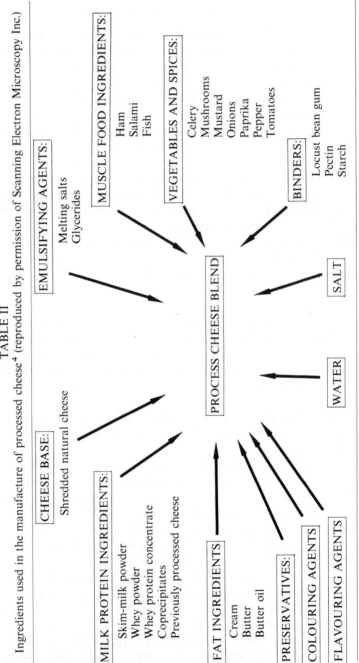

matter, 1·17% lactose) was pasteurized (high temperature–short time, HTST), cooled to 30°C, inoculated with lactic starter and, after 2 h, evaporated at 42°C to 62% dry matter. It was further incubated at 25°C until the pH reached 5·2 and was then packaged in plastic bags under vacuum. The cheese base can be used in processed cheese production at an 80:20 ratio with ripe cheese.

At the Utah State University in the USA, a cheese for processing was manufactured from ultrafiltered whole milk adjusted to pH 5·2–6·6.[8] The melting properties of the product improved with decreasing pH of the milk before ultrafiltration, as was expected from the reduced calcium concentration in the retentate. Chymosin treatment of the UF retentate adversely affected the meltability of the cheese produced. Ostojić and Manić[9] used up to 85% of a Trappist cheese produced from ultrafiltered milk in a processed cheese blend and found no negative influence on the sensory attributes of the final product which had a higher content of essential amino acids.

A well-known curd product, 'Schmelzpack', is manufactured in Germany especially for processed cheese production. It contains 90–100% unhydrolysed casein and can be blended with natural cheeses of diverse type and maturity.[10,11] Good results on the use of chicken pepsin for the 'peptonization' of curd for incorporation into processed cheese have been reported from Bulgaria.[12]

Several enzymic methods for accelerating the ripening of natural cheeses are now in use[13,14] and have been reviewed in detail by Law[14] (see Chapter 10, Volume 1). Acceleration of the ripening process in the production of 'natural' cheese destined for use in processed cheese manufacture is particularly interesting, both technologically and economically. For example, in Cheddar manufacture it was possible to reduce the duration of ripening from a few months to 2–3 weeks.[15] Pasteurized milk was coagulated at 36°C by the addition of chymosin and high quantities of starter culture (up to 4%). After cutting, scalding and whey separation, the curd (at pH 5·1–5·3) was milled, mixed with emulsifying agent to form a plastic mass, filled into containers, paraffined on top and ripened for only a few weeks.

A patent for chemical hydrolysis of cheese trimmings, intended for inclusion in processed cheese blends, was recently granted in the USSR.[16] The trimmings were washed with hot water, centrifuged, comminuted and hydrolysed with 1·4–1·6M-HCl at 110–116°C for 3–5 h. The procedure produced a hydrolysate with about 80% peptides in dry matter and 20% essential amino acids (on a total amino acid basis). Hydrolysate (about 20%

dry matter) was successfully incorporated in the blend up to a maximum of 15%, depending on the type and maturity of the natural cheese used.

Another rapid procedure for the production of a cheese product for processing, based on curd acidification, was developed and patented by Kraft and Ward[17] in the USA. Milk was coagulated, and after whey separation, the curd was immersed in lactic acid ($0.2–1.5\%$ acidity) and heated, with agitation, to 43°C for 6–40 min. The lactic acid solution was drained from the curd, which was washed with water, salted and pressed, and finally stored at 5°C; after 2 days, the pressed curd can be used in processed cheese manufacture.

Shimizu et al.[18] have recently established that the N-terminal peptide obtained from the peptic hydrolysate of α_{s1}-casein (residues 1–23) has high emulsifying ability. These results suggest that hydrolysis of milk proteins (casein) could positively affect the emulsifying properties of processed cheese blends.

All non-dairy ingredients intended for blending (muscle foods, vegetables, spices, etc.) must be sterile and of the highest quality, with typical flavour. Their quantities must be properly prescribed for blending. In addition to the various possible non-dairy components used in processed cheese blends cited in Table II, some attempts have recently been made to incorporate cottonseed flour[19] and dried vegetables.[20]

2.4 Shredding (Grinding, Milling)

This operation enables the emulsifying agent to come into intimate contact with the blend mass during processing.

2.5 Addition of Emulsifying Agents

Addition of emulsifying agents is the last step in preparing the blend for processing. Since the effects of emulsifying agents are responsible for the unique features of processed cheese production, their types and role will be described in a later section.

2.6 Processing

Processing means heat treatment of the blend, with direct or indirect steam, under partial vacuum and with constant agitation. If processing is carried out discontinuously, i.e. in a kettle, the temperature reached is 71–95°C for a period of 4–15 min (Table I), depending on various parameters;[3] this heating also provides a pasteurization effect. A new programmed jacketed processor has recently been developed,[21] which is used to grind, mix and process natural cheeses with other blend components, water and emulsifiers using steam injection and vacuum, at 75°C for 5 min. The processor is programmed via a punch-card for blend formulation and cleaning-in-place. The blend, after cooling, is discharged either by tilting the processor or by aseptic pumping to a packaging machine. When continuously processed, the blend is sterilized at temperatures of 130–145°C for 2–3 s in a battery of stainless steel tubes.[1] Zimmermann[22] obtained a patent in the Federal Republic of Germany which describes a continuous process for simultaneous melting, homogenization and sterilization in processed cheese production without application of pressure. A Japanese patent[23] describes a new method for the post-processing heat treatment (to 100°C) of packed processed cheese, produced in the usual way.

Some chemical, mechanical and thermal parameters in the cheese processing procedure are listed in Table III.

2.7 Homogenization (Optional)

Homogenization improves the stability of the fat emulsion by decreasing the average fat globule size. It also improves the consistency, structure, appearance and flavour of the processed cheese. However, since it involves unnecessary additional capital, operational and maintenance costs, and prolongs the production schedule, homogenization is recommended only for blends with high fat contents.

2.8 Packaging

Processed cheese is usually packed and wrapped in lacquered foil, in cardboard or plastic cartons and occasionally in glass jars. A relatively new development is the continuous slicing and packing of the cheese slices, suitable for sandwiches. Slices may also be obtained by mechanically slicing rectangular processed cheese blocks.

2.9 Cooling

There is a general rule for cooling processed cheeses: it should be as fast as possible for processed cheese spreads and relatively slow for processed cheese blocks (rapid cooling softens the product). However, slow cooling

TABLE III

Chemical, mechanical and thermal parameters as regulating factors in the cheese processing procedures[3] (reproduced by permission of the Food Trade Press Ltd)

Process conditions	Processed cheese block	Processed cheese spread
Raw material		
(a) Average age of cheese	Young to medium ripe, predominantly young	Combination of young, medium ripe, overipe
(b) Water insoluble N as a % of total N	75–90%	60–75%
(c) Structure	Predominantly long	Short to long
Emulsifying salt	Structure-building, not creaming, e.g. high molecular weight polyphosphate, citrate	Creaming, e.g. low and medium molecular weight polyphosphate
Water	10–25%	20–45%
Addition of water	All at once	In portions
Temperature	80–85°C	85–98°C (150°C)
Duration of processing	4–8 min	8–15 min
pH	5·4–5·6	5·7–5·9
Agitation	Slow	Rapid
Reworked cheese	0–2·0%	5–20%
Milk powder or whey powder	0	5–10%
Homogenization	None	Advantageous
Filling	5–15 min	10–30 min
Cooling	Slowly (10–20 h) at room temperature	Rapidly (15–30 min) in cool air

can intensify Maillard reactions and promote the growth of spore-forming bacteria.

2.10 Storage

The final product should be stored at temperatures below 10°C, although such low temperatures may induce crystal formation.

3. EMULSIFYING AGENTS: TYPES AND ROLE

Emulsifying agents (melting salts) are of major importance in processed cheese production where they are used to provide a uniform structure during the melting process. Phosphates, polyphosphates and citrates[2,25-28] are most common but sodium potassium tartrate[2,27] or complex sodium aluminium phosphates of the general formula

$$X\,Na_2O\,.\,Y\,Al_2O_3\,.\,8\,P_2O_5\,.\,Z\,H_2O$$

where $X = 6$–15, $Y = 1\cdot5$–$4\cdot5$ and $Z = 4$–40,[2] are also used. Sodium potassium tartrate, trihydroxyglutaric acid or diglycolic acid are rarely used. Some characteristics of the most commonly used emulsifying agents are presented in Table IV.

These compounds are not emulsifiers in the strict chemical sense (i.e. they are not surface active compounds), and since emulsification is not their only ability, melting salts are conditionally termed 'emulsifying agents'. However, true emulsifiers may be included in commercially-produced emulsifying agents, which are usually mixtures of compounds (Table II).

The essential role of the emulsifying agents in the manufacture of processed cheese is to supplement the emulsifying capability of cheese proteins. This is accomplished by:

1. removing calcium from the protein system;
2. peptizing, solubilizing and dispersing the proteins;
3. hydrating and swelling the proteins;
4. emulsifying the fat and stabilizing the emulsion;
5. controlling pH and stabilizing it; and
6. forming an appropriate structure after cooling.

The ability to sequester calcium is one of the most important functions of emulsifying agents. The principal caseins in cheese (α_{s1}-, α_{s2}-, β-) have non-polar, lipophilic C-terminal segments, while the N-terminal regions, which contain calcium phosphate, are hydrophilic (Fig. 1, Ref. 23). This structure allows the casein molecules to function as emulsifiers.[29-31] The solubility of casein in water, and hence its emulsifying capacity, are increased by reducing the Ca phosphate content; when calcium in the Ca–paracaseinate complex of natural cheese is removed by the ion exchange properties of melting salts, insoluble paracaseinate is solubilized, usually as Na caseinate. The affinity, i.e. sequestering ability, of the common emulsifiers for calcium increases in the following order: NaH_2PO_4, Na_2HPO_4, $Na_2H_2P_2O_7$, $Na_3HP_2O_7$, $Na_4P_2O_7$, $Na_5P_3O_{10}$.

Polyvalent anions (phosphates, citrates) have a high water-sorption ability. They become bound via calcium to protein molecules, providing them with a negative charge; basic salts also increase the pH of cheese. Both changes, i.e. increased negative charge and pH, result in higher water

TABLE IV

Emulsifying salts used in the processing of cheese[1,2,4] (reproduced by permission of Scanning Electron Microscopy Inc.)

Group	Emulsifying salt	Formula	Mol. mass	P_2O_5 content (%)	Solubility at 20°C (%)	pH value (1% solution)
Citrates	Trisodium citrate	$2Na_3C_6H_5O_7.11H_2O$	714·31	—	High	6·23–6·26
Orthophosphates	Monosodium phosphate	$NaH_2PO_4.2H_2O$	156·01	59·15	40	4·0–4·2
	Disodium phosphate	$Na_2HPO_4.12H_2O$	358·14	19·80	18	8·9–9·1
Pyrophosphates	Disodium pyrophosphate	$Na_2H_2P_2O_7$	221·94	63·96	10·7	4·0–4·5
	Trisodium pyrophosphate	$Na_3HP_2O_7.9H_2O$	406·06	34·95	32	6·7–7·5
	Tetrasodium pyrophosphate	$Na_4P_2O_7.10H_2O$	446·05	31·82	10–12	10·2–10·4
Polyphosphates	Pentasodium tripolyphosphate	$Na_5P_3O_{10}$	—	57·88	14–15	9·3–9·8
	Sodium tetrapolyphosphate	$Na_6P_4O_{13}$	—	60·42	14–15	9·0–9·5
	Sodium hexametaphosphate (Graham's salt)	$(NaPO_3)_n$	—	69·60	infinite	6·0–7·5

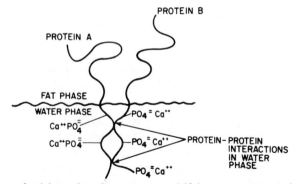

Fig. 1. Effect of calcium phosphate as an emulsifying agent on protein–protein interactions in processed cheese. According to Shimp[29] (reproduced by permission of the author and the Institute of Food Technologists).

sorption by the proteins. The concentrations of Ca and P are about twice as high in the insoluble phase of processed cheese as in the natural cheese from which it was made. The reactivity between the emulsifier and protein is defined by the ratio of insoluble to total proteins in the natural cheese and in the processed cheese.[25] The affinity of protein for the cations and anions of melting salts is determined by the valency of the ions.[32]

Salts consisting of a monovalent cation and a polyvalent anion possess the best emulsifying characteristics. Although some salts have better emulsifying properties than others, they may have inferior calcium-sequestering abilities or may not solubilize and hydrate the protein sufficiently. It is necessary to combine two or more salts into mixtures to achieve optimal emulsifying and melting characteristics simultaneously and to produce a homogeneous and stable processed cheese. An appropriate pH value is important for several reasons. It affects protein configuration and solubility and the extent to which the emulsifying salts bind calcium.[29] The pH of processed cheeses varies within the range 5·0–6·5. At pH $\sim 5·0$, which is near the isoelectric point of the proteins, the texture of the cheese may be crumbly, probably due to weakening of protein–protein bonds but the incidence of fat emulsion breakage is reduced. At pH $\sim 6·5$, the cheese becomes excessively soft and micro-biological problems may be encountered also. The effect of pH on the texture of processed cheese was clearly demonstrated by Karahadian,[33] using mono-, di- and trisodium phosphates, the respective pH of 1% solutions of which were 4·2, 9·5 and 13·0. Cheese made with the NaH_2PO_4 (low pH) was dry and crumbly whereas cheese made with Na_3PO_4 (high pH) was moist and elastic; the texture of cheese made with Na_2HPO_4 was intermediate. Similar pH-dependent effects apply also to other emulsifiers.[29]

Some emulsifying agents exhibit bacteriological effects. Monophosphates have a specific bacteriostatic effect which is even more pronounced with higher phosphates and polyphosphates.[1,2] Citrates lack such effects and may even be subject to bacterial spoilage. Since the usual heat treatment during processing is relatively mild, processed cheeses are not sterile; although the final product contains no viable bacteria, it may contain viable spores, including *Clostridia*, which may originate from the natural cheese or from added spices.[1,2,34] Orthophosphates suppress the germination of *Cl. botulinum* spores in processed cheese whereas citrates have no effect.[35] Differences in processing conditions, e.g. type of emulsifier, pH and moisture level, also affect spore germination.

The characteristics of individual melting salts and their mixtures have been studied extensively;[1,34,36-44] the effects of some emulsifying agents are summarized in Table V.

3.1 Phosphates

Two types of phosphates are used:

(a) Monophosphates (orthophosphates), e.g. NaH_2PO_4; Na_2HPO_4; Na_3PO_4.

(b) Condensed polyphosphates:
—polyphosphates
—metaphosphates—rings, e.g. $Na_3P_3O_9$; $Na_4P_4O_{12}$
—condensed phosphates—rings with chains and branches.

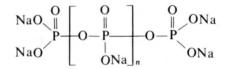

The ability to sequester calcium is closely related to the ability to solubilize protein. According to von der Heide,[45] the solubilization of fat-free rennet casein was 30% with orthophosphate, 45% with pyrophosphate and 85% with polyphosphate. Similar findings were made by Daclin.[46] The concentration of soluble nitrogen increased with the concentration of polyphosphates added in the range from 1 to 3%.[47] Hydrolysis of polyphosphates to orthophosphates in processed cheese was evident after

TABLE V

Characteristics of emulsifiers most commonly used in the manufacture of processed cheese and related products[1] (reproduced by permission of Scanning Electron Microscopy Inc.)

Emulsifier[a]	Characteristics
Sodium citrate	Versatile: produces cheese with good melting properties; inexpensive; best qualities
Disodium phosphate	Good firming, buffering and melting properties; poor creaming properties, least expensive
Trisodium phosphate	Highly alkaline; improves sliceability when used in combination with other emulsifiers; good buffering capacity; used at low concentrations
Sodium hexametaphosphate (Graham's salt)	Produces tartish flavour and a very firm body; product does not melt easily; least soluble of all; bacteriostatic
Tetrasodium diphosphate	Good creaming properties; strong buffering capacity; high protein solubility; excellent ion exchange; tartish flavour

[a] Other emulsifiers permitted by the US Federal Standards of Identity are: sodium acid pyrophosphate, sodium potassium tartrate, tetrasodium pyrophosphate, dipotassium phosphate, potassium citrate, calcium citrate and sodium aluminium phosphate.

cooling. The calcium-sequestering ability of sodium metaphosphate is markedly lower than that of sodium tetrametaphosphate; a smooth homogeneous processed cheese is obtained with the latter salt.[48,49] Differences in depolymerization of casein and changes in the flow properties of processed cheese are related to differences in calcium complexation between mono- and tetrapolyphosphates.[50]

Melting rate, ultrafiltrable calcium concentration and textural properties (stress/relaxation, hardness, gumminess and elasticity) of processed cheese are affected more by varying the condensed phosphate than the polyphosphate concentrations.[51] Scharpf[52] suggested that the emulsifying effect of chain phosphates is associated with their interaction with paracasein in such a way that phosphate anions form bridges between protein molecules.

Processed cheese of good quality can be produced using 1% of a surface-active monoglyceride preparation in combination with 50% of the usual amount of phosphate.[53] A processed cheese with improved rheological properties and storage stability can be produced using an emulsifier consisting of tripolyphosphate and monoglycerides.[54] Addition of monoglycerides to the cheese blend increases the hydrophilic properties of the cheese immediately after processing as well as during storage.[55]

All condensed polyphosphates hydrolyse in aqueous solutions; hydrolysis also occurs during melting and afterwards. The degradation of polyphosphates increases with the duration of processing, irrespective of the rate of stirring and the temperature used.[56] About 50% of the polyphosphates added are hydrolysed during the melting procedure and the remainder are hydrolysed after 7–10-week storage.[57]

3.2 Citrates

Of the many citrates available, only trisodium citrate, alone or in combination with other salts, is used as an emulsifying agent in processed cheese production; citric acid may be used to correct the pH of the cheese. Potassium citrate imparts a bitter taste to the finished product. Monosodium citrate is reported[2] to cause emulsion breakdown during cheese melting because of its high acidity, while disodium citrate leads to water separation during solidification of the melt, also because of high acidity. Comparison of the effects of sodium citrate, sodium citrophosphate and sodium potassium tartrate on chemical changes in processed cheese showed[26] that the highest and the lowest acidity were obtained with citrophosphate and tartrate, respectively. Soluble nitrogen was higher in all three processed cheeses than in the initial natural cheese and was highest when Na citrate was used as emulsifier.

Trisodium citrate and Na_2HPO_4 have similar effects on cheese consistency and yield softer cheeses than several polyphosphates; the effect of the latter on cheese firmness increases with the degree of phosphate condensation.[58] The effects of citrate, orthophosphate, pyrophosphate, tripolyphosphate and Graham's salt $[(NaPO_3)_n.H_2O]$ on the physico-chemical properties of processed cheese were examined by Kairyukshtene *et al.*[25] The pH values of 3% solutions of these salts were 8·16, 8·89, 6·61, 9·31 and 5·49, respectively. Soluble protein contents in processed cheeses were increased and the water-binding capacity and plasticity of the cheese blends during processing were markedly improved by the use of the alkaline salts. The finest fat dispersions were obtained with citrate, tripolyphosphate or orthophosphate in the processing of fresh curds or green cheese, and by using citrate or Graham's salt with well-ripened cheese.

Addition of citrate, orthophosphate, pyrophosphate or sodium potassium tartrate, all at 3%, to curds obtained from concentrated milk led to products with poor sensory attributes, although citrate at 2% gave satisfactory results.[27]

3.3 Salt Combinations

As already mentioned, salt mixtures are used to combine the best effects of their individual components.[34,36-38,40-44] Some early results[40,42] seem to favour citrate in melting salt combinations but more recent studies emphasize the desirable effects of phosphates.

According to Shubin,[40] a combination of sodium citrate, trihydroxy-glutarate and Na_2HPO_4 gave best results in the manufacture of processed cheese. Earlier work[42] showed that orthophosphates and pyrophosphates were generally unsatisfactory, whether used alone or in a combination, but citrate was useful to a limited extent; polyphosphates were satisfactory in every respect.

Thomas *et al.*[43] produced processed cheeses with a 3% addition of disodium phosphate, tetrasodium diphosphate, pentasodium triphosphate or trisodium citrate or equal quantities of sodium polyphosphate and tetrasodium phosphate. The general acceptability of all cheeses was about the same but cheeses made with disodium phosphate, tetrasodium diphosphate or pentasodium triphosphate had elevated contents of water-soluble nitrogen compared to the other cheeses. When the melting salts were used at 2% or 4%, no differences were detected in the levels of water-soluble nitrogen in any of the processed cheeses or in their stickiness, crumbliness, sliceability or general acceptability.

In general, polyphosphates yield processed cheese with superior structure and better keeping quality than other emulsifying agents,[36] apparently due to their ability to solubilize calcium paracaseinate because of their high calcium-sequestering capacity. Pyrophosphates and, in particular, orthophosphates contribute undesirable sensory attributes to the processed cheese and although citrates are as efficient emulsifiers as polyphosphates, they lack their bacteriostatic effect.

Sood and Kosikowski[44] investigated the possibility of replacing cheese solids with untreated or enzyme-modified skim-milk retentates in the manufacture of processed Cheddar cheese. Casein in the retentates was largely insoluble, and therefore the retentates cannot be used alone for processing. However, cheese containing up to 60% of retentate solids (treated with fungal protease and lipase preparations) had better sensory attributes than the reference cheese; a combination of sodium citrate (2·7%) and citric acid (0·3%) was the best emulsifier for retentate-containing cheese. Increasing the retentate content to 80% resulted in an unacceptable product with a hard, long-grained texture.

4. MICROSTRUCTURE OF PROCESSED CHEESE

Optical microscopy has been used to observe various stages of cheese processing, from assessing the suitability of natural cheeses for processing to checking the finished product. Boháč[59] suggested that the selection of natural cheeses for processing should be based on their interaction with melting salt solutions during heating to 85–95°C. The interactions were observed using a polarizing microscope equipped with a heated stage. A movie camera attached to the microscope made it possible to record the behaviour of the samples using time-lapse photography. Several phenomena were observed, such as the disintegration of some cheese samples along curd granule junctions as the temperature was increased above 70°C or the formation of a diffuse zone consisting of protein and fat. Some cheese samples were found to contract at 60–70°C but not to melt until the temperature reached 95–98°C. Rapid diffusion of ripe and over-ripened cheeses into the melting salt solution was commonly observed even before the melting temperature had been reached. The amount of fat released from the cheese sample under study and the temperature at which

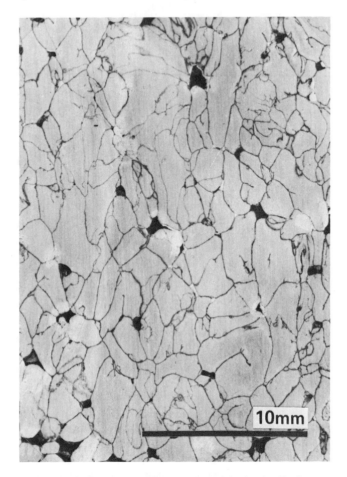

Fig. 2. Curd granule junctions (dark lines) in Brick cheese. Dark areas are air pockets in the cheese.

the cheese melted were taken into consideration when assessing a particular cheese for processing.

Solubilization of regular as well as instantized melting salts during cheese processing was also investigated using polarizing microscopy.[59] Light micrographs of various defects in processed cheeses, particularly the development of salt crystals, have been reproduced by Meyer.[3]

Electron microscopy has been used to study the microstructure of natural and processed cheeses in greater detail than is possible by optical

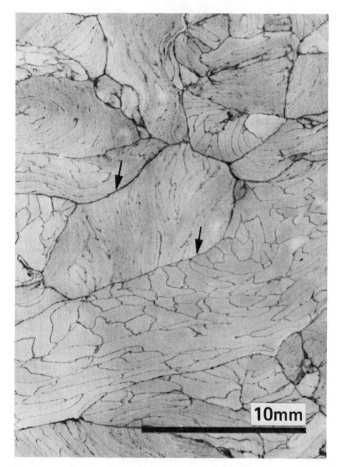

Fig. 3. Curd granule junctions (thin lines) and milled curd junctions (thick lines—arrows) form characteristic patterns in Cheddar cheese depending on manufacturing conditions.

microscopy. One of the most suitable techniques used to prepare cheese samples for scanning electron microscopy (SEM) involves so-called freeze-fracturing.[60] This procedure provides smooth fracture planes by which the extent of fat emulsification and the distribution of fat globules may be evaluated and other processed cheese components such as various crystalline inclusions, lactic acid bacteria and some other corpuscular ingredients may be detected. For transmission electron microscopy (TEM), the cheese is embedded in a resin; thin sections obtained from the embedded

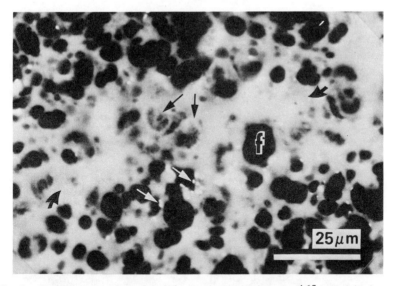

Fig. 4. Fluorescence microscopy of a curd granule junction[4,67] in Brick cheese (light area between large black arrows). f = fat globules; small black arrows point to calcium phosphate crystals and white arrows point to lactic acid bacteria appearing as white dots (courtesy of S. H. Yiu).

cheese are stained and examined. TEM makes it possible to study cheese samples at magnifications considerably higher than those attainable by SEM. Taneya *et al.*[61] replicated freeze-fractured cheese with platinum and carbon and examined the replicas.

Natural cheese slices, fixed in glutaraldehyde, defatted, dried and polished, reveal characteristic curd granule patterns when examined under an optical microscope at a very low magnification.[62–65] The patterns are simple in stirred-curd cheeses such as Brick cheese (Fig. 2) but are more complex in Cheddar cheese (Fig. 3), where an additional kind of so-called 'milled curd junction' develops as the result of milling cheddared curd. Optical as well as electron microscopy[62,63,66,67] reveal that curd granule junctions are areas depleted of fat (Figs 4 and 5). Fat globules in young natural cheese retain their membranes even when the globules occur in large clusters (Fig. 6).

Through electron microscopy, it is known that curd granule junctions and fat globule membranes disappear during processed cheese manufacture as the result of heating, melting and stirring. Calcium-sequestering agents convert the relatively insoluble proteins of natural cheese into a

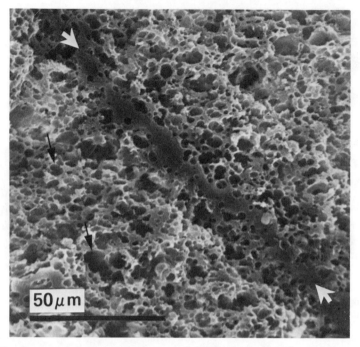

Fig. 5. Scanning electron microscopy of Brick cheese reveals a curd granule junction as a relatively compact protein structure between white arrows.[4] Extraction of fat globules during preparation of sample for microscopy left void spaces (black arrows) in the protein matrix.

smooth and homogeneous mass of partially solubilized proteins in processed cheese. As the emulsifying properties of the cheese proteins are improved in the presence of the melting salts, fat becomes emulsified into small globules,[68,69] which may be only several micrometres in diameter (Figs 7, 8 and 11–14).

Some crystalline inclusions present in natural cheese,[70–73] particularly those composed of insoluble calcium phosphate, are not affected by processing (Fig. 7). In addition to calcium phosphate aggregates, which can be as large as 30 μm in diameter, other inclusions may consist of calcium lactate (in randomly arranged aggregates up to 80 μm in diameter),[71,72] or crystalline amino acids such as tyrosine[74] or calcium tyrosinate.[2]

During processing, calcium which is present in the natural cheese reacts with soluble phosphates of the emulsifying agents to form insoluble calcium phosphate crystals.[1] Such crystals are apparent in processed cheese

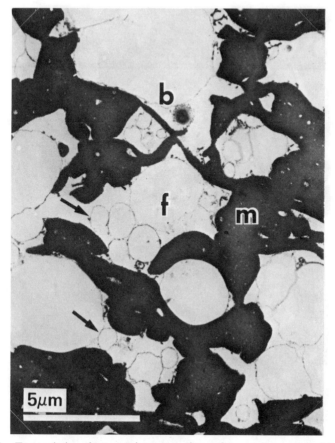

Fig. 6. Transmission electron microscopy shows the protein matrix (m) in 1-day-old Cheddar cheese interspersed with fat globules (f) encased in fat globule membranes (arrows).[4]

through microscopy (Figs 7–10 and 12). Yiu[67] identified calcium phosphate crystals in processed cheese by optical microscopy using Alizarin Red as a stain specific for calcium (Fig. 10). When sodium diphosphate was used as a melting salt,[69] the calcium phosphate crystals which were initially present in the cheese continued to grow and developed fine spikes on the crystal surfaces (Fig. 10). Anhydrous phosphates were reported to absorb water and form large aggregates.[1] Tinyakov and Barkan[75] established that the incidence of insoluble crystals in processed cheese which was made with sodium citrate as the emulsifying agent was lower, and crystal aggregates

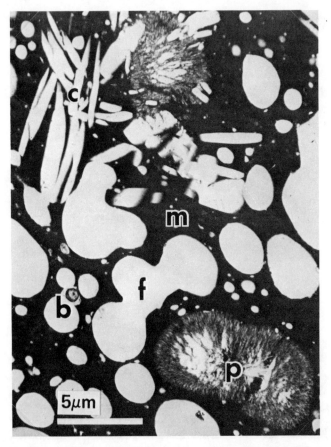

Fig. 7. During processing, fat (f) in the cheese becomes emulsified; crystalline sodium citrate (c) added as an emulsifying agent gradually dissolves in the aqueous phase of the protein matrix (m). Calcium phosphate crystals (p) are insoluble (transmission electron microscopy of a thin section[4]).

were smaller, than in processed cheese which was made with sodium phosphate.

Small white crystals identified as calcium citrate occasionally develop on the surface of processed cheese as early as one week after manufacture.[76] The development of such crystals was prevented by eliminating sodium citrate from the emulsifying agent used. Crystals of a tertiary sodium calcium citrate, $NaCaC_6H_5O_7$, in a processed cheese were identified and reported by Klostermeyer *et al.*[77]

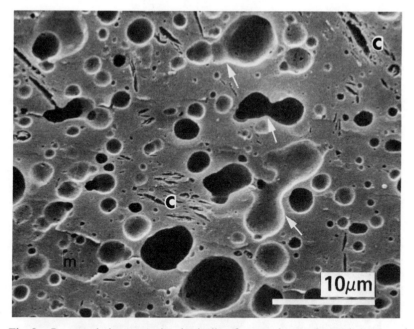

Fig. 8. Processed cheese consists basically of a protein matrix (m) interspersed with fat globules. Arrows point to incompletely emulsified fat particles. Needle-like void spaces (c) indicate that an emulsifying salt such as sodium citrate was used in excess (scanning electron microscopy of a defatted sample).

Melting salt crystals may be present in processed cheese as the result of using an excessively high concentration of the melting salt or because the salt does not dissolve completely in the cheese during processing.[78] Melting salt crystals usually appear different from the crystals of calcium phosphate which are present initially in the natural cheese. Sodium citrate may occur as needles (Fig. 11); being soluble in water, the crystals are washed out of the cheese during preparative steps for electron microscopy. Void spaces in the fixed protein matrix (imprints) are visualized by electron microscopy (Figs 7 and 11) but the crystals themselves are not.

Examination of three commercial processed cheeses (one sample of processed Cheddar cheese and two samples of processed Gruyère cheese) by SEM revealed considerable differences among the samples as far as emulsification of fat and the incidence of melting salt crystals were concerned[4] (Figs 12–14). Salt crystals were quite rare in the processed Cheddar cheese sample which was made with the declared use of sodium

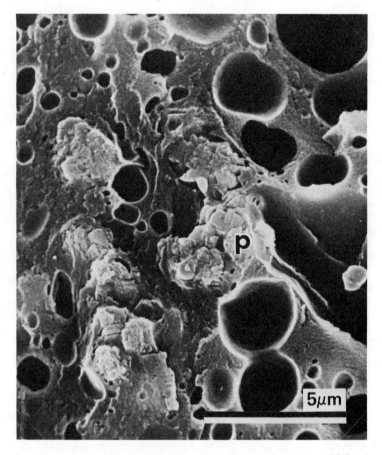

Fig. 9. Calcium phosphate crystals (p) may originate from the initial natural cheese or develop in processed cheese made with phosphate-based emulsifying agents (scanning electron microscopy).

phosphate, sodium-aluminium phosphate, sodium triphosphate and sodium citrate. It was assumed, based on their appearance, that most of the salt crystals observed originated in the natural cheese (Fig. 12). However, energy dispersive spectrometry of some of the crystals revealed the presence of aluminium (Fig. 15). Fat was emulsified to a greater extent in both samples of processed Gruyère cheese than in the processed Cheddar cheese, where fat globules up to 20 μm in diameter were found. In the processed Gruyère cheeses (Figs 13 and 14), the fat globules

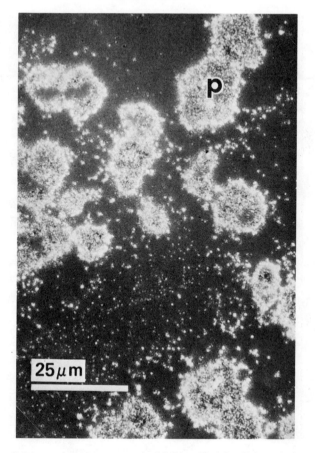

Fig. 10. Calcium phosphate crystals (p) identified by light microscopy using staining with Alizarin Red specific for calcium[4] (courtesy of S. H. Yiu).

did not exceed $5\,\mu m$ in diameter. SEM also revealed the high incidence of salt crystals in both the Gruyère cheeses. Crystal aggregates were larger (Fig. 13) and were spaced at greater distances in the cheese made with sodium-calcium citrate than in the cheese made with sodium citrate (Fig. 14). Interestingly, the citrate crystals in the latter processed Gruyère cheese had not been washed out during preparative steps for electron microscopy, and calcium, phosphorus, sodium and sulphur featured prominently in energy dispersive spectra of those crystals present.

In contrast to the commercial processed cheese examined, no salt crystals

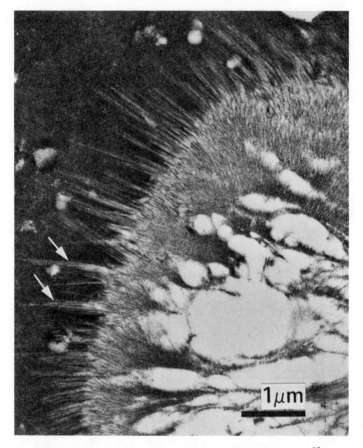

Fig. 11. Salt crystallization (arrows) as observed by Rayan *et al.*[69] in processed cheese made with disodium phosphate used as an emulsifying agent.

were present in processed cheese made by heating a cheese blend with direct steam.[4]

Electron microscopic studies on protein matrices[61,77,79] of soft and hard processed cheeses using thin-sectioning and freeze-fracturing techniques showed that protein in a soft cheese (made with a mixture of 1·0% sodium citrate and 1·5% polyphosphate) consisted predominantly of individual particles (Fig. 16) whereas the protein matrix of a hard cheese (made with 2·2% polyphosphate) contained a high proportion of protein in the form of long strands (Fig. 17). The authors[61,77,79] assumed that the protein strands

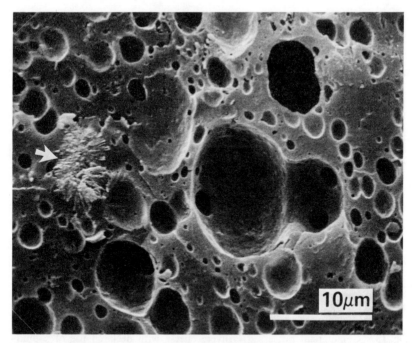

Fig. 12. Commercial processed Cheddar cheese with declared use of sodium phosphate, sodium-aluminium phosphate, sodium triphosphate, and sodium citrate. Fat globule dimensions vary widely (up to 20 μm in diameter). The incidence of salt crystals (arrow) is very low.

in the hard-type processed cheese contributed to the ability to retain its shape upon heating. Heertje *et al.*[80] confirmed the existence of protein in the form of strands in processed cheese. Abundant protein strands were also found in a soft processed cheese made using a combined phosphate–polyphosphate emulsifying agent and direct steam heating (Figs 18 and 19; Kaláb and Carić, unpublished results). The use of White cheese (made by acidifying hot milk and having a characteristic core-and-lining ultrastructure of the casein particles[81,82]) in the blend could be detected in processed cheese. Tinyakov[83] reported that processed cheese contains microvacuoles, the variation in size and shape of which depends on the type of the cheese being examined. A fibrous structure resulted in cheese made using sodium citrate.

In spite of the apparent abundance of information on the microstructure of processed cheese presented in this section, microscopists have not given processed cheese the attention it deserves. Yet, microscopy can contribute

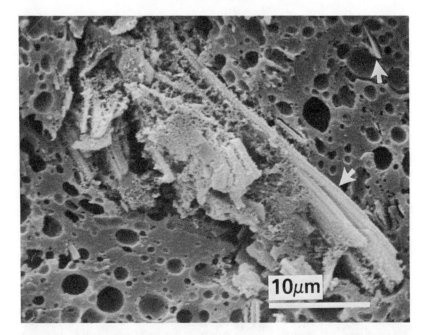

Fig. 13. Commercial processed Gruyère cheese with declared use of sodium-calcium citrate. Fat globules are smaller than in the preceding cheese but salt crystals (arrows) are abundant.

to a better understanding of the many changes taking place at all stages of cheese processing and storage, including changes leading to the development of defects and their prevention. It may be assumed that specific staining techniques will some day be used routinely in optical microscopy of processed cheese and the rapid technique of fluorescence microscopy, which is capable of detecting ingredients and contaminants with great sensitivity, will be used to a greater extent. An extended use of energy dispersive spectrometry and digital image analysis in association with electron microscopy is also anticipated.

5. QUALITY DEFECTS OF PHYSICO-CHEMICAL AND MICROBIAL ORIGIN

A good processed cheese should have a smooth, homogeneous structure, a uniform colour and be free from fermentation gas holes.

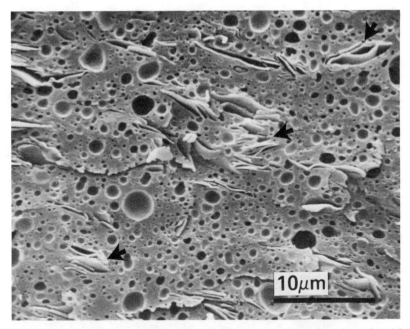

Fig. 14. Commercial processed Gruyère cheese of another brand made with sodium citrate. Fat is emulsified into minute globules. Abundant small foliate crystals (arrows) are oriented in one direction.

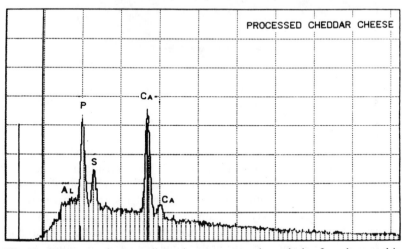

PROCESSED CHEDDAR CHEESE

Fig. 15. Diagram of energy dispersive spectrometric analysis of a salt crystal in commercial processed Cheddar cheese,[4] showing the peaks of aluminum (Al), phosphorus (P), sulphur (S), and calcium (Ca) (courtesy of S. H. Yiu).

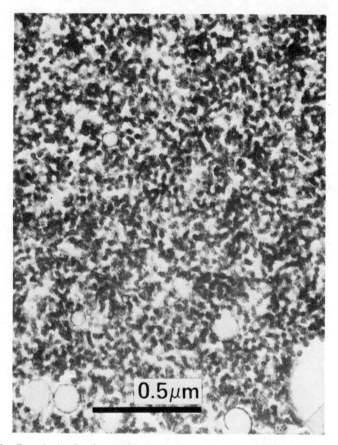

Fig. 16. Protein in the form of individual particles in the matrix of processed cheese of the soft type made with a mixture of 1% sodium citrate and 1·5% sodium polyphosphate[4] (courtesy of T. Kimura).

Various factors can cause physico-chemical or microbial defects. The most important factors are (a) an unsuitable blend arising from the use of poor quality or contaminated natural cheese, a bad relationship of blend components, cheese containing poor-quality proteins, an improper protein/fat ratio, irregular quality or quantity of emulsifying agent, incorrect values for pH, moisture content or quantity of reworked cheese; and (b) inadequate processing, e.g. unsuitable time–temperature regimes, inadequate agitation, improper cooling, unsuitable storage. The first step towards the solution of the problem is to identify the cause by checking all

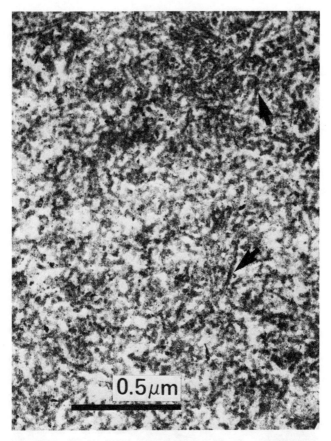

Fig. 17. Protein strands (arrows) present in the matrix of a processed cheese of the hard type made with 2·2% sodium polyphosphate[4] (courtesy of T. Kimura).

parameters which could be responsible for the defect. Although processing parameters might be changed unintentionally during processing, causing quality defects in the final product, most frequently the reason for defects is related to an improper blend.

Possible defects of physico-chemical and microbial origin in processed cheese, their causes and suggestions for their correction are presented in Table VI. Many of the defects described are carry-overs from the natural cheese used in the blend and some can be avoided by proper processing. Once the cause has been established and eliminated, the defect will disappear in subsequent batches. Processed cheese with certain minor

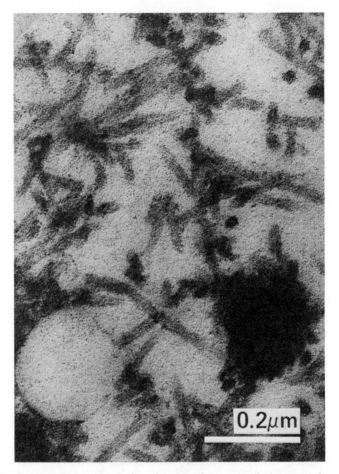

Fig. 18. Long protein strands found in a soft processed cheese made using a combined sodium phosphate–polyphosphate emulsifying agent and direct steam heating (M. Kaláb and M. Carić, unpublished results).

defects can be recovered by reworking small quantities of it into subsequent batches but more severe defects cannot be corrected as they make processed cheese unsuitable for human consumption (e.g. microbial changes, presence of metal ions, excessive Maillard browning) or even dangerous to human health (e.g. *Cl. botulinum* toxin). Crystal formation and discoloration are among the most common physico-chemical defects in processed cheese.

Crystal formation, sometimes visible to the naked eye, is a serious defect

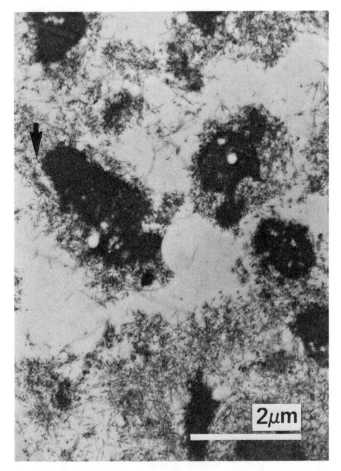

Fig. 19. The use of white cheese in the cheese blend may be detected in processed cheese by transmission electron microscopy on the basis of a characteristic core-and-lining ultrastructure[81,82] of casein particles (arrow) (M. Kaláb and M. Carić, unpublished results).

in processed cheese. A common reason for crystal formation is a low solubility of the emulsifying agent used. This condition is aggravated by the use of excessive amounts of emulsifying agent, a high calcium content in the natural cheese, a high pH and storage of the processed cheese at low temperatures. A poorly soluble component in the emulsifying agent either dissolves incompletely during processing or recrystallizes during cooling.

TABLE VI
Defects in processed cheese[1-3]

Defect	Cause	Correction (solution)
Flavour		
Mouldy	Air contamination, mouldy raw cheese	Use hermetically sealed foils; eliminate all mouldy cheeses from the blend
Empty	Too much young cheese in blend	Correct blend composition
Sharp	Too much mature cheese in blend	Correct blend composition
Bitter, rancid	Over-ripe cheese, mould-ripened cheese or off-flavoured butter in blend	Change blend composition, e.g. add young cheese
Sour, slightly bitter	Sour raw cheese in blend	Add more mature cheese (with higher pH); use emulsifying agent with higher pH
Salty	Salty raw cheese or other components; too much emulsifier	Add young, unsalted cheese or fresh curd to blend; decrease the quantity of emulsifier
Chemical flavour	Off-flavoured natural cheese; certain preservatives; unclean steam; impure emulsifying agent	Remove bad-flavoured components from blend; check steam for purity
Sweet	Blown raw cheese; blowing in processed cheese	Correct cheese blend composition
Sweet-salty	Too much whey concentrate or whey	Reduce quantity of whey products in blend
Soapy	High pH value (>6·2)	Add younger cheese (with lower pH value); use emulsifying agent with lower pH value
Putrid	Over-ripe and putrid raw cheese; presence of *Clostridia* in processed cheese	Proper selection of raw cheese blend
Metallic, oily	Traces of metal ions (Cu, Fe, etc.) which oxidize the fat; presence of other oxidants	Eliminate component(s) containing traces of metal ions
Burnt	Overheating in the presence of lactose and by indirect steam (thermal degradation of lactose)	Keep the heating temperatures <90°C and use indirect steam up to 70°C when the blend contains lactose
Burnt with browning	Maillard reaction (lactose and amino acids); usually when very young cheese or whey products are present	Use processing temperatures <90°C; cool processed cheese immediately after packaging; avoid large containers; store <30°C; avoid high pH value in final product

Texture (body, consistency)

Too soft	High moisture; improper emulsifier; insufficient emulsifier; high pH; fast cooling; excess ripe cheese in blend; prolonged processing. Slow agitation	Reduce water content; use suitable emulsifier; increase emulsifier content; decrease pH; slower cooling; increase proportion of young cheese in blend; reduce processing time; increase agitation speed
Too hard	Low moisture; improper emulsifier; excess emulsifier; low pH; slow cooling; improper blend; excess creamed or over-creamed, reworked cheese	Increase water content; use proper emulsifier; decrease emulsifier content; increase pH; faster cooling; change blend composition; avoid addition of creamed or over-creamed reworked cheese
Gum-like (cheese spread)	Excess young cheese; improper emulsifier; absence of reworked cheese in blend; all water added at once; short processing; slow agitation	Increase proportion of ripe cheese; use of proper emulsifier; add reworked cheese to blend; add water in more increments; increase processing time; increase agitation speed
Hard, showing water leakage during storage	Colloidal change in cheese structure ('overcreaming'); bacteriological action leading to reduced pH	Remove all factors which effect excess creaming; choose blend components carefully; keep processing temperatures >85°C
Inhomogeneous (grainy)	Unsuitable blend; improper emulsifier; insufficient or excess emulsifier; low pH; short processing time; low processing temperature; improper amount of added water; inadequate agitation; colloidal or bacteriological changes caused by improper storage	Add younger cheese; use suitable emulsifier; correct emulsifier quantity; correct pH; prolong processing time in order to provide a homogeneous mass; increase processing temperature >85°C; increase the amount of added water; continue agitation during processing and filling; cold storage without pressure or freezing
Water separation	Colloidal change in cheese structure ('overcreaming'); bacteriological growth; unsuitable storage	Remove all factors which cause excess creaming; choose blend components carefully; keep processing temperatures >85°C; cold storage without pressure or freezing

(continued)

TABLE VI—contd.

Defect	Cause	Correction (solution)
Fat separation	Overripe raw cheese; insufficient or excess emulsifier; hydrolysis or poor calcium-binding capacity of emulsifying agent; low moisture; processing time too long or too short	Increase proportion of young cheese; correct quantity of emulsifier; use correct emulsifying agent; increase amount of water added; use binding agents
Sticky (adhering to lid foil)	Sticky foil, insufficiently impregnated; excessively high pH; processed mass left hot too long without agitation	Change aluminium foil; decrease water addition and if possible add in two portions; increase proportion of ripe cheese or cause better creaming; keep pH <60; continue agitation until packaging
Appearance Holes (blown)	Bacteriological changes (growth of *Clostridia*, coliform or propionic bacteria); physical changes (occluded air, CO_2 from emulsifier mixture (citrates), holes filled up with fluid from emulsifying agent having low solubility); chemical changes (hydrogen from reaction between processed cheese and Al foil)	Select cheese blend components carefully; keep processing temperatures >95°C; use proper vacuum; preheat citrate emulsifier before processing; extend processing time; test porosity of Al foil and if necessary, change it
Crystals	Calcium diphosphate and calcium monophosphate crystals (when these anions are used in emulsifying agent); calcium crystals (when citrates are used in emulsifying agent); further crystal formation when sandy reworked cheese is used in blend; crystals due to undissolved emulsifying salt; large crystals due to excess emulsifier; lactose crystal formation, caused by excess whey concentrates or low water content; light coloured, soft, grainy precipitate of tyrosine (very mature cheese in blend)	Avoid mono- and diphosphates as emulsifying agents, or combinations with higher phosphates and polyphosphates; exclude citrates from emulsifying agent; exclude sandy reworked cheese from blend; distribute emulsifying agent better; increase processing time; add emulsifying agent in solution (if necessary); use prescribed quantity of emulsifier, reduce level of whey products and increase water content; exclude raw cheese which contains tyrosine crystals
Mottles	Mechanical faults due to filling; physico-chemical changes (only when citrate is used as emulsifier)	Continuous filling; empty filler hopper before filling with a new charge; use equal mass and processing parameters in different cookers; use strong, short agitation before filling; eliminate ~~air~~ ~~from emulsifying agent~~

Some emulsifying agents react with calcium in the cheese, producing insoluble calcium salts (e.g. calcium phosphate and calcium tartrate). Using electron microscopy, light microscopy, energy dispersive spectrometric analysis, Debye–Scherrer X-ray analysis and other instrumental methods, crystals in processed cheese have been characterized and chemically identified as calcium phosphate, calcium citrate, sodium calcium citrate or disodium phosphate.[1,4,43,69,76,77] Crystal formation in processed cheese as influenced by the presence of emulsifying agents is shown in Figs 7–15.

In addition to the emulsifying agents, lactose and free tyrosine may be responsible for the development of crystals in processed cheese, particularly if these substances are present at excessively high concentrations.[1,2]

Discoloration or browning is a defect in processed cheese caused by the Maillard reaction (non-enzymic browning), when the product develops a dark brown or pink colour. It starts at elevated temperatures and continues autocatalytically. Since the main reactants in Maillard browning are amino compounds and reducing sugars, the products most susceptible to these changes are blends containing high levels of young cheese (and thus a high concentration of lactose) and other lactose-containing ingredients. Comparing the intensity of non-enzymic browning in processed cheese spreads and processed cheese blocks, Thomas[2] points out that more intense browning occurs in spreads because of higher processing temperatures, longer processing times, a higher water content, a higher lactose content and a higher pH.

Bley *et al.*[84] found a high correlation ($r = 0.929$) between the galactose content and brown colour intensity in processed cheese and showed that the intensity of the browning reaction could be reduced by using a galactose-fermenting strain of *Str. thermophilus*, together with a mesophilic lactic starter culture, in curd production. On the other hand, a high salt concentration increased browning, possibly by suppressing the activity of the lactic acid starter culture. However, the Maillard reaction did not occur to a significant extent in processed cheese, regardless of the sugar or salt contents, if it was cooled very quickly.

Borlja[85] investigated the development of non-enzymic browning in industrial processed cheeses using an unusually severe laboratory heat treatment (95°C, 110°C or 120°C for 60 min) after manufacture. Increasing the heat treatment intensified the Maillard reaction, which started during processing, showing the functionality of a square polynome:

$$y = M - Nx + Ox^2 \quad \text{(Ref. 2)}$$

where M, N and O are constants, which were calculated for each sample.

The total thermal treatment to which processed cheese containing a high level of reworked cheese is exposed is more severe than normal and, consequently, the Maillard reaction is more extensive. Most noticeable are the levels of melanoidins in sterilized processed cheese, even if it is cooled immediately after production and stored, hermetically packed, at low temperature.[86]

Microbial defects in processed cheese are caused by spore-forming bacteria, which usually originate in the cheese milk and enter the processed cheese blend through the natural cheese used for blending; other sources of microbial contamination, e.g. water supply, equipment or additives, are less common.[1-3,87,88] Contamination after processing is not common since the processing temperature is high enough to destroy vegetative bacterial cells and pasteurize the wrapping material (aluminium foil). Recontamination by viable bacteria or moulds can occur only if the foil is defective or becomes damaged.

The most important spore-forming bacteria, which cause defects in processed cheese by producing gas, with or without off-odours, belong to the genera *Clostridium* (*Cl. butyricum*, *Cl. tyrobutyricum*, *Cl. histolyticum*, *Cl. sporogenes*, *Cl. perfringens*) and *Bacillus* (*B. licheniformis*, *B. polymyxa*). Some of these species also cause discoloration or proteolysis in processed cheese, or produce toxins. Karahadian *et al.*[89] found that glucono-δ-lactone, added for acidity, delayed toxinogenesis in processed cheese. Whether produced continuously or in a batch cooker, processed cheese is not sterile. Although it is well known that heat treatment weakens spores, some authors have reported an increased germination ability following heat treatment, due to the destruction of inhibitory factors or due to stimulation by heat treatment. Germination of spores after processing is influenced by various factors, e.g. blend composition, NaCl concentration, type and concentration of emulsifying agent, water level, pH, the presence or absence of natural inhibitors. However, there are a number of possible ways to prevent spore outgrowth: preservatives in the cheese blend, sterilization of the processed cheese or an increased redox potential of the blend (effective against clostridial spores).

6. PROCESSED CHEESE ANALOGUES

Nowadays, there are two recognized groups of products which do not belong to the classical range of dairy products: (a) modified dairy products, and (b) substitute (or imitation) dairy products.[90-92] In modified dairy products, only one dairy component, e.g. protein or fat, is substituted by a non-dairy component for economic or nutritional reasons. Imitation products are based on novel components, frequently produced by newly-developed technological procedures. Some imitation products contain no dairy components. Although traditionally oriented experts still hold reservations on imitation products, these products have found their 'raison d'être' in both developed and developing countries. In the USA, processed cheese analogues exist on the market in parallel with 'conventional' cheese products, and have been used in the National School lunch programme. As Kosikowski[1] says, by 1990 we will need all the proteins and joules that can be obtained through conventional and novel food sources.

Processed cheese belongs to the group of dairy products where substitution of one or more dairy ingredients does not cause technical or technological problems. From the nutritional viewpoint, the blend for modified or imitation (simulated) processed cheeses can easily be enriched with necessary or desirable microcomponents, e.g. vitamins and minerals. On the other hand, the blend can be tailored in such a way as to yield a less expensive product and, therefore, be economically attractive. Essential components are: casein and caseinates (Na, Ca, etc.) and also other proteins (soya, coconut, gluten, etc.), suitable vegetable fats, flavourings, vitamins and minerals, food grade acids (e.g. lactic, citric) to correct the pH to 5·8–5·9, and emulsifying agents. Similar processing parameters (Table I) and equipment are used as for traditional processed cheeses, giving a product of similar physico-chemical and microbiological characteristics. The common composition of processed cheese analogues is given in Table I.

Numerous investigations have recently been carried out in order to find new possibilities in this new field. Rosenau[93] developed a method for the successful pilot plant production of a processed cheese based on dairy, non-cheese components: skim-milk was acidified with HCl to pH 4·6, the coagulum was separated and processed in the usual way with emulsifying agents and other additives. Kirchmeier *et al.*[94] investigated the solubility, dispersibility and colloidal stability of sodium and calcium caseinate dispersions; the rheograms obtained showed that the sol state of these dispersions was the same as that of processed cheese. Egyptian workers[95] included 20% Ras cheese (manufactured from recombined milk using a microbial enzyme) in a processed cheese blend containing the following ingredients: 20% natural cheese, 40% dried skim-milk curd, 7% butter oil, water and 3% emulsifier. Modification of processed cheese by incorporating vegetable oil in the blend improved cheese flavour and resulted in a 25–50%

saving of butter.[96] Various attempts have also been made to develop combined food products which contain processed cheese but with different basic characteristics. For example, a nutritious chocolate product, composed of 50% bitter chocolate and 50% processed cheese, emulsified, solidified, frozen and coated with chocolate, was developed and patented in the UK.[97]

ACKNOWLEDGEMENTS

The authors thank Dr L. A. Shimp, Dr S. H. Yiu and Dr T. Kimura for permission to reproduce micrographs in Figs 1, 4, 10, 16 and 17; Fig. 1 is reproduced with permission from *Food Technology* (Institute of Food Technologists, Chicago) and Figs 4–7, 10, 11 and 15–17 are reproduced with permission from *Food Microstructure and Scanning Electron Microscopy* (SEM Inc., Chicago). The authors wish to acknowledge the assistance of Dragoljub Gavarić, M.Sc., Spasenija Milanović, M.Sc., Ljiljana Kulić, B.Sc., and Zorka Kosovac, Chem. Techn., Dairy Department, Faculty of Technology, Novi Sad, in studying emulsifying agents and developing new commercial mixed agents for application in processed cheese production. Assistance in microstructural studies provided by Paula Allan-Wojtas, B.Sc., is also acknowledged. The Electron Microscope Centre, Agriculture Canada in Ottawa, provided facilities. This is contribution 671 from the Food Research Centre in Ottawa.

REFERENCES

1. Kosikowski, F. V., *Cheese and Fermented Milk Foods*, 2nd edn, F. V. Kosikowski and Associates, Brooktondale, New York, pp. 282, 470, 1982.
2. Thomas, M. A., *The Processed Cheese Industry*, Dept. of Agriculture, Sydney, New South Wales, Australia, pp. 1, 93, 1977.
3. Meyer, A., *Processed Cheese Manufacture*, Food Trade Press Ltd, London, pp. 58, 283, 1973.
4. Carić, M., Gantar, M. and Kaláb, M., *Food Microstruc.*, 1985, **4**, 297.
5. Thomas, M. A., *Aust. J. Dairy Technol.*, 1970, **23**, 23.
6. Gouda, A., El-Shabrawy, S. A., El-Zayat, A. and El-Bagoury, E., *Egyptian J. Dairy Sci.*, 1985, **13**, 115.
7. Rubin, J. and Bjerre, P., German Federal Republic Patent Application, 1983, DE 32 24 364 A1.
8. Anis, S. M. K. and Ernstrom, C. A., *J. Dairy Sci.*, 1984, **67**, 79.
9. Ostojić, M. and Manić, J., *Mljekarstvo*, 1985, **35**, 355.

10. Meyer, A., *Dte Molkerei Ztg*, 1961, **82**, 531.
11. Meyer, A., *Nord. Mejeritidsskr.*, 1961, **27**, 133.
12. Dimov, N. and Mineva, P., *XVII International Dairy Congress, München*, 1966, Vol. D, p. 175.
13. Robinson, R. K., *Dairy Microbiology, Vol. 2, Microbiology of Dairy Products*, Elsevier Applied Science Publishers, London, p. 232, 1981.
14. Law, B. A., *Dairy Ind. Int.*, 1980, **45**, 5.
15. Kimovskii, I., *Moloch. Prom.*, 1954, **15**, 22.
16. Kunizhev, S. M., Kimova, E. T., Kushkhova, M. Kh. and Kunizheva, Sh. M., *USSR Patent*, 1983, SU1 003 795.
17. Kraft, N. and Ward, P. J., *US Patent*, 1956, 2 743 186.
18. Shimizu, M., Lee, S. W., Kaminogawa, S. and Yamauchi, K., *J. Food Sci.*, 1984, **49**, 1117.
19. Abou-Donia, S. A., Salam, A. E. and El-Sayed, K. M., *Indian J. Dairy Sci.*, 1983, **36**, 119.
20. Brezani, P. and Herian, K., *Zborník Prác Výskumného Ustavu Mliekarského v Žiline*, 1984, **8**, 173.
21. Anon., *Dairy Record*, 1984, **85**, 92.
22. Zimmermann, F., German Federal Republic Patent Application, 1983, DE 31 24 725 A1.
23. Hayashi, T., Shibukawa, N., Yoneda, Y. and Musashi, K., Japanese Examined Patent, 1982, JP 57 55 380 B2.
24. Meyer, A., *Dte Molkerei Ztg*, 1961, **82**, 1649.
25. Kairyukshtene, I., Ramanauskas, R., Antanavichyus, A., Butkus, K. and Lashas, V., *Trudy. Litov. Filial Vsesoyuz. Nauchno-Isled. Inst. Maslodel. Syrodel. Prom.*, 1973, **1973**(8), 85.
26. Kapac-Parkačeva, N., *Sotsijal. Zemjodel.*, 1969, **21**, 49.
27. Lapshina, A. D. and Poplavets, P. I., *Nauch. Trudy. Omskii Sel'skokhoz. Inst. Im. S.M. Kirov*, 1976, **158**, 46.
28. Steinegger, R., *Landwirt. Jahrbuch Schweiz.*, 1901, **15**, 132.
29. Shimp, L. A., *Food Technol.*, 1985, **39**(5), 63.
30. Ellinger, R. H., *Phosphates as Food Ingredients*, CRC Press, The Chemical Rubber Co., Cleveland, p. 69, 1972.
31. Bonell, W., *Dte Molkerei Ztg*, 1971, **92**, 1415.
32. Lee, B. O., Paquet, D. and Alais, C., *XXI Int. Dairy Congress, Moscow*, 1982, Vol. 1, Book 1, p. 504.
33. Karahadian, C., M.Sc. thesis, University of Wisconsin, Madison.
34. Carić, M., Gavarić, D., Milanović, S., Kulić, Lj. and Kosovac, Z., Investigations of the Possibilities of Imported Additives Substitution in Processed Cheese Production, Faculty of Technology, Novi Sad, Yugoslavia, 1984, p. 60.
35. Tanaka, N., Goeptert, J. M., Traisman, E. and Hoffbeck, W. M., *J. Food Prot.*, 1979, **42**, 787.
36. Becker, E. and Ney, K. H., *Z. Lebensmittel Unters. Forsch.*, 1965, **127**, 206.
37. Carić, M., Gavarić, D., Milanović, S., Kulić, Lj. and Radovančev, Ž., *Mljekarstvo*, 1985, **35**, 163.
38. Kapac-Parkačeva, N., *Godisen. Zb. Zemjod-Šum. Fak., Univ. Skopje-Zemjodel, Yugoslavia*, 1969, **22**, 49.
39. Kicline, T. P., Stahlheber, N. E. and Vetter, J. L., *US Patent*, 1967, 3337347.

40. Shubin, E. M., *Isv. Vyss. Ucheb. Zaved. Pishch. Tekhnol.*, 1961, **1961**(3), 70.
41. Shubin, E. M. and Kracheninin, P. F., *Trudy. Tsentral. Nauchno-Issled. Inst. Maslodel. Syrodel. Prom.*, 1960, **1960**(6), 75.
42. Kiermier, F., Z. *Lebensmittel Unters. Forsch.*, 1962, **118**, 128.
43. Thomas, M. A., Newell, G., Abad, G. A. and Turner, A. D., *J. Food Sci.*, 1980, **45**, 458.
44. Sood, V. K. and Kosikowski, F. V., *J. Dairy Sci.*, 1979, **62**, 1713.
45. von der Heide, R., *Dte Molkerei Ztg*, 1966, **87**, 974.
46. Daclin, J. P., Thesis No. 96, Ecole Nat. Vet. d'Alfort, France, 1968.
47. Lee, B. O. and Alais, C., *Lait*, 1980, **60**, 130.
48. Ney, K. H. and Garg, O. P., *Jahresfachheft Molkereiwesen*, 1970, **72**, 1.
49. Ney, K. H. and Garg, O. P., *Fette Seifen Anstrichmittel*, 1970, **72**, 279.
50. Kirchmeier, O., Weiss, G. and Kiermeier, P., Z. *Lebensm. Untersuch.*, 1978, **166**, 212.
51. Nakajima, T., Tatsumi, K. and Furuichi, E., *J. Agr. Chem. Soc. Japan*, 1972, **46**, 447.
52. Scharpf, I., *The Use of Phosphates in Cheese Processing. Symposium— Phosphates in Food Processing*, 1971, AVI Publishing Co., Inc., Westport, Connecticut.
53. Zakharova, M. P., *Trudy. Uglich*, 1979, **27**, 105.
54. Gavrilova, N. B., *Zernoper. Pishch. Prom.*, 1976, **1976**(6), 131.
55. Zahkarova, N. P., Gavrilova, N. B. and Dolgoshchinova, V. G., *Trudy. Uglich*, 1979, **27**, 108.
56. Glandorf, K., *Dte Molkerei Ztg*, 1973, **94**, 1020.
    Roesler, H., *Milchwissenschaft*, 1966, **21**, 104.
58. Swiatek, A., *Milchwissenschaft*, 1964, **19**, 409.
59. Boháč, V. In: *The Collection of Papers from the Dairy Research Institute in Prague 1978–1983* (Ed. L. Forman), Technical Information Centre for the Food Industry, Prague, Czechoslovakia, p. 203, 1984.
60. Kaláb, M., *Scanning Electron Microsc.*, 1981, **III**, 453.
61. Taneya, S., Kimura, T., Izutsu, T. and Buchheim, W., *Milchwissenschaft*, 1980, **35**, 479.
62. Kaláb, M., *Milchwissenschaft*, 1977, **32**, 449.
63. Kaláb, M. and Emmons, D. B., *Milchwissenschaft*, 1978, **33**, 670.
64. Kaláb, M., Lowrie, R. J. and Nichols, D., *J. Dairy Sci.*, 1982, **65**, 1117.
65. Rüegg, M., Moor, U. and Schnider, J., *Schweiz. Milchw. Forschung*, 1985, **14**, 3.
66. Taranto, M. V., Wan, P. J., Chen, S. L. and Rhee, K. C., *Scanning Electron Microsc.*, 1979, **111**, 273.
67. Yiu, S. H., *Food Microstruc.*, 1985, **4**, 99.
68. Rayan, A. A., *Diss. Int. B*, 1981, **41**, 2954.
69. Rayan, A. A., Kaláb, M. and Ernstrom, C. A., *Scanning Electron Microsc.*, 1980, **III**, 635.
70. Blanc, B., Rüegg, M., Baer, A., Casey, M. and Lukesch, A., *Schweiz. Milchw. Forschung*, 1979, **8**, 27.
71. Bottazzi, V., Battistotti, B. and Blanchi, F., *Milchwissenschaft*, 1982, **37**, 577.
72. Brooker, B. E. In: *Food Microscopy* (Ed. J. G. Vaughan), Academic Press, New York, p. 273, 1979.
73. Brooker, B. E., Hobbs, D. G. and Turvey, A., *J. Dairy Res.*, 1975, **42**, 341.

74. Fluckiger, E. and Schilt, P., *Milchwissenschaft*, 1963, **18**, 437.
75. Tinyakov, V. G. and Barkan, S. M., *Izv. Vyss. Ucheb. Zaved., Pishch. Tekhnol.*, 1964, **1964**(5), 62.
76. Morris, H. A., Manning, P. B. and Jenness, R., *J. Dairy Sci.*, 1969, **52**, 900.
77. Klostermeyer, H., Uhlmann, G. and Merkenich, K., *Milchwissenschaft*, 1984, **39**, 195.
78. Uhlmann, G., Klostermeyer, H. and Merkenich, K., *Milchwissenschaft*, 1983, **38**, 582.
79. Kimura, T., Taneya, S. and Furuichi, E., *XX Int. Dairy Congress, Paris*, 1978, Vol. E, p. 239.
80. Heertje, I., Boskamp, M. J., van Kleef, F. and Gortemaker, F. H., *Neth. Milk Dairy J.*, 1981, **35**, 177.
81. Harwalkar, V. R. and Kaláb, M., *Scanning Electron Microsc.*, 1981, **111**, 503.
82. Kaláb, M. and Modler, H. W., *Food Microstruc.*, 1985, **4**, 89.
83. Tinyakov, V. G., *Izv. Vyss. Ucheb. Zaved., Pishch. Tekhnol.*, 1970, **2**, 165.
84. Bley, M. E., Johnson, M. E. and Olson, N. F., *J. Dairy Sci.*, 1985, **68**, 555.
85. Borlja, Z., M.Sc. thesis, Faculty of Technology, Novi Sad University, Novi Sad, 1980.
86. Milić, B., Carić, M., Vujičić, B. and Jakovljević, J., *Non-enzymic Browning in Food Products*, Naučna knjiga, Beograd, 1986.
87. Kršev, Lj., Processed Cheese Meeting, Faculty of Technology, Novi Sad, p. 3, 1985.
88. Todorović, M., Processed Cheese Meeting, Faculty of Technology, Novi Sad, p. 6, 1985.
89. Karahadian, C., Lindsay, R. C., Dillman, L. L. and Deibel, R. H., *J. Food Prot.*, 1985, **48**, 63.
90. Winkelmann, F., *Imitation Milk and Imitation Milk Products*, Food and Agricultural Organisation of UN, p. 117, 1974.
91. Carić, M., *Dairy Technology. I. Concentrated and Dried Dairy Products*, 2nd edn, Naučna knjiga, Beograd, p. 143, 1985.
92. Petričič, A., *Fluid and Fermented Milk*, Udružeije mljekarskih radnika SRH, Zagreb, pp. 189, 200, 1984.
93. Rosenau, J. R., *Energy Management and Membrane Technology in Food and Dairy Processing*, American Society of Agricultural Engineers, Chicago, p. 73, 1983.
94. Kirchmeier, O. and Breit, F. X., *Milchwissenschaft*, 1982, **38**, 80.
95. Hagrass, A. E. A., El-Shendour, M. A., Hammad, Y. A. and Hofi, A. A., *Egyptian J. Food Sci.*, 1984, **12**, 129.
96. Snegireva, I. A., Volostnikova, R. V., Barkar, S. V., Darchiev, B. Kh., Morozova, R. A., Semenova, A. I. and Sarafanova, N. I., *USSR Patent*, 1982, SU 971 216 A.
97. Vajda, G., Ravasz, L., Karacsonyi, B. and Tabajdi, G., UK Patent Application, 1983, GB 2 113 969 A.

Index

Acetic acid, 293
Aerobacter aerogenes, 305
Afghanistan, 313
African cheeses, 314–21
Algeria, 321
Anari, 327
Aoules, 321
Appenzeller, 93, 94, 106, 113, 117
Argentina, 331–2
Aroma compounds
  mould-ripened cheeses, 136–9
Arthrobacter, 159, 162, 169, 170
Asadero, 330
Ash-in-cheese moisture, 207
Asiago, 223
Asian cheeses, 311–14
Aspergillus versicolor, 62
Autochthonous cheese varieties, 185
Awshari cheese, 325
Ayib, 320
Azeitão, 211
Azul de oveja cheese, 194

Bacillus, 378
Bacillus mesentericus, 258
Bacterial ripened cheeses, 199–205
Bacterial surface-ripened cheeses,
    151–84
  coryneforms, 169–74
  curing, 154–5

Bacterial surface-ripened
    cheeses—*contd.*
  FDM, 153
  influence of smear, 152, 174–82
  microbiological composition of
    smear, 155–62
  micrococci, 168–9
  micro-organisms present in smear,
    162–74
  moulds, 166–8
  organoleptic properties, 152
  pH effects, 153, 160, 175–9
  ripening, 152, 154–5
  size of cheese, 153–4
  water content, 152–3
  yeasts, 162–6
Bacterium erythrogenes, 157
Bacterium linens, 155, 157
Badaya cheese, 205
Balkan cheese varieties, 257–76
Bel Paese, 71, 223
Beli sir u kriškama, 266, 269
Bixa orellana, 53
Biza, 326
Bjalo Salamureno Sirene, 266, 269
Bleu d'Auvergne, 134
Blue cheese, 157, 206, 247
Blue-veined cheeses, 121, 122, 124,
    134, 206–7
  aroma compounds, 136–7
Bola cheese, 185, 200, 209

Brevibacterium, 169
Brevibacterium erythrogenes, 157
Brevibacterium linens, 122, 138, 139,
　　155, 159, 162, 164, 166, 168,
　　170–4, 182
Brick cheese, 153, 157, 168, 169, 179,
　　180, 357, 359, 360
Brie, 205
Brine-salted cheeses, 2, 3
Brinza, 266, 314
Browning, 377
Brucella melitensis, 196
Buffalo's milk, 221, 266, 288, 312
Burgos cheese, 196
Butyric acid
　bacteria, 85–6
　fermentation, 103

Ca-paracasein caphosphate complex,
　　71
Cabrales cheese, 205, 206
Calcium
　citrate, 362, 377
　phosphate, 377
　　crystals, 360–2, 364, 365
Calcium-sequestering agents, 359
Camembert, 121, 125, 126, 132, 134,
　　138, 139, 142, 143, 205, 209
Carbohydrates in Domiati cheese, 283
Carbonyl compounds, 245
Carum carvi, 46
Cephalotyre Ras cheese, 314–17
Cheddar cheese, 1–44, 132, 199, 209,
　　247, 271, 291, 312–14, 358,
　　359, 361
　acid production at vat stage, 7–10
　characteristic texture of, 2
　cheddaring role, 1–2, 11–12, 14, 19
　chemical composition and quality
　　relationship, 20–5
　Dariworld method, 10
　definition, 1
　effect of calcium concentration,
　　27–8
　　coagulant, 6–7
　　fat, 28–9
　　FDM, 25
　　heating (cooking) the curd, 7

Cheddar cheese—*contd.*
　effect of calcium
　　concentration—*contd.*
　　milk composition, 5–6
　　milling, 13
　　MNFS, 22–3
　　moisture, 28–9
　　pressing, 18–20
　　protein, 28–9
　　ripening, 29–30
　　S/M, 24–5
　　salt, 27–8
　　salting, 14
　　starter culture, 5–6
　equilibration of salt, 16
　fat-in-the-dry matter (FDM), 21, 29,
　　31
　flavour of, 30–5
　　effect of milkfat, 31–2
　　protein, 32–3
　　redox potential, 33
　　role of non-starter, 34–5
　　starter, 33–4
　fusion, 17–18
　grading of, 35–7
　granular, 38
　history, 1
　incidence of texture defects, 19
　low fat, 37–8
　manufacture, 3–20
　mellowing after salting, 15–16
　mellowing prior to salting, 13
　moisture content, 34
　New–Way, 9, 10
　non-fat substances (MNFS), 21,
　　28–9
　pH effects, 2, 9, 11, 21, 23–4, 26–8,
　　30, 40
　processed, 356, 363, 364, 367, 369
　quality assessment, 35
　role of calcium, 37
　salt-in-moisture (S/M), 14, 21, 29,
　　34, 35
　salting of milled curd, 14–15
　seaminess, 17–18
　sensory testing, 36
　soluble nitrogen in, 193
　stirred curd, 38
　texture of, 26–30, 35

Cheddar cheese—*contd.*
  traditional, 2–4, 9, 18
  USDA method, 10
  vacuum pressing, 19–20
  variants of, 37–40
  washed curd varieties, 39–40
Chhana, 312
Chiclosa, 330
Chinese cheeses, 313
Chukumara, 321
Citrates, 354–5
Citric acid, 76–8
Clostridium, 378
Clostridium botulinum, 352
Clostridium butyricum, 103
Clostridium sporongenes, 103
Clostridium tyrobutyricum, 50, 51, 53, 85–6, 103
Colby cheese, 39–40, 49
Coliform bacteria, 1, 53, 84, 122, 258, 305
Colloidal calcium, 280–1
Colloidal calcium phosphate (CCP), 71
Comté, 95
Coryneform bacteria, 88–9, 159, 169–74
Cottage cheese, 71, 312
Cow's milk, 185, 186, 196, 199–206, 208, 209, 211, 221, 257, 287, 312
Cream cheese, 312
Crystal formation, 372–3, 377
Cuajada, 195
Cuminum cyminum, 46
Curd granule patterns, 359
Cynara, 204, 212
Cynara cardunculus L., 211
Cyprus, 327–30

Dahi, 312–13
Dakashi, 321
Dambou, 320
Danish Blue, 121, 132, 134
Debaryomyces, 164
Debaryomyces hanseni, 122
Decca, 312
Discoloration, 377

Disodium phosphate, 366, 377
Domiati, 266, 277–309, 314
Dry-salted cheese, 2–3
Dutch-type varieties, 6, 45–92, 199
  brining, 62
  CaCl$_2$ addition, 68
  control of water content, 70
  curd making, 61–2
  curing, 62–4
  definition, 45
  effect of starter, 67
  FDM, 66–7, 69
  fermentation of lactose and citric acid, 76–8
  flavour, 81–2
  hole formation, 83
  lipolysis, 80–1
  main process steps, 54–60
  manufacture of, 50–64
  maturation, 76–83
  mechanization, 61–2
  microbial defects, 83–9
  moulding, 61–2
  nucleation, 83
  pH and water content interrelations, 73–4
  pH control, 71–3
  pH effects, 54, 58, 81, 88
  pressing, 62
  process control, 69–74
  properties of, 47
  protein degradation, 82
  proteolysis, 78–80
  rind treatment, 62–4
  salting, 68–9
  standardization, 64–6
  starters, composition and handling, 74–6
  storage, 62
  texture, 82
  treatment of milk, 50–3
  washing process, 68
  yield factors, 66–70

Edam, 46, 54, 64, 66, 199, 200, 209, 212, 313
  see also Dutch-type varieties
Egyptian cheeses, 314–19

Ekt cheese, 323
Electron microscopy, 357–68
Emmental(er), 93, 94, 98, 99, 102, 104,
    106, 110, 112–15, 117, 199,
    209
Emulsifying agents, 373, 377
    addition of, 346
    characteristics of, 353
    types and role of, 348–56
Enterobacter aerogenes, 84
Epir, 257
Escherichia coli, 203, 258
Ewe's milk, 49, 185, 206
Eyes, 3

Fajy, 326
Fat acidity of different cheese
    varieties, 132
Feta cheese, 266–9, 277–309
Flamengo cheese, 209
Fontina, 223, 243
Free amino acids, pickled cheeses, 290
Free fatty acids
    Italian cheeses, 230, 231, 238, 242–6
    pickled cheeses, 293–7
    white brined cheese, 267
Friesian cheese, 49

Gallego cheese, 199
Gammelost, 124
Gamonedo cheeses, 205
Gel electrophoresis, Italian cheeses,
    247–8
Geotrichum candidum, 122, 130, 133,
    138, 139, 142, 155, 156, 166–8
Goat's milk, 185, 186, 196, 205, 206,
    208, 212, 221, 257, 266, 269
Gorgonzola, 121, 221, 223
Gouda, 2, 3, 5, 46, 49, 54, 66, 77, 79,
    132, 199, 209, 214, 247, 312,
    314, 315
    see also Dutch-type cheeses
Gram-negative bacilli, 157
Grana cheese, 245–7
Gruyère, 93, 94, 106, 110, 112, 113,
    117, 132, 181, 182, 199,
    363–5, 368, 369

Hafnia alvei, 122
Hallonm, 322
Halloumi, 327–30
HEPA (High Efficiency Particulate
    Air) filters, 75
Herregardsost, 95
Heterofermentative lactic acid
    fermentation, 103

Ibores cheese, 205
Idiazábel cheese, 204
Ilha cheese, 209
Imeretinskii, 266
Indian cheeses, 311–13
Iowa-style Swiss cheese, 95
Iran, 326–7
Iraq, 324–6
Israel, 327
Italian cheeses, 221–55
    classification of, 223–33
    free fatty acids (FFA), 231, 238,
        242–6
    gel electrophoresis, 247–8
    lactose metabolism, 235
    lipolysis, 235
    manufacturing protocol for, 226
    pH levels, 229, 236, 243, 249–50
    pregastric esterase (PGE) activity,
        235–8, 243, 245
    production statistics, 221
    proteolysis, 247
    ripening, 233–53
    soluble nitrogen, 248–53

Jagi, 324–6
Japanese cheeses, 313–14
Jarlbergost, 95

Karish, 314, 315, 319
Käsefertiger, 116
Kashkaval, 257–66, 314, 315
    average composition, 258
    casein fractions in, 263
    free amino acid composition, 264

Kashkaval—*contd.*
  manufacturing procedure, 258–9
  monocalcium paracaseinate, 264
  proteinases, 262
  quality defects, 266
  ripening, 259–66
  starter cultures, 259
  texturing, 259
  typical form of, 258–9
  water soluble N, 263
Kaškaval Balkan, 258
Kaškaval Preslav, 257
Kaškaval Vitosa, 258
Kefalotyri, 269–70, 315
Kesong Puti, 313
Kindirmo, 320
Kishk, 314
Kluyveramyces lactis, 122, 131

L. acidophilus, 225
Laban Khad, 314, 315, 318
Laban Rayed, 315, 318
Laban Zeer, 314
Labneh, 322
Lactic acid, 76–8, 134
  bacteria, 95–9, 115, 155, 204, 262
  fermentation, 95–9, 235
Lactic streptococci, 122
Lactobacillus, 50, 51, 86–7, 122, 318
Lactobacillus bifermentans, 89
Lactobacillus brevis, 305
Lactobacillus bulgaricus, 95, 271, 315
Lactobacillus casei, 122, 200, 203, 204, 268, 269
Lactobacillus lactis, 95
Lactobacillus plantarum, 122, 199, 200, 203, 204, 268
Lactose, 76–8, 88
  Italian cheeses, 235
  mould-ripened cheeses, 134–5
Latin American cheeses, 330–4
Leuconostoc cremoris, 74
Leuconostoc dextranicum, 204, 270
Leuconostoc lactis, 74, 203, 204
Leyden cheese, 49
Lightvan, 326
Limanskii, 266

Limburger cheese, 49, 153, 155–60, 162, 167, 168, 176, 180
Lipases, mould-ripened cheeses, 133–4
Lipolysis, 103
  Italian cheeses, 235
  mould-ripened cheeses, 131–4
  pickled cheeses, 293
Long Giang, 313
Lori, 266

Maasdamer, 49, 95
Mahón cheese, 200
Maillard reaction, 377, 378
Majorero cheese, 205
Manchego cheese, 201–3
Marstar culture media, 202
Mastitis, 67
Medaffarah, 322
Mediterranean cheese varieties, 257–76
Melting salt crystals, 363
Memphis, 315
Meria, 326
Mesanarah, 322
Meshanger, 49, 141
Methyl ketones, 245–7
Micrococci, 204
  bacterial surface-ripened cheeses, 168–9
Micrococcus candidus, 168
Micrococcus caseolyticus, 157, 163, 168
Micrococcus freudenreichii, 157, 163, 168
Micrococcus lactis, 204
Micrococcus roseus, 204
Micrococcus saprophyticus, 204
Micrococcus varians, 157, 163, 168
Micro-organisms, 83, 101, 117, 162–74
Middle East cheeses, 322–30
Milk
  disaggregation and dispersion of colloidal phase of, 281
  exchange of colloidal calcium for sodium in, 280–1
  proteinases, 126
Milled curd junction, 359

Mimolette, 53
Minas Gerais, 333, 334
Mish, 279, 318–19
  artificial, 319
Mixed acid fermentation, 103
Mixed milk, 257
Monterey, 39–40, 49
Mould-ripened cheeses, 121–49, 205–7
  amino acid breakdown, 131
  aroma compounds, 136–9
  effect of flora, 121–4, 130–1
    milk proteinases, 126
    Penicillium, 126–30
    rennet, 125–6
  lactic acid, 134
  lactose, 134–5
  lipases, 133–4
  lipolysis, 131–4
  pH effects, 125–6, 133, 140, 142–3
  proteinases, 127–30
  proteolysis, 124–5
  ripening, 141–3
  starters, 122
  texture, 139
Moulds, 88–9, 122, 124
  bacterial surface-ripened cheeses,
    166–8
Mourta, 318
Mozzarella, 2, 221, 223, 228–33, 312,
    314
  free fatty acid (FFA) compositions
    and flavours of, 230
  microstructure and rheological
    properties, 232
Mucor, 124, 142
Mucor miehei, 243, 245

Nata cheese, 200
Nepal, 313
Nigeria, 320–1
Nitrate, 84–5
Nono, 320
North Yemen, 324

Oaxaca, 330
Oospora lactis, 155

Optical microscopy, 361
Osetinskii, 266

P. candidum, 245
P. caseicolum, 123
Paneer, 312
Panir, 312
Paracaseinate–phosphate complex,
    282
Parmesan, 221, 223, 225–8, 235, 242
Parmigiano Reggiano, 235
Paški cheese, 271
Pasta filata, 221, 225–8, 315
Penicillium, 122, 124–30, 133, 134, 140,
    142
Penicillium camemberti, 121–3,
    126–30, 133–5, 138, 140, 142,
    143
Penicillium camemberti sensus stricto,
    123
Penicillium roqueforti, 121–30, 133–5,
    141, 143, 206, 235, 245
Petit Suisse, 209
Philippines, 313
Phosphates, 352–4
Pickled cheeses, 277–309
  carbohydrates in, 283
  changes during pickling, 282–305
  changes in pickle composition,
    298–301
  classification of, 279–80
  defects in, 305
  degradation products, 289
  electrolytic corrosion, 305
  free amino acids, 290
  free fatty acids, 293–7
  gas-forming micro-organisms, 305
  general composition, 282–7
  heat treatment of milk and use of
    reconstituted and
    recombined milks, 285
  lipolysis, 293
  pH levels, 283, 284, 302
  production of, 277
  proteolysis, 287–93
  role of sodium chloride in, 280–2
  salt content, 285

Pickled cheeses—*contd.*
  soft cheese, 279–80
  soluble nitrogenous constituents, 289
  storage period, 285
  storage temperature, 284
  structure, 301–5
  technological differences between, 278
  ultrafiltration, 285–7
  vitamins in, 297–8
  volatile flavour compounds in, 297
Pindos cheese, 269
Pirdop, 257
Pirotski Kashkaval, 257
Pizza cheese, 228
Polarizing microscopy, 357
Polyphosphates, 355–6
Portuguese cheese varieties, 185, 207–14
  characteristics and manufacture of, 209–12
  production statistics, 207–8
Pregastric esterase (PGE) activity, 235–8, 243, 245
Processed cheese, 339–83
  analogues of, 378–80
  blending, 342–6
  computation of ingredients, 342
  cooling, 347–8
  emulsifying agents, 346, 348–56
  general characteristics of, 339–41
  homogenization, 347
  manufacturing principles and techniques, 341–8
  microstructure of, 356–68
  packaging, 347
  processing, 346–7
  quality defects, 368–78
  selection of natural cheese for, 341
  shredding, 346
  storage, 348
Propionibacterium freudenreichii, 98
Propionibacterium shermanii, 270
Propionic acid bacteria, 88
Propionic acid fermentation, 99–100
Protein particles, 366, 370
Protein strands, 371, 372

Proteinases
  Kashkaval, 262
  mould-ripened cheeses, 127–30
Proteolysis, 100–3, 113, 115
  Italian cheeses, 247
  mould-ripened cheeses, 124–5
  pickled cheeses, 287–93
  white brined cheese, 267
Provolone, 228, 235, 238, 253
Puerto Rico, 331

Quarg, 71
Quark, 209
Queijo Serra, 185
Queijo Serra da Estrella, 208, 211
Queso Azul de oveja, 206
Queso Blanco, 266, 331–4
Queso del Pais, 331–4
Queso Fresco, 331–4
Queso Manchego, 185, 201

Ras cheeses. *See* Caphalotyre Ras cheese
Rennet coagulation, 279–80
Rennet coagulum, 7
  moisture removal, 5
Requesón, 195, 196
Ripened cheese varieties, 257–76
Robiola, 124
Romadour cheeses, 153
Romano, 223, 225–8, 233, 235, 238, 240, 241, 243, 245–7, 250, 251, 253
Romy, 315
Roncal cheese, 204
Roos, 326
Roquefort, 121, 123, 132, 205, 212, 221
Rossiiskii cheese, 270

Saccharomyces cerivisiae, 122
Saint-Nectaire, 124
Salmonella-Shigella, 203
Salt combinations, 355–6
Salt crystallization, 366

Salt-in-moisture (S/M) level, 3, 24–5, 197
Samsoe, 95
San Simón cheese, 200
São Jorge cheese, 209
Sarplaninski, 257
Saudi Arabia, 323–4
Scanning electron microscopy (SEM), 358–9, 363, 365
Schmelzpack, 345
Serena cheese, 204
Serpa cheese, 211, 212
Serra cheese, 208, 211, 212
Serra da Estella cheese, 211
Serra velho, 211
Shanikalish, 322–3
Sheep's milk, 186, 200–5, 208, 211, 212, 221, 257, 266, 269, 322, 323
Sjenički, 269
Skyros cheese, 269
Smear cheeses. *See* Bacterial surface-ripened cheeses
Sodium-aluminium phosphate, 364, 367
Sodium calcium citrate, 362, 368, 377
Sodium chloride, 280–2
    interaction with milk and cheese proteins, 281–2
Sodium citrate, 361, 362, 364, 365, 367, 369
Sodium phosphate, 363–4, 367
Sodium phosphate-polyphosphate, 372
Sodium triphosphate, 364, 367
Soluble nitrogen, Italian cheeses, 248–53
Somborski cheese, 271
Sovetskii cheese, 270–1
    starter cultures, 270
Spanish cheese varieties, 185–207
    chemical and physical characteristics, 187–95
    fresh cheeses and related products, 195–7
    industrial production statistics, 187
    stability coordinates, 194
Sremski, 269

Srikhand, 312–13
Srpski, 269
Staphylococci, 204
Staphylococcus aureus, 50, 51, 203
Stilton, 121, 221
Streptococcus, 51, 318
Streptococcus cremoris, 24, 74, 97, 122, 196, 199, 202, 271
Streptococcus diacetylactis, 270
Streptococcus durans, 200
Streptococcus faecalis var. *liquefaciens*, 199
Streptococcus faecalis var. *malodoratus*, 89
Streptococcus lactis, 74, 97, 122, 196, 199, 200, 202–4, 225, 269, 270, 271
Streptococcus lactis var. *diacetylactis*, 74, 202
Streptococcus lactis var. *maltigenes*, 89
Streptococcus thermophilus, 50, 51, 87, 95, 202, 271, 377
Streptomyces natalensis, 63
Stretched curd cheeses, 221
Sudan, 319
Surface-mould ripened soft cheeses, 121, 124
    aroma compounds, 137–9
Swiss-type varieties, 3, 93–120, 199
    body characteristics, 110–15
    carbon dioxide production and diffusion, 104–7
    characteristics of, 93–5
    eye formation, 104–7, 116
    fermentation, 95–107
    flavour factors, 107–10, 117
    fusion, 112
    influences of cheesemaking operations, 115–17
    lactic acid fermentation, 95–9
    mean free amino acid contents, 109
    non-protein nitrogen (NPN), 101
    non-volatile group, 109
    propionic acid fermentation, 99–100
    proteolysis, 100–3, 113, 115
    proteolysis indices, 100
    quality of, 114
    ripening reaction control, 117–18

Swiss-type varieties—*contd.*
  smear-ripened, 99
  storage conditions, 117
  temperature–time relationship
    during manufacture, pressing
    and ripening, 115
  texture, 117
  volatile compounds, 109
  water-soluble nitrogen (WSN), 100
Syneresis, 14
Syria, 322–3

Tafi cheese, 332
Taizz cheese, 324
Taleggio, 124, 223
Teleme(a) cheese, 266, 268, 289, 291,
  327
Tetilla cheese, 199, 200
Thermoresistant streptococci, 87–8
Thistle rennet, 212–14
Tikammarin, 321
Tilsiter, 49
Time-lapse photography, 356
Tome de Savoie, 124
Torta del Casar cheese, 205
Toureg, 321
Transmission electron microscopy
  (TEM), 358–9
Trappist cheese, 163, 165

Travnički, 269
Trichosporon, 163, 164
Turkey, 327

Ulloa, 199, 200
Ultrafiltration, pickled cheeses, 285–7

Villalón cheese, 196
Vitamins in pickled cheeses, 297–8
Volatile fatty acids, Feta cheese, 294
Volatile flavour compounds, in
  pickled cheeses, 297

Wara, 320
Whey cheese, 195, 196
White brined cheese, 266–9
  average composition, 268
  free amino acid content, 267
  free fatty acid concentrations, 267
  proteolysis, 267
  typical form of, 268
White cheese, 373
Witte meikaas, 49

Yeasts, 88–9, 122
  bacterial surface-ripened cheeses,
    162–6